Citizens and the European Polity

Series editors: *Maurizio Cotta and Pierangelo Isernia*
(CIRCaP – University of Siena)

Books in the series include:

The Europe of Elites
A Study into the Europeanness of Europe's Political and Economic Elites
Edited by Heinrich Best, György Lengyel, and Luca Verzichelli

The Europeanization of National Polities?
Citizenship and Support in a Post-Enlargement Union
Edited by David Sanders, Paolo Bellucci, Gábor Tóka, and Mariano Torcal

European Identity
What the Media Say
Edited by Paul Bayley and Geoffrey Williams

Citizens and the European Polity
Mass Attitudes Towards the European and National Polities
Edited by David Sanders, Pedro Magalhães, and Gábor Tóka

Citizens and the European Polity

Mass Attitudes Towards the European and National Polities

Edited by
David Sanders, Pedro C. Magalhães, and Gábor Tóka

OXFORD
UNIVERSITY PRESS

OXFORD
UNIVERSITY PRESS

Great Clarendon Street, Oxford, OX2 6DP,
United Kingdom

Oxford University Press is a department of the University of Oxford.
It furthers the University's objective of excellence in research, scholarship,
and education by publishing worldwide. Oxford is a registered trade mark of
Oxford University Press in the UK and in certain other countries

British Library Cataloguing in Publication Data
Data available

Library of Congress Cataloging in Publication Data
Data available

ISBN 978–0–19–960233–9

Printed in Great Britain by
MPG Books Group, Bodmin and King's Lynn

Series Editors' Foreword

In a moment in which the EU is facing an important number of social, economic, political, and cultural challenges, and its legitimacy and democratic capacities are increasingly questioned, it seems particularly important to address the issue of *if* and *how* EU citizenship is taking shape. This series intends to address this complex issue. It reports the main results of a quadrennial Europe-wide research project, financed under the Sixth Framework Programme of the EU. That programme has studied the changes in the scope, nature, and characteristics of citizenship presently underway as a result of the process of deepening and enlargement of the European Union.

The IntUne Project—Integrated and United: A Quest for Citizenship in an Ever Closer Europe—is one of the most recent and ambitious research attempts to empirically study how citizenship is changing in Europe. The Project lasted four years (2005–2009) and it involved thirty of the most distinguished European universities and research centres, with more than 100 senior and junior scholars as well as several dozen graduate students working on it. It had as its main focus an examination of how integration and decentralization processes, at both the national and European level, are affecting three major dimensions of citizenship: *identity, representation*, and *scope of governance*. It looked, in particular, at the relationships between political, social, and economic elites, the general public, policy experts and the media, whose interactions nurture the dynamics of collective political identity, political legitimacy, representation, and standards of performance.

In order to address empirically these issues, the IntUne Project carried out two waves of mass and political, social, and economic elite surveys in 18 countries, in 2007 and 2009; in-depth interviews with experts in five policy areas; extensive media analysis in four countries; and a documentary analysis of attitudes towards European integration, identity, and citizenship. The book series presents and discusses in a coherent way the results coming out of this extensive set of new data.

The series is organized around the two main axes of the IntUne Project, to report how the issues of identity, representation, and standards of good governance are constructed and reconstructed at the elite and citizen levels, and how mass–elite interactions affect the ability of elites to shape identity, representation, and the scope of governance. A first set of four books will examine how identity, scope of governance, and representation have been changing over time at elites, media, and public level, respectively. The next two books will present cross-level analysis of European and national identity on the one hand and problems of national and European representation and scope of governance on the other, in doing so comparing data at both the mass and elite level. A concluding volume will summarize the main results, framing them in a wider theoretical context.

M.C. and P.I.

Contents

Contents

List of Illustrations

List of Tables

List of Boxes

List of Contributors

Paolo Bellucci (Professor, University of Siena, Italy)

Eduard Bonet (Junior researcher, Pompeu Fabra University, Barcelona, Spain)

Irena Fiket (Fellow, University of Siena, Italy)

André Freire (Professor, ISCTE-IUL, Lisbon University Institute, Portugal)

Andrija Henjak (Assistant Professor, University of Zagreb, Croatia)

Pierangelo Isernia (Professor, University of Siena, Italy)

Pedro C. Magalhães (Researcher, Institute of Social Sciences, University of Lisbon, Portugal)

Vincenzo Memoli (Assistant Professor, University of Molise, Italy)

Jordi Muñoz (Fellow, Autonomous University of Barcelona, Spain)

Hans Rattinger (Professor, University of Mannheim, Germany)

David Sanders (Professor, University of Essex, United Kingdom)

Hermann Schmitt (Professor, Mannheim Centre for European Social Research—MZES, Germany)

Fabio Serricchio (Fellow, University of Siena, Italy)

Markus Steinbrecher (Assistant professor, University of Mannheim, Germany)

Gábor Tóka (Professor, Central European University, Budapest, Hungary)

Mariano Torcal (Professor, Pompeu Fabra University, Barcelona, Spain)

Bettina Westle (Professor, Marburg University, Germany)

List of Abbreviations

9/11	Terrorist attacks of 11 September 2001 on the United States
ANOVA	analysis of variance between groups
AR(1)	autoregressive function of lag one
CCEB	Candidate Countries Eurobarometer
CP	Comparative Politics
CSES	Comparative Study of Electoral Systems
EB	Eurobarometer
EC	European Community
ECS	European Community Study
ECU	European Currency Unit
EEC	European Economic Community
EES	European Election Studies
EMU	European Monetary Union
EP	European Parliament
EPE	European Parliament elections
EU	European Union
EU6	The six founder member states of the EU (then EEC)
EU9	The nine member states of the EU in 1973
EU12	The twelve member states of the EU in 1986
EU15	The fifteen member states of the EU in 1995
EU27	The current member states of the EU
FEVD	fixed-effects vector-decomposition (model)
FGLS	feasible generalized least square (model)
GDP	gross domestic product
GESIS	German Social Science Infrastructure Services
GLS	generalized least square (model)
GNI	gross national income
IDEA	Institute for Democracy and Electoral Assistance

List of Abbreviations

IntUne	*Integrated and United* (project)
IPE	Informal Political Engagement
ISSP	International Social Survey Programme
LDV	lagged dependent variable
LSDV	least square dummy variable
LM	Lagrange multiplier
NES	national election studies
NPE	national parliament elections
OECD	Organisation for Economic Co-operation and Development
OLS	Ordinary least squares
PCSE	Panel-corrected standard errors
PPP	purchasing power parity
PRS	Political Risk Service
Stata	name of statistical software package
TSCS	time-series cross-section (analysis)
USD	US dollars
WVS	World Value Survey
WW2	Second World War
xtpcse	linear regression with panel-corrected standard errors
xtreg	fixed-, between-, and random-effects and population-averaged linear models
xtregar	fixed- and random-effects linear models with an AR(1) disturbance
xtscc	robust standard errors for panels with cross-sectional dependence

1

Introduction: Citizens and the European Polity

Pedro C. Magalhães, David Sanders, and Gábor Tóka

In the last two decades, the nature of the European integration project has changed very significantly. After the fall of the Berlin Wall, enlargement took place at an unprecedented pace, raising the number of EU member states from twelve to twenty-seven. A common European currency was created, which is shared today by most of the member states. Institutionally, nobody today would be able to describe the European Union as a mere intergovernmental organization managing a common market and common trade policies. Instead, the EU has become a fully fledged multilevel system of governance, in which policy-making authority in a broad number of areas is shared by supranational and national authorities in an increasing number of policy areas. And yet, the full picture of developments in the last twenty years can hardly be described as rosy. In the same period, European Union countries witnessed civil war erupting close to their own borders, remained powerless to prevent it, and, most disturbingly, struggled in vain to find a common position as it unfolded. Such divisions were only exacerbated as fundamentalist Islamic terrorism posed a renewed threat to the world and the United States intervened in the Middle East. Free trade, the modest economic performance of many EU member states, the rise of the economic potential of industrializing nations in the East and the South, and monetary union and its convergence criteria have put enormous pressure on the previous consensus around "embedded liberalism" in Europe, arguably replacing it with an increasingly orthodox and monetarist consensus. However, the recent debt crisis only served to expose how fragile that consensus also was in terms of the actual budgetary policies pursued by member states, as well as the weakness of the political and institutional mechanisms installed to ensure a feasible common monetary policy. As the economic and financial crisis fully unfolded, the internal contradictions of the European project and the conflicts of interest between member states have again brought something that has become familiar in the last two decades: European policy paralysis. At the time of this writing, the challenges posed both to the survival of the euro and to the preservation of the standards of policy delivery in the European welfare states seem the most daunting ever faced.

The core motivation behind this volume flows from the clear sense that neither the origins of the current travails of the EU nor their eventual dénouement can be explained any more by simply focusing, as was often the case in earlier phases and crisis of European integration, on the role of political and technocratic elites. In fact, the other fundamental change that seems to have occurred in the last twenty years has been the entry of mass publics as relevant actors in the dynamics of integration. As EU membership widened and integration deepened, signs of the erosion of the previously assumed "permissive consensus" around integration among mass publics have multiplied. Previously high levels of popular support for integration have waned. Whenever voters were asked to participate in referendums concerning European issues, previously unsuspected resistances emerged, leading ultimately, in several cases, to rejections of treaties (Denmark in 1992, Ireland in 2001, France and Netherlands 2005, Ireland in 2008) or of entry in the eurozone (Denmark in 2000 and Sweden in 2003). In domestic party politics, political challenges to integration—some of a populist and nationalist nature—emerged in several member states. Both instances—the outcome of domestic referendums and the emergence of a resilient party-based Euroscepticism in many countries—brought home the notion that, in accordance with the shift towards multi-level governance referred to above, the European mass public's views of integration are now clearly connected to the dynamics of public opinion and political attitudes at the domestic level. Support for, trust in, and evaluations of national and European institutions seem to be inextricably linked. Voting behaviour in European elections and referendums is dominated by considerations and themes arising in domestic political arenas. At the same time, although it is not yet widely politicized, a growing ideological cleavage over Europe does appear to be emerging among mass publics at the national level.

There is no shortage of excellent individual studies addressing these trends in the political cultures and mass public opinions in Europe. However, a general and encompassing overview of these transformations in book form is still missing. Broad comparative volumes—like the one contained in the seminal *Beliefs in Government* series, dedicated to *Public Opinion and Internationalized Governance* (Niedermayer and Sinnott 1995)—focused on developments prior to the early 1990s and mostly on Western European nations. Those works preceded both the deepening and enlargement transformations that followed the collapse of the Iron Curtain, as well as the main events and trends—monetary union, economic stagnation and the questioning of the European social model, civil war in Yugoslavia, and 9/11—that have affected the European polities since then. Furthermore, the most important volumes that have resulted from the cross-national study of voting behaviour and political culture written in the last decade have either focused on the small core of more industrialized and fully established European democracies (see, for example, Thomassen 2005a) or, instead, have tended to neglect the inter-play and contamination between attitudes towards domestic and towards supranational European institutions.

The *Integrated and United* (IntUne) project, which originated the series in which this volume, *Citizens and the European Polity*, is integrated, allowed us to re-examine all these developments in Europe from the vantage point of the end of the first decade of the twenty-first century. In this particular volume, our focus is on describing and explaining variations concerning mass attitudes in the last two decades, and the extent to which the crucial political, eco-nomic, and social changes we have described played any significant role. On the side of the *explananda* addressed in this book, we look into different categories of political attitudes where, especially in what concerns integration and the EU, the absence of clear theoretical distinctions has often been the source of considerable confusion. Obviously, as many others before us, we are interested in mass publics' generalized attitude towards European integration, which has almost invariably been captured by survey items where respon-dents express their views about whether their country's membership has been "a good thing" or a "bad thing". However, one common aspect of the entire IntUne project is the notion that "citizenship", and its fundamental cultural and attitudinal basis, requires additional distinctions: those between *identity, representation,* and *policy scope.* "Identity" concerns people's feelings about belonging to a particular political community. "Representation" relates to people's sense of the extent to which a particular set of institutions and elites articulates their preferences, allows chances at participating, and is responsive to popular preferences. And "policy scope" concerns the extent to which people award legitimacy to a particular set of political structures situated at this or that level of governance to become the main locus of policy making. To put it differently, we are addressing what Scharpf has long ago identified as the deficits in the input-legitimacy of the EU (Scharpf 1999). To what extent has a "sense of collective identity" emerged among Europeans? To what extent does "the lack of Europe-wide policy discourses, and the lack of a Europe-wide institutional infrastructure that could assure (...) political accountability" impinge on feelings concerning representation by European institutions? And how do both aspects relate to the overall legitimacy awarded to the EU as a policy-making authority? Furthermore, as we pointed out earlier, the

3

sense that developments in European integration are increasingly entwined with aspects of domestic politics has also led us to focus on several crucial attitudinal and behavioural variables that have more commonly been addressed in the study of national politics: support for democracy, ideological preferences and polarization, and political engagement.

On the side of the *explanantia*, following in the footsteps of, for example, Hooghe and Marks (2005), we also want to contribute with this volume and the entire IntUne project to some badly needed clarification. Put together, the different chapters address alternative explanations of public attitude formation and change. First, they focus on the extent to which variations across time, countries, and individuals can be explained by *instrumental rationality*, i.e. calculations about political or economic costs and benefits of alternative situations and course of action. They also discuss the role of *cueing rationality*, i.e. the use of heuristic and cognitive shortcuts under conditions of limited information, through which individuals rely on information conveyed by trustworthy sources and from realities close to their experience to form judgments about complex and more distant phenomena. *Affective/identitarian* factors, particularly feelings of attachment to groups and organizations, constitute a third tier of explanations that will be addressed in several chapters. *Cognitive mobilization*, citizens' level of exposure to information and formal education, is also treated as a factor potentially leading to a more cosmopolitan view of politics and, thus, potentially favourable to integration. Finally, several chapters also focus on *equity/fairness* considerations as drivers of political attitudes, particularly in what concerns perceptions of the workings of political institutions and policy outcomes. These five tiers of explanations are used in different ways in different chapters, depending on availability of survey and other data and on the specific theoretical agenda that our disciplines have developed concerning the different dependent variables. However, all chapters systematically ask the same basic set of questions:

- What trends can be found in the last two decades, and do they prolong or reverse trends found for the 1970s and 1980s?

- Are there events and external shocks that can be meaningfully and plausibly proposed as causes of observed changes?

- What cross-national differences emerge, and are those differences structured around the distinction between older and newer EU member states or deeper and more theoretically meaningful distinctions?

- What sort of explanations—economic, political, cultural, or social—can be found for the observed variations, and what do they tell us about how individuals form judgements and develop attitudes towards the domestic and European levels of government?

Chapter 2—*The Determinants of Democracy Satisfaction in Europe*, by Paolo Bellucci, Vincenzo Memoli, and David Sanders—places us right in the middle of what has been often treated as the most basic dimension of political attitudes: support for the regime and, in particular, citizens' satisfaction with democratic performance. One of the core findings of the *Beliefs in Government* series, based precisely on this indicator, was that there was little sign of a "legitimation crisis" either in Western (Fuchs, Guidorossi, and Svensson 1995) or in the nascent Eastern European democracies (Tóka 1995). However, support for democratic regimes seemed increasingly dependent on their ability to deliver sound economic performance, and the fall of the Iron Curtain raised the possibility that the disappearance of an external enemy resulted in "increasing criticism and political pressure" (Kaase, Newton, and Scarbrough 1996: 228). In the years that followed, such a possibility seemed to have become a reality, as scholars detected the rise of "critical citizens" (Norris 1999a) and "dissatisfied democrats" (Klingemann 1999). Bellucci and Memoli re-examine the available evidence, placing "satisfaction with democracy" within the context of other constructs capturing other dimensions of regime support and looking for cross-national variations. Furthermore, they use a panel analysis of survey data since 1995, looking not only for general trends in this respect but also asking the question of whether variations through time and between countries are fundamentally due to economic performance or, instead, whether citizens are also sensitive to other more stable features of the polity, such as their electoral system and the political performance of their institutions of governance.

Chapter 3—*Informal Political Engagement in Europe, 1975–2007*, by David Sanders and Paolo Bellucci—focuses on levels of political engagement across European societies. In this respect, the detection of secular trends in the past seems to have depended very much—and understandably so—on where and when such trends are being sought. While studies looking at evidence until the 1980s seemed to detect a rise in political involvement (Kaase and Marsh 1979), later studies pointed, again, to a fundamental lack of any major trends in political interest (Gabriel and Van Deth 1995), and to the prevalence of cross-national discrepancies (Van Deth and Elff 2004). In this chapter, Sanders and Bellucci use the long series provided by the Eurobarometer data on political discussion, persuasion, and media use to gauge these trends, and consider not only the impact of political events but also the rival merits of explanations based on cognitive mobilization, equity/fairness considerations, and instrumental rationality.

Chapter 4—*Ideological Polarization: Different Worlds in East and West*, by Hermann Schmitt and André Freire—addresses a second crucial theme in the literature of political attitudes in democratic regimes. It is a theme where, as with the issue of regime support, the existence of secular trends in Western democracies has often been hinted at, as part of an "end of ideology" (Bell 1960). However, the *Beliefs in Government* project showed that left–right materialist orientations remained relevant throughout the 1970s and 1980s (Knutsen 1995), while other analyses suggested the absence of any secular trend in ideological polarization (Klingemann 2005). Schmitt and Freire examine the most recent evidence, looking not only for general trends but also for a potential contrast between the Western democracies and those in Eastern Europe, where younger and less institutionalized party systems would lead us to expect different trends and different economic and political correlates of polarization.

Chapter 5—*Electoral Turnout at the National and European Levels*, by Markus Steinbrecher and Hans Rattinger—focuses on one of the central behavioural dimensions of contemporary democratic politics: turnout, in both national and European elections. Earlier studies have been sceptical about dramatic statements concerning the decline of turnout in Western democracies: while some saw no decline whatsoever (Topf 1995b), others saw a decline that, albeit real, was nonetheless relatively moderate (Franklin 2002). However, the most recent elections, especially those to the European Parliament, have again made evident that a broad trend towards disengagement from formal means of political participation may indeed be taking place. Steinbrecher and Rattinger discuss the possibility that, in spite of variations caused by obvious institutional causes, turnout in European elections is driven by factors both common to national elections and specific to the EP election, i.e. European attitudes. This helps relate this chapter to all the previous ones—particularly those focusing on political engagement, EU attitudes, and ideological polarization—and provides important clues as to why turnout has declined in a more pronounced way than previously thought.

As the volume completes its overview of the basic developments in general political attitudes most commonly addressed in the study of *national* politics—support for democracy, political engagement, ideology, and electoral participation—it then moves to the core four dimensions of specifically *European* attitudes: identity, representation, policy scope, and generalized support for membership. In Chapter 6—*But Still It Does Not Move: Functional and Identity-Based Determinants of European Identity*—Pierangelo Isernia, Irena Fiket, Fabio Serricchio, and Bettina Westle examine data from the early 1970s until 2007 on the intensity with which individuals identify with Europe. Earlier broad comparative studies had shown that, while attachment to Europe was not contradictory with identification with other levels of government, it lagged clearly behind other indicators of European support, displayed a moderate ebb and flow around comparatively low levels, and showed little relationship with the length of a country's membership of the EU (Duchesne and Frognier 1995). Isernia and his co-authors re-examine these conclusions in light of a large array of data, confronting the hypotheses derived both from a "neo-functionalist" approach—which assumes that EU identity would build up with time and the accumulated perception of benefits from integration—and from an alternative approach that allows for the role of short-term economic and political factors, reconducing to the instrumental and cue-rationality approaches that have been advanced as explanations of European attitudes.

Chapter 7—*Trust in the European Parliament: From Affective Heuristics to Rational Cueing*, by Mariano Torcal, Jordi Muñoz, and Eduard Bonet—turns our attention to the second dimension of European attitudes addressed in this volume, *EU representation*. We know from previous research that Europeans' views about the democratic performance of EU institutions have been either sceptical or, when more sanguine—as in the case of the European Parliament—rooted in a very low level of information and understanding about the object of such support (Niedermayer and Sinnott 1995). Torcal and his colleagues, however, ask the question of whether individuals change the basis on which they judge the extent to which the European Parliament is indeed a trustworthy institution of representation over time. They look not only at trends in the overall levels of trust in the European Parliament but also at trends in the attitudinal basis of that trust, testing the hypothesis that time and/or membership in the euro have changed it from affective but cognitively shallow judgments to more rational-instrumental assessments.

Chapter 8—*Support for European Integration*, by Andrija Henjak, Gábor Tóka, and David Sanders—looks into the more conventionally employed measure of European support: generalized support for EU membership. This is, of course, a very well-trodden road in the literature, and the source of most of the extant theoretical approaches to account for attitudes vis-à-vis Europe. Tóka, Sanders, and Henjak revisit them using data since 1973, documenting how variation in the domestic political system and its performance, national economic conditions, and welfare-state entitlements, as well as successive waves of enlargement have influenced the degree to which citizens endorse further European integration or wish to see a reversal of this process. They are particularly concerned, however, in ascertaining the extent to which different theoretical approaches fare differently in different contexts, revealing how different mechanisms operate uniformly or unevenly across countries and periods, thus providing a more complete specification of the models accounting for generalized EU support.

Chapter 9—*Europe à la Carte? Public Support for Policy Integration in an Enlarged European Union*, by Pedro C. Magalhães—focuses on our last dimension of European support, policy scope. We know from previous studies that the preference for assigning policy areas to the European level has varied significantly from policy to policy and from country to country (Sinnott

1995). Magalhães uses data from the late 1980s to test well-known hypotheses concerning the nature of policy areas themselves, i.e. the extent to which their Europeanization is intrinsically beneficial, testing whether citizens tend to make cogent rankings of policies from that point of view. However, he extends his analysis to the detection and explanation of variations through time and between countries, testing for the impact of economic and political variables that may account for the astounding—and highly consequential—diversity of preferences among European publics concerning what kind of political Europe they actually desire.

Finally, Chapter 10—*Summary and Conclusions: Europe in Equilibrium—Unresponsive Inertia or Vibrant Resilience?* by David Sanders, Pedro C. Magalhães, and Gábor Tóka—concludes the volume. It revisits and presents the relevant long-term trends in all the dependent variables treated in the volume and pulls together the conclusions reached in each of the previous chapters. More generally, it revisits previous notions about the fundamentals of the political attitudes of European mass publics and tests them against the changes that have occurred in the last two decades. When summarizing the remarkable efforts of the seminal *Beliefs in Government* project, Kaase, Newton, and Scarbrough (1996: 228) noted, in a perhaps undramatic but characteristically precise fashion, how the overall evidence favoured "political stability, continuity, and adaptation, rather than fundamental or wholesale transformation, even though there has been major and rapid social and economic change in the same period". In Chapter 10, we ask if this general assessment still holds true. We focus on the trends, events, and external shocks, and national and individual-level variations and their correlates as identified by the chapters in this volume. Did the remarkable adaptability that European publics have exhibited in the past to political, economic, and social change persist in the last two decades? Has the same occurred with the well-known cross-national and individual-level variations in political attitudes? And what does that tell us about the likely consequences of the enormous political and economic upheaval that has been experienced in Europe as a result of the financial and budgetary crisis of the last few years? These are the questions addressed in the concluding chapter.

2

The Determinants of Democracy Satisfaction in Europe

Paolo Bellucci and Vincenzo Memoli

1. Satisfaction with democracy and political support

Since the publication of *The Crisis of Democracy* (Crozier, Huntington, and Watanuki 1975), the debate on the prospects of democratic polities has not abated. Moreover, and somewhat paradoxically, the more that democracy extends to formerly authoritarian regimes, the more citizens' disillusion with democratic rule ostensibly advances in both established and new democracies (Norris 1999a; Pharr and Putnam 2000). To be sure, profound differences exist between concerns voiced in the mid-1970s and those of the 1990s. The original emphasis on "government overload"—and its implications for effective governance threatened by rising social participation, erosion of traditional values, and declining support for political institutions—has now translated into more sober concerns over the extent to and the conditions under which popular disaffection may undermine democratic legitimacy.

In Western Europe, contrary to pessimistic expectations, no challenge to representative democracy was evident up to the 1980s. A thorough analysis of the many dimensions underlining the relationship between citizens and the state which appeared in the mid-1990s (Klingemann and Fuchs 1995) detected a "relationship transformed", rather than a crisis. Mass political disengagement was not expanding, though popular attachments to political parties fluctuated, and no serious decline of support for the democratic system emerged. There was certainly a decline in trust for governmental institutions—and to a lesser extent also a decline of trust in politicians—but rather than posing a challenge to the legitimacy of democracy, the evidence pointed to a closer connection between popular support and the actual performance and functioning of democracy. Later analyses on an enlarged panel of countries confirmed this prognosis, describing the rise of "critical citizens" who support and value democratic ideals but remain dissatisfied with the performance of the political system (Norris 1999b).

In contrast to these "revisionist" assessments of the "crisis of democracy", recent research (Dalton 2004) re-emphasizes the severity of the growing scepticism and cynicism among mass publics and their distrust of political institutions. Dalton criticizes the commonly advanced causal accounts of these trends (economic and political performance, media effects, social capital) as weak explanations of the falling trend in political support, which, in Dalton's view, may hamper democratic life through political disengagement and a lack of social compliance.

Behind this scholarly disagreement on the state of popular evaluations of democracy lie many differences in the concepts employed, the time horizons used, and the countries analysed. In this chapter we look at long-term trends in popular satisfaction with the functioning of democracy at national and European levels across European countries. The chapter is organized as follows: we discuss first the conceptual meaning of democratic support; then we analyse long-term trends in support; and, finally, we test some explanatory hypotheses for satisfaction with democracy in both national and European arenas.

2. The meaning of satisfaction with democracy

What does satisfaction with democracy mean? According to Norris (2006: 6) it means "public evaluations of how well autocratic or democratic governments work in practice". In the large literature on democratic support, "satisfaction with democracy" is one of the most used indicators, employed in surveys over an extended period of time.[1] This should imply that its interpretation is clear. On the contrary, its use: " ... is more complicated than many scholars perhaps would like to admit" (Linde and Ekman 2003: 404) and its meaning is frequently ambiguous. Past research has indeed disagreed on what theoretical concept the "satisfaction with democracy" measure operationalizes. The measure correlates with specific and diffuse support (Klingemann 1999; Kornberg and Clarke 1994), with political trust (Dalton 1999), and with perceptions of economic satisfaction (Castillo 2006). It also reflects partisan and/or ideological disagreement with the incumbent government (Montero and Gunther 1994). Although satisfaction with democracy apparently measures system support at a low level of abstraction (Fuchs, Guidorossi, and Svensson 1995; Anderson 1998b), it has been claimed that it should be considered an expression of short-term evaluations of the outputs of the democratic system (Waldron-Moore 1999), and that it is useful as a measure of the discrepancy between democratic norms and the actual democratic process (Wagner, Dufor, and Schneider 2003). Despite all this, it has proved difficult to separate, at the empirical level, the assessment of satisfaction/efficacy from the opinions that citizens have of the legitimacy of democratic regimes (Gunther and Montero 2001).[2]

Easton's conceptualization of political support (Easton 1965, 1975) is the starting point for assessing the theoretical meaning of satisfaction with democracy. Easton distinguished support for three levels of political objects, namely community, regime, and authority. Support for the "political community" refers to a basic attachment or a sense of belonging to a political system and is seen as the essential precondition for the foundation of any stable nation state (Linz and Stepan 1996). "Regime" refers to the main authority institutions and public attitudes toward the constitutional order. "Authorities", instead, identifies the current incumbents of authority roles—it includes evaluations of elected politicians and the performance of party leaders, prime ministers, and heads of state.

As is well known, Easton also proposed a distinction between diffuse and specific support: the first is a deep-seated loyalty to the citizen's own political community, while the second is based on the fulfilment of demands or satisfaction with political outputs. While diffuse support is less susceptible to daily governmental performance, specific support, conversely, is related to politicians' daily actions. In this way, when diffuse support is high, dissatisfaction with government outputs does not necessarily destabilize the political system. However, Easton's argument that all political objects might be recipients of both specific and diffuse support has raised additional problems of interpretation and operationalization (Torcal and Montero 2006).

To overcome these difficulties, an elaboration of the Eastonian framework has been proposed by Norris (1999c) and Dalton (2004). Adopting a fivefold frame, they expanded the original conceptualization of political regime, and distributed the objects of support along a unidimensional axis ranging from diffuse to specific support (see Figure 2.1). In terms of support for the political regime, the framework differentiates among three different objects of political support: (a) *regime principles*, which express the normative values of the political system and support for which can be measured by agreement with the idea of democracy as the best form of government or the most preferred political system (Dalton 1999); (b) *regime performance*,[3] which represents how democratic governments work in practice, and approval of which is measured in performance terms (satisfaction with the way democracy works—see Norris 1999c) or in evaluation terms (satisfaction with democracy itself);[4] and finally, (c) *regime institutions*, support for which refers to trust and confidence in private and public institutions.[5]

11

	Level of Analysis	Affective Orientations	Evaluations
Diffuse Support ↑	Political Community	National pride Sense of national identity	Best nation to live in
	Regime: Principles	Democratic values	Democracy best form of government
	Regime: Performance	Participatory norms Political rights	Evaluations of rights **Satisfaction with democratic process**
	Regime: Institutions	Institutional expectations Support party government Output expectations	Performance judgments Trust in institutions Trust party system Trust bureaucracy
Specific Support	Authorities	Identify with party	Candidate evaluations Party support

Figure 2.1. Levels of political support and content of people's attitudes
Source: Norris (1999a) and Dalton (2004)

This framework clearly assumes that political support is a multidimensional concept, and nicely accounts for differences among distinct objects of support. As Figure 2.1 indicates, "satisfaction with democracy" is conceptualized as an evaluation of regime *performance*. It should not tap, therefore, either adherence to democratic ideals or confidence in regime *institutions*. Nevertheless, as one of the proponents acknowledges, the item measuring this "middle level" support is: " ... ambiguous ... [and] alternative interpretations of this item are possible ... This survey item taps both support for 'democracy' as a value ... and also satisfaction with the incumbent government" (Norris 1999c: 11).

One way to resolve this controversy is to use survey data in order to ascertain whether public opinion does indeed distinguish among different objects of support. Klingemann's (1999) confirmatory factor analysis—based on the World Values Surveys, 1994–7—discovered a three-factor dimensional structure of support. Citizens are able to distinguish among support for the political community, for democracy as an ideal form of government, and for the performance of the regime. This last dimension includes both satisfaction with democracy as well as incumbent and institutional support (for the parliament and the government). On this account, public satisfaction with democracy does not tap abstract ideals but rather the performance of institutions, that is, how democracy functions in practice (thus confirming the analysis in Fuchs, Guidorossi, and Svensson 1995). In terms of Easton's original typology, this implies that institutional support—that is, confidence in the main institutions of democracy (parliament, government, the judiciary, and so on)—is not separated from the performance of the incumbents of those roles. This would mean that people's support for democratic institutions would be contingent, dependent on performance and/or partisan allegiance. In contrast, Dalton's (2004) analysis—based on a subset of Western democracies in the World Values Surveys, 1995–8—shows a four-dimensional structure of support, with confidence in institutions clearly distinct from incumbent performance evaluations. Unfortunately, the "satisfaction with democracy" measure was not included in this survey, which prevents any direct comparison being made between Dalton's findings and the results reported here.[6]

In order to provide additional insight into these issues, we undertake an analysis of European public opinion attitudes, based on the European and World Values Surveys, 1999–2002.[7] The goal of this exercise is to reassess: (1) the dimensionality of democracy support in Europe; (2) the empirical reference for the "satisfaction with democracy" item (Does it operationalize regime performance or institutional trust?); and (3) its interpretation as an indicator of specific or diffuse support.

The analysis is based on thirteen indicators[8] available for studying the five dimensions of democracy support elaborated by Norris (1999c) and Dalton (2004). As Table 2.1 shows, a five-dimensional solution is produced, thus confirming the multidimensional nature of political support. Specifically:

- The first dimension (which explains 8 per cent of the total variance) taps *support for political community*, and correlates with national pride and interest in compatriots' conditions of life.

- The second dimension (11 per cent of the total variance) identifies *support for democratic principles*, and correlates with adherence to democratic ideals.

- The third factor describes *confidence in public institutions*, which explains 17 per cent of the variance.

- The fourth dimension taps *regime performance*, correlating with the two measures of satisfaction with government performance and the way democracy has developed.

- Finally, variables tapping *involvement with the political system*[9] load on the fifth dimension.

The results of the analysis confirm, as in previous research (Klingemann 1999, Dalton 2004), the effective differentiation of the dimensions of democratic support. This suggests that citizens do have the capacity to distinguish among different aspects of democratic support, implying significant levels of political sophistication.[10] In terms of the actual dimensions of democratic support, in accordance with Dalton (2004), confidence in institutions is separated from support for regime performance. European citizens, in short, appear to

Table 2.1. Components of democracy support

	Political community	Regime: Democratic principles	Regime: Institutions	Regime: Performance	Regime: Political authority
National pride	0.667				
Interest in compatriots' living conditions	0.776				
Have a democratic political system		0.834			
Democracy best form of government		0.829			
Confidence in parliament			0.749		
Confidence in civil service			0.758		
Confidence in justice system			0.669		
Confidence in police			0.662		
Satisfaction with how democracy developed				0.673	
Satisfaction with government performance				0.644	
Location on the left–right continuum					0.718
Turnout					0.669
Belonging to political parties				−0.438	0.460
Eigenvalue	1.069	1.443	2.229	1.336	1.287
% of variance explained	8.2	11.1	17.4	10.3	9.9
Kaiser–Meyer–Olkin Test	0.742				
Barlett's Test (Sig.)	0.000				
N	32.316				

Note: Table entries are Varimax rotated factor readings of a principal component analysis (missing data are replaced by mean scores). The KMO measures the sampling adequacy and the Barlett's Test examines if correlation matrix is an identity matrix. The countries included are: Austria, Belgium, Czech Republic, Denmark, Estonia, Finland, France, Germany, Greece, Hungary, Ireland, Italy, Latvia, Lithuania, Luxembourg, Malta, Netherlands, Poland, Portugal, Slovakia, Slovenia, Spain, Sweden, United Kingdom.
Source: European and World Values Survey, 1999–20

differentiate between the trust they express for political institutions and their evaluations of the performance of the democratic process. Furthermore, satisfaction with the functioning of democracy is closely connected to the evaluation of government performance. This leads us to infer the following:

- Satisfaction with democracy is a measure of citizens' support for the actual working of democracy in their respective countries. It expresses people's evaluations of the performance of incumbent governments and, more broadly, of the actual achievements of the democratic process. It does not, therefore, measure adherence to democratic ideals or generalized confidence in the democratic institutions. It is a measure of *regime performance*.

- The association of democracy satisfaction in the same factor dimension with government performance, and its distinctiveness from institutional confidence, implies that it is closer to specific rather than to diffuse support. Indeed, the factor results suggest that the democracy satisfaction measure is best regarded as an indicator of *specific support for regime performance.*

- This in turn implies that the location of the "satisfaction with democracy" measure along the diffuse–specific continuum of political support in Figure 2.1 needs to be moved closer to the specific-support end of the continuum. The sequence of the levels of support in the revised Eastonian framework should then read (from diffuse to specific support) as Political community, Regime principles, Regime institutions, Regime performance, and Authorities.

Before moving to a trend analysis of "satisfaction with democracy", it is of interest to see how European countries are located along the dimensions of political support outlined above.[11] Table 2.2 shows the relative ranking of countries along the five support dimensions, ordered from diffuse to specific.

The first panel of Table 2.2 ranks countries according to their level of support for the political community. Here, as well as in the other panels, the ranking derives from national average factor scores on the dimension. Rather than absolute values, these scores express deviations from the mean.[12] Ireland, Malta, and Portugal show above-average values of support for the *political community* while the scores for Denmark and Latvia locate these countries at the opposite end of the continuum. The countries' spread is much narrower concerning support for *democratic principles*, thus showing a strong generalized commitment of European citizens to democratic values. Moving from diffuse to more specific measures of political support, confidence in democratic institutions shows a more differentiated pattern, where support tends to decline passing from Northern Europe towards Southern European countries and towards the more recent democracies of Eastern Europe. Finally, *support for regime performance* locates the recent democracies towards the more pessimistic end of the continuum—where also some more-established democracies, such as Belgium and Italy, are also placed—while average or above-average values characterize the remaining European countries.

A clearer view of the mapping of political support is offered by placing European countries in the space defined by the dimensions of support. Our focus here is not so much on the causal relationship among dimensions of support, but rather on the description of countries' patterns of association among the various types of support across Europe, particularly between satisfaction with regime performance and the rest.

The location of European countries in the space defined by *regime performance and support for the political community* (Figure 2.2) shows a clear independence between the two types of support. Relatively lower levels of community support coexist with lower performance satisfaction in just a

Table 2.2. Countries' rankings on dimensions of political support

Diffuse support						Specific support			
Political community		Democratic principles		Institutions		Regime performance		Political authority	
Ireland	0.414	Greece	0.289	Denmark	0.557	Malta	0.525	Netherlands	0.495
Malta	0.395	Netherlands	0.198	Luxembourg	0.513	Netherlands	0.460	Sweden	0.338
Portugal	0.395	Austria	0.174	Finland	0.355	Portugal	0.455	Malta	0.275
Poland	0.388	Denmark	0.166	Sweden	0.354	Luxembourg	0.394	Belgium	0.176
Slovenia	0.383	Sweden	0.143	Austria	0.322	Finland	0.322	Slovakia	0.143
Greece	0.216	Germany	0.142	Ireland	0.297	Germany	0.292	Austria	0.136
Italy	0.198	Italy	0.131	UK	0.205	Austria	0.244	Denmark	0.129
Spain	0.178	Luxembourg	0.108	Germany	0.137	Denmark	0.240	Finland	0.109
Sweden	0.168	Spain	0.081	Malta	0.129	Ireland	0.214	Germany	0.050
Slovakia	0.049	Malta	0.058	Portugal	0.119	Spain	0.115	Czech R.	0.032
Hungary	0.001	Czech R.	0.042	France	0.084	UK	0.009	Luxembourg	0.032
Czech R.	-0.040	Lithuania	-0.012	Netherlands	0.077	France	-0.011	Ireland	-0.021
Austria	-0.080	Belgium	-0.016	Spain	0.019	Greece	-0.061	UK	-0.051
UK	-0.082	Estonia	-0.025	Belgium	-0.010	Sweden	-0.115	Greece	-0.102
Germany	-0.088	Ireland	-0.026	Slovakia	-0.062	Poland	-0.119	Portugal	-0.126
Finland	-0.102	France	-0.085	Latvia	-0.062	Estonia	-0.188	Spain	-0.142
Luxembourg	-0.108	Slovenia	-0.086	Hungary	-0.084	Belgium	-0.193	Estonia	-0.159
France	-0.132	Portugal	-0.096	Italy	-0.149	Latvia	-0.206	Poland	-0.159
Lithuania	-0.189	UK	-0.096	Estonia	-0.189	Czech R.	-0.211	France	-0.160
Netherlands	-0.309	Latvia	-0.205	Poland	-0.198	Slovenia	-0.221	Lithuania	-0.214
Belgium	-0.363	Finland	-0.244	Slovenia	-0.259	Italy	-0.322	Italy	-0.221
Estonia	-0.391	Poland	-0.327	Greece	-0.557	Hungary	-0.395	Latvia	-0.225
Denmark	-0.428	Slovakia	-0.341	Czech R.	-0.671	Lithuania	-0.669	Hungary	-0.360
Latvia	-0.522	Hungary	-0.345	Lithuania	-0.773	Slovakia	-0.677	Slovenia	-0.456

Source: European and World Values Survey, 1999–2002. Numerical values reported are average national factor scores

few countries—in Latvia, Estonia, and France. In contrast, Portugal and Malta are characterized by higher levels of both satisfaction and community support. Overall, however, no discernible pattern emerges: for instance, Slovenia and Ireland show similar (high) levels of community support while significantly diverging in terms of performance satisfaction. Conversely, Denmark and Spain have similar (medium) levels of performance support, while showing opposite rates of support for the political community.

A similar image emerges if the countries are plotted against support for *democratic principles and for regime performance* (Figure 2.3). The majority of European nations share high levels of adherence to democratic norms (in the upper quadrants of Figure 2.3) while showing, at the same time, different levels of performance satisfaction. As expected, diffuse and specific measures of political support are relatively weakly related. Note, however, that for a subgroup of nations—mainly the most recent democracies, but also the UK and France—a relatively lower level of democratic support is associated with a somewhat restricted satisfaction with regime performance.

Lastly, and moving to a more "specific" measure of political support, the pattern of association between *generalized support for political institutions* and *democratic performance* shows an apparently closer relationship (Figure 2.4): growing satisfaction with democratic performance reinforces generalized support for political institutions. However, this relationship is mainly due to the location of a few countries (Lithuania, Czech Republic, and Greece) which show very low levels of both satisfaction and institutional support. For the rest of the countries, average or above-average levels of institutional support

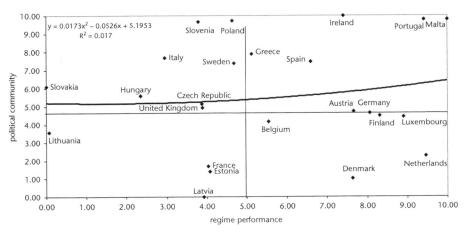

Figure 2.2. Location of EU countries in the space defined by support for political community and regime performance (1999–2002)

Source: European and World Values Survey, 1999–2002

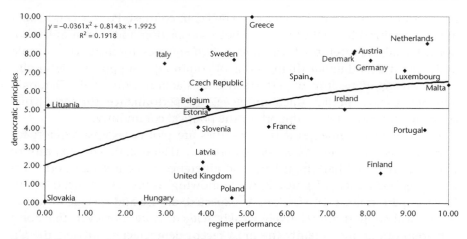

Figure 2.3. Location of EU countries in the space defined by support for democratic principles and regime performance (1999–2002)

Source: European and World Values Survey, 1999–2002

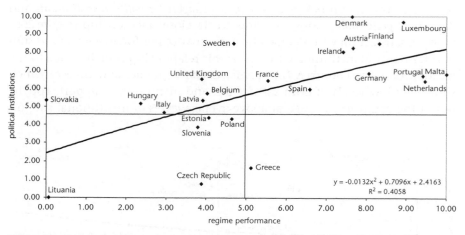

Figure 2.4. Location of EU countries in the space defined by support for political institutions and regime performance (1999–2002)

Source: European and World Values Survey, 1999–2002

coexist with a significant variance in satisfaction for regime performance: for example, France's and the United Kingdom's medium levels of institutional support are similar to those in Portugal and the Netherlands—yet satisfaction with democratic performance is much higher in the latter two countries.

In conclusion, EU countries differ in their patterns of political support. Citizens of European member states show, on the one hand, high levels of adherence to democratic principles and, with a more pronounced variability, of support for their respective political communities. On the other hand, a greater differentiation is evident in relation to confidence in political institutions and satisfaction with democratic performance. Crucially, however, when political support is broken down in its analytical components there is a weak relationship between measures of diffuse and specific support. The weakness of this relationship, which would otherwise make democratic legitimacy directly dependent on performance and therefore vulnerable to the ebbs and flows of policy achievements, sheds a reassuring light on democracy in Europe.

3. Trends in political support

Satisfaction with national democracy

Having ascertained that one of the most widely used indicators of political support—"satisfaction with democracy"—is a measure of specific support for democratic performance, we can now assess its trend over time. Writing in the mid-1990s, Fuchs and Klingemann (1995) noticed that the generally stable level of support after 1976 saw a sharp deterioration between 1989 and 1994. They wondered whether "the extent of the erosion of satisfaction suggests that the 'crisis of democracy', rather than being a matter of rhetoric, is actually materialising" (Fuchs and Klingemann 1995: 441). They provided a negative answer and the available evidence afterwards confirmed their evaluation.

Figure 2.5 shows the aggregate trend of satisfaction with national democracy between 1974 and 2006 in the European countries, differentiated according to their accession to the EU.[13] Among established democracies, the downward trend singled out by Fuchs and Klingemann actually worsened up to 1996, to reverse afterwards and then reach a peak of satisfaction around 2004. After 2004, we observe an improvement in Austria and Northern Europe, some erosion in Southern European polities and stability in the rest of Europe. As Table 2.3 shows, in the 2000s the average rate of satisfaction among established democracies was higher (62 per cent) than in the preceding decades (1970s: 53 per cent; 1980s: 54 per cent, 1990s: 54 per cent). So the erosion of support for the performance of democracy that Europeans experienced during the 1990s has been fully reversed.

Among the more recent democracies of Central Europe, satisfaction with the functioning of democracy stands at lower levels than among established ones (on average, 41 per cent in the 2000s; Table 2.2). This result is not surprising if we take into account two factors. On the one hand, citizens of new democracies have been socialized in undemocratic regimes, characterized by low levels of interpersonal and political trust (Bielasiak 2002) and by restricted experience of democratic politics (Mishler and Rose 2002). On the

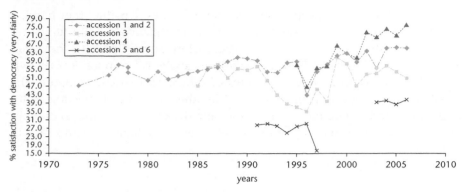

Figure 2.5. Satisfaction with national democracy (1973–2006)

Notes:
Accession 1: Belgium, France, Germany, Italy, Luxembourg, the Netherlands; Accession 2: Denmark, Ireland, United Kingdom; Accession 3: Greece, Portugal, Spain; Accession 4: Austria, Finland, Sweden; Accession 5: Czech Republic, Cyprus, Estonia, Hungary, Latvia, Lithuania, Malta, Poland, Slovakia, Slovenia; Accession 6: Bulgaria, Romania.

Source: Xezonakis (2008); European World Value Survey Integrated File (1999); Eurobarometer 44.3OVR (1996)–58.1 (2002)–60.1 (2003)–61 and 62 (2004)–63.4 (2005); 65.2 (2006); Central and Eastern Eurobarometer (1990–1997; 2003.4)

other hand, very high expectations in the new democratic political elite were perhaps not followed by effective reforms, causing some disillusionment in the citizenry. In particular, this disillusionment is evident in respect to the anticipated benefits of democracy, aspects that, in turn, have slowed down the democratic consolidation process (Waldron More 1999) and the relative satisfaction with it. However, it is remarkable how the Central European trend closely follows—albeit with a lag—that of established democracies. Unfortunately, due to the lack of survey data, we cannot track the crucial period of recovery between 1997 and 2003, which is followed by higher levels of support. Nonetheless, as late as 2006, Central and Eastern European citizens still evaluated their democracies some 20 percentage points lower than did their Western and Northern European counterparts.

These aggregate trends necessarily mask some predictable differences across countries. In the established democracies, Denmark and Luxemburg show the highest levels of satisfaction with democracy (hovering around 70 per cent between the 1970s and the 2000s). By contrast, satisfaction is lowest in Italy (27 per cent on average), while the remaining countries occupy an intermediate position. Among the recent democracies, the 1990s were characterized by low levels of support (though not lower than Italy's), while in the early 2000s satisfaction has improved moderately (reaching, on average, 41 per cent). Slovenia stands out. Helped by its economic growth of recent years, it is the only ex-communist country that has risen into the World Bank's "high

Table 2.3. National democracy satisfaction (% very and fairly satisfied; decade averages)

	1970s	1980s	1990s	2000s	Average 1970s–2000s	N of time points
Austria	—	—	59	67	64	12
Belgium	53	47	46	63	51	32
Denmark	60	68	78	82	73	32
Germany	71	72	49	52	60	32
Great Britain	48	51	50	52	50	32
Greece	—	55	36	54	48	27
Finland	—	—	54	71	62	14
France	43	46	45	54	47	32
Ireland	60	51	68	71	62	32
Italy	19	24	22	42	27	32
Luxembourg	62	70	73	77	71	32
Netherlands	62	59	69	68	65	32
Portugal	—	53	53	37	48	22
Spain	—	52	49	67	55	22
Sweden	—	—	56	71	65	12
Average	*53.1*	*54.0*	*53.8*	*61.9*	*56.5*	
Bulgaria	—	—	21	21	21	13
Czech Republic	—	—	41	47	43	13
Cyprus	—	—	—	67	67	4
Estonia	—	—	33	40	35	12
Hungary	—	—	23	36	27	13
Latvia	—	—	26	42	31	12
Lithuania	—	—	33	30	32	12
Malta	—	—	75	53	57	5
Poland	—	—	36	29	34	13
Romania	—	—	41	47	43	11
Slovakia	—	—	24	22	23	13
Slovenia	—	—	37	55	43	11
Average	—	—	*35.5*	*40.8*	*38.0*	

Note: The question format is: "On the whole, are you very satisfied, fairly satisfied, not very satisfied or not at all satisfied with the way democracy works in <country>? Would you say you are . . . ?"

Source: Xezonakis (2008); European World Value Survey Integrated File (1999); Eurobarometer 44.3OVR (1996)–58.1 (2002)–60.1 (2003)–61 and 62 (2004)–63.4 (2005); 65.2 (2006); Central and Eastern Eurobarometer (1990–1997; 2003.4)

income" category and whose "political situation has become substantially more stable than that of many former ex-communist countries" (Inglehart 2006: 7).

The available long-term data suggest a general change in the level of satisfaction with democracy across European countries. Although based on different periods across the countries, the evidence shows that democratic support is indeed increasing in many European polities. However, a within-Europe gap is also manifest: gauged by its linear trend (regressing for each country the level of satisfaction on time), we see a clear improvement over time in established democracies while the reverse is true in many of the recent ones (Table 2.4). Among the former, the slope is positive in twelve out of fifteen countries. The notable exceptions are Germany and Portugal, which show a statistically significant drop over time (respectively b = –0.97 and b = –1.28).

Table 2.4. Trend in satisfaction with national democracy (% very and fairly satisfied)

Nation	b	SE	Period	N of time points
Austria	1.57**	0.44	1995–2006	12
Belgium	0.34	0.21	1973–2006	32
Denmark	0.88***	0.16	1973–2006	32
Germany	−0.97***	0.22	1973–2006	32
Great Britain	0.13	0.11	1973–2006	32
Greece	−0.17	0.28	1980–2006	27
Finland	2.35***	0.32	1993–2006	14
France	0.32*	0.14	1973–2006	32
Ireland	0.74***	0.13	1973–2006	32
Italy	0.65***	0.14	1973–2006	32
Luxembourg	0.53***	0.11	1973–2006	32
Netherlands	0.45**	0.12	1973–2006	32
Portugal	−1.28**	0.34	1985–2006	22
Spain	1.05**	0.33	1985–2006	22
Sweden	2.41***	0.41	1995–2006	12
Bulgaria	−0.84	0.78	1990–2006	13
Czech Republic	0.09	0.79	1991–2006	13
Cyprus	−1.70	1.47	2003–2006	4
Estonia	0.93	0.45	1991–2006	12
Hungary	1.29*	0.52	1990–2006	13
Latvia	1.48	0.73	1991–2006	12
Lithuania	−1.93*	0.92	1991–2006	12
Malta	−3.99	2.09	1999–2006	8
Poland	−0.26	0.62	1990–2006	13
Romania	−0.95	0.77	1991–2006	11
Slovakia	−0.79	0.69	1990–2006	13
Slovenia	1.94	0.94	1992–2006	11

* $p<0.05$; ** $p<0.01$; *** $p<0.001$.

Note: b is the unstandardized regression coefficient of satisfaction with time, with associated standard errors in the SE column.

The question format is: "On the whole, are you very satisfied, fairly satisfied, not very satisfied or not at all satisfied with the way democracy works in <country>? Would you say you are...?"

Source: Xezonakis (2008); European World Value Survey Integrated File (1999); Eurobarometer 44.3OVR (1996)–58.1 (2002)–60.1 (2003)–61 and 62 (2004)–63.4 (2005); 65.2 (2006); Central and Eastern Eurobarometer (1990–1997; 2003.4)

The German case, particularly, reflects the strong difficulties of integration among Germans, where the different evaluation of the political system expressed by former East and West German citizens continues to affect their level of democracy support (Kluth 2005). On the other hand, a rise in satisfaction with democracy is particularly evident in Sweden (b = 2.41), Finland (b = 2.35), and Denmark (b = 0.88), but also in Spain (b = 1.05), Italy (b = 0.65), and France (b = 0.32).

The picture is more blurred among recent European democracies. With the exceptions of Hungary (b = 1.29), Estonia (b = 0.93, but not statistically significant), and Slovenia (b = 1.94, not significant), all other polities show, albeit mostly non-significant, negative slopes, implying stagnation or decline rather than an improvement in citizens' support for democratic performance. However, the much shorter time series prevents us from deriving a clear interpretation beyond that of "no improvement over time" in levels of democracy satisfaction are already low in comparison with those observed in established democracies.

Satisfaction with European Union democracy

Citizens in the European Union live in in a system of multilevel governance that ranges from local through regional, national, and finally supranational institutions. In this multilevel system of governance, EU institutions have traditionally enjoyed a somewhat restricted popular support which, matched by the lack of clear mechanisms of direct popular accountability, has in the past raised concerns about an EU democratic deficit that could endanger the legitimacy of the EU project (Blondel, Sinnot, and Svensson 1998; Thomassen and Schmitt 1999). However, institutional changes after the Maastricht and Amsterdam treaties, which widened the powers of the European Parliament, might have positively affected popular support for the European Union (Steinbrecher and Rattinger 2007).

Evidence of such an evolution is potentially provided by responses to the question on "satisfaction with the way democracy works in the EU", which was introduced in the Eurobarometer survey starting in 1993, where an upward trend is clearly detectable (see Figure 2.6). This pattern is confirmed by the results reported in Table 2.5. The average level of satisfaction per decade moved upward from 50 per cent in the 1990s to 57 per cent in the 2000s among established democracies. It stands at an even higher level—62 per cent—among the citizens of more recent member states.

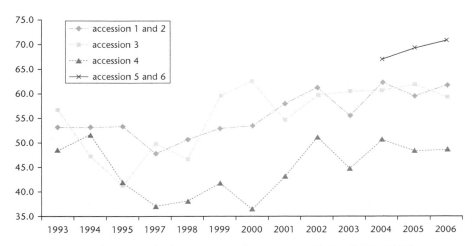

Figure 2.6. Satisfaction with democracy in the European Union (1993–2006)
Notes: see Figure 2.5

Table 2.5. Satisfaction with democracy in the EU (% very and fairly satisfied; average values per decade)

	1990s	2000s	Average 1990s–2000s	N of time points	2000s difference satisfaction EU–National
Austria	52	50	51	11	−17
Belgium	50	66	58	13	3
Denmark	43	58	51	13	−24
Germany	41	47	44	13	−5
Great Britain	50	52	51	13	0
Greece	46	58	52	13	4
Finland	44	44	44	13	−27
France	46	52	49	13	−2
Ireland	79	81	80	13	10
Italy	47	57	52	13	15
Luxembourg	66	68	67	13	−9
Netherlands	47	50	48	13	−18
Portugal	52	50	51	13	13
Spain	53	71	63	13	4
Sweden	26	45	38	11	−26
Average	*49.5*	*56.6*	*53.3*		*−5.3*
Bulgaria	—	66	—	4	45
Czech Republic	—	60	—	4	13
Cyprus	—	65	—	4	−2
Estonia	—	59	—	4	19
Hungary	—	58	—	4	22
Latvia	—	62	—	4	20
Lithuania	—	63	—	4	33
Malta	—	55	—	4	2
Poland	—	65	—	4	36
Romania	—	74	—	4	27
Slovakia	—	50	—	4	28
Slovenia	—	67	—	4	12
Average	—	*62.0*	—		*21.2*

Note: The question format is: "On the whole, are you very satisfied, fairly satisfied, not very satisfied or not at all satisfied with the way democracy works in the European (Community) Union? Would you say you are . . . ?"

Source: Xezonakis (2008);–60.1 (2003)–61 and 62 (2004)–63.4 (2005); 65.2 (2006); Central and Eastern Eurobarometer (2003.4)

The strong positive image of the EU among new democracies' citizens is perhaps not surprising given that the transition to democracy in Central and Eastern Europe has taken place within the framework of the prospective EU accession process. Indeed, in these countries, satisfaction with EU democracy outpaces evaluations of national democracy. Earlier research (Niedermayer and Sinnot 1995) found a strong correlation between satisfaction with national and European democracy, and inferred that the two measures tapped a general system evaluation of democracy rather than an evaluation of the actual working of democracy in the two different political arenas. However, subsequent research found substantial variation in the correlation of the two measures across countries, observing greater approval of European rather than national democracy in some Western European countries (Karp, Banducci, and Bowler 2003; Steinbrecher and Rattinger 2007). This finding is now extended to most of Central and Eastern Europe. The last column of Table 2.5 shows the difference between the percentage of people expressing satisfaction with democracy in Europe and in their own country. With the exception of Cyprus, substantial proportions of people (ranging from a difference of 45 percentage points in Bulgaria to 22 points in Hungary to a low of 2 points in Malta) express more support for European democracy than for the national one. On average, in Central and Eastern Europe, 21 per cent of citizens are more positive about the performance of democratic institutions at the European level than at the national level. By contrast, among established polities, national democracy enjoys an average satisfaction lead of 5 percentage points. But here we observe a great variance. At one end of the continuum, in Italy and Portugal one out of six people is more confident in the democratic performance at the European level than at the national level. At the opposite end, in Sweden and Denmark one citizen in four expresses more satisfaction with the working of democracy at the national rather than European level. Apparently, this gap unfolds along a Northern–Southern European distinction. It can be explained by the differentiated level of governance effectiveness associated with different histories of democratic politics. However, the fact that Northern European countries such as Belgium or Ireland display relatively high levels of dissatisfaction with national compared to European democracy suggests we need to search for further explanatory factors.

4. Explaining satisfaction with democracy

What factors, then, could explain the observed trends of satisfaction with democracy in the national and European arenas? Recalling that this variable measures *specific support for regime performance*, a review of the literature suggests three sets of possible explanatory variables, grouped in the theoretical perspectives of *instrumental rationality*, *political mobilization* and *equity/fairness*.

Instrumental rationality

Instrumental rationality simply assumes that when the general context in which people live is positively (negatively) evaluated, citizens express their support for (criticism of) the political system. In essence, the better the system performance, the higher citizens' satisfaction with democracy will be. There are a number of dimensions that could be relevant for describing the general context and the well-being of a society. We focus here on two key dimensions of a polity: the economy and the rule of law. As to the economic side, an extensive literature relates public support for political authorities and governments to the country's economic performance. Previous research has shown that the economy is a powerful factor in the determination of citizens' attitudes with respect to the many facets of the democratic process (Clarke, Dutt, and Kronberg 1993; Anderson and Guillory 1997). Studies that have focused on the relationship between democracy support and the economy—from a sociotropic or egocentric perspective (see Lockerbie 1993; McAllister 1999; Lewis-Beck and Stegmaier 2000; Curtin 2002)—assume a logic of reward/punishment: the electorate rewards or punishes political authorities with its support as a function of personal or national economic conditions (Clarke, Mishler, and Whiteley 1990). On this account, when government performance falls below citizens' expectations, democratic support is damaged (Dalton 2004).

In this analysis we focus on GDP growth at constant prices, inflation and unemployment rates, and the public budget deficit. Previous research shows that among these economic indicators, GDP growth exercises a significant effect on support for democracy among consolidated democracies, while muffled effects are registered among Central and Eastern European countries (Bandeli and Radu 2006).[14] This set of economic variables is expected to co-vary positively (with the exception of the public deficit) with satisfaction with democracy at both national and European levels. In the supranational arena our expectations stem from the previous framing of European integration as mainly an economic process, which should have improved European prosperity. It is also clear, however, that people and nations who obviously benefit from European integration—with economic gains exceeding costs—should be more satisfied with supranational democracy. We accordingly include, as a further predictor of satisfaction at the European level, the *Net Transfer of Financial Resources from the EU*, which we expect to co-vary positively with satisfaction with European democracy.

The second factor that—according to the instrumental perspective—could affect citizens' evaluations of the way democracy works is the extent to which the rule of law is exercised in their respective polities. From this perspective, corruption is one of the key behaviours that contradicts the rule of law and it is an issue of serious concern not only in new democracies (Linde and Ekman 2005). When corruption penetrates the political, administrative, and judicial branches of government, good democracy is at risk (Morlino 2003). It affects behaviour in both the public and private sectors and undermines the legitimacy of governments and institutions (Newton 2006). Corruption, as Uslaner (2006) argued, is a plague on good government, since it leads to lower rates of economic growth and political distrust (Della Porta 2000; Albritton, Bureekul, and Gang 2005). Moreover, corruption is associated with higher rates of crime and tax evasion, closed markets, lower economic growth, less-efficient government institutions, and lower satisfaction with democracy (Uslaner 2004).

Citizens in countries with higher levels of corruption tend to express less confidence in the political system and less satisfaction with the way democracy works (Mungio-Pippidi 2006). To assess law enforcement and the extent of corruption in each country, we employ the Quality of Government Index,[15] with the expectation that it correlates positively with level of satisfaction at the national level. Its impact at the European level, however, is more uncertain. As we argue below, the impact of satisfaction with national governance on satisfaction with European democracy can operate in two different ways: people can transfer and extend a positive evaluation of their own country's democratic performance to the European system (of which they are, after all, members), but a negative evaluation of domestic governance can also rationally push people to express *more* satisfaction with European democracy (applying a sort of substitution or compensation mechanism), since it represents a larger political system which might positively ameliorate domestic shortcomings.[16]

Political mobilization

The second theoretical perspective we rely on to explain satisfaction with democracy is political mobilization. Under this heading we consider both behavioural and system-level features. As to the former, we include as a predictor informal political engagement, operationalized as the extent to which people discuss politics. Political discussion is a key component and also a consequence of the cognitive mobilization process with has transformed European societies in the second half of the twentieth century (Inglehart 1990). Discussing politics implies a minimum of information and a willingness to engage with the political system, both expressively and instrumentally; it is a form of political participation which nurtures representative democracy, allowing dissenting opinions to be voiced and heard (Topf 1995a). We therefore expect that the more widespread informal political engagement is, the more people are likely to register satisfaction with the national political system that allows and encourages them to express their views freely.

Next, we consider system-level indicators of political mobilization: duration of democracy and electoral volatility. A longer tradition of democratic politics is assumed to be associated with higher levels of satisfaction since people have had more opportunities to be socialized into a democratic polity and to appreciate it. This expectation is consistent with individual-level findings, which show that after an election the level of satisfaction with democracy increases (Nadeau et al. 2000). This pattern even occurs—though to a lesser extent—among voters who "lost" the election (Anderson et al. 2005)—a reflection of the legitimizing function of elections as a means of solving political controversies peacefully, and to the depolarization of opinions which follows the electoral contest. The implication is that more experiences of participating in democratic consultations reinforce satisfaction with democracy.[17]

The impact of electoral volatility on the level of democratic satisfaction is more controversial. On the one hand, changes in parties' vote share may testify to the accountability of democracy, and to the power that citizens hold in expressing either loyalty to parties that rule well or voicing their discontent (by voting for the opposition) about those that do not (Hirschmann 1970). As such we might expect political systems that experience greater electoral volatility to be endowed with *greater* levels of satisfaction with democracy among their citizens. On the other hand, previous empirical research has mainly framed electoral volatility as a *malaise* with mainstream political parties, reflecting partisan dealignment, erosion of traditional ideological and social cleavages but also dissatisfaction with parties' performance (Dalton, Flanagan, and Beck 1984). Increasing volatility in established democracies is on this account signalling popular discontent (though see, *contra*, Bartolini and Mair 1990) and, although this can be expressed and channelled in the electoral arena, it may impact negatively on the stability of the political system. This is particularly evident in recent democracies, where electoral volatility reflects the low institutionalization of party systems and may affect their viability and democratic performance (Mainwaring and Zoco 2007). On balance, we consider it more appropriate to interpret volatility negatively—as an indicator of an unstable, fluid party system—rather than as a positive opportunity to voice discontent. Our expectation, therefore, is that electoral volatility should be negatively associated with democratic satisfaction.

The political mobilization factors that are hypothesized to influence satisfaction with democracy need to be supplemented by other relevant predictors when our dependent variable is satisfaction with *European democracy*. Previous research highlights the importance of trust in European institutions but also of satisfaction with domestic democracy (Karp, Banducci, and Bowler 2003). These evaluations can be thought of as forms of soft rationality, cognitive shortcuts that allow people to express attitude towards distant or unfamiliar subjects. The image of Europe and trust in its institutions operate in such a way, with feelings of being represented by EU institutions enhancing satisfaction with European democracy (Rohrschneider 2002). Our indicator of trust in EU institutions is calculated as the average number of EU institutions trusted by respondents. It is expected to be positively associated with EU democracy satisfaction. Domestic satisfaction, on the other hand, may operate differently. As noted above, it is possible that people satisfied (dissatisfied) with their national democracy may extend their satisfaction (dissatisfaction) to the European level (Anderson 1998b). But it is equally possible that people dissatisfied with national democracy may translate their negative evaluations into greater satisfaction for the working of European democracy, seen as a source of improvement of national governance.

Equity/fairness

The last theoretical perspective we consider is that of equity/fairness. This perspective was originally employed to investigate alternative models of citizenship, explaining political participation and individual attitudes towards rights and obligations (Pattie, Seyd, and Whiteley 2004). We borrow from this, asking whether equality—as both a perception and a system-level feature—can be a source of democracy satisfaction. Equity and fairness are constitutive goals (and promises) of democracy, although each actual democratic polity may stand at quite different levels of fulfilment. Equality of social and economic opportunities and fair access to political representation define the context in which democratic citizenship develops. Of course, such goals are not easily obtained and policies aimed at achieving them are not always successfully implemented. Nor are economic and social resources fairly distributed in society. As a consequence, political inequality may arise (Verba, Schlozman, and Brady 1995) and relative deprivation among social groups may stir feelings of injustice, which in turn may motivate political involvement (Gurr 1970) or withdrawal (Hirschmann 1970). We employ as measures of equity/fairness individual perceptions of subjective well-being and, at the system level, the character of the electoral system.

Happiness and life satisfaction are often considered as a *dependent* variable, under the hypothesis that democracy enhances individual happiness (Inglehart 2006). Democracy, it is argued, fosters both political (by granting freedom and rights) and material well-being (by stimulating economic growth). This sense of well-being in turn translates into personal subjective perceptions of happpiness. The causal order is here reversed, and we employ the perception of one's own satisfaction with life[18] as a predictor of democracy satisfaction, under the assumption that if the well-being "promises" of democracy are to an extent fulfilled, people will express satisfaction with the performance of the democratic regime.

The second component that may affect public satisfaction with the working of democracy within the equity/fairness framework is the system of political representation. The classical claim is that proportional representation facilitates the inclusion of the relevant societal and ethnic groupings far more effectively than electoral systems based on plurality rules, thus fostering feelings of fairness of representation (Lijphart 1999). However, research on the effect of electoral systems on satisfaction with democracy has not reached unique conclusions. On the one hand, Anderson and Guillory (1997), analysing Eurobarometer data, found a positive relationship between proportional representation and satisfaction with democracy. On the other hand, using a different dataset (World Values Study), Norris (1999a: 233) claims that "majoritarian institutions tended to produce greater institutional confidence than consociational arrangements". Aarts and Thomassen's (2007) recent research based on Comparative Study of Electoral Systems data, challenges both previous works, showing that satisfaction with democracy impinges upon the individual's perception of the representative function of elections, but that perceptions of representation are higher among people living in majoritarian systems (while, puzzlingly, perceptions of accountability are associated with proportional electoral institutions). Aarts and Thomassen conclude that "macro-level satisfaction with democracy is primarily affected by the age of the democracy one lives in" (p. 5). Testing this claim here, we will include in our model the Disproportionality Index (Gallagher 1991), with the expectation that it varies negatively with democracy satisfaction, while we already control for age of democracy.

5. Findings

We turn now to a test of the impact of potential predictors, according to the theoretical perspectives outlined above, on the level of satisfaction with democracy. We use a pooled time-series cross-section design at the aggregate level, where our dependent variables are the country's yearly percentage of respondents who describe themselves as "very" or "fairly" satisfied with the way democracy works (a) in their country and (b) at the European level. The independent variables are country averages or scores by year of the relevant predictor variables. Unfortunately, data are not available for all countries and for all years.[19] Aggregating the various available survey data, we built a data matrix that includes the *national democracy satisfaction* scores for the EU9 countries[20] over a time span of 30 years, from 1976 to 2006. A second data matrix includes the EU27 countries for the shorter period 2004–6. As an exploratory strategy we also analysed an unbalanced matrix where relevant variables appear over time, with increasing sample size N × T. Available data for *satisfaction with European democracy* allow for a matrix that includes the EU9 countries between 1999 and 2006 and the EU27 countries between 2004 and 2006. Given the nature of the data, Prais-Winsten regression with panel-corrected standard errors (PCSE)[21] is used to estimate the parameters in the models.

National satisfaction

Table 2.6 Model A reports the estimates from a linear cross-section time-series model of satisfaction with national democracy in the EU9 countries between 1976 and 2006. The results show large, robust, and statistically significant effects for most of the variables considered, with 57 per cent of the variance explained. Satisfaction with national democracy is a function of citizens' evaluations and system-level characteristics—as hypothesized by the instrumental rationality, political mobilization, and equity/fairness perspectives. Almost all of the system performance variables are statistically significant, with the exception of the public deficit, and correctly signed. When the economy improves, citizens' satisfaction moves in tandem: a 1 percentage point increase in GDP increases satisfaction with democracy by 1.1 percentage points; likewise, a unitary increase in inflation or unemployment depresses

Table 2.6. Satisfaction with national democracy in the European Union member states (linear cross-sectional time-series model; Model A: H-corrected standard errors; Model B: correlated panel-corrected standard errors; Model C: H-corrected standard errors)

	Model A: EU9 1976–2006		Model B: EU27 2004–6		Model C: EU27 1976–2006 (unbalanced panel)	
	b	SE	b	SE	b	SE
System performance						
GDP growth	1.16****	0.30	0.52	0.65	1.03****	0.27
Inflation	−1.42**	0.25	0.01	0.45	−0.10	0.29
Unemployment	−1.32****	0.22	−0.53	0.52	−1.02****	0.28
Budget deficit	−0.01	0.01	1.26**	0.51	0.00	0.00
Governance quality	0.01****	0.00	30.41***	10.61	21.64**	10.18
Political mobilization						
Political discussion	0.71****	0.19	0.61**	0.29	0.16	0.15
Electoral volatility	−0.28**	0.11	−0.28****	0.07	−0.17**	0.08
Democracy duration	0.48****	0.07	0.19	0.13	21****	0.07
Equity/fairness						
Life satisfaction	0.07	0.08	0.10i	0.30	0.12	0.10
Disproportionality	−1.02****	0.15	0.57	0.58	−0.15*	0.08
Constant	25.98***	9.56	14.91	20.96	22.18**	10.44
R^2	0.57		0.67		0.43	
Spearman's Rho			0.16		0.54	
N	9		27		27	
Time	30		3		3–27	

* p<0.10; ** p<0.05; *** p<0.01; **** p<0.001.

Note: The period considered for Model A is 1976–2006; countries include Belgium, Denmark, France, Germany, Ireland, Italy, Luxembourg, Netherlands, United Kingdom. The countries considered in Model B, estimated for the 2004–6 period, are the EU27. The countries considered in Model C, estimated for the 1976–2006 period, are the EU27; unbalanced panel, T varies between 3 and 30, with an average of 15.
  Missing data in 1996 for "satisfaction with democracy" and "life satisfaction" have been interpolated with the 1995 and 1997 values.

Source: The Mannheim Eurobarometer trend (1970–2002); European World Value Survey Integrated File (1999); Eurobarometer 44.3OVR (1996)–58.1 (2002)–60.1 (2003)–61 and 62 (2004)–63.4 (2005); 65.2 (2006); Central and Eastern Eurobarometer (1990–1997; 2003.4).

citizens' evaluations by roughly the same amount. The impact of quality of government on satisfaction with democracy shows a positive relationship: where the corruption level is low, satisfaction with democracy is high. Citizens living in "difficult" democracies are therefore likely to express dissatisfaction with their country's democratic performance—though in Europe corruption is relatively low (EuroTopics 2006).

Political mobilization variables also have a direct impact. Higher levels of political involvement of the citizenry are associated with greater satisfaction ($b = 0.71$). Democratic history also has a positive significant effect ($b = 0.48$). So, within the EU9 countries, satisfaction with democracy depends on the extent to which their citizens are politically engaged. Beyond that, electoral volatility shows a significant effect in the expected negative direction, with party-system instability depressing satisfaction with democracy. Turning, lastly, to equity/fairness explanations, life satisfaction does not show a significant impact, while the disproportionality index does: in line with Anderson and Guillory (1997), countries with proportional electoral systems enable their citizens to feel more satisfied with the working of democracy ($b= -1.02$).

Are these findings confirmed if we take into account all EU member states, although reducing the length of the time period considered? Table 2.6 Model B reports the estimates of the previous model applied to the 2004–6 period. The results indicate that the equity/fairness perspective does not hold, while some of the variables with which we have operationalized instrumental rationality and political mobilization exert the expected impact. In terms of instrumental rationality, both quality of government and public budget deficit increase satisfaction. Contrary to our expectations, however, public budget deficit is positively correlated with performance satisfaction. Although these aggregate estimates do not allow us to speculate on individual behaviour, this finding lends support to the notion that deficit spending is not perceived as involving the government's failure to balance the budget, rather as a more neutral tool to find resources in order to perform state and welfare-related, functions. Finally, among the political mobilization variables, political engagement and electoral volatility impact significantly, while democratic history does not.

There are evident differences in the reported results, according to the length of the time series and the number of countries included in the analysis, which may explain the variations in findings. Observing the relationship between satisfaction with democracy and economic performance in a *limited* period, where the economy is stagnant for all, depresses the effects of economic variables. Conversely, including in the sample a large number of recent democracies with fluid party systems enhances the significance of electoral volatility. We clearly need to wait for longer time series in order to reach firmer conclusion on whether the model employed to explain the trend of satisfaction with the democracy in established democracies can be extended to all Europe. But we cannot be oblivious to the important consistent results in the two models: quality of governance and political engagement consistently boost democratic satisfaction.

As indicated above, we also tried to explore the stability of previous findings by fitting the same model to an unbalanced panel, characterized by increasing the number of observations with time. Rather than having missing cases scattered randomly, the structure of the data reflects the various waves of accession to the EU so that T ranges from 31 to 22, 12, and finally 3. This affects the findings, which must be interpreted with extreme caution and taken just as illustrative. However, Table 2.6 Model C shows that most of the relationships retain their significant effects, with the notable exceptions of political discussion and life satisfaction.

In conclusion, assuming (as we do) that satisfaction with democracy is a good indicator of the performance of democratic rule, these results show that satisfaction is increasing over time and that a good economy, low corruption, political engagement, and adequate political representation can instil among citizens confidence in the workings of democratic institutions.

Supranational satisfaction

Moving to the supranational European arena, the estimates are consistent with most of the causal effects proposed by the instrumental rationality, political mobilization, and equity/fairness theoretical models. Most important, however, the findings highlight the difference between satisfaction with European democracy and national democracy, and their reciprocal relationships within a multilevel system of governance. Table 2.7 Model A reports findings for the EU9 countries in the 1999–2006 period. First, the impact of instrumental rationality variables is clearly modified in comparison with domestic satisfaction. Countries' economic performance levels do not directly impinge upon European satisfaction, while the benefits accruing from the country do, as shown by the statistically significant coefficient of Net Financial Transfers from the EU (b = 4.69). Second, Quality of Government has a negative impact, which means that people living in polities with lower control over corruption and with restricted bureaucratic accountability express greater support for European democracy. The story told by the instrumental rationality variables about European democratic satisfaction is contingent on people's expectations that they will gain from EU membership, both economically and politically.

But political mobilization factors also add to the story. Political engagement and democratic history boost support, implying that European democracy is nurtured by a vibrant democracy at home. However, when vibrancy of

Table 2.7. Satisfaction with European democracy in the EU member states (linear cross-sectional time-series model, panel-corrected standard errors (PCSE))

	Model A: EU9		Model B: EU27	
	1999–2006		2004–6	
	b	SE	b	SE
System performance (instrumental rationality)				
GDP growth	0.02	0.34	−0.41 **	0.19
Inflation	0.75	0.57	0.60	0.44
Unemployment	0.21	0.96	0.04	0.19
Budget deficit	−0.37	0.31	−0.05	0.16
Net EU transfers	4.69*	2.59	−0.90	1.22
Governance quality	−35.45***	12.42	−12.76*	7.76
Political mobilization I				
Political discussion	0.26	0.15	0.17	0.13
Electoral volatility	−0.39****	0.11	−0.09 *	0.03
Duration of democracy	0.36****	0.08	0.00	0.04
Political mobilization II (soft rationality)				
Trust in European institutions	18.52****	2.30	15.08 ****	1.66
National democracy satisfaction	0.18***	0.07	0.04	0.06
Equity/fairness				
Life satisfaction	0.22*	0.14	0.22****	0.02
Length of EU membership				
Accession 1970s	0.39	1.54	3.34 **	1.50
Accession 1980s			−0.23	1.24
Accession 1990s			−0.92	3.86
Accession 2004			−1.22	1.96
Accession 2006			−0.03	0.68
Constant	−25.70	13.26	−3.19	8.27
R^2	0.78		0.76	
Spearman's Rho	0.34		0.35	
N	9		27	
Time	8		3	

* p<0.10; ** p<0.05; *** p<0.01; **** p<0.001.

The period considered for Model A is 1999–2006; countries include Belgium, Denmark, France, Germany, Ireland, Italy, Luxembourg, Netherlands, United Kingdom.

The countries considered in Model B, estimated for the 2004–6 period, are the EU 27.

Source: Xezonakis (2008); European World Value Survey Integrated File (1999); Eurobarometer 44.3OVR (1996)–58.1 (2002)–60.1 (2003)–61 and 62 (2004)–63.4 (2005); 65.2 (2006); Central and Eastern Eurobarometer (1990–1997; 2003.4).

domestic politics is associated with party-system instability—as measured by increasing national electoral volatility—evaluations of European democracy are depressed (b = −0.39). The relevance of national political instability for *European* democracy can be further appreciated if we contrast its negative impact with that of satisfaction with national democracy and with life in general. Both national democracy satisfaction and life satisfaction positively influence European satisfaction (respectively: b = 0.18; b = 0.22). This means that the relationship between domestic and supranational arenas is contingent on different aspects: well-being and democratic good government encourage confidence in European governance, while domestic party instability discourages it. Lastly, in keeping with previous research, trust in European institutions strongly affects satisfaction with European democracy (b = 18.5), effectively linking a positive image of Europe—net of all other factors—to perceptions of good governance.

When the same model is applied to the EU27 countries (Table 2.7 Model B), the overall picture is not significantly changed, although some variables lose statistical significance. Across the full membership of the EU, citizens evaluate European democracy on the basis of the extent to which they trust EU institutions. However, they also employ a substitution mechanism, turning to supranational governance when national government is failing. In contrast, satisfaction is depressed by domestic political instability, while personal well-being improves people's confidence in Europe.

6. Conclusion

The aims of this chapter have been to clarify the tangled concept of satisfaction with democracy, and to evaluate its theoretical and empirical implications, analysing its distribution among European citizens and explaining its trend over time. Following Easton, we have ascertained that satisfaction with democracy is a measure of citizens' support for the actual working of democracy in their countries. Analysing a dataset of twenty-four European countries, the results obtained show that EU countries differ in their patterns of political support, as other scholars have also claimed. We find high levels of adherence to democratic principles and political community across Europe, and significant differences concerning confidence in political institutions, and satisfaction with democratic performance. Yet the weak relationship between measures of diffuse and specific support confirms claims that democratic legitimacy does not directly depend on performance.

Looking at different measures of democracy support and at the location of "satisfaction with democracy" along the diffuse–specific continuum of political support, our results suggest that its place in the continuum defined by Easton and revisited successively by Norris should be moved towards the specific-support pole of the continuum. The sequence, reading from diffuse to specific support, should then be: Political community, Regime principles, Regime institutions, Regime performance, and Authorities.

Across established European democracies, and with the partial exception of Germany (due to the recent integration of the two Germanies), the trend of satisfaction with democracy is positively increasing rather than decreasing. However, the process of democratic consolidation which characterizes Central and Eastern European democracies shows that their citizens still express lower levels of democratic support. The determinants of the trend of satisfaction with *national* democracy show that it depends on a complex set of economic, political, and social factors which we have investigated within three theoretical perspectives: instrumental rationality, political mobilization, and equity/fairness. Each of them adds to the overall explanation. Satisfaction with national democracy increases when economic performance is strong, when corruption is low, when citizens are politically engaged, and when the electoral institutions ensure fair and wide representation. In these circumstances, satisfaction with national democracy flourishes and increases over time. Satisfaction with *European* democracy reflects the aspiration that the integration process will produce benefits for both the economic well-being and the political effectiveness of the national political institutions. Such rational and soft-rational motivations are then supplemented by political engagement, showing that an active citizenry does sustain support for European democracy.

Notes

1. The standard format of the question, employed in the *Eurobarometer* series, the *Central and Eastern Eurobarometer* and the *Candidate Countries Eurobarometer* (CCEB), is: "On the whole, are you very satisfied, fairly satisfied, not very satisfied, or not at all satisfied with the way democracy works in (your country)?"
2. Mishler and Rose (2001: 306), for instance, suggested comparing, in newer democracies, the public evaluation of the current regime against the previous regime, without referring to "democracy" per se, since this provides a common standard in each country.
3. It is also denominated regime norms and procedures (see Dalton 2004).
4. Some doubts could emerge concerning the validity of these two measures, especially if we compare old democracies with new democracies: in the former, satisfaction with democracy tends to be more stable than in the latter (Anderson 2001).
5. On this political object there are differentiations in measures: some scholars prefer to measure it using only public institutions (Dalton 2004), while others include both private and public institutions (Norris 2006).
6. The measure of satisfaction available in the survey, and employed by Dalton, is the following: "People have different views about the system for governing this country. Here is a scale for rating how well things are going: (1) means very bad and (10) means very good. Where on this scale would you put the political system as it is today?" However, the lack of reference to "democracy" prevents interpretation of this question as equivalent to the "satisfaction with democracy" item.
7. The twenty-four countries are: Austria, Belgium, Czech Republic, Denmark, Estonia, Finland, France, Germany, Greece, Hungary, Ireland, Italy, Latvia, Lithuania, Luxembourg, Malta, Netherlands, Poland, Portugal, Slovakia, Slovenia, Spain, Sweden, United Kingdom.

8. The indicators used are: national pride, interest for compatriots' conditions of life, approval democratic ideals; democracy is the best form of government; satisfaction with the way democracy develops; confidence in public institutions (police, parliament, justice systems, civil service); satisfaction with government performance; positioning on the left–right continuum, electoral turnout, and party membership.

9. Given the lack of suitable measures of support for political actors, positioning on the left–right continuum, turnout, and party membership have been employed as subjective behavioural indicators of involvement with the political system (Dalton 2004: 24).

10. As in Luskin (1987: 860–1) we interpret political sophistication as "the extent to which [a person's personal belief system] is large, wide-ranging, and highly constrained" and "the political case of a more general variable cognitive complexity or expertise").

11. We replicate Dalton's (2004: 61) research design over EU countries.

12. These are standardized factor scores, not actual values of the component variables. For instance, the range of the national pride (per cent respondents who are proud of being a [national] citizen) shows a restricted variance, and varies from a high of 97.4 per cent in Poland to a low of 81.4 per cent in Latvia. Their ranking therefore reflects deviation from the average mean for all countries, compound across the variables which load on the factor. In Figures 2.2–2.4, factor scores have been rescaled to 0–10.

13. Which corresponds to data availability in the Eurobarometer series. Data plotted is the percentage of respondents who are very or fairly satisfied with the way democracy works in their country, computed including missing values. Unweighted data. Source: Xezonakis (2008); Eurobarometer 44.3OVR–49–53–54.1–56.2–58.1–59.1–60.1–62.2–63.4; Central and Eastern Eurobarometer (1990–1997; 2003.4).

14. A different situation is found among Latin democracies, where GDP effects on the democratic process show that the economy is not able to explain variations in support for democracy (see Latinobarometro 2003).

15. This index, from International Country Risk Guide by The PRS Group, measures control of corruption, rule of law, and bureaucratic accountability. It varies from 0 (high corruption) to 1 (low corruption). See www.prsgroup.com.

16. Sanchez-Cuenca (2000) shows that people living in low government quality countries express greater confidence in European institutions.

17. Duration of democracy is measured by the number of years the country was under a democratic regime since 1900.

18. Satisfaction with life is measured as the percentage of people answering "very" or "fairly" to the question: "On the whole, are you very satisfied, fairly satisfied, not very satisfied, not at all satisfied with the life you lead?"

19. The sources used are: Xezonakis (2008); European World Value Survey Integrated File (1999); Eurobarometer 44.3OVR (1996)–58.1 (2002)–60.1 (2003)–61 and 62 (2004)–63.4 (2005); 65.2 (2006); Central and Eastern Eurobarometer (1990–7; 2003–4).

20. The countries are: Belgium, Denmark, France, Germany, Ireland, Italy, Luxemburg, Netherlands, United Kingdom.
21. We used Stata 8 to estimate the model. The Prais estimators are generalized least-squares estimators, but they are fairly restrictive in that they permit only first-order autocorrelation in the disturbances. In this way, Prais-Winsten AR(1) estimator is used to reduce the problems commonly found in time-series analysis caused by serial correlation. It does so by transforming both the dependent and explanatory variables in the regression by subtracting a proportion, ρ, of the variable's value in the previous period. For thorough discussion see Beck and Katz (1995).

3

Informal Political Engagement in Europe, 1975–2007

David Sanders and Paolo Bellucci

The decline in electoral turnout that has affected most European countries in recent decades has prompted some observers to conclude that European mass publics are becoming less engaged with politics and the political process. If this were indeed the case, it would be a matter of some concern for the operation of conventional democratic politics, since an engaged citizenry plays an important role in holding politicians to account. This chapter focuses on European citizens' informal engagement with politics by considering the extent to which they discuss politics with other people and/or attempt to persuade them to change their political views. Using Eurobarometer and European Social Survey data from 1975 to 2007, we explore the individual-level and macrostructural determinants of people's informal engagement with the political process. Part 1 of the chapter shows that, although there has been a clear decline in voter turnout in national elections across the EU since the early 1960s, citizens in many EU countries have, if anything, become more engaged in informal political activity since the early 1970s. Part 2 develops a set of multilevel models that seek to explain why people vary in their patterns of political discussion and persuasion, both individually and across countries and over time. These models assess the explanatory power of five sets of factors: individual-level demographic and ideological characteristics; the condition of the domestic macroeconomy; the core political characteristics of the state; the relationship between the state and the EU; and significant "external" events. Part 3 presents our empirical results. These show that at the individual level, informal political engagement is strongly affected by gender, labour market position, and left–right ideology. In terms of macro-level effects, engagement is affected by the condition of the domestic economy, by the quality of the domestic democratic process, and by the size of the EU's net contributions to the respondent's country. We also show that large-scale changes in the international system can invoke a temporary but significant increase in informal political engagement among mass publics. Controlling for a wide range of other factors, in Western Europe at least (no suitable data exist for Central and Eastern Europe), the end of the Cold War appears to have produced a discernable increase in political discussion and persuasion between 1990 and 1993.

1. Trends in political engagement in Europe, 1945–2007

It is well known that, over the last fifty years or so, electoral turnout has declined in most advanced democracies. Figure 3.1 shows the overall pattern between 1945 and 2009 for the fourteen largest West European countries described in the international IDEA database.[1]

The graph shows average turnout over each five-year period from 1945–9 to 2005–9. The simple message of Figure 3.1 is clear. Between 1945 and the early 1970s, turnout in national elections across Western Europe was fairly constant, averaging around 85 per cent of eligible voters. From the mid 1970s, however, a clear trend decline set in, so that by the 2005–9 period, turnout was averaging some 10 percentage points less, giving rise to fears about the possible "democratic legitimacy" of governments that are elected on the basis of relatively low levels of electoral participation. Figure 3.2 describes the trends for the EU member states, broken down by accession wave. Although the

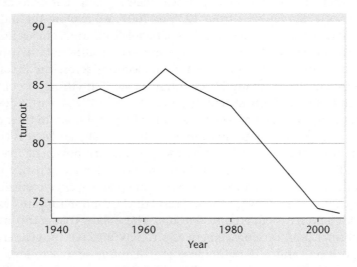

Figure 3.1. Average turnout in legislative elections in 14 West European countries, 1945–2009

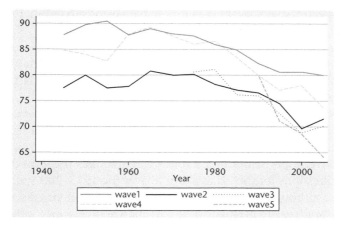

Figure 3.2. Average turnout in major legislative elections by accession wave, 1945–2009

Notes: Wave 1: Joined EEC/EC/EU 1957 (France, Germany, Italy, Netherlands, Belgium, Luxembourg)
Wave 2: Joined EEC/EC/EU 1973 (Denmark, Ireland, UK)
Wave 3: Joined EEC/EC/EU 1980s (Greece, Spain, Portugal)
Wave 4: Joined EEC/EC/EU 1995 (Austria, Finland, Sweden)
Wave 5: Joined EEC/EC/EU post 2000 (Cyprus, Czech Republic, Estonia, Hungary, Latvia, Lithuania, Malta, Poland, Romania, Slovakia, Slovenia)

average level of turnout is higher among the founder members (Wave 1) and among those states that joined the EU in the 1990s (Wave 4), the overall trend—downwards—is clearly evident among five groups. The sources of this decline are analysed in Chapter 5, so we do not discuss them here. The key question for our purposes, however, is whether or not this decline in voting has been accompanied by a commensurate decline in other, more informal, forms of political activity.

There are obviously many ways in which citizens in democratic countries can engage in political activity beyond the simple act of voting. These "action repertoires" inter alia include political party and interest group activities, signing and collecting petitions, boycotting products and services, making "ethical" purchasing decisions, and participating in demonstrations (Barnes and Kaase 1979). Although a number of cross-national surveys since the early 1990s have attempted explicitly to measure the extent to which mass populations in specific countries engage in these behaviours, there are very few directly comparable data available which allow a relatively large number of countries to be analysed over a reasonably long period of time. Indeed, the only survey source that provides cross-nationally comparable profiles of EU member states over a sufficient time period to enable meaningful over-time analysis is the Eurobarometer series. This series effectively began in 1973 and ran until 2002. Since then, the core questions of the series have been included in the European Social Survey. We employ data using a combination of these two sources, covering the continuous period from 1975 to 2007. Note that the resulting dataset is necessarily "unbalanced", since with each new wave of EU accessions further countries are included. In the 1970s, only the Wave 1 and Wave 2 member states were included in the survey; from 2004 to 2007, all twenty-seven of the current member states are included.

The Eurobarometer/EES provides cross-national time-series data on two key measures of informal mass political engagement: political discussion and political persuasion. Table 3.1 describes the form of the two questions and their respective response options. Table 3.1(a) describes the joint distribution of the two questions for the EU as a whole over the 1975–2007 period. As the table shows, although only 5.1 per cent of EU respondents discuss politics "frequently" *and* seek to persuade others to change their views "often", overall there is a very good "spread" of activity across the cells of the joint distribution, implying that engagement is a variegated phenomenon that requires explanation. Table 3.1(b) shows how we combine these two sets of responses to form a single Informal Political Engagement (IPE) scale.

Figure 3.3 shows how the average scores on the 1–6 IPE scale vary across the twenty-seven EU member states. Informal political engagement was on average highest in the Netherlands (average annual score on the 1–6 scale = 3.78) and in Greece (annual average score = 3.70). Engagement was lowest in the Czech Republic and in Spain (annual average scores respectively of 2.99 and 3.01). Figure 3.4 shows how average informal political engagement across the EU varied on an annual basis between 1975 and 2007. As the graph indicates, although the over-time variations in the series are relatively modest, there is a clear peak in the series during the early 1990s, corresponding to the period immediately after the end of the Cold War. The variations in average annual IPE scores by country are shown in Figures 3.5 to 3.7.

Table 3.1. Measures of political discussion, political persuasion and informal political engagement

Table 3.1(a). The joint distribution of discussion and persuasion

Political discussion[a]	Political persuasion[b]				Total
	Never	Rarely	From time to time	Often	
Never	12.7	7.9	8.1	2.6	31.3
Occasionally	7.8	15.0	24.4	6.0	53.2
Frequently	1.4	2.2	6.8	5.1	15.5
Total	21.9	25.1	39.3	13.7	100.0

[a] *Political discussion.* When you get together with friends would you say you discuss political matters frequently, occasionally or never? Response options: Frequently; Occasionally; Never.
[b] *Political persuasion.* When you (yourself) hold a strong opinion, do you ever find yourself persuading your friends, relatives or fellow workers to share your views? Does this happen: Often; From time to time; Rarely; Never.
Notes: Cell entries record the absolute percentages of respondents who fall in that cell. N = 1,050,378.

Table 3.1(b). The values assigned to the Informal Political Engagement scale

Political discussion	Political persuasion			
	Never	Rarely	From time to time	Often
Never	1	2	3	4
Occasionally	2	3	4	5
Frequently	3	4	5	6

Notes: Cell entries record values assigned for the Informal Political Engagement (IPE) scale. Respondents who failed to respond or answered "Don't know" on either measure were excluded from the analysis. The correlation between the 1–6 point IPE scale and the single factor obtained from a principle components factor analysis of the Political discussion and Political persuasion variables is r = 0.99.

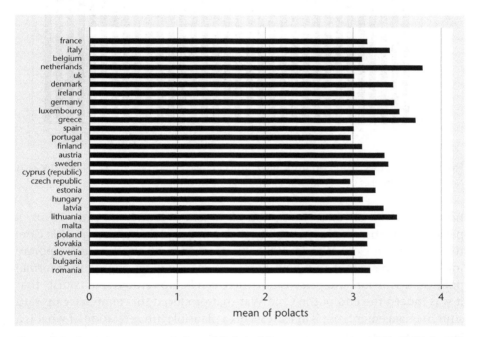

Figure 3.3. Average scores on Informal Political Engagement scale, 1975–2007, by EU Member State

Note: Polacts describes the 1–6 Informal Political Engagement scale

Figure 3.5 reports the variations over the longest time period—1975 to 2007—for founder EEC members and the three states that joined the then EC in 1973. As the graphs suggest, there is no obvious linear trend in informal political engagement in most of the Wave 1 or 2 member states. Although there is a suggestion of growing engagement in the Netherlands, Belgium, and Denmark, for the most part IPE levels are fairly similar at the beginning and end of each series. The intriguing pattern in all of the graphs in Figure 3.5,

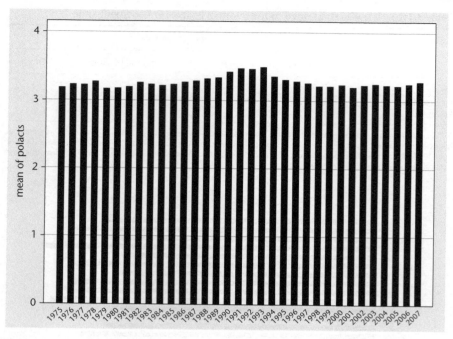

Figure 3.4. Average scores on Informal Political Engagement scale, 1975–2007, by Year

Note: Polacts describes the 1–6 Informal Political Engagement scale

however, is the obvious "hump" in each series around the early 1990s, a pattern suggestive of the possibility that a major global event—in this case, the end of the Cold War in 1989–90—is capable of effecting a temporary increase in the extent to which European mass publics engage in informal political discussion and persuasion. There can be no certainty, of course, that it was indeed the end of the Cold War that produced this temporary upward shift in engagement, but it at least seems a plausible interpretation of what is a very distinct pattern. We test more explicitly for the effect, with appropriate statistical controls, later in the chapter. Figures 3.6 and 3.7 report the corresponding graphs for the remaining EU countries. Since each of the series is shorter than in Figure 3.5 (ranging from 1980–2007 for Greece to 2004–7 for the Wave 5 accession countries), it is more difficult to discern much patterning in the data. Nonetheless, in the cases of both Spain and Portugal (though not in Greece), there also appears to be some sort of temporary increase in engagement in the early 1990s. In the remaining countries, each series is too short for any sensible inferences about over-time shifts to be drawn.

The obvious question that follows from these various patterns is why political engagement varies across individuals and countries and over time. It is this question that we consider in the next section.

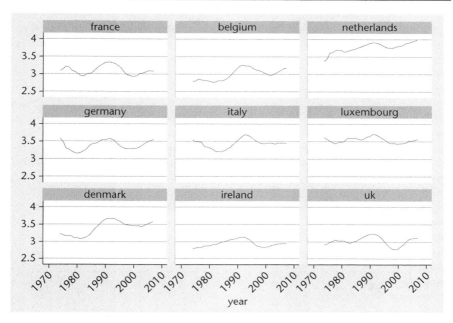

Figure 3.5. Annual variations in informal political engagement, 1975–2007; accession Waves 1 and 2

Note: Graphs smoothed using a rolling five-year window.

2. Specifying models of informal political engagement

People's general interest in politics is typically used in scholarly research as an explanatory rather than as a dependent variable. Although political interest often appears as a predictor variable in models of voting turnout (e.g. Clarke et al. 2004 and 2009), civic engagement (Huckfeldt and Sprague 1995) and unconventional political actions such as political protest (Barnes and Kaase 1979), relatively few studies have focused on either political interest or informal political engagement as objects of study in their own right.[2] Here we develop a series of individual-level and societal-level hypotheses about the sources of informal political engagement. Our broad approach is similar to that adopted by Van Deth and Elff (2004), though our model specifications and empirical conclusions are very different from theirs.

Individual-level sources of informal political engagement

There is a well-established tradition of social research, going back to at least the 1930s, that connects people's political and social attitudes and behaviours

45

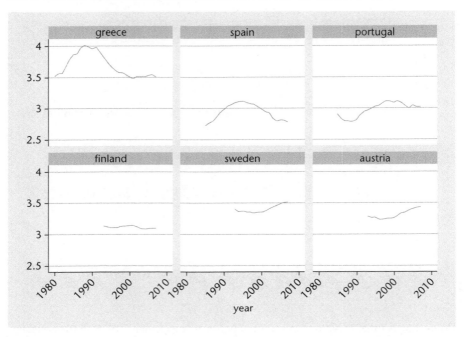

Figure 3.6. Annual variations in informal political engagement, 1980–2007; accession Waves 3 and 4

Note: Graphs smoothed using a rolling five-year window.

to their respective positions in the social structure. Given the data available in the Eurobarometer series, we can consider the possible effects on political engagement of four sets of *social-structural factors*. The first of these is *age*. It could be argued that younger people are more likely to have both the energy and the social contacts that facilitate relatively high levels of political engagement—in which case it might be hypothesized that age, *ceteris paribus*, should have a *negative* effect on engagement. Alternatively, it could be argued that older people have been exposed to a longer socialization process about politics and that therefore they should be more likely, other things being equal, to engage with politics—that there should be a *positive* effect of age on IPE. A third possibility is that the relationship between engagement and age is curvilinear, with engagement rising from youth through to middle age but then declining as people reach old age. We test these various possibilities by expressing the effects of age as a quadratic of the form $Y = a + b_1X + b_2X^2$. If the effects of age on engagement are negative (positive), then b_1 will be significant and negative (positive); and b_2 will be non-significant. If the effects are curvilinear as suggested, then b_1 will be positive and b_2 negative, with both coefficients significant.

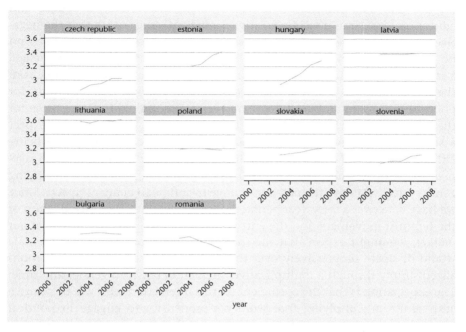

Figure 3.7. Annual variations in informal political engagement, 2000–2007; accession Wave 5

Note: Graphs smoothed using a rolling three-year window.

A second possible social-structural source of IPE is *education*. The obvious expectation here is that more educated people, since they are in general more "cognitively mobilized", are more likely to engage in political discussion and persuasion than their less-educated counterparts. Given the difficulties of generating cross-nationally comparable measures of educational attainment, we measure education as a three-point scale based on the age at which the respondents completed their formal education.[3] Our simple expectation is that education will exert a positive effect on engagement.

A third individual-level source of engagement is *gender*. The most obvious expectation about gender effects on IPE is that in societies like most of those in the EU, where politics has until relatively recently been a generally male-dominated activity, women should be less likely to be politically engaged than men. This would imply that being female should have a *negative* effect on engagement. This overarching influence, however, is likely to be qualifed by other, ameliorating or exaggerating, gender effects. The first of these relates to the possible interaction between gender and education. The expectation here is that the IPE levels of highly educated women will be less different from men's than those of women with limited education. This implies that a multiplicative interaction term between being female and education level should yield a positive coefficient—suggesting that the negative effect of being female is reduced among more-educated women. A second potentially qualifying gender effect relates to women who have either pursued a "traditional" gender role as "homemaker" within the family or retired from the labour market. We would expect that these women's opportunities for political discussion and persuasion are even more limited than are those for their counterparts who are active in the labour market. We accordingly expect a significant negative for the interaction between being female and being either a homemaker or retired, implying that the (negative) effects on engagement of being female are even greater among this group. The final qualifying gender effect relates to the possible change over time in gender impacts. Since we have data over a forty-year period that coincides with the consolidation of the feminist movement and the entry of many more women into the labour market, we might expect that the (negative) effects on IPE of being female would dissipate progressively over time. This hypothesis can be operationalized simply through a multiplicative interaction between gender and time. The expectation is that the coefficient on this interaction term will be positive and significant, implying that women's propensity to engage in political discussion and persuasion increases over time, thereby progressively reducing the gap in IPE between men and women.

The fourth set of potential social-structural effects on engagement involves *labour market positions* more generally. There are certain kinds of labour market position that we might expect, other things being equal, to be associated with either higher or lower levels of informal political engagement. On the one hand, people in professional and managerial positions and the self-employed are more likely to have an incentive to engage in political discussion and persuasion in order to protect their own interests in the face of policy changes either proposed or initiated by the state. We accordingly expect that, in comparison with other occupational groups,[4] professionals, managers, and the self-employed will be more likely to engage in discussion and persuasion. On the other hand, working-class and unemployed people are less likely to have access to the information resources necessary to enable them readily to engage in political discussion and persuasion. We accordingly expect membership of these groups to be negatively associated with IPE.

A further individual-level predictor of engagement, connected to but distinct from social-structural position, is *left–right ideology*. The Eurobarometer series has an extensive set of responses, covering many years and countries, to a question that asks respondents to locate themselves on a 1–10 left–right ideological "left–right" scale, where 1 represents "left" and 10 represents "right". Given the motivating power of ideology across Europe throughout much of the twentieth century, it seems plausible to argue that, ceteris paribus, IPE should be highest among those respondents who place themselves towards either *extreme* of the ideological spectrum, and lowest among those who place themselves relatively close to the ideological centre ground. Those further away from the centre are more likely to be aware of, and to feel strongly about, political matters and are therefore more likely to engage in political discussion or persuasion. This simple proposition again implies a simple curvilinear function, this time of the form IPE = $a - b_1$LeftRight + b_2 LeftRight^2, where b_1 is expected to have significant negative sign and b_2 a significant positive sign.

Our initial model specification combines all of these hypothesized individual-level effects in a single additive equation. In order to take proper account of the different national patterns of informal engagement described in Figure 3.3 and the temporaral variations described in Figures 3.4 to 3.7, this individual-level model includes statistical controls for both nation and year. These take the form of dummy variables for each country in the analysis (with France as the reference category) and for each year from 1980 onwards (with 1975–9 as the reference category). Because we include all these year dummies in the estimation, in order to avoid multicolinearity at this stage we exclude the interaction term between Female and Year referred to above. Our initial specification is therefore:

$$
\begin{aligned}
\text{Informal Political Engagement} = {} & a + b_1\text{Age} + b_2\text{Age}^2 + b_3\text{Education} \\
& + b_4\text{Female/not} + b_5\text{Female*Education Interaction} \\
& + b_6\text{Female*Homemaker/Retired Interaction} \\
& + b_7\text{Professional-Managerial/not} + b_8\text{Self-Employed/not} \\
& + b_9\text{Manual Worker/not} + b_{10}\text{Unemployed/not} \\
& + b_{11}\text{Left-Right Ideology} + b_{12}(\text{Left-Right Ideology})^2 \\
& + \Sigma b_i\text{Country Dummies} + \Sigma b_j\text{Year Dummies} + e_i \qquad [1]
\end{aligned}
$$

where b_1, b_3, b_5, b_7, b_8, b_{12} are expected to be positive; all other numbered coefficients are expected to be negative; and e_i is a random error term.

Societal-level sources of informal political engagement

Equation [1] is intended primarily to establish which of our individual-level hypotheses are consistent with the available data. However, although the Country and Year dummies are useful statistical devices for ensuring that these individual-level effects expressed in b_1–b_{13} are properly estimated, they obviously do not contribute much to the actual explanation of people's propensities to engage in political discussion and persuasion. Equation [1] *controls* for the effects of spatial and temporal context, but it does not *explain* what it is about those contexts that produces variations in engagement over and above any individual-level effects. In an effort to move towards an explanation of how context might affect individual engagement propensities, we consider the possible effects of a series of economic, political, and EU-related factors, in order to build what is in effect a multilevel model of IPE.

Consider, first, possible *macroeconomic* effects on political engagement patterns. It seems reasonable to suppose that macroeconomic conditions might have an effect on people's informal engagement. It is well known that the saliency of economic issues such as unemployment and inflation among mass publics tends to be higher when economic conditions are relatively difficult (see, for example, Sanders 2000). Accordingly, we hypothesize that engagement levels should be higher, *ceteris paribus*, when annual unemployment and inflation are relatively high—and vice versa. A further macroeconomic expectation relates to the level of economic development. Using Eurobarometer data between 1973 and 2002, Van Deth and Elff (2004) report a strong positive effect of economic development on informal political engagement. To take account of these prior findings, we accordingly include a term for economic development (annual GDP/capita), with the expectation that its effect on engagement is positive and significant.

A second set of macro-level hypotheses relates to *national political infrastructure*. Our core assumption here is that people will be more stimulated to engage in political discussion and persuasion if they live in countries where government is in general more responsive to citizens' needs. We hypothesize that such responsiveness helps to produce an intellectual environment in which people are encouraged to express their political opinions to others. We employ three related but distinct indicators of political infrastucture. The first of these is the overall *quality of governance*, which measures, *inter alia*, government effectiveness, political stability, absence of corruption, regulatory quality of the state, and the extent of "voice and accountability".[5] Our assumption here is that these quality measures in combination are conducive to an environment in which individuals will feel more inclined to engage politically with their fellow citizens. The second infrastructure measure is the extent of *social welfare provision*.[6] The expectation here is that a more extensive welfare state will be associated with a more equal society that in turn is more conducive to citizens engaging in mutual political discussion and persuasion. Finally, we hypothesize that the *fairness of the electoral system* will also affect informal political engagement, on the assumption that fairer systems will be conducive to more extensive political discourse among citizens. Our expectation here is that IPE will be higher in systems based on proportional representation than in those based on majoritarian principles.[7]

We noted earlier that, at the individual level, we expect people at the extremes of the left–right ideological spectrum to display higher levels of informal political engagement. The effects of ideology, however, may extend beyond these immediate individual-level effects. It is also possible that the extent of *ideological polarization in a country* might also have an effect on people's informal engagement patterns. It has been suggested that electoral turnout can be affected by the degree of ideological polarization in a country, with high polarization being seen as a stimulus to individual participation (see chapters of this volume). A similar argument can clearly be applied to IPE. The more polarized that opinion is, the more likely it is that people will be motivated to engage in informal political discussion with their fellow citizens. There are clearly different ways of assessing the extent of ideological polarization in a country. One way is to try to characterize the ideological positions adopted by the parties in their election manifestos (Budge et al. 2001). One problem with this approach, however, is that the resultant indices cannot easily measure fluctuations in ideological polarization in the interims between elections. We accordingly prefer to use the extent of ideological polarization *among citizens themselves*, rather than measures based on party positions. We do this by employing the same Eurobarometer left–right ideology measures that were referred to earlier. However, rather than using these data as individual measures, we calculate the standard deviation in individual scores, by country year. These standard deviation scores by definition measure the degree of dispersal of ideological opinion around the country-year mean. We assume that this degree of dispersal reflects the extent to which citizens' ideological opinions are polarized: the lower the standard deviation, the more that opinion is clustered around the mean and therefore the less polarized it is; the higher the standard deviation, the more that opinion is weighted towards the ideological extremes, and therefore the more polarized it is. Our simple expectation is that polarization will have a positive effect on IPE.

Our final set of "societal factors" relates to the European Union and global affairs more generally. There are broadly two ways in which EU membership might be expected to affect people's propensities to engage in political discussion and persuasion. First, membership of the EU by definition brings an additional (supranational) layer of governance to bear on all citizens. Membership therefore increases the range of potential *sources* of public policy, and at the same time potentially increases the *opportunities* for citizens to be stimulated into informal political discourse. It is also likely that the longer that a state has been part of the EU, the more *embedded* these possibilities for discussion become. In these circumstances, we hypothesize that there should be a postive association between the length of time that a state has belonged to the EEC/EC/EU and the level of informal political engagement of its citizens. We operationalize this perodicity of belonging in terms of each member state's "accession wave". Our expectation is that "wave" should have a negative effect on engagement, with later waves displaying lower levels of engagement. A second possible way in which EU membership might affect engagement is through the financial contributions that the EU makes to national economies. It is possible that relatively large net contributions from the EU could stimulate political discussion in the recipient states. We accordingly include a term for net transfers from EU budget in our model specification, with the expectation that this variable will exert a positive effect on informal political engagement. Finally, we include a "global affairs" measure that was anticipated in our discussion of Figures 3.4 to 3.7. In order to reflect the temporary surge in engagement that appears to have occurred in the wake of the end of the Cold War, we include a dummy term that takes the value of 1 for the period 1990–3 and zero otherwise. We expect this effect to be positive and significant.

Combining the individual hypotheses represented in equation [1] with the various macro hypotheses associated with these societal factors gives our second equation:

$$
\begin{aligned}
\text{Informal Political Engagement} = {} & a + b_1\text{Age} + b_2\text{Age}^2 + b_3\text{Education} \\
& + b_4\text{Female/not} + b_5\text{Female*Education Interaction} \\
& + b_6\text{Female*Homemaker/Retired Interaction} + b_7\text{Female*Year} \\
& + b_8\text{Professional-Managerial/not} + b_9\text{Self-Employed/not} \\
& + b_{10}\text{Manual Worker/not} + b_{11}\text{Unemployed/not} \\
& + b_{12}\text{Left-Right Ideology} + b_{13}(\text{Left-Right Ideology})^2 \\
& + b_{14}\text{Unemployment level} + b_{15}\text{Inflation level} + b_{16}\text{GDP/capita} \\
& + b_{17}\text{Quality of Governance} + b_{18}\text{ Percent Social Welfare Spending} \\
& + b_{19}\text{Proportional Representation/not} + b_{20}\text{Ideological Polarization} \\
& + b_{21}\text{EU Wave} + b_{22}\text{Net EU budget transfers} \\
& + b_{23}\text{Cold War/not} + e_i
\end{aligned}
$$

[2]

where the expectations for individual-level effects b_1–b_{13} are as in [1]; b_{14}–b_{23} are macro-level effects that are all expected to be positive, with the exception of b_{21}, which is expected to be negative; and e_i is a random error term.

In the following section, we estimate equations [1] and especially [2] in several different ways, to reflect the varying number of country-year data points that are available over the 1975–2007 period. We begin with a simple estimation of [1] across all the available data points. This enables us to assess the overall robustness of the individual-level components of the model that we are proposing. We then estimate [2], again using all the available country-year data points. As we show, this particular estimation "loses" quite a lot of cases because of missing macro-level data. We accordingly re-estimate a reduced form of [2] which drops the non-significant macro variables from the specification. We then test the robustness of the reduced form specification by subsetting the data by accession wave and by East/West region within Europe. These tests allow us to tell a slightly more nuanced story about the differential impacts of both individual- and macro-level factors in the genesis of informal political engagement across the EU.

3. Empirical results

Table 3.2 reports the results of estimating equation [1] across all twenty-seven EU member states over the period 1975–2007. Note that this time frame is reduced progressively for member states that joined after Wave 2, falling to 1985–2007 for Wave 3; to 1995–2007 for Wave 4; to 2004–7 for Wave 5. The dependent variable is the 1–6 Informal Political Engagement scale. For ease of interpretation of the coefficients, estimation is by robust regression, with robust standard errors estimated by clustering the data by country year. A near-identical pattern of coefficients signs and significance levels is obtained using ordered logit estimation.[8] The values of the coefficients on the country dummies are not reported. Given the large number of cases in the estimation, significance levels need to be interpreted cautiously. For the individual-level effects, we expect coefficients to be significant at p = 0.001 or better for a hypothesized effect to be confirmed.

The individual-level results shown in the table are highly significant and fully consistent with the hypotheses advanced in section 2. Several conclusions are sugggested by the table. First, the significant positive coefficient on age and significant negative coefficient on age^2 indicate that the effects of age on engagement are curvilinear, with the highest levels of informal engagement being associated with "middle" age. Second, the education coefficient is significant and positive (b = 0.20), implying that more-educated individuals tend to be more engaged. Third, the three "female" coefficients are all as anticipated. The "parent" female term is significant and negative (b = –0.51), suggesting that on average women score over half a point less than men on the 1–6 Informal Political Engagement scale. The significance of the two female interaction terms, however, indicates that this average effect tells only a part of the story. The negative effects of being female are reduced for more-educated women (see the positive b = 0.11 for female*education interaction term) and increased for women who are either homemakers or retired (b = –0.15). Fourth, the labour market position terms all behave as expected. Professional/managerial workers (b = 0.20) and the self-employed (b = 0.05) are more likely to engage than the labour market reference group (white-collar workers), while manual workers (b = –0.13) and the unemployed (b = –0.12) are less likely to engage. Finally, the coefficients on the two ideology terms (b = –0.21 for left–right and b = 0.02 for left–right-squared) indicate that people who place themselves towards the extremes of the ideological spectrum are more likely to engage in political discussion and persuasion than those at the ideological centre.

The individual-level results from Table 3.2, then, indicate that gender, labour market, and ideological positions all affect the extent to which people

Table 3.2. Model of informal political engagement in EU countries, 1975–2007; individual-level predictors, with year and country dummies

	b	Robust SE
Individual-level variables		
Age	0.03***	0.00
Age-squared	−0.00***	0.00
Education	0.20***	0.00
Female	−0.51***	0.02
Female*education	0.11***	0.01
Female*homemaker/retired	−0.15***	0.01
Professional/managerial	0.20***	0.01
Self-employed	0.05***	0.01
Manual worker	−0.13***	0.01
Unemployed	−0.12***	0.01
Left–right ideology	−0.21***	0.01
Left–right ideology-squared	0.02***	0.00
Time controls		
Year 1980	−0.07	0.05
Year 1981	−0.05*	0.03
Year 1982	−0.03	0.03
Year 1983	−0.05	0.03
Year 1984	−0.08***	0.03
Year 1985	−0.03	0.04
Year 1986	0.02	0.04
Year 1987	0.04	0.04
Year 1988	0.02	0.04
Year 1989	0.04	0.04
Year 1990	0.13***	0.03
Year 1991	0.14***	0.03
Year 1992	0.14***	0.02
Year 1993	0.17***	0.02
Year 1994	0.05*	0.03
Year 1995	−0.09***	0.03
Year 1996	−0.07**	0.03
Year 1997	−0.08***	0.03
Year 1998	−0.13***	0.03
Year 1999	−0.17***	0.04
Year 2000	−0.09***	0.03
Year 2001	−0.12***	0.03
Year 2002	−0.11***	0.03
Year 2003	−0.10***	0.03
Year 2004	−0.11***	0.02
Year 2005	−0.11***	0.03
Year 2006	−0.07***	0.03
Year 2007	−0.06**	0.03
Constant	0.09***	0.04
R^2	0.12	
N	768,085	
Time period	1975–2009	
Clusters (country years)	449	

* $p<0.1$; ** $p<0.05$; *** $p<0.01$.

Notes: Year variables are all dummies; reference category is 1975–9. Country dummies (not reported) included for Germany, Italy, Netherlands, Belgium, Luxembourg, Denmark, Ireland, UK, Greece, Spain, Portugal, Austria, Finland, Sweden, Cyprus, Czech Republic, Estonia, Hungary, Latvia, Lithuania, Malta, Poland, Romania, Slovakia, Slovenia. France is the reference country. White-collar workers (plus students and "other") are the reference category for labour market position. Estimation of equation [1] is by robust regression, clustered by country year.

engage informally in political discussion and persuasion. The inclusion of country dummies in the specification (coefficients not reported) means that these individual-level effects operate regardless of country-level variations in engagement. The coefficients on the year dummies suggest that, over and above any individual-level and country-specific effects, there were significant over-time variations in levels of political engagement from the 1970s onwards. The non-significance of the various year dummies during the 1980s indicates that there were no significant changes in overall engagement during that decade. However, the significant *positive* effects for the years 1990–3 is suggestive of the possibility, anticipated in the graphs reported earlier, that the end of the Cold War generated an increase in political discussion and persuasion across the (then) EU. The smaller, significant, *negative* effects that are evident for the period from 1995 to 2007 suggest that since 1993 engagement may have dropped back below the levels seen in the "baseline" years of 1975–9. However, given that after 1995 the data include two new waves of EU member states, these negative coefficients need to be interpreted with considerable caution. At this stage, we simply note these negative effects. We return to the implications of the EU's expanding membership below.

Table 3.3 Column (a) reports the results of estimating equation [2]. Column (b) of Table 3.3 re-estimates equation [2], dropping the clearly non-significant variables from Column (a). Recall that the difference between this specification and the one shown in Table 3.2 is that equation [2] includes no specific country or year dummies, but rather, includes a set of macro-level economic and political variables that seek to explain *why* there might be country-by-country and year-by-year variations in engagement. Two points of comparison between the Table 3.2 and Table 3.3 results are worth emphasizing. First, the number of cases, which is $N = 768,085$ in Table 3.2, falls in Column (a) of Table 3.3 to 379,580. This is because the macro-level variables included in the Column (a) model are available only over a restricted set of years. When the non-significant variables from Column (a) are excluded from the specification, the N rises to 756,452—almost back to the level achieved in Table 3.2. The second point of comparison between Tables 3.2 and 3.3 relates to the degree of model fit. The R^2 values, though not high in either, are acceptable, given the number of cases and that the data are at individual level. The key point, however, is that although the specification in Table 3.3 drops the individual country and year dummies, R^2 falls only marginally from the Table 3.2 model ($R^2 = 0.12$) to the Table 3.3 models ($r = 0.10$ in both cases). In short, although the Table 3.3 models are far simpler than the Table 3.2 model, they explain almost as much of the variance in informal political engagement.

Table 3.3. Models of informal political engagement in EU countries, 1975–2007; individual-level and macro-level predictors

	Column (a)		Column (b)	
	b	SE	b	SE
Individual-level variables				
Age	0.03***	0.00	0.03***	0.00
Age-squared	−0.00***	0.00	−0.00***	0.00
Education	0.17***	0.01	0.19***	0.01
Female	−0.30***	0.08	−0.50***	0.03
Female*education	0.09***	0.01	0.10***	0.01
Female*homemaker/retired	−0.17***	0.01	−0.13***	0.01
Professional/managerial	0.22***	0.01	0.22***	0.01
Self-employed	0.06***	0.01	0.06***	0.01
Manual worker	−0.16***	0.01	−0.15***	0.01
Unemployed	−0.13***	0.01	−0.13***	0.01
Left–right ideology	−0.19***	0.01	−0.21***	0.01
Left–right ideology-squared	0.02***	0.00	0.02***	0.00
Macro-level variables				
Unemployment	−0.02***	0.00	−0.02***	0.00
Inflation	0.02***	0.00	0.02***	0.00
GDP/capita	0.00	0.00		
Social expenditure	0.02***	0.00	0.01***	0.00
PR system	0.32***	0.02	0.25***	0.02
Ideological polarization	0.39***	0.10	0.37***	0.06
Governance quality	0.27*	0.16		
Net EU transfers	0.02*	0.01		
EU accession wave	−0.08***	0.01	−0.06***	0.01
End of Cold War (1990–3)	0.14***	0.03	0.18***	0.03
Female*time	−0.01*	0.00	−0.00	0.00
Constant	1.69***	0.26	2.31***	0.14
R^2	0.10		0.10	
N	379,580		756,452	
Time period	1975–2007		1975–2007	
Clusters (country years)	209		442	

* $p<0.1$; ** $p<0.05$; *** $p<0.01$.

What are the substantive implications of the models reported in Table 3.3? The first thing to note about both the Column (a) and Column (b) models is that they produce exactly the same individual-level results as were observed in relation to Table 3.2. Age, education, gender, labour market postion, and ideology behave in exactly the same way in both tables, with all the relevant coefficients correctly signed and clearly significant. In Column (a), however, three of the macro-level variables fail to achieve significance: GDP/capita, quality of governance, and net transfers from EU budget. These findings suggest that these variables do not affect informal political engagement in the way that was hypothesized previously. They are accordingly dropped from the model, which is re-estimated in Column (b).

The model reported in Column (b) of Table 3.3 represents our best estimate of the overall factors that influenced informal political engagement in the EU between 1975 and 2007. As noted, the individual-level coefficients suggest important roles for age, education, gender, labour market position, and ideology. At the macro level, there are important effects for economic, political, and EU factors. Of the *economic factors*, although GDP/capita proves non-significant (in contrast with van Deth and Elff's finding), unemployment and inflation are both significant. The positive coefficient on inflation (b = 0.02) is in line with our earlier suggestion that economic bad news (higher inflation) can increase the level of informal engagement. The negative coefficient on the aggregate unemployment term, however, suggests that this effect does extend to macro measures of unemployment, where the general reaction seems to be similar to that associated with unemployment at the individual level—a greater sense of anomie and a *reduced* propensity to engage in political discussion and persuasion. As far as the *macro-political* effects are concerned, social welfare expenditure, proportional representation and ideological polarization all produced significant and positive coefficients, as hypothesized. The greater social equity implied by higher social welfare provision and the greater electoral fairness implied by proportional representation seem to be associated with higher levels of informal political engagement. Higher levels of ideological polarization among mass publics also seem to engender higher levels of engagement. Of the *EU factors*, the wave variable clearly exerts a significant effect (b = –0.06). Given the way that the variable is coded, this means that informal engagement has been progressively lower with each successive membership accession wave. Mass publics in the newer states appear to be less engaged than their counterparts in the older member states—though whether this is a consequence of EU membership itself or more a reflection of the types of state that have joined the EU at different periods remains a matter for conjecture. Finally, there is also a significant role for the end of the Cold War, where the coefficient of b = 0.18 indicates that average engagement, controlling for a wide range of other factors, rose by 0.18 on the 1–6 scale for the four years from 1990. The only variable which is non-significant in Column (b) of Table 3.3 is the interaction between being female and time.[9] The clearly non-significant coefficient on this interaction term (p = 0.83) provides a strong indication that, across the EU as a whole, there has been no progressive tendency for women to become more engaged in informal political discourse since 1975—notwithstanding the important changes in gender relations in many European countries over that period.

Variations by EU accession wave

As intimated above, the model presented in Table 3.3 Column 2 represents our best overarching summary of the individual and macro-level sources of engagement across the EU over the 1975–2007 period. As we have also suggested, however, these estimates are based on an "unbalanced" dataset in which countries from the first two EU accession waves contribute far more cases to the analysis than those that joined in later waves. The situation is particularly unbalanced with regard to the Wave 5 accession states, for which continous individual-level data are available only from 2003. This asymmetric data pattern means that, in spite of all the controls that are applied in the models reported in Table 3.3, there must always be the suspicion that the relationships displayed in the table place too much emphasis on the Waves 1 and 2 member states (which contribute 525,243 of the 756,452 cases shown

Table 3.4. Models of informal political engagement in EU countries, 1975–2007, by accession wave; individual-level and macro-level predictors

	Accession Waves 1 and 2		Accession Wave 3		Accession Wave 4		Accession Wave 5	
	b	SE	b	SE	b	SE	b	SE
Individual-level variables								
Age	0.03***	0.00	0.03***	0.00	0.01***	0.00	0.03***	0.00
Age-squared	−0.00***	0.00	−0.00***	0.00	−0.00***	0.00	−0.00***	0.00
Education	0.19***	0.01	0.17***	0.01	0.12***	0.01	0.19***	0.02
Female	−0.38***	0.04	−0.61***	0.10	−0.48**	0.19	−0.53	0.92
Female*education	0.10***	0.01	0.15***	0.02	0.11***	0.02	0.10***	0.02
Female*homemaker/retired	−0.14***	0.01	−0.18***	0.02	−0.12***	0.02	−0.11***	0.03
Professional/managerial	0.24***	0.01	0.17***	0.02	0.18***	0.02	0.11***	0.02
Self-employed	0.14***	0.01	0.05**	0.02	0.16***	0.02	0.09***	0.03
Manual worker	−0.16***	0.01	−0.12***	0.02	−0.15***	0.02	−0.08***	0.02
Unemployed	−0.16***	0.01	−0.08***	0.02	−0.09***	0.03	−0.07**	0.03
Left–right ideology	−0.22***	0.01	−0.18***	0.01	−0.17***	0.01	−0.16***	0.02
Left–right ideology-squared	0.02***	0.00	0.01***	0.00	0.02***	0.00	0.02***	0.00
Macro-level variables								
Unemployment	−0.02***	0.00	−0.01**	0.00	−0.04***	0.01	−0.00	0.01
Inflation	0.00	0.00	0.04***	0.01	0.03	0.02	0.01	0.01
Social expenditure	0.01***	0.00	0.05***	0.01	0.03***	0.01	−0.03***	0.01
PR system	0.25***	0.02						
Ideological polarization	0.21***	0.07	0.90***	0.20	0.27*	0.16	0.33***	0.08
End of Cold War (1990–3)	0.21***	0.03	−0.09	0.06				
Female*time	−0.00***	0.00	−0.00	0.00	−0.00	0.01	−0.00	0.03
Constant	2.75***	0.16	0.30	0.30	3.25***	0.43	2.40***	0.19
R^2	0.11		0.15		0.07		0.06	
N	525,243		118,014		64,738		48,457	
Time period	1975–2007		1985–2007		1995–2007		2004–7	
Clusters (country years)	282		73		39		48	

* $p<0.1$; ** $p<0.05$; *** $p<0.01$.

in Column (b)), and insufficient emphasis on data relating to more recent member states.

We address these possible concerns by replicating, as far as possible, the Table 3.3 Column (b) model for each of the accession waves separately. Table 3.4 reports the resultant estimates. Waves 1 and 2 are combined (in Column 1), because from the time that the Eurobarometer started collecting annual data on informal political engagement (in 1975) both Waves 1 and 2 accession states were included in the surveys. The model is estimated for Wave 3 joiners in Column 2; for Wave 4 joiners in Column 3; and for Wave 5 joiners in Column 4. (Note that the wave term from the Table 3.3 model is dropped in Table 3.4 because in each individual model it becomes a constant.) In the Waves 3, 4 and 5 models the terms for end of the Cold War and for proportional representation are dropped for the same reason.

The overall pattern of coefficients across the four-wave grouping shown in Table 3.4 is remarkably consistent. With only two exceptions, the individual-level coefficients produce the same sign and significance patterns across all four wave groups. The coefficients for age, age-squared, education, female, female*education, female*homemaker/retired, professional/managerial, self-employed, unemployed, left–right and left–right-squared are significant and correctly signed in every equation. The only exceptions are the self-employed term in the Waves 1/2 equation (column 1) and the female term in the Wave 5 equation (column 4). The lack of significance of the self-employed term in Column 1 is not of particular import given the correct signs and significance levels of the other labour market position variables. However, the lack of significance of the female term ($p = 0.57$) in the Wave 5 equation represents a substantively important departure from the pattern observed in the rest of the EU member states. One clear characteristic of the states that, for the most part,[10] were part of the Soviet bloc until the early 1990s, is that political discussion and persuasion are not disproportionately a male preserve. The formal gender equality espoused by the communist states of Eastern Europe during the Cold War period maintains a resonance today in the lack of major gender differences in informal political engagement.

The effects of the macro-level variables in the Table 3.4 models are a little more variegated than their individual-level counterparts—but not much more so. The unemployment term is significant and negative in every equation except for that of Wave 5. The social expenditure term is significant and positive in the equations for Waves 1–4, though it is negative in the Wave 5 model (we return to this issue below). The proportional representation and end of Cold War terms are significant and positive in each of the equations in which they appear. The ideological polarization term is significant and positive in every equation except for that of Wave 4 (though even in this context it is significant at $p = 0.10$). However, the inflation term which, as we saw, was clearly significant in the overall model shown in Table 3.3 Column (b), fails to achieve significance in three of the four sub-models (those for Waves 1/2, 4, and 5). This finding casts some doubt on the robustness of the inflation effect reported in Table 3.3. The variable that fails most spectacularly to live up to theoretical expectations is the female*year interaction term. Recall that this term was included to determine whether or not, controlling for other relevant factors, women's disinclination to engage in informal political discussion and persuasion dissipated in the three decades after 1975. The results of the four sub-models show overwhelmingly that this was not the case. In the Waves 3, 4, and 5 sub-models, the female*year interaction term is very clearly non-significant. The only equation in which the term achieves significance is in the Waves 1/2 sub-model (Column 1) where the coefficient is significant (p = 0.01) but negative (b = –0.003). This implies that, if anything, in comparison with men, women in the Waves 1 and 2 countries became even *less* likely, over the 1975–2007 period, to engage in political discussion and persuasion. The clear message is that there has been no systematic closing of the gender gap in informal political engagement since the mid 1970s—even in the long-standing EU member states—notwithstanding the EU's systematic efforts over the years to promote "gender mainstreaming".

Variations across East and West Europe

A more detailed check on the possible differences between Western and East–Central Europe is provided in Table 3.5. The results reported again use equation [2] as the core specification. The results are consistent with those reported in Table 3.4. In both Western and Eastern Europe, informal political engagement is affected by the same set of individual-level factors. The coefficients on age, education, the labour market position variables, and ideology are all significant and correctly signed. As in the Wave 5 model in Table 3.4, the only exception relates to gender effects. In Western Europe, women are significantly less likely to engage than men, though this overall effect is mitigated for more-educated women and exaggerated for women homemakers. In the East, however, the main gender coefficient is clearly non-significant, confirming the suggestion made previously that gender differences in political discussion and persuasion are not as great in the post-communist states as they are in the traditionally more democratic West.

But if similar patterns of effect are evident at the individual level, the same conclusion is not warranted with regard to the macro-level determinants of informal political engagement. In the model for Western countries reported in Table 3.5, the macro effects are identical to those reported in Table 3.3 for the whole of the EU. Controlling for a range of other relevant factors, engagement varies negatively with unemployment but positively with inflation, social

Table 3.5. Models of informal political engagement in EU countries, by East Europe (2004–7) and West Europe (1975–2007); individual-level and macro-level predictors

	East		West	
	b	SE	b	SE
Individual-level variables				
Age	0.03***	0.00	0.03***	0.00
Age-squared	−0.00***	0.00	−0.00***	0.00
Education	0.21***	0.02	0.19***	0.01
Female	−0.74	0.96	−0.42***	0.04
Female*education	0.10***	0.02	0.11***	0.01
Female*homemaker/retired	−0.10***	0.03	−0.13***	0.01
Professional/managerial	0.09***	0.03	0.22***	0.01
Self-employed	0.09**	0.03	0.05***	0.01
Manual worker	−0.06**	0.02	−0.16***	0.01
Unemployed	−0.07*	0.04	−0.13***	0.01
Left–right ideology	−0.16***	0.02	−0.21***	0.01
Left–right ideology-squared	0.02***	0.00	0.02***	0.00
Macro-level variables				
Unemployment	0.00	0.01	−0.02***	0.00
Inflation	0.01	0.01	0.01***	0.00
Social expenditure	−0.03***	0.01	0.01***	0.00
PR system			0.23***	0.02
Ideological polarization	0.33**	0.16	0.35***	0.07
End of Cold War (1990–93)		0.19***	0.19***	0.03
Female*time	0.01	0.03	−0.00**	0.00
Constant	2.37***	0.30	2.26***	0.16
R^2	0.06		0.10	
N	44,468		711,984	
Time period	2004–7		1975–2007	
Clusters (country years)	40		402	

* $p<0.1$; ** $p<0.05$; *** $p<0.01$.

welfare expenditure, proportional representation and ideological polarization. The model for Eastern countries shown in Table 3.5 produces rather different results. The coefficients for unemployment and inflation are non-significant, suggesting that economic factors do not affect engagement in this part of Europe. The social welfare expenditure coefficient is significant but negative— the opposite sign to that observed in the West—implying that in the post-communist states higher levels of social spending serve to reduce people's informal enagement levels. Whereas in the West, the greater social equity associated with state welfare spending appears to stimulate informal political discussion and persuasion, in the East such spending perhaps generates a greater sense of social contentment that in turn reduces informal engagement. This is clearly a matter for further research. In spite of these differences, however, there is one important similarity between the Eastern and Western models. The coefficient on the ideological polarization term in both models is positive and significant, producing a value of b = 0.35 in the West model and b = 0.33 in the East. This suggests that ideological factors play a remarkably similar role in generating informal political discussion across all the EU member states. Economic and political infrastructural factors operate in different ways in different parts of the EU. But ideology, at both the individual and macro levels, appears to be remarkably uniform in its effects.

One final point needs to be made about the role played by gender. Given that there is no general gender effect in the East Europe model in Table 3.5, we would not expect the interaction between being female and time to be significant either. This indeed proves to be the case (see the non-significant coefficient for female*year in the East model in Table 3.5). Given that in the West there is a clear individual-level gender effect, we might still expect that this effect would diminish over time as women's general visibility in labour markets and in politics has risen. The empirical results, however, show this expectation to be incorrect. The female*year coefficient in the West model in Table 3.5 is significant—but it is *negatively* signed. This suggests that, if anything, women in Western Europe have become marginally *less* inclined to engage in discussion and persuasion over the last thirty years or so.

Summary and conclusions

There is no doubt that, over the last four decades, voters in advanced democracies—including those in the EU—have been progressively less prepared to vote in elections. Since the end of the Cold War, the new democracies of Eastern and Central Europe—including those states that joined the EU after 2004—have generally followed the same pattern, displaying relatively low levels of turnout in elections at a variety of different levels. This chapter's first, simple, claim is that this decline in formal, public, citizen participation in politics has not been accompanied by a corresponding fall in formal, largely private forms of political involvement. On the contrary, although informal engagement has fluctuated over time—sometimes increasing systematically, as in the years immediately after the end of the Cold War—it has certainly not been subject to any sort of trend decline, either overall or (as far as the data permit us to judge) in relation to specific countries.

Our core objective in this chapter has been to explain *why* people vary in their propensities to engage in informal political discussion and persuasion. In this endeavour we have sought to identify the key individual-level and societal-level factors that seem to impel people to engage politically with their fellow citizens and friends.

At the individual level, we have established a fairly stable set of relationships that apply across all twenty-seven EU member states. An individual's *social-structural position*, perhaps unsurprisingly, appears to be consistently related to their engagement profile. Age, education, and labour market position all have clear and predictable effects on engagement. The typical highly engaged person is middle-aged, well educated, and from a professional or managerial occupational background. The typical disengaged person is young (or very old), poorly educated, and either from a manual working-class background or unemployed. In Western Europe, there is also a very clear gender pattern. Women are generally much less likely to engage than men, though this effect is strengthened for homemakers (and the retired) and attenuated for women with higher levels of education. Given the subordinate position occupied by women in most Western societies for centuries, this pattern makes sense. However, it also appears to be the case that very little has changed since the mid-1970s. It might have been expected that the slow moves towards women's equality that have taken place over the last three decades would have reduced the gender gap in levels of informal political engagement. The non-significance of the female*year interaction term in our general models in Table 3.3 suggests that this is not the case. The significant negative coefficient on this same interaction term in the West model in Table 3.5 implies that in parts of Europe women's involvement may even have fallen slightly.

Our analysis suggests a continuing major role at both the individual and the societal levels for left–right ideology. In individual-level terms, across all EU accession waves and across both East and West Europe, people who position themselves towards either extreme of the political spectrum are significantly more likely to be engaged than those at the centre. The effects of ideology, however, extend to the macro level too. The degree of ideological polarization in a given society has a positive and clearly significant effect on people's informal political engagement. This finding again applies both across all accession waves and to both East and West European states. In short, ideological debate matters—and it matters in virtually the same way and to the same extent in all parts of the EU.

Finally, it seems to be the case that the macro-level sources of informal engagement vary across the Western and Eastern parts of Europe. In the West, there are clear economic effects (unemployment dampens engagement whereas inflation stimulates it) and clear political infrastruture effects (the greater equity/fairness associated with both higher social welfare expenditure and proportional representation electoral systems seems to elicit greater engagement). In the East, however, social welfare spending seems to *reduce* engagement and economic effects appear not to operate at all. These differences may reflect nothing less than the different historical experiences of the East and West of Europe. It is also possible, however, that the apparent differences in macro-level effects between East and West are the consequence of the very limited number of time points available (2004–7) for analysing public preferences and behaviours in Eastern Europe. If this is indeed the case, then we may find, as more data accumulate, that the same macro-level factors that clearly affect citizens in the "older" more established EU states also affect mass publics in the East. Inevitably, this is a matter for further future research.

Notes

1. The countries are Austria, Belgium, Denmark, Finland, France, Germany, Greece, Ireland, Italy, Netherlands, Portugal, Spain, Sweden, UK.
2. One notable exception here is Van Deth and Elff (2004).
3. The three categories of the education scale are: Educated up to age 15; Educated to between age 16 and 19; Educated up to age 20+.
4. The base category that we use for estimating these various labour market positions is a combination of "white-collar workers", "homemakers", and "other".
5. Our measures of quality of governance are based on a series of World Bank indicators which are combined into a single index. For details, see Appendix to this volume.
6. We measure this operationally as the percentage of GDP allocated to social welfare spending.
7. Our operational measure here is whether or not legislative elections to the national assembly are in part or wholly based on proportional representation.
8. For details, see link to website for logit version of equation [1].
9. The gender*time interaction is at the margin of significance in Column (a) and clearly non-significant in Column (b). The reason for this stark difference lies in the extra cases that are included in the Column (b) model—extra cases that are brought into play because the quality of governance, GDP/capita, and net transfers from EU budget terms, for which data are available over a shorter time period for some countries, have been dropped, thereby reducing the number of missing cases.
10. Of the twelve new member states that acceded to the EU after 2000, ten were from the former Soviet bloc; Malta and Cyprus were the exceptions.

4

Ideological Polarization: Different Worlds in East and West

Hermann Schmitt and André Freire

Effective electoral representation requires, on the supply side of politics, that citizens at election time are offered a choice between competing contenders for public office.[1] Because representative democracy is, at its core, a mechanism for collective decision making on public policy, this choice must have recognizable and significant policy implications (APSA 1950; Kirkpatrick 1971; Miller et al. 1999). Currently, however, there is concern that this necessary component of the electoral verdict—a substantial policy choice—is eroding. In some parts of Europe at least, political parties seem to become more and more alike regarding the issues they emphasize and the policies they propagate (Schmitt and Wüst 2006). Under those conditions, voter preferences for any of the competing parties can hardly be based on issue or policy considerations. This raises questions about the policy content of the vote, about the well-functioning of political representation, and more generally about the meaningfulness of electoral choices (Schmitt and Wessels 2005).

The opposite problem is also well known: there have been historical situations in which electoral choice options were "too meaningful". This occurs when the issue agendas of relevant parties are so different and ideological splits between them so deep that they cannot peacefully be bridged. This is what Giovanni Sartori (1976) referred to as "polarized pluralism"—a type of party system which he described as characterized by centrifugal competition, the existence of anti-system parties and by irresponsible competitors engaging in the "politics of outbidding". In such a constellation the democratic order in general is in danger, as is the regular organization of free and fair elections that is at its core. The most disastrous example that comes to mind here is the breakdown of the Weimar Republic in the 1930s as a result of the rapidly accelerating polarization between the NSDAP under the leadership of

Adolf Hitler on the one hand, and the left—Social Democrats and Communists—on the other.

This is the argument that the present paper tries to put forward: that electoral choice options can be both too distinct and not distinct enough, and that the quality of electoral democracy suffers at both ends of the scale. We proceed in five steps. First, we further discuss the association between ideological polarization and the performance of electoral democracy, and formulate a number of hypotheses in an effort to identify the antecedents of ideological polarization. Second, we present the data and the methodological tools that we use to analyse them in order to test how well our hypotheses can adequately describe the empirical reality. Third, we identify national trends in ideological polarization, for four groups of European countries and for the USA and Australia.[2] Fourth, we test our hypotheses, first in a bivariate and then in a multivariate perspective. Fifth and finally, we summarize our findings and propose some tentative conclusions.

1. Theory and hypotheses

Electoral choices need to be distinct in terms of issues and policies in order to satisfy one important precondition of electoral representation. The "degree of distinctiveness" of electoral choices is also known as ideological polarization (or, as it is called in the US literature, partisan polarization). The difference between these terms is in the level of aggregation: while distinctiveness refers to individual parties, ideological (or partisan) polarization characterizes a *party system*. Individual choice options can be more or less distinct from one another while a whole electoral and party system can be more or less polarized.

The core of any definition of polarization refers to the spread of relevant electoral choice options around some measure of central tendency (usually mean or median) of the dominant ideological dimension (usually the left–right dimension) of a party system.[3] Sartori adds a directional component of party competition to this criterion, namely whether political parties in their struggle for support move away from the ideological centre or towards it (as the dominant median voter theorem of Anthony Downs (1957) assumes). But in any case, a party system is said to be polarized if, and to the degree to which, the relevant parties are apart from one another.

It is the basic proposition of this chapter that ideological polarization is related to the quality of electoral democracy. In mass democracies at least, the latter refers to the effectiveness of political representation or, in other words, the relative congruence of issue agendas and policy positions of elected representatives and their constituents (e.g. Schmitt 2001). But in addition to this substantial dimension of representative democracy, there is also an important procedural dimension of electoral democracy more broadly conceived. This procedural dimension points to such basic requirements as the rule of law, freedom of speech, and free and fair elections, among other things (for an overview, see Kaufmann, Kraay, and Mastuzzi 2007). Both aspects of the quality of democracy vary independently from one another: the substantial dimension of representative democracy can score highly in a procedurally poor democracy, and vice versa.

The proposed relationship between ideological polarization and the quality of electoral democracy is, however, expected to be not linear but curvilinear (Hypothesis 1). Low and high polarization should score low in terms of electoral democracy, while a "middle of the road" degree of ideological polarization—i.e. not "too little" and not "too much" of it—should score highest. We can summarize our expectation in graphical form (see Figure 4.1), without, however, having any possibility of knowing the exact form that this curvilinearity might take. The curve that fits the empirical data could resemble an inverted U, it could look like the tent that we choose to display in Figure 4.1, or it could assume yet another more unbalanced form—like an inverted J or L curve.

Regarding the causes of the expected shortcomings of electoral democracy under conditions of low and high ideological polarization, we can formulate some more specific expectations (without, however, being able to test them here).[4] Low-polarization systems should experience a lack of issue congruence

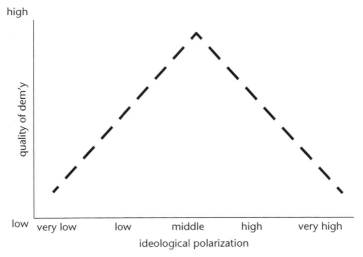

Figure 4.1. Relationship between satisfaction with democracy and ideological polarization

between voters and the parties they vote for, because parties under those conditions lack a distinct issue agenda and policy profile. When the relevant parties—in terms of the issues they are emphasizing and the policies they are pursuing—are very close to one another while their electorates are not, the congruence between electors and elected is bound to suffer.

In high-polarization systems, the symptoms (or indicators) of deficient democracy scores are likely to be different. Rather than the substantive dimension, it might be the *procedural* dimension that is causing problems here. While issue congruence can be expected to be high under the circumstances of intense politicization of the citizenry, more procedural aspects of representative democracy (like rule of law, freedom of speech, etc.) are possibly more endangered than they are in a less-polarized environment.

Socio-economic factors causing polarization. We leave the consequences of polarization behind and move on to the likely causes of it. There are three broad classes of factors that we expect to contribute to ideological polarization. Probably the most prominent of them is about the translation of social divisions into political oppositions. The deeper those social cleavages are, the more polarized we expect a party system to be (Hypothesis 2; see Lipset and Rokkan 1967; Sartori 1976). By implication, polarization is expected to decline over time as a consequence of the ongoing process of partisan dealignment (Hypothesis 2a; Dalton, Flanagan, and Beck 1984; Franklin, Mackie, and Valen 1992) and the ensuing "catch-all" strategies of political parties in electoral competition (Kirchheimer 1965). A related hypothesis involves economic factors. The proposal here is that economic crises reduce the potential for redistribution and thereby increase social conflict (Hypothesis 3). With or without the vehicle of sociopolitical cleavages, this is likely to express itself in electoral support for ideologically more extreme parties (e.g. Pelizzo and Babones 2007).

Political-structural factors causing polarization. Here we move to the somewhat crowded class of political-structural factors that are said to contribute to ideological polarization. The first factor is a numerical one: it is the argument of Giovanni Sartori (1976) that ideological polarization is restricted to multi-party systems (more precisely: to systems with five or more parties). We thus expect that the larger the number of relevant parties in a party system is, the higher is its degree of polarization (Hypothesis 4). The format of party competition depends to a large extent on the electoral system applied (Duverger 1951). We therefore predict that the more proportional an electoral system is, the higher is the ideological polarization in the party system in which it is applied (Hypothesis 5).

Another group of political-structural factors refers to the existence of veto players in a system (Tsebelis 1995, 1999, 2002). While Tsebelis focuses his veto player theory on the ability of political systems and governments to produce "significant laws" as the main dependent variable, we underscore one of his side arguments which suggests that the existence of veto players affects ideological polarization. This is so because more veto players impose a greater need for compromise and conciliation among political actors, and thereby reduce the distinctiveness of electoral choice options and contribute to the depolarization of party and government systems. There are a number of factors on the level of the political regime and at the level of the actual government that are likely to increase the number of veto players, and all of them are expected to decrease ideological polarization: among them are presidential and semi-presidential systems as opposed to parliamentary governments (Hypothesis 6a; but see Linz in Linz and Valenzuela 1992 for a partly opposite perspective); federal as opposed to unitary states (Hypothesis 6b); a bicameral as opposed to a unicameral house (Hypothesis 6c); and EU membership (Hypothesis 6d).

Regarding the level of the actual government, there are again several factors that contribute to polarization or the opposite of it. One of them is coalition government (Hypothesis 6e) and another is divided government (Hypothesis 6f; but see Jacobson 2000 for the complementary argument that partisan polarization, by affecting the calculus of the vote, causes divided government).

2. Data and methods

The empirical evidence that we draw upon in the following rests on aggregate data. We use a variety of different data sources to test our hypotheses. Regarding our first hypothesis on the democratic consequences of ideological polarization, we use the quality of democracy index scores provided by EUI (2008), which combines more specific scores from five sub-dimensions.[5] Those democracy scores are then confronted with ideological polarization index scores derived from the second wave of the Comparative Study of Electoral Systems post-election surveys (CSES II). The CSES covers a wide variety of electoral systems which also differ regarding the quality of democracy scores that can be attributed to each of them.

With respect to the causes of ideological polarization we are also interested, in addition to cross-national differences, in variation over time—a domain in which the CSES is not very informative. For those analyses, we rely on the databases of national programmes of election studies which often have been conducted over several decades.[6] Extending the European Voter database (Thomassen 2005c, 2005b) by adding countries and elections,[7] we were able to identify ideological polarization scores for 135 national elections held in eighteen countries—sixteen from the North, the South, and the East of

Table 4.1. Election years for which left-right party positions can be estimated from voters' left-right self-placements

Norway	Sweden	Denmark	Great Br.	Netherlands	Germany
2001	2002	2005	2005	2006	2005
1997	1998	2001	2001	2003	2002
1993	1994	1998	1997	2002	1998
1989	1991	1994	1992	1998	1994
1985	1988	1990	1987	1994	1990
1981	1985	1984	1983	1989	1987
1977	1982	1979	1979	1986	1983
1973	1979	1977	1974	1982	1980
	1976		1974	1981	1976
	1973			1977	1972
[8]	[10]	[8]	[9]	[10]	[10]
Portugal	Spain	France	Italy	Greece	Hungary
2005	2008	2002	2006	2004	2006
2002	2004	1997	2001	2000	2002
1999	2000	1993	1996	1996	1998
1991	1986	1981	1994	1993	1994
1987	1993	1978	1992	1990	1990
1985	1989	1973	1987	1989	
	1986		1983	1985	
	1982		1979	1981	
			1976		
			1972		
[6]	[8]	[6]	[10]	[8]	[5]
Poland	Czech R.	Slovenia	Croatia	USA*	Australia
2007	2006	2004	2003	2004	2007
2005	2002	2000	2000	2000	2004
2001	1998	1996	1995	1996	2001
1997	1996	1992	1992	1992	1998
1993	1992		1990	1988	1996
1991				1984	1993
				1980	1990
				1976	1987
				1972	
[6]	[5]	[4]	[5]	[9]	[8]

*: Liberal-conservative positions.

Europe, and two non-European (the USA and Australia; see Table 4.1). We might have missed out a few elections and countries for which sufficient information would have been available, but overall we claim that for the time being the polarization database that we have collected is quite exhaustive.

Both for the CSES-generated data and for the national election studies (NES) data, we use a polarization index that has proven to be useful in earlier work (van der Eijk, Schmitt, and Binder 2005).[8] The position of a party on the left–right scale is at the base of it. It can be determined in a number of ways. We used two different ones: for the CSES surveys, we identified party positions on the basis of the mean voter perceptions of where the parties stand; for the 135 NES datasets that we analyse subsequently, we identified party positions on the basis of the mean self-placements of the voters of these parties. In the online appendix to this volume we present a cross-validation effort which clearly shows that the party-based and the voter-based polarization scores co-vary strongly—which is to say: they seem to measure the same thing. Interestingly enough, the voter-based scores quite regularly identify a somewhat stronger degree of polarization than do the party-based scores.[9]

Last but not least, we move on to the predictors of ideological polarization. They again come from different sources. Most of the institutional characteristics of the systems under study are from Armingeon et al. (2008) and Gallagher (undated). Data on party strength and parliamentary representation are taken from official election statistics as available online. The economic data are from the OECD. Cleavage strength is estimated as Nagelkerke's Pseudo R^2 from multinomial logistic regressions of the vote recall (only relevant choice options included) on social-structural characteristics of respondents of the election surveys under study (Table 4.1 again). The instrumentation of social background variables differs between countries and sometimes also between surveys within countries. While this can certainly be an issue, we proceed under the assumption that national study directors will have included the locally relevant social-structural predictors of the vote in their questionnaires.[10]

3. Findings

Trends in ideological polarization across countries

In this section, we identify the major trends in ideological polarization across countries. To that purpose the polarization index introduced above is used. As we focus on over-time trends, we use the arithmetic mean of party voters' left–right self-placements as an indicator of their parties' left–right positions and compute the polarization index on this basis.

We divide the countries into five groups. These groups not only share (by and large) common trends in terms of ideological polarization, they also share some historical, geopolitical, and political features (Almond et al. 2006; Tiersky and Jones 2007; Rose and Munro 2003; Arter 2006; Bruneau et al. 2001). However, this is perhaps less pronounced for two of our five groups, i.e. for group three (continental Western Europe and the United Kingdom) and for group five (USA and Australia). The scatter plots with the five sets of countries, as well as some of the information from the OLS regressions (beta coefficients and respective levels of significance), are presented in Figures 4.2 to 4.6.

The first group (presented in Figure 4.2) includes a set of countries from Central and Eastern Europe. In all of these countries, the levels of polarization

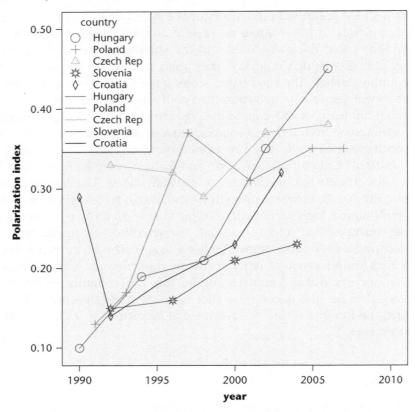

Figure 4.2. Trends in ideological polarization in Central and Eastern Europe

Sources: pre- and post-election surveys as indicated in Table 4.1.

Notes: Regressing polarization on time produces the following results: Hungary – $R^2 = 0.958$, $\beta = 0.979$, $p < 0.01$; Poland – $R^2 = 0.666$, $\beta = 0.816$, $p < 0.05$; Czech Republic – $R^2 = 0.469$, $\beta = 0.685$, $p > 0.2$; Slovenia – $R^2 = 0.940$, $\beta = 0.969$, $p < 0.05$; Croatia – $R^2 = 0.176$, $\beta = 0.419$, $p > 0.4$.

increase over time; for the majority of these countries we even find a strong increase. These democracies not only share important historical legacies resulting from their communist past; they are also new democracies and as such share several other political and institutional characteristics to which we will turn in greater detail shortly. While they are all characterized by upward trends in ideological polarization, in the cases of the Czech Republic and Croatia the (always positive) coefficients are not significant and the trend lines do not show a strong increase. For Hungary, Slovenia, and Poland—the other three countries included in this group—there is a clear and strong upward trend. In these three countries the beta coefficients are not only positive but also statistically significant in spite of the limited number of observations in each case. One further observation might be relevant. For

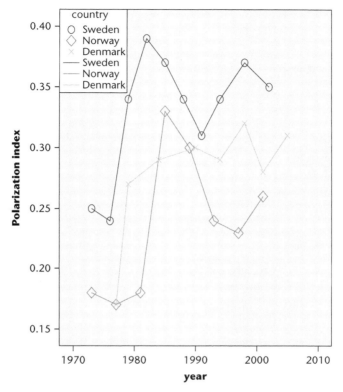

Figure 4.3. Trends in ideological polarization: Scandinavia

Sources: pre- and post-election surveys as indicated in Table 4.1.
Notes: Regressing polarization on time produces the following results: Sweden – R^2 = 0.691, β = 0.557, $p < 0.1$; Norway – R^2 = 0.251, β = 0.501, $p < 0.2$; Denmark – R^2 = 0.465, β = 0.682, $p > 0.1$.

Hungary, Slovenia, and Poland, ideological polarization starts from a rather low level (index values around 0.10; recall that the polarization index that we use varies between 0 and 1). The situation is very different in both the Czech Republic and Croatia where polarization starts at an index score of 0.3 or above.

As we said before, a particular feature of this first subgroup of five countries is that all of them are new democracies. New democratic regimes are less likely to exhibit high levels of party-system institutionalization—stable and legitimized party organizations, regular patterns of party competition, and the existence of relatively strong attachments to existing parties on the part of voters (Dalton and Tanaka 2007; Dalton and Weldon 2007; Mainwaring and Torcal 2005; Rose and Munro 2003). Where these elements are absent, parties' and citizens' ideological placements tend to be less clear and widespread, and

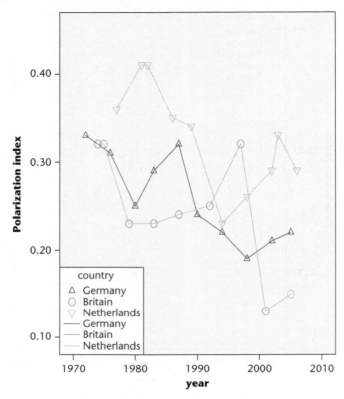

Figure 4.4. Trends in ideological polarization; Continental Western Europe and Great Britain

Sources: pre- and post-election surveys as indicated in Table 4.1.

Notes: Regressing polarization on time produces the following results: Germany – R^2 = 0.691, β = −0.831, p < 0.01; Britain – R^2 = 0.439, β = −0.662, p < 0.01; Netherlands – R^2 = 0.490, β = −0.700, p < 0.05.

also to exhibit higher levels of instability (Barnes 2002; Freire, Lobo, and Magalhães, 2009; Freire 2006a).

Moreover, in these new regimes other dimensions of competition (for example, related with the support vs contestation of the democratic regime) might reduce the salience of the left–right divide, at least in the first years (Moreno 1999). However, there is evidence of a learning process, and with the passage of time the parties tend to present clearer and more consistent policy alternatives to voters, and the citizens also tend to have a clearer view not only about the content of the left–right divide but also about parties' location in that dimension of competition (Barnes, McDonough, and Pina 1985; Freire 2006a). Summing up, in new democracies we should expect clearer and more distinctive left–right placements of both parties and electors as the years pass

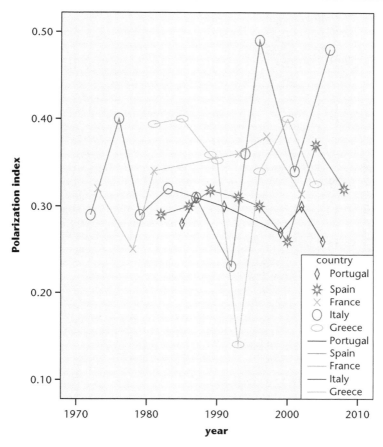

Figure 4.5. Trends in ideological polarization: Southern Europe—New and Old

Sources: pre- and post-election surveys as indicated in Table 4.1.

Notes: Regressing polarization on time produces the following results: Portugal – R^2 = 0.256, β = −0.506, p > 0.3; Spain – R^2 = 0.129, β = 0.360, p > 0.3; Greece – R^2 = 0.047, β = −0.021, p > 0.6; Italy – R^2 = 0.251, β = 0.476, p > 0.1; France – R^2 = 0.225, β = 0.474, p > 0.3.

over the transition to democracy. This element might help us to explain the presence of five new democratic regimes in this set of five countries with rising polarization scores. Of course, the cases of the Scandinavian countries (group 2, Figure 4.3), Italy (group 3, Figure 4.4), and Australia (group five, Figure 4.6) tells us also that not everything can be explained by the age of the democratic regime (in a similar vein, see Freire 2008).

The second group comprises the three Scandinavian countries (Figure 4.3), which not only share several political and institutional characteristics[11] (Pappi and Schmitt 1994; Arter 2006), but also similar upward trends regarding ideological polarization. As these three countries are all very old and

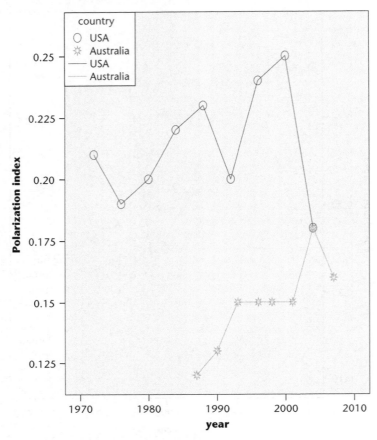

Figure 4.6. Trends in ideological polarization: USA and Australia

Sources: pre- and post-election surveys as indicated in Table 4.1.

Notes: Regressing polarization on time produces the following results: USA – $R^2 = 0.055$, $\beta = 0.234$, $p > 0.5$; Australia – $R^2 = 0.741$, $\beta = 0.861$, $p < 0.01$.

consolidated democracies, increases in ideological polarization here cannot be explained by the newness of the democratic regimes. It rather seems that the tradition of consensual policy making that was characteristic of Scandinavian politics until the 1980s (Luebbert 1986) is eroding as a result of new socio-political conflicts—taxation and immigration being just two examples—with significant repercussions on the format and direction of party competition. Moreover, the usual existence of congruent coalitions (alternative coalitions of either left-wing parties—social democrats and radical left, greens, etc.—or "bourgeois coalitions" of right-wing parties, with centre parties and/or "social liberal parties" sometimes integrating both) has also contributed to the increased clarity of policy (and party) alternatives in Scandinavia.

We note that the upward trend in ideological polarization is stronger in Sweden and Denmark (positive and significant beta coefficients) than in Norway (positive but not significant beta coefficient). In addition, there seems to be some ranking between the countries in terms of the degree of polarization (Sweden on the top, Norway at the bottom, and Demark in between), and the changes between the 1970s and 2000s do not transform this hierarchy.

The third group comprises three countries from continental Western Europe plus the United Kingdom (Figure 4.4). It is more heterogeneous in terms of institutional characteristics such as the different types of electoral and party systems; the different types of democratic models, with some being more majoritarian (like Britain) and the remainder being more consensual. But the group is nonetheless rather homogeneous in terms of trends towards depolarization: Germany, Britain, and the Netherlands all consistently exhibit strong negative and significant beta coefficients.

The fourth group comprises the countries of Southern Europe. Part of this group ("The New Southern Europe", i.e. Portugal, Spain, and Greece) shares a common historical legacy: all of them are middle-aged democracies after democratic transitions in the mid-1970s with a historical record of right-wing authoritarian dictatorships. They also share some majoritarian trends in the political system (especially in terms of Lijphart's "executive-parties dimension") since the mid-1980s (Bruneau et al. 2001; Freire and Teperoglou 2007). Figure 4.5 shows that they also seem to share some stable trends in ideological polarization. Although Portugal and Greece[12] have negative beta coefficients, and Spain has a positive one, in all cases the absolute values of the coefficients are low and, above all, not significant. This is partly due to strong ups and downs. Thus, the situation in this group is perhaps best described as trendless fluctuation.

Despite the fact that the countries of the New Southern Europe are relatively young democracies as well, we do not find here the increasing trends in ideological polarization that we identified in the post-communist democracies of Eastern Europe. However, whatever we say about the link between party system institutionalization and ideological polarization in the new democracies of Eastern Europe should also apply to these three countries from the mid-1970s on. And yet this is not what we find when we look at Figure 4.5: there is no secular increase in polarization there. We have no satisfactory explanation for this deviant situation, but will at least offer a speculation. First, we observe that we lack polarization estimates that cover the very early period of post regime change in the countries of the New Southern Europe. Thus we cannot rule out that polarization increased there too and we simply do not have the necessary data points to recognize it. One supportive hint in this direction could be seen in the fact that polarization is already relatively high when our trend lines start in the 1980s.

Overall, we would underline that the level of polarization is rather high, with frequent ups and downs. This is also characteristic of the other two Southern European countries that belong to this group, Italy and France. Although ideological polarization there does show some increase (positive beta coefficients), again the trend is not totally clear (many ups and downs, and above all no significant beta coefficients) and we should perhaps more properly refer to these two countries as also displaying trendless fluctuation.

The final group, presented in Figure 4.6, comprises our two mature non-European democracies, the USA and Australia. As noted, we decided to include these two non-European countries in order to increase the variance in some characteristics of the institutional set-up of the set countries under study.[13] If only modestly and on a comparatively low level, ideological polarization seems to be on the rise in both countries.

While the increase in "partisan polarization" at the elite level is a much-debated feature of the US political process over the past three decades or so (e.g. Thierlaut 2008), it is equally well known that ideological polarization among US citizens is much less pronounced (e.g. Jacobson 2000; Fiorina and Levendusky 2006). Our polarization index, based on the self-placement of US voters on the liberal–conservative scale, shows a slow increase in ideological polarization from the 1970s to the beginning of the 2000s, followed, however, by significant downfall of polarization in the 2004 election (the second George W. Bush election). In any case, compared to the levels of ideological polarization in Southern Europe which we have just examined, there is not much ideological polarization in the USA even after the increases that our data reveal.[14] And there is even less polarization in Australia. There, our time series starts later and at a considerably lower level (around 0.10). However, the Australian trend is clearly upward (indicated by a strong and significant beta coefficient).

Overall, considering that in a total set of sixteen countries only three—Germany, Britain, and the Netherlands—do show a clear decline in ideological polarization, we must conclude that this evidence does not support the "end of ideology hypothesis". In a similar vein, see, for example, van der Eijk, Schmitt, and Binder 2005; Berglund et al. 2005; Dalton 2006; Freire 2006a, 2006b, 2008; Gunther and Kuan 2007; Knutsen and Kumlin 2005.

Ideological polarization and the quality of democracy

But why is it relevant at all to study the evolution of ideological polarization in a number of democratic regimes? It is our argument that ideological polarization and the quality of electoral democracy are systematically related to one another. More specifically, we argue in our first hypothesis that electoral democracy is in trouble under conditions of high ideological polarization—this is as far as Giovanni Sartori (1976) goes—as well as when polarization reaches particularly low levels (i.e. when the issue and policy offers of relevant electoral-choice options are so similar that the voter faces a situation in which "meaningful choices" are hard to make. (Schmitt and Wessels 2005).

This latter aspect of the quality of electoral democracy is not directly covered by the available indices (like the ones issued by Freedom House or the World Bank or the one we use here, which has been compiled by *The Economist*). All of those indices focus on more procedural—as opposed to substantive—aspects of electoral democracy because they lack the empirical evidence that would enable them to evaluate the degree of issue congruence between voters and parties (or candidates). However, the former are likely to be related to the latter. Moreover, we know from earlier work that low levels of ideological polarization go hand in hand with low effects of the left–right scheme on vote choices (van der Eijk, Schmitt, and Binder 2005; Lachat 2008). As representative democracy rests on the importance of issue and policy considerations for the calculus of the vote (e.g. Schmitt 2001), we can read this as indirect evidence supporting our claim that low polarization is bad for representative democracy as long as it is based on general elections.

This seems to be supported by our confrontation of CSES-based polarization data and the composite quality of democracy scores issued by *The Economist* (Figure 4.7). A polarization score could be determined for thirty-three

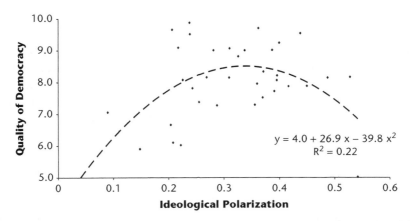

Figure 4.7. The curvi-linear association between ideological polarization and quality of democracy

Sources: Polarization estimates based on CSES II data

democracies in which the CSES II module was administered. When plotted against the relative quality of democracy, these scores clearly identify the expected curvilinear pattern, which confirms our first hypothesis. While the strength of the coefficient of determination (R^2) is rather modest, both regression terms are statistically significant (at $p < 0.05$).

The causes of ideological polarization: bivariate analyses

We leave the democratic consequences of ideological polarization behind and move on to the causes of it. We begin by considering the bivariate correlations between levels of ideological polarization across countries and time and various predictors as specified in the hypotheses spelt out above. Correlations are presented separately for "consolidated" Western democracies and for the post-communist systems of Eastern Europe. The reason for this segmented procedure is that the antecedents of ideological polarization in both groups are so different that a combined ("pooled") analysis was found to conceal more than to reveal.

We start out with the strength of cleavage anchoring. Contrary to our Hypothesis 2, cleavage strength—operationalized as the effect of social inequalities on the vote—does not seem to have any relevance for the level of polarization, at least not in terms of the bivariate perspective that we apply here (Table 4.2). Related to the cleavage strength hypothesis, we expected that polarization would be declining over time along with the ongoing dealignment between social divisions and party systems (Hypothesis 2a). Again, this expectation is clearly disconfirmed. For the consolidated West, there is no significant trend in polarization whatsoever, while we find a strong effect in the post-communist East that points in the *opposite* direction: polarization there increases strongly—rather than decreasing—over the two decades that elapsed after the breakdown of communism. The time period for which election study evidence is available is, of course, highly collinear with the age of the democratic regime and thus with the learning process we mentioned above for both parties and voters. This is why we find roughly the same correlations between age of democracy and polarization that we found before between year of election and polarization.

Our third hypothesis predicts a positive effect of economic crises on ideological polarization. We find traces of this in the West, with borderline-significant correlations between economic growth and inflation on one hand and ideological polarization on the other: growth tends to reduce polarization while inflation tends to increase it. Again, the situation is reversed in the post-communist East. There, economic growth goes along with increasing polarization, and rising inflation and unemployment are associated with decreasing polarization, and all of this is statistically significant despite the

Table 4.2. The correlates of ideological polarization

	"Consolidated"	Western systems	Post-communist	Eastern systems
	r (p)	N	r (p)	N
Society				
Cleavage strength[1]	0.02 (0.805)	110	0.01 (0.983)	20
Secular decline				
Year of election	−0.05 (0.600)	110	0.69 (0.000)	25
History				
# years democratic[2]	−0.17 (0.082)	110	0.74 (0.000)	23
Economy				
GDP growth	−0.17 (0.082)	110	0.52 (0.009)	24
Unemployment	0.14 (0.157)	102	−0.42 (0.058)	21
Inflation[3]	0.16 (0.096)	109	−0.59 (0.010)	18
Electoral and party system				
Effective number of parties[4]	0.28 (0.003)	110	−0.56 (0.004)	25
Disproportionality[5]	−0.25 (0.008)	110	−0.27 (0.198)	25
Veto players				
Type of regime[6]	−0.18 (0.060)	110	−0.31 (0.130)	25
Federalism[7]	−0.49 (0.000)	110	–	–
Type of parliament[8]	−0.15 (0.126)	110	0.15 (0.475)	25
EU membership length[9]	0.28 (0.003)	110	0.52 (0.008)	25
One party majority[10]	−0.27 (0.004)	110	−.40 (0.075)	21
Divided government[11]	−0.06 (0.511)	110	0.02 (0.937)	25
National experience divided government[12]	−0.08 (0.399)	110	0.23 (0.277)	25
Number of veto players[13]	−0.01 (0.946)	110	0.22 (0.294)	25
Consequences of polarization				
Turnout (vap)[14]	0.29 (0.003)	109	−0.37 (0.069)	25

Note: See the appendix for variable definitions

limited number of cases we can analyse in this group. Correlation and causation are two different things, of course, and we might be confronted here with purely coincidental phenomena. However, as we shall see in a moment, these adverse associations of economic development and ideological polarization do not disappear when we proceed to a more encompassing multivariate model of analysis, which is why we will then try to identify some reason behind those coefficients.

We move on to our Hypotheses 4 and 5 which predict that increasing numbers of relevant parties and, related to that, decreasing levels of disproportionality of the electoral system, should set favourable conditions for ideological polarization. These hypotheses are confirmed for the consolidated Western systems under study. The correlations are not strong but they are statistically significant, and they point in the right direction. The world looks again very different in the post-communist systems of Eastern Europe. Polarization there increases when the number of relevant parties decreases, which is exactly the opposite of what we expected. The reason for this unanticipated result might be that the number of effective parties is exceptionally high in the post-communist systems. Moreover, not only are there many parties to keep an eye on; they also keep changing their names, labels, and ideological orientations over and over again (see again Rose and Munro 2003; Tworzecki 2002). This is likely to create confusion on the part of the voters who might find it difficult to orient themselves. In any case, the fluidity of the party systems is likely to decrease the clarity of political alternatives and thereby decrease rather than increase ideological polarization. Disproportionality, at least in a bivariate perspective that we apply here, does not have a statistically significant effect on the degree of ideological polarization in our five post-communist systems.

Our last set of hypotheses concerns the contribution of veto players to the degree of ideological polarization of a system. Borrowed from Tsebelis, the argument is that veto players, individually and jointly, reduce the level of polarization as they impose compromise and conciliation as the predominant style of decision making—i.e. the opposite of ideological polarization. We can quickly run through our six sub-Hypotheses (6a–6f), as most of them are disconfirmed. Both in the West and the East, parliamentary rather than presidential or semi-presidential regimes go along with lower levels of polarization—which disconfirms Hypothesis 6a. Federalism reduces polarization strongly and significantly (this is testable only for the West as none of our post-communist systems is organized as a federation), and Hypothesis 6b is the only one that is confirmed here. The type of parliament is not significantly related to polarization, neither in the West nor in the East, a finding which disconfirms Hypothesis 6c. Length of EU membership increases rather than decreases polarization, which disconfirms Hypothesis 6d. One-party majority governments—i.e. the opposite of coalition governments—decrease rather than increase polarization both in West and East, which disconfirms Hypothesis 6e. Divided government does not significantly contribute to depolarization, which disconfirms Hypothesis 6f. And, last but not least, the summary indicator counting the number of veto players that operate in a political system is not related to depolarization either (disconfirming the more general idea of our Hypotheses 6a–6f).

The causes of ideological polarization: multivariate analyses

Do these results hold when we move on from bivariate correlations to a multivariate model? This is where we finally turn. There are, of course, a number of ways in which such a multivariate analysis can be approached.

Table 4.3. The antecedents of ideological polarization

predictors of polarization	Consolidated democracies in the West	Post-communist systems
	b	b
Duration of democracy	−0.12	0.89
Cleavage strength	−0.09	0.07
Economic growth		0.15
Unemployment	0.26	
Political regime	0.10	−0.08
Federalism	−0.52	—
EU membership length		0.07
Effective number of electoral parties		−0.68
Single party majority government	−0.32	−0.05
Divided government		0.08
R2 (for the polarisation equation)	0.38	0.98
Fit Indices (for the overall equation system)		
Bentler-Bonett Normed Fit Index	0.925	0.907
Bentler-Bonett Non-Normed Fit Index	0.908	1.096
Comparative Fit Index (CFI)	0.962	1.000

Note: Results from EQS structural equations modelling effort; effect coefficients from the standardized solution are given for the polarization equation; fit indices are reported for the overall model.

The standard option, given the measurement properties of our dependent variable, would probably have been an OLS multiple regression. As we are interested not only in the direct effects of our predictors but even more so in their total effects—i.e. direct plus indirect effects taken together—we chose a different analytical strategy and specified structural equations models. There were a few decisions to be taken on the way. First, we decided to stick to our two-group strategy because the results at the bivariate level were already so different that anything else did not make much sense. Second, a number of the predictors used in bivariate analyses are strongly correlated (a good example here is election year and age of democracy). In those cases, we decided to use the more powerful predictors (as evidenced by bivariate analysis) in the multivariate setting. Third, for the sake of simplicity we decided to focus the presentation of our results on the polarization equation, and document all the rest of our findings in the online appendix to this volume.

In formal terms, three main results emerge from this step of our analysis (see Table 4.3). The first is that our bivariate findings by and large survive the multivariate test. The second is that we seem to understand the causes of polarization in post-communist systems much better than we do in mature Western systems, statistically speaking at least. And the third is that we are able to account for a sufficiently large proportion of the co-variances of the variables in the equation system so that our models—including the polarization equation—fit the data quite well.

What then are the causes of polarization and depolarization in these two very different worlds of democratic politics? In the Western world, federalist veto players are very effective in pulling polarization down. A badly running economy which produces high unemployment rates works in the opposite direction. This comes very much as expected. Unexpected is the depolarizing effect of single-party majority governments, and, by implication, the polarizing effect of coalition governments. There are minor effects that we will not dwell upon at this stage. Obviously, large proportions of variance in the degree of ideological polarization remain unexplained in mature democracies: we cannot account for them. Party elite strategies certainly are just one candidate for an important unobserved variable; there might be many more.

Moving on to the post-communist systems of Eastern Europe, we must keep in mind that liberal democracy and free and fair elections in these systems are a mere twenty years old. Given this short time frame, we see again a strong trend towards ideological polarization in post-communist electoral systems that starts with regime change and progresses almost linearly over time under democratic rule. This is the single most important effect in the equation: the greater the distance of an election from 1990, the higher the ideological polarization. In addition, ideological polarization obviously profits from the *concentration* of post-communist party systems: the fewer relevant parties there are in such a system, the higher are the polarization scores that we identify for it. These two main effects obviously run counter to any orthodox conception of the antecedents of ideological polarization. They suggest, however, that in an environment of volatile and fragile electoral systems, a clear pattern of ideological opposition first needs to evolve and flourish before it becomes subject to the more conventional factors affecting ideological polarization in mature democracies.

Conclusion

If often neglected, ideological polarization is an important property of electoral systems. It is known to affect the behaviour of individual voters: issue considerations have a better chance of affecting vote choices in ideologically polarized environments. As issue effects on the vote are important prerequisites for representative democracy (because electoral representation can only be effective if vote choices carry some issue or policy content), polarization strengthens the effectiveness of representative democracy.

On this aggregate level, however, things are less clear cut than they might seem at first sight. While too little polarization can certainly be a problem for the effectiveness of representative democracy, we know from Sartori (1976) that too much polarization might equally be a problem as it might endanger the survival of electoral democracy. It is our argument, therefore, that the relationship between ideological polarization and the quality of electoral democracy is not linear but curvilinear: both high and low scores of ideological polarization can be detrimental for the democratic process. We have tested this claim against available data and found that it is supported by empirical evidence.

The consequences of ideological polarization are one thing; its causes are another. Drawing from the relevant literature, we propose a few hypotheses. First, we claim that polarization is a function of the strength of sociopolitical cleavages and, as dealignment is progressing over time, that polarization should decline with the passage of time. Second, we claim that the economy has an impact on polarization because bad economic conditions are likely to accentuate existing social divisions, and thus to increase polarization. Last but not least we claim that institutional veto players reduce ideological polarization, because they—jointly and separately—tend to switch the mood of policy making from confrontation to compromise and conciliation.

When confronting these theoretical expectations with empirical evidence, we detect two separate worlds—consolidated democracies and emerging democracies in the post-communist world. The antecedents of polarization appear to be very different in these two worlds. While our predictors—social conflict, time, economic conditions, and even to some degree the veto player idea—seem to describe the Western reality quite well, they completely fail for the post-communist world of Eastern Europe. There, consolidated voter–party alignments and stable party systems first need to emerge before we can expect them to behave as such.

In the meantime, we must not forget the curvilinear shape of the effects of ideological polarization on the quality of electoral democracy. We find polarization steadily rising in Eastern Europe, a fact which at some point can even put democratic principles and procedures into question. The integration of many of these countries in the European Union, however, will make any attack on the democratic order very difficult.

Notes

1. We would like to acknowledge the excellent research assistance of Sascha Adam, Andrea Fiege, Inês Lima, Filipa Seiceira, and Maximilian Zorn. A seminar on the same topic taught by the first author at the University of Mannheim in the winter of 2009–10 contributed many stimulating ideas.
2. Although our focus is on EU countries, we include data on the USA and Australia in order to assess the extent to which our substantive conclusions can be extended to other mature democracies.

3. There are some more detailed operational questions associated to that definition which we will turn to in the subsequent section of data and methods.

4. This will be the topic of a further paper, in which we intend to distinguish empirically between these two aspects of the quality of democracy and test explicitly that policy congruence suffers when polarization is low; and that free and fair elections and their prerequisites are in danger when polarization is high.

5. These five sub-dimensions of democracy are: the electoral process and pluralism; functioning of government; political participation; democratic political culture; and civil liberties.

6. Where no consolidated election study programme was available, we used nationally representative surveys that were conducted at around election time (+/– three months from election day).

7. And paving the way for the COST Action "The True European Voter", see www.true-euopean-voter.eu.

8. The formula reads as follows: IP = (Σ |LRm-LRpx|*EPpx)/IPmax, where:

   IP = ideological polarization
   LRm = the numerical centre of the left–right scale;
   LRpx = the position of party x on the left–right scale;
   EPpx = the proportion of party x of the valid vote in the last election; and
   IPmax = maximal ideological polarization defined by two equally strong parties that are located at opposite poles of the ideological spectrum.

   Note that all relevant parties are being considered, relevancy being defined by parliamentary representation.

9. We cannot go into the details of this observation here, but will elaborate on this phenomenon in a separate research note.

10. The predictors normally include some indictors of age, sex, rural/urban residence, education, class, religiosity, and wealth. Where relevant and available, denomination and ethnicity are also included. A list of the social-structural predictors of the vote that were used for each individual study is available from the authors upon request.

11. Among them: proportional representation, multipartism, a relatively strong level of cleavage anchoring, especially in terms of the class cleavage, strong unions, "neocorporatist" institutional arrangements, etc.

12. In the Greek case, the 1993 election seems to be an outlier due to the very low level of polarization. Instead of thinking of a measurement problem here, however, we should bear in mind that this 1993 election followed two elections (1989 and 1990) after which both the communists (KKE) and the right (ND: Nea Demokratia) joined forces in so-called "*catarse* governments" to unseat the discredited PASOK (Clogg, 1987). When both the left (KKE) and the right (ND) get together to form a coalition government, polarization must be expected to reach a particularly low level.

13. Both the USA and Australia use majoritarian electoral systems and join forces in that regard with the United Kingdom; these two countries are organized as federations and join Germany in that regard; and the USA is the second presidential system in our sample next to France.

14. We note in passing that some of the US studies on partisan polarization at the mass public level analyses the correlation between citizens' evaluations of the two parties rather than directly the ideological views of these parties' voters. However, the increasingly strong and negative correlations between the evaluations of Democrats and Republicans might well measure some sort of inter-party hostility rather than ideological polarisation. And while the two are certainly related, they are not the same thing.

5

Electoral Turnout at National and European Levels

Markus Steinbrecher and Hans Rattinger

Introduction

Turnout is one of the key behavioural components of political activity. However, the first thing of interest after an election is the distribution of votes among parties and what this means for the future government. Turnout rarely comes under closer scrutiny after national elections, yet it has always been important for the analysis of electoral behaviour at the European level. Politicians and media commentators have often regarded turnout in European Parliament elections (EPE) as an indicator of support for European integration, for European institutions, and even for the policies conducted at the European level. Thus, the decline of turnout rates in European elections since 1979 has frequently been attributed to rising levels of dissatisfaction with the EU in the public discourse. However, these popular assumptions are only supported by a limited number of studies (Blondel, Sinott, and Svensson 1998; Frognier 2002) and are questioned in many others (Oppenhuis 1995; Rosema 2007; Schmitt and Mannheimer 1991; Schmitt and van der Eijk 2003).

At the micro level, conventional predictors of turnout have included social structure, societal norms, instrumental evaluations, interest in politics, and non-EU-related political attitudes (e.g. Steinbrecher, Huber, and Rattinger 2007; Steinbrecher and Rattinger 2012). At the macro level, several scholars have focused on political system characteristics like compulsory voting, Sunday and postal voting (e.g. Blais 2000; Geys 2006; Mattila 2003; Oppenhuis 1995; van der Eijk, Franklin, and Marsh 1996), or the timing of the European election in the electoral cycle of the national parliament (Reif and Schmitt 1980) when explaining the differences in national turnout levels. Only recently, aggregate levels of support for European integration have been integrated into macro-level analyses of turnout and have proven their analytical potential (Flickinger and Studlar 2007).

The main goal of this chapter is to test the importance of EU-related attitudes for turnout in European Parliament elections at the micro and macro levels in comparison with the standard predictors over the period 1979–2009. This chapter will thus proceed as follows. Section 1 introduces the database for the analysis. It outlines the theoretical relevance of the independent variables examined, and provides an overview of their operationalization as well. Section 2 is primarily descriptive and focuses on the development of turnout between 1979 and 2009. The first subsection concentrates on European elections, while the second describes the development at the national level. The third subsection highlights the most important differences in turnout at the two electoral levels. This is necessary because European elections are just one specific type of election in a system of multilevel governance with independent, but related, elections at every political level. Section 3 presents the empirical analyses. We first focus on the explanation of differences between member states with a macro-level analysis. The second part of Section 3 concentrates on micro-level factors and thus sheds light on the importance of Europe-related attitudes for turnout from a citizen perspective. The chapter ends with a summary and discussion of the findings.

1. Theory and data

This section provides information about data and the theoretical background of predictors in the macro and micro analyses. At the macro level we collected turnout rates for the whole EU as well as for individual EU member states from official data sources and providers. These included the statistical offices of the EU and the member states, as well as internet sources like the Institute for Democracy and Electoral Assistance (IDEA) and "Parties and Elections in Europe" (http://www.parties-and-elections.de/). The individual-level data come from Eurobarometer (EB) surveys and the European Election Studies (EES) conducted in the immediate aftermath of European Parliament (EP) elections, between 1979 and 2009. All our seven datasets feature the respondents' recollection of voting in EP elections, but differ in the range of predictor variables available. The consequences of this problem are discussed below.

It is a well-known fact that turnout rates in European elections differ widely across countries. Hence, we will run a macro-level analysis. Previous research has identified several political system characteristics that explain national differences in the level of electoral participation (Blais 2000; Blondel, Sinott, and Svensson 1998; Fauvelle-Aymar and Stegmaier 2008; Flickinger and Studlar 2007; Franklin 1996, 2001; Geys 2006; Mattila 2003; Oppenhuis

1995; van der Eijk, Franklin, and Marsh 1996). Compulsory voting has a strong positive effect on turnout rates. Positive effects can be expected from Sunday voting, too, as people have more free time to go to the polls than on weekdays. Simultaneous nationwide elections also help to boost turnout at the European level, when European elections profit from the higher perceived importance of national parliament or nationwide regional elections. Several scholars have identified a "first-time boost" for turnout, if European elections are held for the first time (Franklin 2001: 312; Reif 1984: 7; van der Eijk, Franklin, and Marsh 1996) as the new kind of election attracts voters to show up at the polls. The last political system characteristic is related to the position of the European election in the first-order election cycle. According to the second-order election model, turnout is lower if European elections are held close to or at the first-order mid-term due to a lower level of general political mobilization (Reif and Schmitt 1980; Reif 1984).

We add four other variables to our macro-level analysis. *Communist past* is included to account for the different historical background of the countries and the turnout gap between the accession countries of 2004 and 2007, on the one hand, and the countries of the EU15, on the other. Our main variable of interest is national aggregate support for EU membership. According to previous research (Flickinger and Studlar 2007), we expect this variable to have a positive impact on turnout. Two further political culture characteristics are *satisfaction with the working of democracy* and *left–right polarization*.[1] The causal connection with turnout of the latter variable is quite obvious. If a political system is less polarized, people should be less motivated to vote and thus turnout should be lower. The impact of the level of satisfaction with democracy is less clear. If findings for the micro level also apply to the macro level with people transferring their support for the national political system to the European level (Rohrschneider 2002; Sanchez-Cuenca 2000; Schmitt 2003b; see below) there should be a positive causal relationship with turnout.

For our general indicator of EU attitudes, we use "Support for EU membership" to gauge if a respondent thinks that the membership of their country in the EU is a good thing, a bad thing, or neither. We chose this indicator as it was the only EU-related attitude available in all the datasets that we analyse. The assumption that turnout in European elections is affected by support for the EU and the European integration process is in line with theoretical considerations offered by Easton (1965) and Almond and Verba (1963). They stated that the stability and performance of a democracy are dependent on the fundamental willingness of citizens to support the political system. This is particularly likely to be the case for the European level of governance since it is still quite new and rather remote for many Europeans. Citizens who are satisfied with the European political system may thus be more likely to cast a ballot in EP elections than the dissatisfied. Moreover, if all or almost all parties are in favour of the integration process, non-participation in European elections will be the only way of expressing opposition to the European political system and the integration process (Schmitt and van der Eijk 2003: 281f.).

The importance of our EU-support indicator will be assessed below in comparison with other micro-level variables whose impact on individual turnout in national and European elections has been well demonstrated in previous research (Franklin 1996; Kleinhenz 1995; Oppenhuis 1995; Rosenstone and Hansen 1993; Steinbrecher, Huber, and Rattinger 2007; Wolfinger and Rosenstone 1980). Ideally, we would have liked to test the explanatory power of the five main theoretical approaches—instrumental rationality, cueing rationality, affective/identitarian factors, cognitive mobilization, and equity/fairness considerations—that are covered in other parts of this volume. However, due to the limited availability of items over time, our predictors belong to just two of these dimensions: political cues and cognitive mobilization.

We use four political cue variables in our models: strength of party identification, left–right extremity, satisfaction with democracy, and materialist value orientations. The first indicator is part of the social-psychological approach to electoral analysis, in which attachment to a party is considered to promote psychological involvement in the political process: the stronger the party identification, the higher the probability of casting a ballot (Campbell et al. 1960: 97f.).

The second political cue variable is left–right extremity. It can be assumed that people with a more extreme self-placement either to the left or the right have a higher probability of showing up at the ballot box. The main reason why we decided for this operationalization of ideological orientation is that we want to test if the macro-level relationship between ideological polarization and turnout hypothesized above also exists at the individual level.

The third political cue variable is satisfaction with democracy. Research on support for European integration has demonstrated that the quality of national institutions (Rohrschneider 2002; Sanchez-Cuenca 2000; Schmitt 2003) has an impact on attitudes towards European integration, but also on turnout itself in European elections (Schmitt and van der Eijk 2003). It is expected to have a positive effect on EU electoral participation. If the act of voting is regarded as an indicator of system support, citizens will transfer support for the national political system to the European political system (Schmitt 2003b: 76ff.).

The fourth political cue variable is based on Inglehart's theory of a *Silent Revolution* (1977a, 1990) and his well-known materialism index based on four items. According to Inglehart's hypotheses, materialists should tend to participate in conventional forms of political participation like turnout while post-materialists should be more active in unconventional participation forms. Thus, the materialism index in our analysis should have a positive impact on the probability of turnout. Unfortunately this index is only available in some of the datasets that we analyse.

The second major group of predictor variables relates to cognitive mobilization. Many of these variables can be derived from the social-psychological approach, if one applies a wider understanding of it. Among these predictors are political interest and media consumption. Politically interested people and heavy media users have a higher probability of electoral participation (Campbell et al. 1960: 101). Political efficacy is a further possible predictor in this context. A distinction has traditionally been drawn between internal and external efficacy (Converse 1972). Both aspects correlate positively with turnout: the higher that someone evaluates their capabilities and/or the responsiveness of the political system and its actors, the more likely it is that s/he will participate in elections (Campbell et al. 1960: 105). Unfortunately, efficacy indicators are available only very rarely in the surveys at hand and thus are part of the analysis on some occasions only.

Due to limited availability of cognitive mobilization indicators in the older Eurobarometer studies, we use another construct, the so-called opinion leadership index that combines the frequency of political discussions with other people and the frequency of convincing friends. The theoretical background for this indicator is the work by Lazarsfeld and his colleagues who, in *The People's Choice*, identified the central role of opinion leaders in the two-step flow of communication (1968: 150ff.). As opinion leaders are involved in politics to a high degree, we suppose that they are more active and thus have a higher probability of participating in elections.

Social structural variables are not as important as attitudinal variables for the prediction of individual electoral behaviour, but they should not be omitted from the analysis (Steinbrecher, Huber, and Rattinger 2007: 210ff.). Variables like class membership, religiosity, and urbanization can be directly linked to the micro- and the macro-sociological approach (Lazarsfeld, Berelson, and Gaudet 1968). Education and class membership (as a proxy for income and occupation) are part of socio-economic status (Verba and Nie 1972; Verba Schlozman and Brady 1995), which is an important positive predictor of political participation. Gender and age are not directly connected to the two theoretical approaches, but are nevertheless germane to the sociological approach in general. While men traditionally show higher participation rates, age is, according to the start-up–slow-down model, correlated in a curvilinear way with turnout (Verba and Nie 1972: 138ff.). In addition, religiosity can be used as a proxy variable for the perceived duty to vote, which is usually among the strongest positive predictors of national turnout. Unfortunately, the latter has not been part of the present Eurobarometer and EES surveys. As the perceived duty to vote is correlated with holding particular values (Rubenson et al. 2004: 410), religiosity can be regarded as an adequate proxy.

2. Descriptives: the development of turnout between 1979 and 2009

This section gives an overview of the development of turnout rates in European and national parliament elections (NPE) between 1979 and 2009. We look at both electoral levels first and test whether there are linear trends in the development of turnout in the period of our analysis. We then compare the level and stability of turnout at both levels and inspect if the turnout gap between elections at both levels has broadened in recent years or not.

Development of turnout in European Parliament elections

The first task of this chapter is to focus on the development of turnout rates in the period between 1979 and 2009. In the whole EU, mean turnout is 54 per cent during the thirty-year period. Turnout clearly declines after the first election in 1979. The difference between the maximum in 1979 (63 per cent) and the minimum in 2009 (43 per cent) is 20 percentage points. The biggest drop between two elections occurred from 1994 to 1999 (7 percentage points). After 1999, less than half of the EU's voters went to the EP polls. The very low turnout rates in 2004 and 2009 are also related to the accession of Central and Eastern European countries. The separate calculation of averages for old and new member states reveals that electoral participation is at a much lower level in the latter group of countries in the 2004 and the 2009 elections (see Table 5.1).

Belgium and Luxembourg are clearly the countries with the highest turnout rates—they are close to or even above 90 per cent on average. The reason for the extraordinarily high turnout is the application of compulsory voting in both countries. Malta has an average turnout of 80.6 per cent. Italy and Greece follow with 76.2 per cent and 71.2 per cent, respectively. Then there is a large group of countries with mean turnout rates between 50 and 65 per cent: France, Germany, Denmark, Ireland, Spain, Austria, and Cyprus. Another large group of countries is characterized by mean participation rates between 40 and 50 per cent. Here we find the Netherlands, Portugal, Sweden, Finland, and Latvia. Exceptionally low participation rates appear in the United Kingdom and in almost all Eastern European countries. While the British reveal the lowest willingness to cast a ballot (33.6 per cent) among Western Europeans, less than one-third of the eligible voters show up at the polls on average in

Table 5.1. Turnout in European Parliament Elections (EPE) 1979–2009 (EU-27)

Country	1979	1984	1989	1994	1999	2004	2009	Mean	Standard deviation
France	60.7	56.7	48.7	52.7	47.0	42.8	40.6	49.9	7.3
Belgium	91.6	92.2	90.7	90.7	91.0	90.8	90.4	91.1	0.6
Netherlands	57.8	50.6	47.2	35.6	30.0	39.3	36.8	42.5	9.7
Germany	65.7	56.8	62.4	60.0	45.2	43.0	43.3	53.8	9.7
Italy	84.9	83.4	81.5	74.8	70.8	73.1	65.1	76.2	7.3
Luxembourg	88.9	88.8	87.4	88.5	87.3	89.0	90.8	88.7	1.2
Denmark	47.8	52.4	46.2	52.9	50.4	47.9	59.5	51.0	4.5
Ireland	63.6	47.6	68.3	44.0	50.5	58.8	58.6	55.9	8.8
United Kingdom	32.3	32.6	36.2	36.4	24.0	38.8	34.7	33.6	4.8
Greece	78.6	77.2	79.9	71.2	75.3	63.4	52.6	71.2	9.9
Spain		68.9	54.6	59.1	63.0	45.1	44.9	55.9	9.7
Portugal		72.4	51.2	35.5	40.0	38.6	36.8	45.8	14.2
Sweden				41.6	38.8	37.8	45.5	40.9	3.4
Finland				60.3	31.4	39.4	40.3	42.9	12.3
Austria				67.7	49.4	42.4	46.0	51.4	11.3
Malta						82.4	78.8	80.6	2.5
Poland						20.9	24.5	22.7	2.5
Czech Rep.						28.3	28.2	28.3	0.1
Slovakia						17.0	19.6	18.3	1.8
Estonia						26.8	43.9	35.4	12.1
Latvia						41.3	53.7	47.5	8.8
Lithuania						48.4	21.0	34.7	19.4
Hungary						38.5	36.3	37.4	1.6
Slovenia						28.3	28.3	28.3	0.0
Cyprus						71.2	59.4	65.3	8.3
Bulgaria						29.2	39.0	34.1	6.9
Romania						29.5	27.7	28.6	1.3
EU	63.0	61.0	58.5	56.8	49.8	45.7	43.0	54.0	7.8
EU-15	63.0	61.0	58.5	56.8	49.8	48.8	46.6	54.9	6.0
EU-15 +						27.8	28.8	28.3	0.7

Source: Statistics offices of the EU and the member states, IDEA, http://www.parties-and-elections.de/.
Note: Means for EU, EU-15, and EU-15 + are weighted by population size.

Poland, Czech Republic, Slovakia, Slovenia, and Romania. A general finding that applies to many countries is the decline of participation rates in the more recent elections: France, Portugal, Spain, Finland, Greece, and Germany are the clearest cases of this development (see Table 5.1).

Overall, the member countries show different patterns for the development of turnout in the period since 1979. On the one hand, countries like Belgium, Luxembourg, Denmark, Sweden, and the United Kingdom have quite stable participation rates. However, the levels are quite different for each country. Luxembourg and Belgium show the most stable turnout patterns because of the compulsory vote, with a standard deviation of about 1 percentage point. Turnout in Sweden is at a much lower level, ranging between 38 and 45.4 per cent and exhibiting a standard deviation of 3.4 percentage points, while Denmark's and the United Kingdom's turnout fluctuations are 4.5 and 4.8 percentage points, respectively. On the other hand, turnout has been quite variable in Finland, Austria, the Netherlands, Portugal, Germany, Greece, and Spain. The high standard deviations for all these countries, with the exception of Germany, result from the very high turnout in the respective first European election that perhaps was caused by a "first-time boost" due to the excitement accompanying the novel experience of European elections (see Franklin 2001: 312; Reif 1984: 7; van der Eijk, Franklin, and Marsh 1996). Considering the standard deviation, Austria, Finland, and Portugal show the most unstable development of turnout. Quite interesting developments can be reported for Germany and especially Ireland. While Ireland shows a continuous up and down from election to election, the situation in Germany can be separated into two periods. From 1979 to 1994 turnout varies around 60 per cent, while it is close to 45 per cent since 1999. Finally, the United Kingdom is the country with the lowest turnout until the accession of Eastern and Central European countries in 2004.

It is interesting to test whether a linear trend explains the development of turnout since 1979. Table 5.2 thus displays the results of linear regression analyses with turnout as the dependent variable for the EU15 between 1979 and 2009. The predictor variable in this model is the time passed since 1979. As the table shows, there are four countries where the linear model explains either none or very little of the variance in turnout: Luxembourg, Ireland, the United Kingdom, and Sweden. For France, Italy, Germany, Greece, Austria, and the whole EU15, the explanatory power of the linear model is very good or almost perfect, with above 70 per cent or even close to 90 per cent in some cases. However, the most interesting finding is not the level of explained variance, but the significance of the regression coefficients for time. For five

Table 5.2. Regression analysis for turnout in EPE 1979–2009 (EU 15)

Country	R^2	Constant	Time
France	0.91	59.51	−0.64**
Belgium	0.56	91.71	−0.04
The Netherlands	0.66	53.49	−0.73*
Germany	0.80	65.77	−0.80**
Italy	0.92	85.95	−0.65*
Luxembourg	0.16	88.03	0.04
Denmark	0.27	47.77	0.22
Ireland	0.01	57.03	−0.07
United Kingdom	0.01	32.78	0.05
Greece	0.74	82.98	−0.79*
Spain	0.64	70.39	−0.83
Portugal	0.63	66.88	−1.21
Sweden	0.16	36.11	0.21
Finland	0.30	66.25	−1.04
Austria	0.68	83.82	−1.44
EU	0.94	64.50	−0.70**

*: $p < 0.05$, **: $p < 0.01$, ***: $p < 0.001$.

Source: own calculations.

countries the analysis reveals a significant negative trend over time. Interestingly, four out of these five countries belong to the group of the founding fathers of the EU: France, the Netherlands, Germany, and Italy show a decline of turnout between 0.64 and 0.8 percentage points per year. This significant linear trend also applies to Greece (–0.79) and to the EU15 as a whole with a b-value of –0.70. In the rest of the countries the b-values are not significant, but there are negative signs in at least eleven of the fifteen countries, which account for the negative trend over time.

Development of turnout in national parliament elections

In order to compare the national and the European electoral levels in the next subsection, a look at national turnout rates and their development over time is the next step. Table 5.3 shows the turnout in all national elections since 1979 in the countries of the EU27 as well as mean and standard deviation of turnout by country. There is no country with a mean participation rate below 67 per cent in national parliament elections among the EU15. Belgium and Luxembourg are the countries with the highest mean turnout rates in Western Europe as a result of compulsory voting, which also explains why variations in turnout rates are very low in both countries. With the Netherlands, Germany, Italy, Denmark, Sweden, and Austria there is a large group of countries with a mean turnout above 80 per cent in the period analysed. However, for all these countries a trend of decline can be observed, especially during the 1990s and the 2000s. There is another large group of countries with mean turnout rates between 70 and 80 per cent: Greece, Portugal, Spain, and Finland are all included in this group. The EU15 countries with the lowest mean turnout rates are the United Kingdom (69.7 per cent), Ireland (69.5 per cent), and France (67.9 per cent). Turning to variation over time there are only three countries among the EU15 that show relatively volatile turnout rates, i.e. the United Kingdom (7.5 percentage points), France (6.0 percentage points), and Portugal (9.3 percentage points). In the United Kingdom and Portugal this is mainly due to the strong linear decline of turnout rates. While this development starts in the second half of the 1990s in the former, the latter is hit by the turnout decline that started during the early 1980s. The other twelve countries of the EU15 have very stable turnout rates (standard deviation below 5 percentage points) over the whole period analysed.

Malta and Cyprus, with their longer democratic histories, stand out among the accession countries of the 2000s. They have mean turnout rates above 90 per cent and their turnout practically does not vary at all compared to the Central and Eastern European countries. For Malta the main reason is a strong polarization of the electorate between just two parties. For Cyprus it is, once again, compulsory voting. As with European elections, electoral participation

Table 5.3. Turnout in national elections 1979–2009 (EU 27)

Country	1979–1984	1984–1989	1989–1994	1994–1999	1999–2004	2004–2009	Mean	Standard deviation
France	70.9	78.5 66.2	68.9	68.0	62.4	60.2	67.9	6.0
Belgium	94.6	93.6 93.4	92.7	91.1 90.6	91.6	91.1	92.3	1.4
The Netherlands	87.0 81.0	85.8	80.3 78.7	73.2	79.1 80.0	80.4	80.6	4.0
Germany	88.6 89.1	84.3	77.8	77.9 82.2	79.1	77.7	82.1	4.8
Italy	89.0	88.9	87.4 86.1	82.9	81.4	83.6 80.5	85.0	3.3
Luxembourg	88.9	88.8	87.4	88.5	86.5	91.7	88.6	1.8
Denmark	85.6 87.8 88.4	86.7 85.7	82.8	83.4 86.0	87.1	84.5 86.6	85.9	1.7
Ireland	76.2 73.8	73.3 68.5	68.5	66.1	62.6	67.0	69.5	4.6
United Kingdom	72.7	75.3	77.7	71.4	59.4	61.4	69.7	7.5
Greece	81.5	83.8	84.5 84.3 83.0	76.3	75.0	76.5 74.1	79.9	4.3
Spain	80.0	70.5	69.7 76.4	77.4	68.7 75.7	73.9	74.0	4.1
Portugal	87.5 85.4 78.6	75.4 72.6	68.2	66.3	61.0 62.8	64.3	72.2	9.3
Sweden	90.7 91.4	89.9 86.0	86.7	88.1 81.4	80.1	82.0	86.3	4.2
Finland	81.0	76.4	72.1	71.9 68.3	69.7	67.9	72.5	4.7
Austria	91.3	88.8	83.6	80.2 84.0	80.4 84.3	78.5 78.8	83.3	4.4
Malta	94.6	96.1	96.1	96.3 95.4	96.2	93.3	95.4	1.1
Poland			62.1 43.2 52.1	47.9	46.3	40.6 53.8	49.4	7.3
Czech Rep.			96.3 85.1	76.4 74.0	57.9	64.5	75.7	13.8
Slovakia			95.4 85.0	45.5 84.0	70.1	54.7	72.5	19.3
Estonia			78.2 67.8	68.9 57.4	58.2	62.0	65.4	7.9
Latvia			81.2 89.9	71.9 71.9	71.2	61.0	74.5	9.9
Lithuania			75.2	52.9	58.2	46.0 48.6	56.2	11.6
Hungary			75.5 68.9	56.7	73.5	67.8	68.5	7.3
Slovenia			85.9	73.7	70.4	60.5 63.1	70.7	10.0
Cyprus	95.7	94.6	94.3	90.1	91.8	89.0	92.6	2.7
Bulgaria			83.9	75.2 58.9	66.6	55.8	68.1	11.6
Romania			76.3	76.0	65.3 58.5	39.2	63.1	15.3

Source: National Statistics Offices, IDEA, http://www.parties-and-elections.de/.

in Poland is very low with a mean of 49.4 per cent, while the Czech Republic, Latvia, and Slovakia have the most active citizens (average turnout above 70 per cent) among the accession countries of the 2000s. Nevertheless, turnout seems to be very unstable in the most eastern of these countries, where it seems highly dependent on the specific circumstances around a particular election. The most extreme cases with respect to *variation* are Romania (15.3 percentage points) and Slovakia (19.3 percentage points).

As was the case with turnout in European elections, linear regressions for turnout in *national* elections have been calculated with time as the explanatory variable (Table 5.4). Again, the results vary strongly from country to country. In Luxembourg, Denmark, Spain, Malta, and Hungary the linear regression model explains none of the variance in turnout. The linear model fits the data perfectly or almost perfectly in Belgium, Germany, Italy, Ireland, Greece, Portugal, Sweden, Finland, and Austria, which exhibit R^2 values above 0.70. The signs of the regression coefficients are negative in all countries except Luxembourg. Effects are significant in France, Belgium, Germany,

Table 5.4. Regression analysis for turnout in national elections, 1979–2009 (EU 27)

Country	R^2	Constant	Time
France	0.61	75.19	−0.51*
Belgium	0.79	94.38	−0.14**
The Netherlands	0.35	84.25	−0.25
Germany	0.78	88.89	−0.50**
Italy	0.82	90.77	−0.34**
Luxembourg	0.05	88.81	−0.04
Denmark	0.05	86.38	−0.04
Ireland	0.75	75.06	−0.42**
United Kingdom	0.56	77.77	−0.56
Greece	0.76	86.43	−0.46**
Spain	0.02	75.00	−0.06
Portugal	0.87	82.55	−0.86***
Sweden	0.82	91.56	−0.42**
Finland	0.85	80.54	−0.50**
Austria	0.73	89.12	−0.37**
Malta	0.07	95.94	−0.03
Poland	0.14	56.64	−0.39
Czech Rep.	0.85	114.47	−2.11**
Slovakia	0.26	101.11	−1.59
Estonia	0.61	82.92	−0.94
Latvia	0.69	100.02	−1.39*
Lithuania	0.67	87.70	−1.50
Hungary	0.06	73.61	−0.27
Slovenia	0.86	101.59	−1.47*
Cyprus	0.84	96.29	−0.26*
Bulgaria	0.62	92.38	−1.24
Romania	0.90	111.20	−2.29*

*: $p < 0.05$, **: $p < 0.01$, ***: $p < 0.001$.
Source: own calculations.

Italy, Ireland, Greece, Portugal, Sweden, Finland, Austria, Czech Republic, Slovenia, Cyprus, and Romania. The overall trend in the period is negative in every country. However, the trend is not significant in all cases and the magnitude of the trend effect varies widely. Obviously, the negative trend is stronger in the accession countries of the 2000s. In the Czech Republic and Romania, turnout decreases by more than 2 percentage points per year. In Western Europe, Belgium exhibits the weakest significant decline, with 0.14 percentage points per year. Turnout declines most strongly in Portugal, with 0.86 percentage points per year. Comparing the results for this analysis with those for the European level shows that the proportion of states for which the linear model applies is much higher for national elections than for European elections. Obviously contextual influences seem to be more important for the latter.

Differences between turnout in European and national parliament elections

Since European and national elections occur in a system of multilevel governance, a comparison of turnout at both electoral levels is important for an overall assessment. Table 5.5 below compares average turnout rates and standard deviations at the two levels since 1979 for the countries of the old EU15. In addition, we calculate a linear regression with the difference between national and European election turnouts as the dependent variable and time

Table 5.5. Differences between mean turnout and standard deviation of turnout in European and national elections, regression analysis for the differences in turnout between European and national elections, 1979–2009 (EU 15)

	Difference mean NPE-EPE	Difference standard deviation NPE-EPE	R^2	Constant	Time
France	18.0	−1.3	0.08	13.60	0.15
Belgium	0.7	1.6	0.64	2.41	−0.09*
The Netherlands	37.5	−5.5	0.72	25.09	0.80**
Germany	27.1	−3.8	0.28	19.23	0.41
Italy	8.7	−4.0	0.59	3.38	0.22*
Luxembourg	−0.5	0.9	0.24	−0.48	0.06
Denmark	34.9	−2.7	0.04	37.07	−0.07
Ireland	13.6	−4.3	0.03	16.20	−0.17
United Kingdom	35.4	2.3	0.70	47.49	−0.74*
Greece	7.8	−4.9	0.25	2.03	0.24
Spain	18.1	−5.6	0.25	4.52	0.59
Portugal	25.3	−4.6	0.64	−2.02	1.21*
Sweden	45.3	0.8	0.05	45.79	−0.14
Finland	29.6	−7.6	0.54	−22.95	2.03
Austria	31.9	−6.8	0.83	−9.10	1.71*

*: p<0.05, **: p<0.01, ***: p<0.001.

Source: own calculations. NPE = National Parliament Elections EPE = European Parliament Elections

since 1979 as the independent variable. This model tests whether there is a linear trend in the development of turnout differences over time.

The numbers in Table 5.5 underscore what we have reported in the two preceding subsections. Strong differences exist between the two electoral levels in most of the countries. Exceptions include all countries that apply compulsory voting: the mean differences are almost non-existent in Luxembourg and very low in Belgium. An additional reason for the parity of average turnout at both levels in Luxembourg is that both elections are always held simultaneously. Compared to the rest of the 15 countries, Italy and Greece are exceptional cases with a difference of 7.8 and 8.7 percentage points between the means for both electoral levels. This may be due to the former application of compulsory voting in both countries that seems to have caused a relatively strong obligation to vote among Italians and Greeks. The other countries show rather strong differences between mean turnout in EPE and national parliament elections (NPE): in France, Ireland, and Spain these are below 20 percentage points. Portugal (25.3 percentage points), Germany (27.1 percentage points), and Finland (29.6 percentage points) have differences below 30 percentage points. Differences in Austria, the United Kingdom, Denmark, and the Netherlands are between 30 and 38 percentage points. In Sweden, the gap between both mean values is the highest of all EU15 countries, at 45.3 percentage points. The United Kingdom and Sweden are the only countries where turnout rates in national elections are more than twice as high as in European elections.

Regarding *differences between standard deviations at both levels*, there is a group of four countries where turnout varies more strongly at the national than at the European level. While the difference is quite low in Belgium, Luxembourg, and Sweden, it is 2.3 percentage points in the United Kingdom. The rest of the countries exhibit more unstable turnout in European elections. The difference between the participation levels is almost negligible in France. Denmark, Greece, Germany, Italy, Ireland, and Portugal show moderate differences below 5 percentage points, and in the Netherlands, Spain, Austria, and Finland turnout is much more stable at the national than at the European level. Finland is the most outstanding example in this group, with a difference of about 8 percentage points. In sum, these findings are obvious: with the exception of the countries that apply compulsory voting, average turnout is much higher at the national than at the European level. In addition, turnout rates at the European level are much more unstable and vary much more strongly across the 1979–2009 period.

Another interesting point is the development of the differences over time for the EU15 during the period from 1979 to 2009. Positive coefficients for time in Table 5.4 indicate a linear increase in the turnout gap. Given that, as seen previously, turnout *declines* in elections at both levels, a *positive* coefficient means that the decline is *stronger* in European Parliament than in national parliament elections. Conversely, a negative coefficient means that the turnout gap gets smaller in recent years. The latter is the case in one-third of the EU15 countries. However, *significant* negative effects occur in Belgium and the United Kingdom only. Turnout rates of both elections *converge* in both countries, but especially in the United Kingdom (–0.7 percentage points per year). Ten countries reveal an *increase* in the turnout gap over time. This development is significant in the Netherlands, Italy, Portugal, and Austria. In Austria and Portugal the widening of the gap is particularly strong, with 1.2 and 1.7 percentage points per year, respectively. These results show that, despite the decline of turnout rates at both levels, the participation gap between the European and the national levels increases in a majority of countries.

3. Analyses of turnout in European Parliament elections 1979–2009

This section presents results of our empirical analysis. As outlined previously, we focus on the explanation of turnout from two different perspectives. The first subsection explains the *cross-country* differences in European election turnout, while the second subsection provides results regarding causes of differences in the *individual* willingness to cast a ballot.

Explaining aggregate turnout in European Parliament elections 1979–2009

We have reported strong national differences with respect to turnout in the previous section. The goal of the subsequent analysis is to identify the reasons for these differences. We have already highlighted one of the obvious causes, the application of compulsory voting in some member states. The regression analysis in Table 5.5 includes several additional variables whose expected effect has been reported in Section 1 of this chapter. We have run two separate analyses, one for all countries and elections between 1979 and 2009 and the other for the countries of the EU15.[2] The dependent variable is turnout at the national level in the European elections of that period. The predictive quality of the model for all countries and elections is quite high, with an adjusted R^2 of 0.71. The direction of the effects of the political system characteristics is as expected. There is a first-time boost for European election turnout. Holding European elections distant from the first-order mid-term, compulsory voting, Sunday voting and simultaneous nationwide elections all help to increase turnout rates. The communist-past variable accounts for the turnout gap between Western and Eastern European countries and also has the expected sign. High aggregate support for EU membership boosts turnout considerably.

Satisfaction with democracy and left–right polarization also have positive effects on turnout. That countries with a high satisfaction with domestic democracy show higher turnout rates in European elections confirms findings on the transfer of satisfaction with national institutions to the European level as reported by Karp, Banducci, and Bowler (2003).

However, most of the predictors mentioned do not reveal statistically *significant* effects. The model is strongly dominated by compulsory voting (beta = 0.60). Communist past is the second strongest predictor, followed by the fact that an election is the first-ever election to the European Parliament and support for EU membership. The separate analysis for the countries of the EU15 reveals that some effects are more pronounced, like the first-time boost, compulsory voting and aggregate support for EU membership. Sunday voting and satisfaction with democracy's performance gain significance. Surprisingly, the effect of left–right polarization changes direction and more polarized countries have lower turnout in Western Europe. This might be due to the exclusion of the highly polarized Eastern European states from the analysis. The whole model certainly works better in the countries of the EU15, with an adjusted R^2 of 0.79. All in all, our analysis shows that aggregate support for EU membership has a significant positive effect on national turnout levels, even when traditional macro-level predictors like compulsory voting are entered into the models.

Explaining individual turnout in European Parliament elections 1979–2009

The macro-level analysis in the previous subsection has revealed the substantial importance of aggregate support for European integration for cross-country differences in European Parliament election turnouts. This subsection shifts attention to the individual level. It is interesting to see whether different levels of individual support influence the willingness to cast a ballot in European elections between 1979 and 2009 when controls are applied for other important individual-level characteristics.

The analysis at the micro level suffers from several shortcomings. The most important problem is related to the lack of important predictors of turnout in Eurobarometer surveys and European Election Studies. Unfortunately, explaining turnout was not the focus of the European Commission and electoral research, so theoretical constructs like efficacy, the perceived duty to vote, and even interest in politics were rarely if ever part of these surveys. This shortcoming is particularly important for a comparative analysis over time. Due to the absence of some attitudes, the models presented here are dominated by social structural characteristics. Nevertheless, the models differ somewhat due to item availability as the early Eurobarometers in particular had a very limited repertoire of items.

Table 5.6. Regression analysis for aggregate level turnout in EPE 1979–2009

Predictor	EU-27		EU-15	
	b	Beta	b	Beta
First EPE	7.51**	0.15	11.27***	0.22
Distance first-order mid-term	1.39	0.02	−3.50	−0.06
Compulsory voting	27.62***	0.60	29.61***	0.72
Sunday voting	0.83	0.02	7.48**	0.17
Simultaneous nationwide election	5.68	0.10	3.66	0.07
Communist past	−19.08***	−0.34	—	—
Support EU membership	11.10*	0.12	18.92***	0.24
Satisfaction with national democracy	5.61	0.03	22.47*	0.11
Left-right polarisation	1.56	0.02	−6.25	−0.06
Constant	35.49**	—	31.67**	—
Adjusted R^2	0.71	—	0.79	—
N	118	—	94	—

*: $p<0.05$, **: $p<0.01$, ***: $p<0.001$.

The following tables (Table 5.7 to Table 5.9) present results of logistic regression analysis at the national level. Obviously, we cannot display all logistic regression coefficients as this would result in a vast array of numbers that we would not be able to describe effectively. We rely on cumulated information instead.

Tables 5.7 to 5.9 display the share of positive and negative logistic regression coefficients for each item in all countries. Effects are further divided into significant (probability level <0.05) and non-significant effects. Relative frequencies offer the advantage that results are comparable across all European Parliament elections, although the number of countries in the analysis changes over time. Variables in the tables are grouped according to the theoretical concept to which they belong. At the top of each table, we use evaluations of EU membership as a proxy for EU-related attitudes. It is followed by items belonging to cueing rationality, cognitive mobilization, and socio-demographics. In addition to the share of the respective effects, we report the range between minimum and maximum Nagelkerke's R^2 as additional information for the predictive quality of the logistic regression models presented. The tables thus provide a good overview about the direction and uniformity of effects in all European member states.

Our most important concern is the effect of support for EU membership. Its effect is predominantly positive over the whole period of analysis, with at least two-thirds of the countries revealing positive effects for that item in every election. This means that people who evaluate the membership of their country positively have a higher probability of participating in European Parliament elections. However, the share of significant positive effects seems to be higher in the earlier elections. Nevertheless, this result shows that

Table 5.7. Positive and negative effects of predictor variables in logistic regressions for individual probability of turnout in EPE 1979 and 1984

Predictor	1979				1984			
	+ sig. (%)	+ non sig (%)	−non sig (%)	−sig. (%)	+ sig. (%)	+ non sig (%)	−non sig (%)	−sig. (%)
EU membership benefit	55.6	11.1	0.0	33.3	50.0	50.0	0.0	0.0
National democracy satisfaction	11.1	66.7	0.0	22.2	30.0	40.0	0.0	30.0
Left-right polarisation	33.3	44.4	0.0	22.2	10.0	60.0	0.0	30.0
Strength of PID	55.6	44.4	0.0	0.0	80.0	20.0	0.0	0.0
Materialism index	22.2	44.4	0.0	33.3	10.0	0.0	0.0	90.0
Opinion leadership index	0.0	66.7	11.1	22.2	20.0	60.0	10.0	10.0
Male	0.0	44.4	0.0	55.6	10.0	60.0	10.0	20.0
Age	44.4	33.3	0.0	22.2	50.0	40.0	0.0	10.0
Education	22.2	66.7	0.0	11.1	20.0	50.0	0.0	30.0
Urbanisation	0.0	77.8	22.2	0.0	0.0	0.0	30.0	70.0
Religiosity	—	—	—	—	30.0	60.0	0.0	10.0
Range Nagelkerke R^2		0.04–0.21				0.09–0.26		

Source: EB 12, 22.

Notes: Level of significance: p<0.05. — Variable not part of respective survey.

Table 5.8. Positive and negative effects of predictor variables in logistic regressions for individual probability of turnout in EPE 1989 and 1994

Predictor	1989				1994			
	+ sig. (%)	+ non sig (%)	−non sig (%)	−sig. (%)	+ sig. (%)	+ non sig (%)	−non sig (%)	−sig. (%)
EU membership benefit	16.7	50.0	8.3	25.0	25.0	66.7	0.0	8.3
National democracy Satisfaction	16.7	75.0	0.0	8.3	8.3	66.7	16.7	8.3
Left-right polarisation	8.3	58.3	8.3	25.0	0.0	41.7	0.0	58.3
Strength PID	66.7	33.3	0.0	0.0	50.0	50.0	0.0	0.0
Materialism index	8.3	25.0	8.3	58.3	—	—	—	—
Interest in politics	33.3	41.7	8.3	16.7	41.7	58.3	0.0	0.0
Opinion leadership index	8.3	58.3	0.0	33.3	—	—	—	—
Male	8.3	41.7	8.3	41.7	16.7	25.0	8.3	50.0
Age	50.0	33.3	0.0	16.7	66.7	25.0	0.0	8.3
Education	8.3	33.3	0.0	58.3	16.7	50.0	0.0	33.3
Urbanisation	0.0	25.0	16.7	58.3	8.3	25.0	25.0	41.7
Religiosity	16.7	50.0	0.0	33.3	50.0	41.7	0.0	8.3
Class	0.0	50.0	8.3	41.7	0.0	66.7	0.0	33.3
Range Nagelkerke R²		0.12–0.47				0.06–0.28		

Source: EB 31A, 41–1.

Notes: Level of significance: p<0.05. — Variable not part of respective survey.

Table 5.9. Positive and negative effects of predictor variables in logistic regressions for individual probability of turnout in EPE 1999 and 2004

Predictor	1999				2004			
	+ sig. (%)	+ non sig (%)	−non sig (%)	−sig. (%)	+ sig. (%)	+ non sig (%)	−non sig (%)	−sig. (%)
EU membership benefit	20.0	60.0	0.0	20.0	31.8	63.6	4.5	0.0
National democracy satisfaction	13.3	40.0	0.0	46.7	9.1	81.8	4.5	4.5
Left-right polarisation	6.7	60.0	0.0	33.3	22.7	54.5	9.1	13.6
Strength PID	66.7	26.7	0.0	6.7	31.8	63.6	0.0	4.5
Internal efficacy	46.7	33.3	0.0	20.0	—	—	—	—
Interest in politics	46.7	53.3	0.0	0.0	45.5	54.5	0.0	0.0
Media consumption	33.3	53.3	6.7	6.7	28.6	71.4	0.0	0.0
Male	6.7	33.3	6.7	53.3	22.7	18.2	22.7	36.4
Age	100.0	0.0	0.0	0.0	90.5	9.5	0.0	0.0
Education	13.3	46.7	6.7	33.3	31.8	50.0	9.1	9.1
Urbanisation	6.7	33.3	26.7	33.3	25.0	30.0	25.0	20.0
Religiosity	21.4	50.0	0.0	28.6	18.2	72.7	0.0	9.1
Class	13.3	53.3	0.0	33.3	13.6	59.1	4.5	22.7
Range Nagelkerke R^2		0.08–0.41				0.11–0.33		

Source: EES 1999, 2004.

Notes: Level of significance: $p<0.05$. — Variable not part of respective survey.

EU-related attitudes are important predictors of turnout, even when other theoretically relevant variables are controlled for. In addition, it shows that dissatisfaction with European unification can be a reason for individual abstention in European Parliament elections.

Turning to the other variables, most of them reveal the expected or hypothesized effect. Among the cueing rationality variables, the most dominant patterns appear for strength of party identification. This item has a positive effect in a large majority of the countries in all elections analysed here, so that citizens with a stronger party identification have a higher probability to cast a ballot. Figures for non-significant and significant positive effects combined add up to at least 89 per cent of the countries.

Satisfaction with democratic performance also has widespread positive effects, but they are rarely significant. The highest ratio for this variable is 30 per cent in 1984. In all other elections this share does not exceed 17 percentage points. Nevertheless, with the exception of 1999, the positive relationship in general applies to a large majority of the countries. People who are satisfied with their national democracy participate in European elections to a higher degree. This is further evidence for the transfer of motives from the first-order to the second-order arena. General patterns are quite similar for left–right extremity. Except in 1994, there is a majority of positive effects. However, the share of significant positive effects does not exceed 33 per cent (in 1979) and is outbalanced by the share of significant negative effects between 1984 and 1999. Thus, we can report mixed findings for this particular item that do not match our hypothesis in a considerably high number of cases. The materialism index was only part of the analyses for the elections until 1989. The results do not support our hypothesis. We can see an overall dominance of significant *negative* effects, which implies that *post-materialists* have a higher probability of casting a ballot compared to materialists in most of the member states.

Among the indicators of cognitive mobilization we have the most consistent results for *interest in politics*. There are almost no negative effects at all and there is a clear dominance of significant positive effects (ranging between 33 and 89 percentage points). Thus, people with a higher interest in politics have a higher willingness to participate in most countries. There is a dominance of positive effects, too, for the other cognitive mobilization indicators, opinion leadership index and media consumption, so that in most of the countries and elections the people with high values on these items have a higher probability of going to the polls. However, the share of significant effects for both indicators is considerably lower, with a maximum value of 20 per cent (in 1984) for the opinion leader item and 33 per cent (in 1999) for media consumption. The effects of internal and external efficacy are mainly positive as expected, but the share of significant positive coefficients is much higher for internal efficacy (in 1999).

Age is the variable among the socio-demographics for which we find the clearest patterns: its positive effect is at least significant in 81 per cent of the cases in the last three elections. In earlier elections, shares are lower, but there is a large majority of positive effects nevertheless. Results for gender are mixed. There are no dominant patterns over all elections and countries. Findings for education are somewhat at variance with our expectations. The low share of significant positive effects and the appearance of negative coefficients in some countries oppose our hypothesis and previous findings. This might be due to the operationalization of education by age when finished full-time education.

Turning to urbanization, the majority of negative effects for this item matches our expectations that turnout is usually lower in big cities, where there is generally less social control among citizens. Contrary to our hypothesis, religiosity does not work very well as a proxy for the perceived duty to vote. There is a dominance of positive effects, but in most of the countries they are not significant. Class is the final variable to be mentioned. Here, the results are very mixed. Whether people of higher or lower classes are more participatory seems to be heavily dependent on the national context.

The explanatory power of the models differs strongly between countries and elections. In some countries the model does not work at all (minimum Nagelkerke's R^2 of 0.04 in 1979 and 0.06 in 1994), while it works quite well in others. The strong differences are obviously related to the lack of important predictors of turnout and the varying number and quality of predictors in the model. However, our central question can be answered positively. EU-related attitudes have a positive impact on individual turnout in European Parliament elections.

Conclusion

The goal of this chapter was to gauge the importance of EU-related attitudes for turnout in European Parliament elections between 1979 and 2009 in comparison with traditional explanations of electoral participation. We described the development of turnout rates in European and national elections in order to give a comprehensive overview of our dependent variable. Using linear regression analysis we could identify a significant linear decline in five of the EU15 countries for European elections, and in fifteen of the EU27 countries for national elections. This shows that turnout decline in European elections is *not* linear in most of the member countries and thus influenced by contextual factors to a much stronger extent. However, the linear regression analysis for the development of the *gap* between European and national turnout shows that the gap widens over time. Although turnout drops at both electoral levels, *the decline in the European arena is much stronger over time.*

Our analysis then revealed that *turnout is positively related to support for European integration at the macro level.* Turnout rates at the aggregate level are heavily influenced by political system characteristics like compulsory and Sunday voting, but a positive national opinion towards the country's membership clearly leads to higher levels of participation. As support for EU membership has declined particularly in some countries since the fall of the Iron Curtain, as evidenced in Chapter 8 of this volume, the slight removal of support for European integration is probably one of the sources of turnout decline at the European level.

The *micro-level analysis* also shows positive effects of support for EU membership on the individual probability of participating in European elections, too. Traditional predictors of turnout obviously have stronger effects—and show clearer patterns with respect to the share of countries with significant effects—but we found positive effects of support for EU membership in a majority of countries. Thus, *individual abstention is partly caused by dissatisfaction with the European integration process.* This finding supports popular knowledge and contradicts the results of many scientific analyses which proved the lack of importance of EU-related attitudes for turnout in European elections (e.g. Steinbrecher and Rattinger 2012). One reason for our findings might be related to the absence of some traditional powerful predictors, such as the perceived duty to vote, interest in politics, or efficacy, from some or even all of our analytical models. Future Eurobarometer surveys as well as European Election Studies should thus include these variables in order to provide comprehensive answers to the question as to whether or not Europe-related attitudes matter for turnout in European Parliament elections.

Notes

1. We prefer satisfaction with the national democracy over satisfaction with democracy at the European level because the latter has not been included in EB and EES since the first election to the European Parliament in 1979. Left–right polarization has been operationalized as described in Chapter 4 of this volume.
2. A separate analysis for the accession countries of 2004 and 2007 would have led to invalid results due to the limitation of available cases to 24.

6

But Still It Does Not Move: Functional and Identity-Based Determinants of European Identity[1]

Pierangelo Isernia, Irena Fiket, Fabio Serricchio, and Bettina Westle

With the increasing presence of the European Union in the everyday life of its citizens, a sense of European identity is seen by many sources, including the preamble to the Treaty of Lisbon, as necessary to overcome the legitimacy deficit of European institutions as well as a possible source of policy inspiration. This growing attention to issues of European identity is not matched by a consensus over its conceptual nature and empirical content. The concept of "identity" is used by a vast array of disciplines, spanning from philosophy through political science and sociology to psychology, and they all have different perspectives on the topic and attach different meanings to it (for overviews, see Huddy 2001; Brewer 2005; Westle 2010). The adjective "European" adds confusion. Does Europe refer to a geographical entity, whose borders seem rather stretchy? Or does it refer to a set of institutions, the European Union, whose complex and continuously evolving nature defies a clear-cut definition? As such, it is not even clear whether European identity actually exists. These conceptual problems are complicated by the fact that theoretical and empirical discussions apparently ignore much of what their respective counterparts have to say. A further source of confusion stems from the lack of consensus about the operationalization and meaning of the different indicators used to measure the concept.

Therefore, we start with clarifying how we see the concept. Our primary reference point is Deutsch's definition of the "sense of community" as "a matter of mutual sympathy and loyalties, of we feeling, trust, and mutual consideration; of partial identification in terms of self-images and interests; of mutually successful predictions of behaviour, and of cooperative action in accordance with it—in short, a matter of a perpetual dynamic process of mutual attention, communication, perception of needs, and responsiveness in the process of decision-making" (Deutsch 1957: 36). Later research narrowed this very broad concept to a horizontal dimension—the mutual trust that ties together people of a political community, and a vertical one—the identification with a political community (see e.g. Niedermayer and Westle 1995; Scheuer 2005). In this chapter, we focus our attention only on the second of these two dimensions and we will deal exclusively with the intensity of identification, but not with the question of which meanings citizens associate with their identity.

In this chapter, we explore the cross-national evolution of identification with Europe over time and its contextual determinants, proceeding as follows. We start with reviewing the literature about European identity and its dimensions. Without any pretension to systematically reviewing all available studies on European identity issues (for previous efforts, see Duchesne and Frognier 1995; Green 2000, 2007; Herrmann and Brewer 2004; Citrin and Sides 2004a, 2004b; Risse 2005; Scheuer 2005; Westle 2007), we summarize those elements that are especially relevant for our purposes. We argue that two different models can be extracted from the literature regarding the formation and development of European identity: one functionalist and one identity based. Next, we introduce the empirical indicators available to measure identification with Europe and update the results of previous reviews of trends in European identity among the EU member states. Last, we explore a macro-level model that seeks to account for variation in European identity across nations and over time, and which tests both the functional and the identity-based models.

1. Previous findings on European identity

The study of European identity started in the early 1950s and has gone through three different stages, each corresponding to a different theoretical perspective—the functionalist and neo-functionalist, the rational choice, and the social-psychological approaches, respectively.

The functionalist approach

The first (and still ongoing) stage has seen European identity as a consequence of satisfaction with concrete policies. Both "founding fathers" of integration theory—Haas and Deutsch—saw the creation of a truly European identity as a crucial element in the formation of a European political community (Risse 2005). Yet Deutsch (1957) *assumed* European identity as a central precondition for an integrated community, whereas Haas (1958) expected it as an *end-state* of a process largely determined by the political and technocratic elites. Guetzkow (1955) offered an early theoretical analysis of political identity, especially of identification with international organizations, as one among many identities, and Easton (1965) introduced the distinction between specific and diffuse support, suggesting that diffuse support can develop over time as a spillover effect of enduring instrumental evaluations.

The empirical results of this wave of studies were far from unequivocal, however, and they are of only limited relevance for our discussion about European identity. Studies in this period (e.g. Lindberg and Scheingold 1970; Sheperd 1975; Hewstone 1986; Wildgen and Feld 1976) focused mainly on support and its dimensions, and not on identity. As a result, they could not really advance our understanding of the sources of European identity, not least because they did not use explicit measures of identity in their empirical analyses but rather subsumed conceptually the notion of identity in the difficult-to-handle notions of "diffuse" or "affective" support. Only Inglehart (1970a, 1970b) departs from these works in that he does not integrate identity into a concept of support and stresses the importance of situational determinants instead. Using a question about geographical attachment, he pointed to three factors to explain the rising degree of identification with Europe in the 1950s and 1960s: the length of time spent in the EU, cognitive mobilization, and emerging post-materialist values.

The economic approach[2]

From the 1980s, a new wave of studies, inspired by the *political economic* models in voting behaviour research, claimed that support for European integration was mostly driven by utilitarian, economic considerations. This approach either ignored questions of identity or declared them irrelevant for the European Union. The early focus of European integration on trade and market issues seemed to justify the search for the determinants of support for European integration among individual and collective costs and benefits accruing from Europe (Eichenberg and Dalton 1993; Gabel 1998c). This research explored both situational and contextual, national and European, economic and political factors affecting support based on cost–benefit calculus but typically avoided dealing with identity (e.g. Handley 1981; Eichenberg and Dalton 1993). Gabel (1998c) tested the Eastonian model of political support, including identity. He concluded that citizens do indeed organize their orientations towards the European Union along the model proposed by Easton, but that only a few of them show strong affective ties to the European Union, implying that support for the EU mainly rests on utilitarian evaluations. McLaren (2006) also found that egocentric individualism and sociotropic utilitarianism were important sources of EU attitudes.

The economic approach is mainly associated with the analysis of support for EU integration as a dependent variable. Such an approach would appear quite distant from research on social identities. However, identification can also be seen as an instrumental choice (Kelman 1969), and people who perceive membership in the European political community as a sustained source of benefit (both personal and for their own country) may develop a higher intensity of attachment to Europe. Ruiz-Jimenez et al. (2004) indeed showed that instrumental support for membership correlates with European identification.

The social-psychological approach

More recently, psychological theories of self-categorization and reference groups also entered the study of European identity. These studies (e.g. Break-well and Lyons 1996; Herrmann, Risse, and Brewer 2004; Mummendey, Wenzel, and Waldzus 2007), were largely inspired by social identity theory as first developed by Tajfel and Turner (1979; Tajfel 1981; Turner et al. 1987). They start with the central argument that an individual's memberships in social groups are relevant elements of the individual's self-concept and thus contribute to the individual's self-esteem, self-respect, and dignity. Such memberships, and the social identities derived from them, are something upon which people might feel the need to act. European identity is no different: it is an additional self-definition available to European citizens, which is evolving alongside, and may be intertwined with, pre-existing regional and national identities. Research on European identity thus started with the relationship between national and European identity and then moved on to explore how multiple social identities can coexist (Deschamps 1977).

Some of these ideas were also disseminated in political science and most contemporary analyses concur that national and European identity are not necessarily in conflict. Duchesne and Frognier (1995: 202–6) found a weak or non-existent relationship between the two variables and most successive studies have not only confirmed this but some even reported a positive relationship between them (Weiler 1999; Diez Medrano and Gutiérrez 2001, Westle 2003a, 2003b; Castano 2004; Citrin and Sides 2004a; Hooghe and Marks 2004; Bruter 2005; Risse 2005; McLaren 2006; Green 2007; Kaina 2009). However, Hooghe and Marks (2005) find a negative impact of exclusively national attachment on support for the EU, while Carey (2002) and McLaren (2002, 2006) report that national identification hinders favourable attitudes towards Europe. A few studies attempted to link the causes of conflicting versus coexisting identities to factors like party divisions over Europe, immigration, and collective benefits to a country from European integration (Hooghe and Marks 2005; Garry and Tilley 2009), essentially suggesting that the link between different identities is a matter of political framing (Díez Medrano 2003).

To explore the conditions under which multiple social identities can coexist, political psychology has suggested different balancing mechanisms. Following this, Westle (1999, 2003a, and 2003b) and Herrmann and Brewer (2004) point to a possible hierarchy of attachments, contrasting a model of clear separation with "nested" and cross-cutting models, while Risse (2005) suggests the "marble-cake model", which would impose salience and coherence to a set of cumulative multiple attachments. Waldzus and Mummendey (2004) and Wenzel, Mummendey, and Waldzus (2007) propose an "in-group projection model" whereby people project in-group prototypes to the wider superordinate group. Battistelli and Bellucci (2002) find that the subjective meaning of national attachments constrains or facilitates the development of European identification in Italy. Citizens relying on ascribed factors (cultural traditions) in defining their national identity exhibit weaker identification with Europe than citizens who rely on acquired traits of national attachment.

In conclusion, these three waves of research have offered some empirically informed ideas about European identity but also left many open questions and raised new ones. Obviously, we cannot deal with all of them. We focus on two different lines of reasoning that emerge from these debates and that can help to explain the development of a European identity. The first line of argument—mainly advocated by functionalists—is about the role of utilitarian support for European integration in promoting European identity. In this view, European identity is mainly formed as a consequence of a long-term and steady process of institutionalization of practices and norms around the benefits flowing from the process. In this regard, both functionalists and political economic models stress the role of macroeconomic variables in particular. The social-psychological approach, in contrast, stresses the importance of the sense of belonging to other institutions, namely the nation state, as an active promoter of or deterrent to European identity. European identity in this view is formed as a consequence of the growing relevance of Europe as a group reference point, in a dynamic interplay with other referents, such as the nation. In the following we want to explore how these different models explain the evolution of European identity. Before that, however, we discuss different operationalizations of the concept and chart trends over time.

2. Dimensions of European identity and their measurement

This section reviews the empirical data available on European identification, expanding upon and updating previous efforts (see Duchesne and Frognier 1995; Green 2000; Citrin and Sides 2004a, 2004b; Westle 2003a, 2007). More precisely, we examine aggregate trends at the EU level as a whole and in a set of countries. Special attention is given to distinctive differences related to the EU accession date of countries. We rely on forty-nine datasets with relevant questions, including European Community Studies (ECS 1970, 1971, 1973), standard Eurobarometer (EB 1976–2007), World Value Surveys (WVS 1981, 1990, 1999) and ISSP (2003). Altogether 836 macro-level observations are available for the

Table 6.1. Overall average and standard deviation (SD) of European identifiers by question wording

Question wording	Overall average (N)	Overall SD	SD by year (a)	SD by country (b)	Ratio of (a) and (b)	N
1	15.5	6.3	4.0	5.2	0.77	83
2	52.3	11.8	4.5	11.8	0.38	166
3A	60.8	14.0	7.3	13.2	0.55	147
3B	45.0	11.8	5.2	11.8	0.44	52
4	54.2	10.4	5.3	10.3	0.52	253
5	67.2	10.5	4.6	9.8	0.47	135
TOTAL	52.7	17.7				836

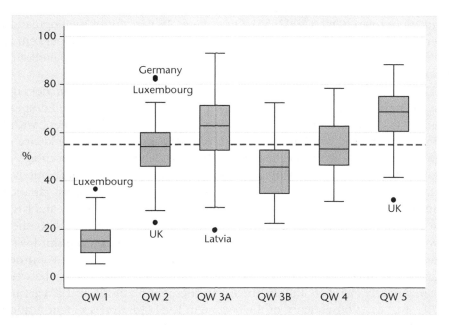

Figure 6.1. Box-plot of country-by-country percentage of European identifiers by question wording (QW)

Note: The horizontal bars towards the middle of each grey box represent the median value of the cross-time averages for the EU member states. The upper and lower ends of each box are defined by the lowest value in the top and the highest in the bottom quartile. Outliers, if any occur, are marked by a dot labelled by the country name.

period between 1971 and 2007.[3] All these observations are displayed in the online appendix to this volume, while Table 6.1 and Figure 6.1 summarize key findings.

The study of trends in European identity is complicated by the number of EU member states growing and the relevant Eurobarometer questions changing back and forth over time. Five different questions will be considered as measures of European identity here (see the section on Chapter 6 in the appendix on question wording), with items about geographical belonging, thinking of oneself as European, sense of attachment to Europe, European vs national identification, and pride in Europe providing our numbered question wordings from one to five, respectively.[4] The fourth item has the longest series (fifteen time points, running from 1992 to 2007 with two gaps), followed by the first, which covers a longer time span (thirteen time points scattered across all the years from 1971 to 2000).[5] Most of the indicators, however, start in 1991–2 only.

The first question wording (QW1) asks for the respondents' first and second choices regarding a *feeling of belonging* to five different geographical entities. The pattern of responses is very much alike across countries. Apparently, Europe is mentioned only by a tiny minority of respondents as first or second choice when it is in an either–or competition with alternatives like their country or town (Green 2007: 53). On average, 15 per cent of the population mention Europe as first or second choice, varying from a low of 6 per cent to an upper end of 36 per cent of the respondents in the UK and Luxembourg, respectively, without any clear trend over time.

The second question wording (QW2), *thinking of oneself as European*, does not put the nation and Europe in competition, but attempts to measure European identity as an addition to the national one. It has been asked 12 times,[6] with a minor variation in wording.[7] This item records a much higher incidence of European identity than the first (see Table 6.1). The average percentage of identifiers—i.e. the respondents who often or sometimes think of themselves as European—is 52 per cent, with a quite wide range of cross-country variation from a low of 23 per cent in the UK to 72 per cent in Luxembourg. By and large, the second-wave accession countries (Denmark, Ireland, and the UK) show lower levels of identification than the founding members and the third-wave (Southern) accession countries. The trend is quite static in all the countries. However, at the EU level the data show some movement, with the gap between the original six members and the three countries joining the EU in 1973 getting closer, first as a consequence of the decline in level of European identification among the original six during the 1980s and, since 1993, because of a process of synchronic increase in identification of both country groups. Italy and France show the biggest downturn in 1992, but in other countries, with the exception of the UK, Spain, and Portugal (the latter two already at appreciably higher levels than the other EU member states), there was a remarkable increase in the percentage of European identifiers after 1992.

The third question wording (QW3A) is about *attachment to Europe*. In some versions of this question "Europe" was replaced by the term "European Union", thus producing QW3B, which records a lower average level of European identification than QW3A (see Figure 6.1).[8] Either way, this item is part of a wider battery of questions asking about the respondent's feelings towards various geographical units (the same as listed under the first question wording). This question was integrated into the Eurobarometer studies with the aim of making it possible for the respondents to articulate their loyalties to different geographical/political units independently from each other and thus allow for the expression of multiple identities (Westle 1999). In this context, we focus only on attachment to Europe. We count those who answered that they are very or fairly attached to Europe as identifiers. This series again shows a somewhat higher average level of European identification (61 per cent) than the two previous ones, with the percentage ranging from 29 per cent in the Netherlands to 92 per cent in Hungary. According to this indicator, the strongest identification is found in the Northern European countries, followed by the original six member states, and the cross-country differences (especially in the case of the ten new Eastern European members) are larger than the question wording suggested. Between 1991 and 1999 an increase of European identifiers can be observed, but after 1999 no further increase occurred either in the all-EU average or in individual countries.

The fourth question wording (QW4), *national versus European*, calls on the respondent to prioritize the nation or Europe, putting them in a head-on comparison. Considering those who do not exclude Europe totally (three categories of four),[9] we see that citizens of the founding countries (and especially those in Italy, Luxembourg, and France) identify with Europe more frequently than those joining in any of the later waves. On average, 54 per cent of Europeans feel in some way "European", and this percentage remains rather stable over time, with a peak only in 1994, mainly due to a temporary rise in the original six founding countries. Yet most of this identification, around 45 per cent on average, is due to the category "nationality (first) and European (second)". Once again, large differences between the countries are present, from 32 per cent in the UK to 78 per cent in Italy.[10]

The last question wording (QW5), *pride in Europe*, produces the highest level of identification of all indicators (an average 67 per cent of the respondents being very or fairly proud of Europe), as well as an increasing trend up to 2002, when the trend reversed.[11]

We can summarize this discussion in three points. First, the degree to which people can be classified as European identifiers appears to be strongly dependent on question wording and, of course, the chosen cut-off point between identifiers and non-identifiers. The fifth question wording produces the highest level of European identity followed by version (a) of the third, then numbers four, two, three (b), leaving number one at the bottom of the list. The percentage of identifiers ranges from 15 per cent, on a cross-country and over-time average for question wording one to 67 per cent for wording five. Figure 6.1 summarizes the dramatic impact of wording on the cross-time average percentage of identifiers in individual countries in a box-plot chart.

Second, despite the huge variation in the number of identifiers among the different indicators discussed here, there is remarkable stability over time *within* each indicator. Even though European integration has passed through profound economic and institutional changes, especially in the period around 1991–2, these changes seem to have produced only small effects on European identity. On the other hand, and this is our third point, substantial differences exist between individual countries that persist across the indicators. Controlling for differences in question wording and the time of the survey, the UK has by far the lowest percentage of people identifying with Europe. Table 6.1 shows quite clearly that variation *over time* is much lower than variation *across countries*. The average within-country standard deviation over time is between one-third and one-half smaller than the variation across countries when controlling for question wording. The most extreme example of this is obtained with the second wording, where the cross-country standard deviation is 11.8 while the over-time average deviation is 4.5.

To assess in a more systematic way the relative importance of these three sources of variation—question wording, time, and country—across all the different observations, and taking into account the nominal nature of two of the three variables, we conducted a three-way ANOVA. As shown by Table 6.2, all three factors are important in explaining variance across observations. But it emerges that question wording and country are far more important than year in accounting for the variations. This result speaks clearly against the neo-functionalist expectation that the length of EU membership, by itself, would lead to identification with Europe/the European Union. Yet it does not invalidate the Eastonian model, because the length of membership does not signal in itself whether membership has been perceived as negative or positive.

Table 6.2. ANOVA model of contextual sources of variation in European Identity

Source	Partial SS	Df	MSE	F	Prob>F
Model	206666.36	61	3387.97	48.44	0.000
Question wording	51192.26	5	10238.45	146.37	0.000
Year	5754.98	30	191.83	2.74	0.000
Country	44608.80	26	1715.72	24.53	0.000
Residual	54140.219	774	69.95		
Total	260806.57	835	312.34		

R^2 = 0.792; Adj R^2 = 0.776; Root MSE = 8.364; N = 836. Eta^2 for Question wording = 0.196; Year = 0.022; Country = 0.171

These results raise the theoretically interesting question of whether such a huge variability in levels of European identity as question wording changes is a consequence of the fact that people have "non-attitudes" as far as European identity is concerned, or, rather, that European identity only has a chance to emerge when it is not put in competition with pre-existing identities. We lean toward the latter explanation, not only because previous studies show how European identity varies systematically, and not randomly, together with several important attitudinal and socio-demographic variables, but also because these questions—as they are constructed—make European identity differently demanding in terms of competition with national identity. The rank-order question clearly sets European identity in explicit competition with national and local identities, forcing people to choose one of the two. This is followed by the national-versus-EU question that allows for different degrees of coexistence between the two. The attachment questions are the least demanding, because they do not raise the issue of competition between the different objects of identification. Overall, the results point to the fact that, for most people, European identity is only one among the several political identities to which they adhere and any attempt to assess its importance as compared to other forms of political identity generates a lower degree of identification with Europe. Whether this fact is, in itself, a sign of weaker attachment to Europe compared with other forms of political identity and what implications to draw from this are something we leave open for now— though we do return to the question in the conclusion.

3. The determinants of European identity: macro-level analysis

With the growing psychological focus on European identity, a greater interest in the sources of variation in European *identity* as distinct from support for European *integration* also appears, although the two dependent variables are often explained using the same variables. Based on the literature discussed in Section 1, we focus on two, partially overlapping, views of the sources of European identity over time: the functional model and the national-context model. According to the functional model, both instrumental support and time are considered to be the fundamental sources of identification with Europe. According to the identity model, European identity has to be seen in joint operation with national identity and identity cannot be reduced to instrumental calculus. Although the causal mechanisms underlying both models are not clearly spelt out, they point to quite different variables in trying to explain how European identity develops.

In this last section we address these sources of cross-national variation through a pooled time-series cross-section (TSCS) analysis of identification with Europe. This aggregate analysis takes for granted the individual-level differences in identification with Europe and concentrates on the aggregate-level cross-national differences, with particular reference to the contrasting views of the functional model and the national-context models in explaining variation in levels of European identification.

The dependent variable

Our dependent variable is based on version A of question wording number four: "In the near future do you see yourself as (NATIONALITY) only, (NATIONALITY) and European, European and (NATIONALITY) and European only?" We chose this as the only series available for a period long enough to allow a meaningful trend analysis that includes all twenty-seven member states. However, in view of the previous discussion about question wording, we cannot ignore the possibility that the choice of question might affect the results. Although we can only speculate here about this possibility, it might be the case that the more demanding the question wording is (i.e. the lower the level of European identification that it detects), the greater the chances are that the identity-based rather than the functional model receives support from this analysis. In this respect, of all possible questions this is the one in which this possible influence is in a way minimized by the fact that the question explicitly sets European identity in competition with national identity, allowing respondents to choose whether and to what extent the two coexist in their minds.

We recoded the answers into two groups, splitting those who answered that they feel only national against all the others (percentages are computed including "Don't know" and no answer), following the approach used by Hooghe and Marks (2005) in measuring "exclusive national identity". The series for this indicator runs from 1992 up to 2007, with two gaps in 1996 and 2006. Data are available for the entire period for the original six members of the EC; the three Northern European countries that entered in 1973 (Denmark, Ireland, and the United Kingdom); and the three Southern European countries that entered in 1981 (Greece) and 1986 (Spain and Portugal). This produces 168 data points.[12] Data for Finland are available from 1993 and for Sweden and Austria from 1994. All data for the remaining member states are available from 2004 (including Bulgaria and Romania). In total, we have 238 data points for an unbalanced panel design. A further problem we have in our data, a problem quite typical in the analysis of such pooled data, is that the level of the dependent variable across units (i.e. countries and years, in our case) is not homogeneous. As shown already in the discussion in the previous section, the variation on the dependent variable across countries is much larger than over time. The ratio of the two standard deviations is in fact approximately 100 per cent higher for between-units variation than over-time variation: 11.8 to 5.2. It is also quite heterogeneous across clusters. This poses severe problems of potential misspecification in using a standard OLS model that will be discussed later on.

The independent variables

The *functional model* states that utilitarian support has, over the long run, a positive effect on European identity. In addition, this tradition, at least since Inglehart (1977b), sees the duration of EC/EU membership as an important determinant of support. As we noted in our discussion of Easton, length of time is just a crude proxy here for accumulated experiences, which are presumed to be predominantly positive on account of what the Eurobarometer series shows about the perceived benefits of integration over the years. All in all, the functional model expects that economic variables should play an important role at the beginning but that their impact on identity should decline progressively as diffuse support builds up as a result of cumulative positive experiences. In other words, the combination of a positive impact of length of time together with a declining impact of the economic variables should vindicate the functional model rather than a simple economic model of support.

The *identity model* of the determinants of European identity looks at the importance of the national context in explaining variation in European identity. Typically captured as a series of dummy variables for nation, this factor contributes in a statistically significant and strong way to all multivariate models built to predict levels of European identity (e.g. Inglehart 1977b; Eichenberg and Dalton 1993; Duchesne and Frognier 1995; Citrin and Sides 2004a; 2004b; Green 2007). In line with what the descriptive analysis in the previous section just showed, countries vary systematically in the level of European identification, with the original six and the Southern European countries showing systematically higher proportions of European identifiers than Northern Europe. It is, of course, not obvious that these national differences stand for the influence of identity (or any other factor that varies across countries but little over time), and they are often treated in empirical analyses as a nuisance that merely needs to be fixed rather than as something to be explained. As aptly stressed by Green (2007: 100), "it would be preferable if conceptual measures could be substituted for nominal nation-state categories in analyses of political culture". This is precisely what we intend to do in this chapter.

Specifically, to explore the determinants of variation in European identity we operationalize the two contrasting models as suggested in Table 6.3. We are aware that for some of the available indicators, their connection to one or other model is debatable, and this is especially the case as far as identity-related variables are concerned. However, given the aggregate nature of our model and the difficulty of finding straightforwardly measured identitarian factors, we preferred to choose those factors that can be plausibly argued to affect identitarian considerations. This strategy has been followed also by others (e.g. Eichenberg and Dalton in measuring national culture with country dummies) and it is in line with recent studies stressing how the impact of identity varies according to domestic or other contextual factors (e.g. Hooghe and Marks 2005; Garry and Tilley 2009). We have included two factors more often considered as important in making group (i.e. national) identity salient: globalization and immigration.

The *functional model* is based on two sets of determinants. On the one hand, there are the economic variables, national and international. The European Union was first and foremost an economic enterprise,[13] and it is perceived as such by the public. The economic benefits of European integration can flow through two processes, one direct and the other indirect. European integration can create favourable conditions for economic growth, price stability, and steady employment in each member state and/or it can provide direct benefits to member states. The growing economic and trade interdependence and the progressive development of a single economic market within the European common economic market are all factors promoting the growth of the member states' economies. To measure these processes we use three different indicators. First, we measure the level of economic development of the country, using GDP per capita. Second, we include two variables usually considered by the political economy literature as the most relevant for explaining support at the aggregate level: inflation and unemployment rates. Third, we include a measure of interdependence among European economies, represented by the share of intra-EU trade in their exports and imports. All these factors, according to this model, should promote greater support for European integration because people should appreciate the positive impact on their lives and the domestic economic context.

The second set of factors has to do with the direct transfer of economic resources to member states. Member states contribute through their taxes to the EU budget and they receive in return a part of these benefits. The ratio of contributions to benefits received has been a source of concern among member states. We expect that these factors, both direct and indirect, should have an impact on European identity, but we also expect that these factors should weigh in less than others as time goes by. According to the functional model, the length of membership has a positive impact on European identity. On this point, the results so far are mixed and point in different directions. Some scholars claim that this is an important predictor of support and identification (Inglehart 1977b; Eichenberg and Dalton 1993). Others find no relationship between these two variables. Duchesne and Frognier (1995: 200–1) show a much bumpier process, in which the evolution of European identity meets turning points, downturns, and upturns, also in older member countries. And still others (Green 2007: 100–1) find a significant relationship between identity and length of membership, but in the opposite direction: the newer countries are by far more likely to identify with Europe than citizens of older member states, a symptom of integration "fatigue". To measure the functional effect of time we include also a second variable, more closely related to the theoretical argument put forward by functionalists: specific support. In line with the functionalist argument, a steady flow of benefits promotes specific support and this, in turn, brings about European identity. To model this process, we also included the EU membership benefit indicator—the percentage of Eurobarometer respondents in each country year who think their own country benefits from the EU.[14]

As to the *identity model*, we look at national political and economic factors that can affect the level of European identity of the different member states: the quality of the governance of the system, the saliency of national identity, the size of the country, a measure of the satisfaction with the way democracy works domestically, and a measure of exposure to globalizing economic trends. They can be related in opposite ways to European identification and their impact on European identity is not clear and unequivocal. We expect that those who are satisfied with the working of democracy at the national level and live in countries where the quality of governance is high are less likely to identify with the EU institutions, since the most effective locus of agency is seen to be the nation state. On the contrary, people living in countries where the quality of the governance and satisfaction with democracy are lower and where they are economically less powerful could see in European identity an outlet for their frustrated sense of belonging. For instance, in Italy, substantial sectors of society have seen Europe as a way to make the Italian state better (Martinotti and Stefanizzi 1995; Ammendola and Isernia, 2005). A positive link between EU identification and national democracy might also arise in the new Eastern member countries, because their EU membership has been justified by arguments about stabilizing these young democracies. We also included a measure of globalization to explore to what extent European identity is affected by the degree of exposure to the challenges of the globalizing economy. Are those countries most exposed to globalization forces also those in which the people are more likely to perceive Europe as a shield against globalizing trends? Or is it rather seen as an obstacle to a growing enmeshing in the world market?

The last indicator is also meant to capture the saliency of national identity for the development of European identity. We look at one possible source of increasing salience of national identity that is represented by a strong presence of immigrants in the country. We argue that as the number of immigrants increases, national identity issues become more salient in the political discourse, either because national identity is raised as an issue by right-wing parties (Howard 2007; Garry and Tilley 2009) or because the impact is a growing sense of competition for scarce resources among the indigenous groups. The main consequence of this process is expected to be growing salience of national identity in contrast to European identity.

Research design

We conduct two sets of analyses. One is based on the 1992–2007 period covering the twelve member states that joined before 1986. With N=12 countries and T=14 data points, this panel is not cross-sectionally dominated (T>N) and has a long enough series to allow for robust estimation.[15] A second analysis has more countries (N=15, including Austria, Finland, and Sweden), but a shorter time period from 1994 to 2007 (T=12), which raises some methodological concerns (Stimson 1985: 820). Both datasets have two gaps in the time series (we miss data for the dependent variable in 1996 and 2006), which makes them unbalanced panels, and yield an unfavourably high ratio of temporal and spatial units to actual cases in the analysis.[16]

In estimating our pooled model we address three possible sources of threats to our inferences: serial correlation, spatial correlation, and panel heteroscedasticity (Plumper, Troeger, and Manow 2005). Unfortunately, no technical quick fix is available in the statistical literature and, if any, the progress of research in TSCS techniques has made the issues even more complicated, rather than cleared them away.[17] To further complicate our estimation problems, we have a greater between-unit than over-time variation in our dependent variable. This between-units heterogeneity inflates the problems of both heteroscedasticity and serial correlation (Stimson 1985: 920–1). In addressing these validity threats, first we explore the error structure of our model, using the OLS residuals as a diagnostic tool. We then discuss different models based on a pooled design, and we choose what we think is the most appropriate strategy: a pooled OLS strategy (with panel-corrected standard errors) with dummies for groups of acceding countries and an AR(1) correction (i.e. an autoregressive function of lag one). Last, to assess the sensitivity of our results to different estimation strategies, we compare our preferred model to a wider set of estimation strategies, using both fixed and random-effect models.[18]

Using a wide spectrum of diagnostics tools,[19] it emerges that serial correlation[20] and heteroscedasticity are both sources of (limited) estimation problems.[21] We proceeded to correct them using two standard approaches—PCSEs with a lagged dependent variable (the so-called Beck and Katz or B&K standard)—and PCSEs with AR(1) correction. As we will discuss in the next section, we ultimately prefer the latter model, but the results do not diverge much from those obtained using the B&K standard. The Hausman test finds that the explanatory variables are uncorrelated with the unobserved unit effects.[22] On the practical basis of efficiency, this last result would suggest the choice of a random-effect model. For the sake of interpretability, however, we steered a middle course between two not always complementary needs. On the one hand, there is the need to replace country effects—usually measured through dummies—with truly substantive contextual variables that can account for the differences in levels and rate of the dependent variable. In a model such as the present one, these dummy coefficients can be seen as manifestations of "specific ignorance" (Maddala 1971)[23] rather than a quick fix for problems of misspecification (Green, Kim, and Yoon 2001). On the other hand, as is often the case in comparative politics, there is a need to address the set of countries not as a sample of possible units about which to infer the distribution parameters, but as a substantive regional group with specific and unique characteristics and history.

To address these two somehow conflicting needs, we adopted a two-step strategy. First, we started with a standard OLS with PCSEs model using either an LDV or AR(1) but, in order to gain in efficiency, instead of including single country dummies, we assessed the impact of accession date on European identity, including dummies for those who joined the EU in 1973 (UK, Ireland, and Denmark), in 1981 (Spain, Portugal, and Greece) and in 1995 (Austria, Finland, and Sweden). On the basis of the diagnostics, we conclude that the best model is an OLS with PCSE and AR(1), the one on which we base our discussion of results. Second, to assess the robustness of our results, we compare them with different fixed and random-effects models. We are aware that we risk some "underspecification of unit effects" (Stimson 1985: 928), but we think that this is counterbalanced by the gain in efficiency of not including so many theoretically uninteresting country dummies in the model.

Results

Our starting point is the workhorse of pooled cross-national analysis: an OLS with panel-corrected standard errors and a lagged dependent variable (Model 1 in Tables 6.3 and 6.4). Tables 6.3 and 6.4 respectively describe the variables and report the results of different models using these estimates. A simple OLS model shows quite clearly—and consistently for both our datasets—the importance of several variables in explaining variation in the dependent variable. Since there are no big differences between the EU12 and the EU15, our discussion will focus on the EU12, the longest time series. Both the functional and the identity models play an important role in explaining variation in aggregate levels of European identity. Several effects expected by

Table 6.3. Variables and indicators for the Identity and Functional Models

Functional Model	Identity Model
INFLATION: Inflation in %. Source: Eurostat. UNEMPLOYMENT: Unemployment, % of labour force. Source: 1990–2007 Eurostat, pre-1990 CP dataset MEMBERSHIP LENGTH: Length of EU Membership in years. EU MEMBERSHIP BENEFIT: % respondents who think their own country benefits from the EU. Source: Eurobarometer, various years NET EU TRANSFERS: Net transfers from EU budget as % of GNI. Source: various European Commission reports. Coverage: 1991–2007 INTRA EU TRADE: trade with EU countries as a % of total trade. Source: Eurostat. Coverage: 1995–2007	- QUALITY OF GOVERNANCE: Quality of Governance index. Since the World Bank governance indicators are only available for (some of the) years after 1995 and the PRS indicators is only available until 2004, this variable provides a single comprehensive measure of governance quality by using the QGPRS score and imputing its missing values from the World Bank indicators of governance SOUTHERN WAVE: Accessing countries Spain, Portugal and Greece ANGLOSAXON WAVE: Accessing countries Denmark, Ireland and United Kingdom NATIONAL DEMOCRACY SATISFACTION: % satisfied (fairly or very) for the way democracy works. Source: Eurobarometer, various years
GDP: GDP per capita in USD (2004 constant prices) at year. Source: Penn World tables Coverage: 1970–2004	FOREIGN WORKERS: Share (%) of foreign workers in total workforce. Source: OECD population database. Coverage: 1996–2005 TRADE OPENNESS: Combined exports and imports of goods and services as % of GDP. Source: 1990–2007 Eurostat, pre-1990 CP dataset

the functional model are statistically significant. The size of intra-EU trade, unemployment, and the perception of benefiting from membership are all positively and significantly related to high levels of European identity, while net transfers drawn from the EU are negatively related to European identity. As shown in Models 2 and 4, when we control for the accession period, the impact of this variable falls, but remains statistically significant. The short-term economic effects, such as unemployment, also exert a role in explaining levels of identity. Apparently, the greater the unemployment level, the higher the number of those who identify with Europe, a possible sign that the European Union is seen as a shield against economic turmoil. Length of membership, another important even if rough and imprecise determinant of identification in the functional model, is an important predictor of European identity. It is significantly related in a positive direction with the aggregate level of European identity when the standard OLS is considered, while it becomes insignificant and changes sign when the dummies for accession groups are included. This is not surprising in the sense that the lagged dependent variable (European identity in the previous year) absorbs much of the variance explained by duration of membership. However, the impact of

Table 6.4. Regression analysis of the determinants of European identity (Pooled sample of 12 countries)

	Model 1		Model 2		Model 3		Model 4	
	OLS with LDV#		OLS with LDV and Accession groups#		OLS with AR(1)†		OLS with AR(1) and Accession groups†	
	b	SE	b	SE	b	SE	b	SE
Lagged dependent variable	0.44**	0.14	0.35*	0.14				
Functional Model								
GDP per capita	0.00***	0.00	0.00***	0.00	0.00***	0.00	0.00***	0.00
Unemployment	1.17*	0.47	1.11**	0.39	2.06***	0.44	1.67***	0.32
Intra EU Trade	0.33***	0.09	0.16	0.11	0.51***	0.11	0.19	0.14
Net EU Transfers	-3.15**	1.13	-1.95*	0.98	-4.23***	1.31	-2.10*	1.01
EU membership benefit	0.35**	0.11	0.35***	0.10	0.54***	0.11	0.49***	0.08
EU membership length	0.17*	0.09	-0.22	0.38	0.33***	0.09	-0.44	0.40
Identity Model								
Trade openness	-0.04	0.03	-0.05*	0.02	-0.07*	0.03	-0.07***	0.02
National democracy satisfaction	-0.01**	0.07	0.01	0.06	-0.05	0.08	-0.00	0.07
Governance Quality	-19.81	12.76	-23.73*	10.38	-25.58	14.80	-31.47***	10.94
Foreign Workers	-0.14	0.08	-0.43***	0.13	-0.19	0.10	-0.61***	0.14
1980–81 group			-8.57	11.45			-16.70	11.68
1973 group			-12.05	7.63			-20.69**	7.57
Constant	-22.61	15.13	-4.68	23.57	-36.28*	16.13	2.75	25.51
R²	0.87		0.88		0.78		0.82	
Wald Chi²	3258.58		8138.86		947.36		1867.10	
Rho					0.223		0.185	
N	88		88		88		88	

* p<0.05; ** p<0.01; *** p<0.001# OLS with PCSE (panel corrected standard error);† Prais-Winston regression (autoregressive error with a time lag of one) with PCSE.
LDV denotes lagged Dependent Variable.

time becomes insignificant and even changes sign once we control for the different accession dates of countries to the EU. The membership benefit indicator has an effect in the expected direction but is barely significant.

The identity model is also important in explaining variations in the level of European identity. Two results stand out from this model. First, the percentage of foreign workers reduces the incidence of European identity. We can explain this result by the fact that in countries with many working immigrants national identity is more strongly activated and militates against the formation of a European identity. The quality of governance index is significantly, and negatively, related to the aggregate level of European identity: identification with Europe is stronger in those countries whose citizens perceive their own government as lacking in efficiency. This may follow the logic of those whom Martinotti and Stefanizzi (1995) call "escapists/innovators" because "they hope either that European integration will provide leverage for innovation or reform in their own national system or they regard it as an escape hatch through which the deficiencies of the national system can be circumvented" (1995: 176–7). These results confirm at the aggregate level what Bellucci, Sanders, and Serricchio (2011) have found, using IntUne individual-level data, about the negative relationship between confidence in national institutions and European identity. An indicator of the exposure to globalization forces, for the openness of the national economy, is the degree of trade openness of a country as measured by import and export as a proportion of GDP. The results show that those who are more exposed to globalization, and might see a possible role for the EU as a shield against globalization, do not identify more strongly with Europe. The coefficient is not statistically significant in every model and has a positive sign when it is: the mass publics of those countries that trade more as a percentage of their economy are also less likely to identify with the EU. These results seem to suggest that globalization, rather than making European identity more salient, increases the salience of national identity and thus reduces European identity. It is also worth noting that within-EU trade has an insignificant but positive effect on European identity.

In both Models 1 and 2 of Table 6.4, the effect of the lagged dependent variable is highly significant and eats up much of the variation in the other time variable, duration of membership in the EU.[24] Since we have no obvious interpretation for this coefficient and it has been shown that lags are problematic (Achen 2000), we re-estimated the model, correcting for autocorrelation with a first-order serial-correlation factor instead. Including this correction does not affect the strength and sign of our main coefficients, however. If we consider that both in terms of the time points available and considering the quite sluggish dependent and independent variables, dynamics are not a major source of variation and the static model with serially correlated errors is probably the most appropriate. In fact, we consider Model 4 as the most appropriate for the data at hand, and the one we will use as a benchmark for our sensitivity analysis to test the robustness of our results.

In general, the comparison of the two explanations for European identity points to the fact that European identity seems stronger when the country is economically more developed, when the economy is going badly, when governance is poorer, and when immigration is modest. The opposite constellation has a depressive impact on European identity. But how stable are these results? In view of the many complex decisions involved in estimating a pooled model, we also explored the extent to which our model's results are robust in the face of different estimation strategies. In particular, given the constraints in measuring the unit effects with dummies and the ambiguous results of the Hausman test, we performed a sensitivity test, with different estimation techniques, following the approach of Wilson and Butler (2007).[25] We used the pooled model with twelve countries, a corrected serial correlation of lag one and the two dummies for different accession years (Model 4) as our benchmark to compare with other models. In particular, we tested our model against a standard least square dummy variable (LSDV) model (with panel-corrected standard errors) with control for the lagged dependent variable (LDV), also known as the standard Beck and Katz model, a generalized least square (GLS) model with an AR(1) correction, a feasible GLS (FGLS) model,[26] and a fixed-effects vector-decomposition (FEVD) model without the LDV.[27] Table 6.5 reports the main results of this analysis and some indicators of the relative performance, based on the distinction Wilson and Butler (2007) suggest between "robust", "weakly robust", and "non-robust" findings.[28]

We assessed our preferred model against a fairly diverse array of estimation techniques, one of which, the LSDV with LDV, is surely the hardest, given the loss of degrees of freedom it involves. However, the analysis shows that the main results, as discussed above, still hold under different estimation techniques. In particular, three coefficients appear particularly robust and consistent across a wide set of estimation techniques: the impact of the net EU transfers; the perceived benefits of EU membership; and the quality of governance. These results stand out under several different estimation techniques. Unemployment and import–export as a percentage of GDP also have robust effects, while GDP per capita's sign flips under the standard fixed-effect model with lagged dependent variable. As to membership duration, a variable whose coefficient sign was shown to be flipping in previous models, the significant and positive sign in these models, is probably a consequence of misspecification, due to the fact that different accession waves bring different levels of European identity into the model, which is not accounted for in the LSDV with lagged dependent variable and the random-effects models. Another factor related to

Table 6.5. Regression analysis of the determinants of European identity (Pooled sample of 15 countries) #

| | Model 1 | | Model 2 | | Model 3 | | Model 4 | |
| | OLS with LDV | | OLS with LDV and Accession groups | | OLS with AR(1) † | | OLS with AR(1) and Accession groups † | |
	b	SE	b	SE	b	SE	b	SE
Lagged dependent variable	0.53***	0.13	0.41**	0.14				
Functional Model								
GDP per capita	0.00***	0.00	0.00***	0.00	0.00***	0.00	0.00***	0.00
Unemployment	0.85*	0.41	0.81**	0.34	1.62***	0.47	1.29***	0.32
Intra EU Trade	0.26**	0.10	0.12	0.12	0.47***	0.13	0.18	0.15
Net EU Transfers	−3.11**	1.30	−1.64	1.12	−3.92*	1.44	−1.50	1.14
EU membership benefit	0.17*	0.09	0.26***	0.09	0.27**	0.11	0.37***	0.08
EU membership length	0.01	0.05	−0.34	0.35	0.14	0.08	−0.57	0.39
Identity Model								
Trade openness	−0.01	0.02	−0.04	0.02	−0.04	0.02	−0.06**	0.02
National democracy satisfaction	−0.00	0.07	0.03	0.06	0.00	0.10	0.03	0.07
Governance quality	−23.19***	12.44	−26.76**	9.90	−33.17**	15.70	−37.70***	10.81
Foreign Workers	−0.15	0.08	−0.41***	0.10	−0.19	0.13	−0.58***	0.13
1980–81 group			−10.66	11.20			−20.64	11.52
1973 group			−13.51	7.76			−23.46***	7.85
1995 group			−13.33	14.15			−25.44	15.31
Constant	−1.41	14.03	10.81	20.63	−3.82	18.62	2.42	2.28
R²	0.85		0.87		0.75		0.80	
Wald chi²	11837.82		55034.36		3573.88		7944.66	
Rho					0.405		0.286	
N	109		109		109		109	

* p<0.05; ** p<0.01; *** p<0.001# OLS with PCSE; † Prais-Winston regression with PCSE.

identity, the percentage of foreign workers, turns out not to be a robust result, flipping from positive to negative and significant only in some specifications and models. A robust non-finding in our model turns out to be the level of satisfaction with the way democracy works in the respondent's country. Contrary to the expectation that satisfaction with democracy might be related to levels of European identity, this variable is never significant. All in all, this sensitivity test supports most of our previous conclusions and it clearly shows that some of the coefficients we have found relevant to explain different levels of European identification withstand different estimation strategies and stand out clearly as important predictors of level of European identity in the different countries.

Conclusions

In this chapter we have explored and discussed three sets of issues related to European identity. We reviewed the theoretical and empirical literature on European identity as it has gone through various stages and found that it can be reconfigured under two major perspectives, the neo-functionalist and the psychological-identitarian one. The first looks at European identity formation as a long-term process of acquisition that starts from the perception of concrete material benefits accruing from European integration and then slowly develops over time into a proper form of political identification. The second, identitarian, looks at European identity as a form of identity created in analogy with national and other forms of political identity, with which it can coexist more or less in competition.

We then discussed the different ways European identity has been measured and traced its evolution, based on various different indicators, from the early 1970s up to 2007. In an attempt to account for the different levels of identity, as measured by these indicators, we have shown that question wording is by far the most important explanation for variation in recorded levels of European identity, followed by nation, and, lastly, time. In our view, the paramount importance of question wording in comparison to cross-national and time-series variation is a consequence of the very nature of this form of identity, and for that matter of all forms of political identity. Many people have multiple political identities whose coexistence is dynamic and in flux. The different levels of identification with Europe reflect the different reactions that respondents produce depending on whether their identification with Europe is addressed in isolation from, or in competition with, other objects of identification. When this competition is more explicit, such as when the respondent is invited to prioritize the order of identification, European identity registers quite low. But when there is no reference to other objects of political

131

identification, levels of European identity grow substantially. This immediately raises the question of when and under what conditions citizens are, in real life, ready to consider themselves as Europeans together with being nationals rather than being in competition with their national identification. This, we think, is an area worth exploring in the future.

Finally, we shifted our attention to the sources of variations in levels of European identity, cross nationally and over time. We chose the indicator which offers the longest time series and an intermediate level of probability, relative to other question wordings, for recording a European identity. Using a pooled design, we tested the functional and the identity models about the genesis of European identity with different estimation strategies. We find, in line with other recent works (Garry and Tilley 2009), that *both* functional and identity components are important in explaining variations in levels of European identity over time and cross nationally. Both the statistical analysis and the sensitivity tests clearly show that European identity is higher when countries are wealthy, but in economic trouble, when they are less exposed to globalization, and when the quality of governance is lower. Moreover, economic globalization seems to be more important than political globalization, as measured by the level of immigration.

Given the aggregate nature of our data and our short time series, we were unable to explore interaction effects among these two dimensions, but our results clearly show that in order to explain levels of European identity there is no point in attempting to disentangle what works better among political and economic determinants. They work equally well. Our results also suggest that, over time, there is *no* clear sign that economic factors are receding in importance while political determinants are becoming more important. Cross-national sources of variations are much more important than time-relevant changes. A puzzling consequence of these results is that, although identity factors have recently started to attract the attention of both policy makers and scholars, still a long-term perspective shows no clear sign that sense of attachment to Europe is moving up over the last two decades. Finally, the length of duration of EU membership is not significantly related to the aggregate level of European identity. The membership benefit indicator and the intra-European trade measure are both in the right direction, although barely significant and, in the latter case, often insignificant.

These results raise some interesting, but also puzzling, questions about the role and future developments of European identity in the greater scheme of things related to Europe. As our analyses show—and in line with more than twenty years of research in this field—European identity has been remarkably stable over time and across countries. The small upward blips we detected in the positive effect of duration of membership on level of European identity (see Model 1 in Table 6.3) were in fact consequences of the different accession periods of different waves of countries. The United Kingdom, Ireland, and Denmark started their EC membership with markedly lower levels of popular identification with Europe in comparison to both the founding members and the countries acceding to the EC/EU later on. Once we controlled for this factor, the upward EU-wide trend disappears.

Descriptively, the evidence that we find shows that most of the variation in levels of European identification reflects either the economic situation and the benefits accruing to the member states by the integration process or the perceived need for Europe as a substitute for the deficiencies of the national political system. In contrast, when national identity is activated through immigration or globalization, European identity levels may drop lower. The main implication of this state of affairs is that, contrary to what both functionalists and identitarian theorists seem to expect, there is no sign that European identity is progressively taking hold in Europe with the increase in European integration. Structural factors related to the economic compact of the member states as well as their distinctive political situations explain the differences in level of identification with Europe. These results, however, are also puzzling in what they imply. On the one hand, European identity seems to be related to factors such as the quality of governance and the relevance of national identity that are invariant or slowly changing. On the other hand, variation in levels of identification with Europe seems to be exposed to the vagaries of the economic situation, increasing when the economic situation deteriorates (as measured by levels of unemployment) and decreasing when things go better. This should induce more temperate expectations about the ability of institutions—at both the national and European levels—to foster European identity and, in general, about the capacity of European identity to play the role that scholars and policy makers attribute to it in filling the gap in legitimacy that Europe presently has.

Notes

1. We thank Pedro C. Magalhães, David Sanders, and Gábor Tóka for their careful reading of and very useful comments on different versions of this chapter. Some preliminary results of this paper have been presented to the *Seminario Permanente di Teoria Politica*, Department of Political Science, University of Pavia, 10 March 2010. All analyses have been done using Stata 11.0.
2. Although the economic approach as such does not say anything more useful about identity, still it is an important contribution to the discussion about the sources and determinants of public opinion on European integration that deserves to be briefly discussed.

3. An observation is a single question asked in a specific year, country, and question wording.

4. Percentages here reported are based on the total number of cases, including "no answer" and "don't know". We report data for EU countries only, excluding accession countries and Norway.

5. For a few years, question wording 1 has been part of the questionnaire in some but not all member states, and we decided to drop these observations from the analysis. Thus, the years covered by this series are just 1971, 1973, 1976, 1978, 1979, 1981, 1990, and 1999.

6. A similar question has been asked in EB 41.1 (1994) but using a 1–10 scale.

7. The only potentially troublesome source of differences could be the term "citizen of Europe" in 1983, while in all the other years the question reference was to "European". In EB 37, the two versions of the question were asked from one half of the sample each, and they generated almost identical responses (Chi^2 = 8.821 significant at the level 0.066; for a similar evaluation see Duchesne and Frognier 1995). See our online appendix for the results of all experiments discussed in the text.

8. The two different versions were asked together in 1991 and as a split-half experiment in 2006. While in 1991 the two questions produced almost the same results, as a possible consequence of carry over effects, in 2006 there is a big difference between the two versions (Chi^2 = 576,731 significant at the 0.000 level). The reference to the EU generates an identification ranging from 25% to 75% with an average of 45%, while the reference to Europe produces an identification ranging from 29% to 92% with an average of 61%. This difference in the results holds up for all accession waves. See our online appendix for details.

9. This recoding is often used in research (e.g. Citrin and Sides 2004a; Green 2000, 2007). Yet it seems debatable: one could as well dichotomize in the middle, especially because most of the respondents choose the lowest intensity of European identification through giving preference to their nation before Europe.

10. Twice in 2004 (EB 61.0 and EB 62.0) the question was split, with half of the sample being offered only three alternatives, dropping the item "European and (Nationality)". The results, shown in the online appendix to this volume, are not very different.

11. A fifth alternative—"I do not feel European"—was offered to the respondents in 2006.

12. Eichenberg and Dalton used the semi-annual nature of the Eurobarometer data to increase their sample size. We stuck to the annual nature of most of the aggregate data, averaging the European identity indicators when there were two time points in a single year.

13. This is true for most of the period covered by studies of support for European integration, from the early 1970s on. It is probably less true for explaining support for European integration in the 1950s and 1960s, when political factors were probably more important (see Isernia 2008 for the Italian case).

14. We tested a model with a one-year lag, but the results are identical to the one without lags. Theoretically, there is nothing in the Guetzkow–Easton argument that leans toward a lagged impact of specific support on European identity.

15. We must note, however, that our results are based on quite a small number of time points. Since pooled methods are asymptotic in T, a large number of time points would be useful and estimates based on T<10 should be considered with caution (Beck 2001: 274). For this reason, we rely on several analyses, based on different sets of countries. They all produce converging results.

16. As an example, to fully address the problems of TSCS using Beck and Katz's suggestion, we should create 13 time dummies and 11 country dummies for the longest TSCS series (88 cases) and 2 time dummies and 26 country dummies for the shortest and widest series (133 cases), a heavy toll in terms of degrees of freedom.

17. For a quantitative description of the growing interest in TSCS, see Adolph, Butler, and Wilson (2005: 2–5). For relevant Monte Carlo simulations see Beck and Katz (2004), Judson and Owen (1999), Kristensen and Wawro (2003) and Adolph, Butler, and Wilson (2005).

18. We used the OLS model in different variants for the fixed-effects model and the GLS and FGLS for the random-effects model. For a discussion of the rationale of this choice, see below.

19. We performed the pooled Durbin–Watson d (Sayrs 1989: 19) and the Lagrange multiplier test for serial correlation. To assess panel heteroscedasticity we test for groupwise homoscedasticity (Kittel 1999) and used the likelihood ratio test. We also computed the average contemporaneous correlation of residuals to test for serial correlation, which produces an average Pearson correlation coefficient of 0.371 for absolute values of the dyadic correlations. Finally, we run the Hausman test to compare random- vs fixed-effects models.

20. The pooled Durbin–Watson d is 2.723, which—with 8 regressors and 12 cases for each regression—shows no evident problem of serial correlation. But the Lagrange multiplier test returns a Chi^2 value of 12.038, which—with one degree of freedom—is significant below the 0.001 level, and therefore we reject the null hypothesis of no serial correlation.

21. The Lagrange multiplier test value is 14.959, which—with 11 degrees of freedom—is not significant, while using the likelihood ratio test, the critical value is 105.161; that is, significant at the level 0.05.

22. The Hausman test for 12 countries (1992–7) has a $Chi^2 = 8.26$, significant at level 0.604 and the same test for 15 countries (1994–2007) has a Chi^2 of 14.10, significant at the level 0.168.

23. We have also run an OLS (with PCSEs) with all country dummies, but we neither present it here nor discuss it in the analysis since due to efficiency problems all coefficients become insignificant. Including all country dummies absorbs many degrees of freedom, seriously impairing the efficiency of the estimates. However, a joint F-test of the cluster of nation dummies with 11 covariates and 66 degrees of freedom produces a Chi^2 of 5.79 significant at the level 0.001, pointing to the relevance of these country differences for our model.

24. We tested for stationarity using an LM test, as suggested by Beck (2006) and we found no sign of it in the data (with the residual of the dependent variable with a coefficient of .329, significant at the level 0.011).
25. We should note that our sensitivity analysis is not so much directed to address the dynamic aspects of the model (given the slowly changing nature of our dependent variable and since we found lagging of the independent variables inconsequential) but rather the choice between fixed effect, random effects, or no controls for unit effects at all, given the results of the Hausman test.
26. This is clearly the most problematic estimation technique in our case as the ratio of time points to cases is close to 1, making the estimates for contemporary serial correlation quite inaccurate (Beck and Katz 1995: 634; Kittell 1999: 228–9). However, as discussed before, contemporary correlation is not a dramatic problem in our case.
27. We tested these models also for N=15. Since the results are not different, we do not report them, but they are available upon request from the authors.
28. A robust finding is when coefficients all have the same sign, the range of coefficients is low, and the number of statistically significant coefficients is high. A "weakly robust" finding has at least 3 significant findings, with no sign reversal. A "non-robust" finding has several sign variations, the range of estimate is high, and statistical significance is uncommon.

Table 6.6. Sensitivity of the b coefficients to different estimation techniques[†]

VARIABLE	OLS with PCSE and AR (1)[#]	LSDV with PCSE and LDV	GLS with PCSE and AR (1)	FGLS with PCSE and AR (1)	FEVD	Average	SD	Range	Range in no. of standard errors	N models with significant effect	Robustness*
LDV		0.11									NA
Functional Model											
GDP per capita	0.00	−0.00	0.00	0.00	0.00	0.00	0.00	−0.001–+0.002	8.93	3	Weakly robust
Unemployment	1.67	0.26	1.78	1.76	0.23	1.14	0.82	+0.262–+1.780	4.78	3	Robust
Intra-EU trade	0.19	0.11	0.48	0.43	0.10	0.26	0.18	+0.103–+0.483	2.66	2	Weakly robust
Net EU transfers	−2.10	−1.07	−3.69	−3.56	−5.48	−3.17	1.68	−5.477–−1.069	4.37	4	Robust
EU membership benefit	0.49	0.30	0.50	0.54	0.56	0.48	0.10	+0.300–+0.555	3.11	5	Robust
EU membership length	−0.44	1.08	0.39	0.45	0.30	0.36	0.54	−0.436–+1.082	3.80	4	Weakly robust
Identity Model											
Trade openness	−0.07	0.07	−0.07	−0.07	−0.10	−0.05	0.06	−0.095–+0.065	7.65	4	Weakly robust
National democracy satisfaction	−0.00	0.06	0.01	−0.04	0.00	0.01	0.03	−0.004–+0.058	1.41	0	Robust non-finding
Governance Quality	−31.47	−11.51	−29.04	−25.73	−39.65	−27.48	10.30	−11.511–−39.652	2.57	4	Robust
Foreign Workers	−0.61	−0.35	−0.12	−0.04	0.21	−0.18	0.31	−0.606–+0.208	5.84	2	Not robust

[†] Significant coefficients (at p <0.05) in bold and italics.
[#] Results based on Model 4 in Table 6.4 and 6.5.
* We use the criteria suggested by Wilson and Butler (2007).

Box 6.1 EUROPEAN IDENTITY QUESTIONS

Question wording/Source/Survey Date

(1) Geographical belonging

ECS: 1971, 1973
EB: 6–1976, 10A–1978, 12–1979

WVS: 1981, 1982, 1990, 1995, 1996, 1997, 1999, 2000

Question

To which of these geographical groups would you say you belong first of all? And the next?
– Locality or town where you live,
– Region or country where you live,
– Your country as a whole,
– Europe,
– The World as a whole,
– (Don't Know)
Europe 1st choice; Europe 2nd choice; Europe not chosen

(2) Thinking of self as European
(a) EB: 17–1982

(b) EB: 19–1983, 24–1985, 26–1986, 37–1992

(c) EB: 27–1987, 30–1988, 31–1989, 33–1990

(d) EB: 36–1991, 37–1992, 64.2–2005, 66–2006

(e) EB: 41.1–1994

(a) Do you ever think of yourself as a citizen of Europe?
often, sometimes, never, (don't know)

(b) Do you ever think of yourself not only as a (nationality) citizen but also as a citizen of Europe? often, sometimes, never, (don't know)

(c) Does the thought ever occur to you that you are not only (nationality) but also European? Does this happen often, sometimes, never, (don't know)

(d) Do you ever think of yourself as not only (nationality), but also European? Does this happen often, sometimes, never, (don't know) [1990, 1991, 2005, 2006]

(e) Does the thought ever occur to you that you are not only (nationality) but also a European?
10-point scale: not at all also European. . . . very much also European (don't know)

(3) Attachment to Europe/European Union
(a) EB: 36–1991, 51–1999, 54–2000, 60–2003, 63–2005, 65.2–2006, 67.1–2007,
ISSP 2003
(b) EB: 36–1991, 56.3–2002, 58.1–2002, 65.2–2006

(a) How attached (or: close/emotionally attached/identifying with) do you feel to Europe?

(b) How attached (or: close/emotionally attached/identifying with) do you feel to the European Union?
(a and b): very attached/very close, fairly attached/close, not very attached/not very close, not at all attached/not close at all, (don't know)

(4) National versus European
(a) EB: 37.0–1992, 40–1993, 42–1994, 43.1–1995, 44–1995, 46.0–1996, 47–1997, 49–1998, 50–1998, 52–1999, 53–2000, 54–2000, 56–2001, 57–2002, 58.1–2002, 59.1–2003, 60.1–2003, 61.0–2004, 62.0–2004, 64.2–2005, 67.1–2007

In the near future do you see yourself as . . . ?
(a) (nationality) only, (nationality) and European, European and (nationality), European only, (don't know)

(b) EB: 61.0–2004

(b) (nationality) only, (nationality) and European, European only, (don't know) [split ballot with version a) in EB 61.0 2004]

(c) EB: 62.0–2004

(c) (nationality) only, firstly (nationality) and then European, firstly European and then (nationality), European only, as (nationality) as European (spontaneous), (don't know) [split ballot with version a) in EB 62.0, 2004] And would you say you are very proud, fairly proud, not very proud, not at all proud to be European?

(5) PROUD TO BE EUROPEAN

(a) very proud, fairly proud, not very proud, not at all proud, (don't know)
(b) additionally: I do not feel European (spontaneous)

(a) EB: 54–2000, 56–2001, 57–2002, 60–2003, 62–2004, 64.2–2005,
(b) EB: 66.1–2006

ECS = European Community Studies; EB = Eurobarometer; WVS: World Values Survey

7

Trust in the European Parliament: From Affective Heuristics to Rational Cueing

Mariano Torcal, Jordi Muñoz, and Eduard Bonet

Since Easton (1965), the literature on political support has stressed the relevance of confidence in political institutions. Given that confidence refers to the citizen's assessment of core political democratic institutions, it has been said that it entails an evaluation of the most relevant institutional attributes: credibility, fairness, transparency, and openness. As Newton and Norris (2000) put it, confidence in institutions is the main indicator of the underlying feelings of the general public about its polity and is a central component of political trust. Its opposite, political disaffection, impinges on many aspects of the relationship between citizens and their polity (Torcal and Montero 2006). In this chapter, we look at the level of trust expressed by Europeans in the European Union's (EU) main institutions and, more specifically, in the European Parliament (EP). However, this chapter is not only about trust in a major EU institution: it is also about the general topic of public opinion formation in the EU.

Scholars have dealt extensively with political confidence in national parliaments, but very little work has been done on the EP. This is probably because of the theoretical and empirical hurdles to studying the topic. The EU and the workings of its institutions are far removed from what most average European citizens think about when it comes to politics and thus many of their attitudes are poorly thought out (Janssen 1991: 467; Anderson 1998a: 573). Furthermore, the European integration process has been evolving from its outset, both deepening and expanding the power of the new institutions, making the consequences of their decisions more conspicuous and increasing the number of member states. This evolution yields a portrait of a non-stable polity with changing institutional settings that may be difficult for citizens to understand, evaluate, or even to become affectively engaged with (Anderson 1998a: 574).

Finally, the level of political information on the EU among average citizens is very low (Janssen 1991: 454; Franklin, Marsh, and McLaren 1994: 458).

So, how do Europeans form their opinions about the EP and other EU supranational institutions when it comes to expressing trust? As has been argued by some scholars (Hurwitz and Peffley 1987: 1114; Zaller 1992: 24), the fact that citizens are so ignorant about issues related to politics in general and foreign policies in particular is precisely the reason that individuals must often fall back on core values and general postures to instruct their opinions. We argue here that this is the case for expressing trust in the EP. Citizens tend to fall back on attitudes relating to their general support for the EU in order to express their degree of trust in the EU institutions.

Easton (1965) argued that citizens could give two types of support to basic institutions and political objects: diffuse and specific support. This theoretical distinction has also been used for the study of attitudes on European integration, and scholars have distinguished since then between (a) "diffuse/affective" support and (b) "evaluative/utilitarian" or "instrumental/specific" support (Lindberg and Scheingold 1970; Inglehart 1977a; Inglehart and Rabier 1978). The latter is based on cost–benefit analysis and requires higher levels of knowledge and sophistication, while the former could be the result of overall support for the EU integration process. For some years, scholars have argued that affective support has dominated when it comes to studying general support for the EU. They have called this unconditional support for the European integration process the "permissive consensus" (Lindberg and Scheingold 1970). This initial permissive consensus could be the reason behind the initial limited impact of party positions on attitudes toward EU integration found originally by some scholars (Wilgden and Feld 1976).

However, this permissive consensus has been declining since the implementation of the Maastricht Treaty and the Economic Monetary Union (EMU) (Niedermayer 1995a; Franklin, Marsh, and McLaren 1994; Dalton and Eichenberg 1998; Ray 2003a) and two groups of alternative explanations have emerged to explain this decline. First, scholars have highlighted evaluations based on cost–benefit analysis of either objective economic and social benefits (whether for individuals or groups) or of subjective perceptions of those benefits (Gabel and Palmer 1995; Anderson and Reichert 1996; Gabel 1998c and 1998b; Christin 2005). Additionally, a growing number of works highlight the importance of national cueing factors (political and institutional) driving increasing change (Anderson 1998a; Sánchez Cuenca 2000; Rohrschneider 2005). These are the so-called national political cues, which consider that the EU is just an extension of domestic politics (Hooghe and Marks 2005: 420). Among those factors, there has been increasing interest in the effects of party competition and the evaluation of national incumbents (Duch and Taylor 1997; Gabel 1998c; Ray 1999, 2003a and 2003b; Hug and Sciarini

2000), the impact of national or sub-national identities (Díez Medrano and Gutierrez 2001; Kriesi and Lachat 2004) and the consequences of the evaluation of national representative institutions (Anderson 1998a; Sánchez Cuenca 2000; Rohrschneider 2002 and 2005; Christin 2005). Often both aspects—the increasing level of instrumental evaluations and the incremental effects of national politics—seem to be interconnected when it comes to explaining trends in EU support. This interaction is the result of the increasing politicization of the European integration process in many of the member states (Franklin, Marsh, and McLaren 1994; Sanchez Cuenca 2000; Hooghe and Marks 2005 and 2008), where political parties play an increasingly important cueing role (Ray 1999 and 2003a).

We argue in this chapter that individuals fall back on a set of core attitudes and values to express their support for the EP: one affective heuristic (affective assessments of the EU integration process) and one political cue (the perceived benefit of the integration process). More importantly, we also argue that: (1) citizens' use of these proxies in placing trust in EU institutions has varied over time; (2) these variations reflect both the increasing impact of the EU on national politics and heightened public awareness of this development. We therefore posit that *as citizens become better acquainted with the EU in general and with the EP in particular, they will rely more on perceived subjective benefits (political cues) and less on affective heuristics when it comes to trusting the EP.* So, citizens' support for the EU and its institutions is becoming more strongly linked to subjective evaluations of EU general outcomes (interacting with national political and institutional cues) rather than with general support for the integration process. The growing impact of these factors on trust in the EP is the result of both greater *political awareness*[1] of the consequences of the EU and the related politicization of the EU issue. As Hooghe and Marks (2008) and Kriesi (2008) have recently argued, political awareness of the consequences of EU integration is the first step towards politicization of EU integration. In turn, greater politicization raises public awareness. However, politicization of EU integration depends on many contextual political factors, varying over time by country (Ray 2003a and 2003b) and is thus inherently unstable. This is why political awareness of EU integration is often out of step with more volatile national political cues. So this chapter will try to demonstrate increasing EU awareness and instrumental evaluation of the process, which may lead to further politicization.

The analysis is confined to the period 1994 to 2006 given data availability limitations and the nature of the research design. The fact that EU integration has already been under way for decades makes it difficult to extrapolate this argument to the future. Furthermore, one should note that the time frame chosen encompasses periods of significant change in EU integration, thus providing a kind of natural quasi-experimental setting for testing our hypothesis.

The first section of this chapter discusses the theoretical framework of the analysis. Second, we describe: (1) the trends in country-level trust in the EP over the period (1994–2006) and (2) the bearing of the aforementioned political cues and heuristics on that trust. The third section tests whether trust in the EU parliament is increasingly a function of support based on a subjective evaluation of the benefits of EU integration. Last, we test rival hypotheses to our main argument, namely whether trust in the EU is merely a matter of time (this might be termed the "socialization hypothesis") and/or the timing of each country's accession to the EU.

1. The theoretical framework: the three basic proxies for evaluating the EP

Easton came up with the idea of a dual conceptualization of political support that could account for both evaluations of the authorities' performance (specific support) and more basic and fundamental aspects of the political system (diffuse support). In his own words, "support was not all of a piece" (Easton 1975: 437) and its constituent classes could vary independently from one another. Specific support can be object-specific in two ways: first, it is assumed that people are aware of the political authorities working on behalf of the system; second, it takes into account the perceived decisions, policies, actions, utterances, and style of the authorities. In this sense, the members of a political system can rationally decide whether the authorities' actions address their needs and demands. Specific support can only exist in societies whose institutions allow authorities to be held accountable for their actions and their consequences. Accordingly, citizens' awareness of the consequences of the decisions taken by these authorities will fluctuate according to their satisfaction and perception of the benefits. In short, each political object could be supported by either diffuse or specific arguments, or both, depending on each individual's level of *political knowledge, information, and acquiescence*.

This model of political support has been applied to the discussion of support for the EU and its integration process and distinguishes between affective support and instrumental support for the EU (Lindberg and Scheingold 1970). The first analyses of support for the EU found that European citizens blindly supported EU integration (affective support). This was put down to a kind of "permissive consensus" among citizens, which mostly led to unquestioning support for elite-driven decisions on European integration (Lindberg and Scheingold 1970; Wilgden and Feld 1976; Inglehart 1977a; Inglehart and Rabier 1978).

This permissive consensus, however, has been waning since the Maastricht Treaty and the Economic Monetary Union (EMU) came into force (Eichenberg and Dalton 1993; Niedermayer 1995a; Franklin, Marsh, and McLaren 1994; Dalton and Eichenberg 1998).[2] Two reasons are usually cited for this declining support. The first is that Europeans are becoming more aware of the consequences of the integration process as its results become more obvious (for instance, the impact of the EMU) (Hooghe and Marks 2008; Ray 2003a: 990). The second is that citizens are increasingly weighing up the decisions taken by the elite. In this context, one should note that some scholars argue that a country's share of EU trade plays a part in such support (Gabel and Palmer 1995; Gabel 1998b). Others point to the direct effects of other economic factors such as inflation or unemployment (Eichenberg and Dalton 1993; Dalton and Eichenberg 1998; Anderson and Kaltenthaler 1996; Bednar, Ferejohn, and Garret 1996; Gabel 1998c). Yet others consider the economic and social winners and losers in each country as a result of given EU policies (Gabel and Palmer 1995; Anderson and Reichert 1996; Gabel 1998b and 1998c; Hooghe and Marks 2005).

Leaving aside some of the empirical evidence regarding the absence of such direct effects (Bosch and Newton 1995), there are two problems with these purely instrumental approaches, especially when it comes to explaining support for the EU and its institutions. As other scholars have shown, such instrumental support is the result of subjective perceptions, even though many citizens know little about the EU, its policies, the way it works, and its decision-making processes. Second, in the absence of deep-seated values, well-thought-out attitudes, and direct personal experience of EU politics, these perceptions and evaluations are shaped by *national* political cues such as the actions of national political parties and institutions (Janssen 1991; Anderson 1998a; Ray 2003a; Hooghe and Marks 2005; Rohrschneider 2002 and 2005).[3]

We argue here that Europeans' trust in the EP is increasingly determined by two cues—subjective instrumental evaluations and the evaluation of national institutions—and that the affective component is waning. These cues might be interrelated but they also independently influence Europeans' trust in the EP. However, the relative weight of these factors is changing slowly as EU citizens become more aware of community integration and the EU issue becomes more politicized. If we are right, we should expect to see a shift away from the affective component and towards subjective instrumental support based on the benefits of EU integration cued by the impact of national politics and institutions. While the aggregate *levels* of trust in the EP do not show major changes over time, the instruments used to express trust may well do so, shaped as they are by national political awareness of the impacts of EU integration and the politicization of the issue this leads to in member states. This is why subjective instrumental evaluations play a greater role in defining the level of trust in the EP. This finding confirms the trends noted by other scholars, who have detected the rising importance of subjective instrumental calculations cued by national politics when it comes to making an overall appraisal of EU integration. This could be the most conspicuous consequence of the shift from a permissive consensus to a "constraining dissensus" on the EU among citizens (Hooghe and Marks 2008).

We therefore hypothesize that changes in the use of these evaluating instruments may be changing in response to public awareness of the results of EU policy. In other words, the greater the level of citizens' political awareness and interest in the consequences of European integration, the lower their affective support for the EP. So, *the more national publics are exposed to institutional and political discussion of EU policies and the outcomes of EU integration, the more they will base their evaluation on instrumental calculations and national political cues, and less on affective support.*

With regard to national political cues, we focus attention on the relationship between trust in national parliaments and trust in the EP. Europeans might transpose their own views on national institutions and their performance to the supranational level. However, this process could cut both ways. While some might argue that trust levels range across institutional tiers (in this case, supranational ones), others argue just the opposite and in particular, that lower evaluations of national institutions vis à vis European ones will foster support for European institutions by reducing the perceived costs of transferring power to the latter (Anderson 1998a: 577). This relationship has also been found in connection with national identity and support for European integration (see Carey 2002; Citrin and Sides 2004b; Díez Medrano and Gutiérrez 2001; Marks and Hooghe 1999; Van Kersbergen 2000). However, the impact of national politics varies constantly and is affected by fleeting factors such as party strategies, elections, government policies and so on (Ray 2003b). Thus, in both cases, the effect will be unstable since citizens' views on the performance of EU institutions may be affected by their national government's support of and views on community bodies—something one might expect to vary across member states.

2. Trust in the European Parliament—trends

Citizens know little about European political institutions. That is why any analysis of the nature of citizens' support for these bodies should focus on the EP. This is because, as a wealth of survey data demonstrates, it is the European institution citizens know best. Indeed, some Eurobarometer surveys asked interviewees whether they had ever heard about several European Union institutions and the results again show that the European Parliament is the

Table 7.1. "Have you heard of . . . ?" (Column percentages)

	EB52 (1999)		EB53 (2000)		EB57.1 (2002)		EB61.0 (2004)	
	Parliament	Commission	Parliament	Commission	Parliament	Commission	Parliament	Commission
Yes	93.9	85.6	92.6	81.9	90.8	80.4	92.6	83.2
No	6.1	14.4	7.4	18.1	9.2	19.6	7.4	16.8
N	15,586		16,078		16,012		16,082	

most familiar institution for EU citizens.[4] Table 7.1 shows the comparison between the EP and the European Commission for four Eurobarometer surveys.

We start with an exploration of trust trends in the EP between 1994 and 2005 for every member state, using Eurobarometer data.[5] The trends are presented by groups of countries according to their accession date (Niedermayer 1995a: 53–72). This way of presenting the information allows comparisons to be made between newcomers and old members and to check whether trust in institutions depends on how long a country has been part of the EU (i.e. the older the EU membership, the greater the support), as well as the impact—if any—of when each group joined the EU and of the level of domestic consensus on EU integration. As some scholars have argued (Anderson and Kaltenthaler 1996: 184–5), citizens of countries that joined the EU at different times and for different political and economic reasons might not only present different levels of European support but they might also react in dissimilar ways to the impact of integration, having been exposed to a longer and more positive initial process of socialization (Anderson and Reichert 1996: 237; Anderson and Kaltenthaler 1996: 177). Therefore, observing trends in trust in the EP among these groups of countries may give a clearer picture of the way citizens have responded to the various milestones in European integration and the consequent politicization process.

As shown by Figure 7.1, trust in the EP has risen among the six founding members, confirming findings in these countries concerning EU support. The former two German states (East Germany, of course, was not an EU member) have seen a remarkable growth in trust, though Luxembourg is the country that displayed the highest levels of trust in the EU throughout the period studied. If we consider the period from 1999 to 2006, trust in the EP remained between 50 and 70 per cent of the population. As shown by Figure 7.2, although trust began from much lower levels, the same trend can be seen in the three countries that joined the EU in the 1970s (Denmark, the United Kingdom, and the Irish Republic). These exhibit a slight increase in trust throughout the period depending on whether one begins the series in 1994 or in 1999.[6] The United Kingdom is a glaring exception, where overall levels of

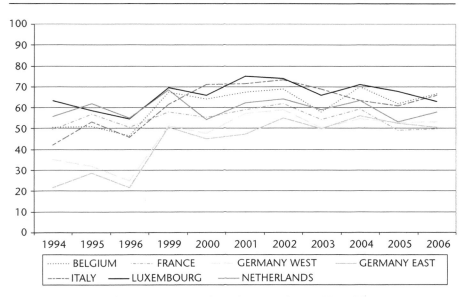

Figure 7.1. Trust in the EP among the founding members, 1994–2006

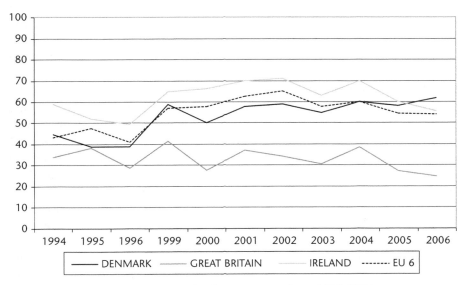

Figure 7.2. Trust in the EP among the first wave members, 1994–2006

147

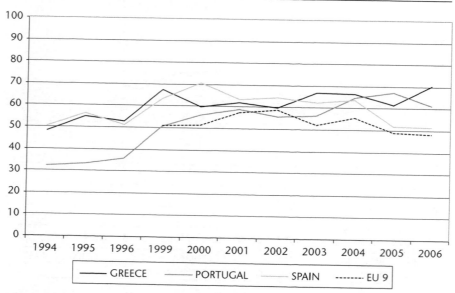

Figure 7.3. Trust in the EP among second-wave members, 1994–2006

trust were around 30 per cent and gradually declining. Even though EU integration is still an issue in some of these countries, it does not affect the level of general trust in the EP, as pointed out recently by other scholars regarding general support for the European integration process (Hooghe and Marks 2008: 9–10).

As Figure 7.3 shows, the second wave of EU accession countries during the 1980s (Greece, Spain, and Portugal) shows the same trends as the old nine member states. In this group, Portugal has gone from having the lowest percentage of people trusting the EP to having one of the highest ones (32 per cent to 68 per cent). Despite the differences, it should be noted that these three countries have a larger trusting population than the old nine members of the EU and the countries in the first wave of expansion (with the exception of the Irish Republic). However, the rise in trust in the EP has also been much more notable in the countries joining the EU in the 1980s, the only exceptions being the two German states and, to a lesser degree, Ireland.

Are the newcomers in general more prone to trust the EP because of the timing of their accession? Did they tend to improve the average trust in the EP because of when they joined? Figure 7.4 shows that third-wave members (Austria, Finland, and Sweden) have much lower average levels of support for the EP, although this rose markedly from 1999. Figure 7.5, which includes the ten post-communist countries that became new member states in the fourth wave, reveals that these had higher levels of trust in the EP, varying

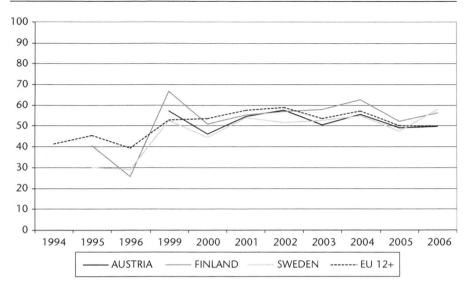

Figure 7.4. Trust in the EP among third-wave members, 1994–2006

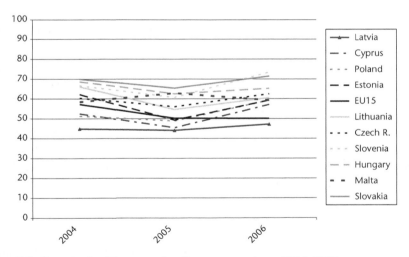

Figure 7.5. Trust in the EP among fourth-wave members, 1994–2006

between 50 and 70 per cent. In this case, it is better not to jump to conclusions about trust trends over time because only three time points are involved.

These data, then, show that there has been a slight tendency towards increasing trust in the EP in all countries, or at least relative stability after an initial surge (with the exception of nine of the ten first EU members). The increase was more dramatic among "the less-developed newcomers", although the last ten accession countries, from the former post-communist bloc, break the pattern one might expect among poorer newcomers. Contrary to the findings observed in support for European accession (Anderson and Kaltenthaler 1996), one cannot say that higher levels of trust in the EP are consistently associated with either those countries that formed the EU at the outset, with those that joined in a given wave of accessions, or with those that had particular political and economic reasons for entering the EU. Likewise, one cannot say that older members of the EU display a markedly more positive reaction to EU integration in terms of expressing greater trust in the EP—something that has been pointed out by various studies on general support for the EU integration process (Anderson and Reichert 1996; Anderson and Kaltenthaler 1996).

3. The correlations between trust in the EP and affective and subjective instrumental evaluations of the EU

The simple preceding analysis of the country-by-country trends in trust in the EP does not reveal how European citizens manage to express trust or distrust in the EP when they have no information with which to form a judgement. In order to test our central hypothesis, we explored the trend in the relationship between trust in the EP and our three variables: *trust in national parliaments* (as a cue of the political performance of the national system); the *desired speed of unification* (as an indicator of affective support for the EU); and evaluations of the *benefits received* by one's country from the EU (as an indicator of subjective instrumental evaluation). Before launching into the analysis, it should be pointed out that the use of the desired speed of unification to measure affective support for the EU integration process is an uncommon approach to researching attitudes towards the EU—though there are some exceptions to the rule (for instance, Sánchez-Cuenca 2000). However, there are at least three reasons why we consider this to be a better measure than the common Eurobarometer measure of support for EU unification. First, its wording remained constant across the time period analysed in this study, whereas the Eurobarometer surveys switched from referring to EU unification to European political union. Second, our indicator incorporates a more refined seven-point scale instead of the coarse "either/or" Eurobarometer approach. Third, the dynamic nature of our measure takes into account the evolving nature of the EU unification process (Malang 2010: 16). Our reasoning here is based on the idea that our preferred "unification speed" item measures support for EU expansion *and therefore itself changes with EU enlargement*. However, as we show in Figure 7.6, the average desired unification speed has remained largely stable throughout the period studied despite major EU expansion. This

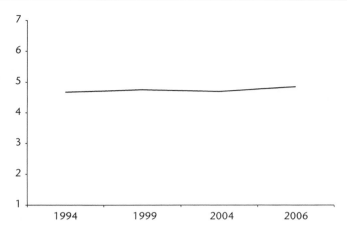

Figure 7.6. Trend in desired unification speed 1994–2006; (all-EU mean)

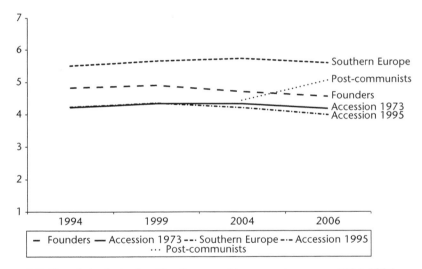

Figure 7.7. Trends in desired unification speed by accession wave, 1994–2006

can be interpreted as indicating a general continuation of the same underlying attitude in 1994 and 2006. Moreover, if the analysis is performed for groups of countries (see Figure 7.7), we can gather additional evidence for a steady pace in the integration desired by EU members. An exception to this is the post-communist group of countries, which sought faster integration between 2004 and 2006.

The correlations between trust in the EP and each of our three main predictor variables for the period 1999–2006 are shown in Figures 7.8, 7.9, and 7.10.

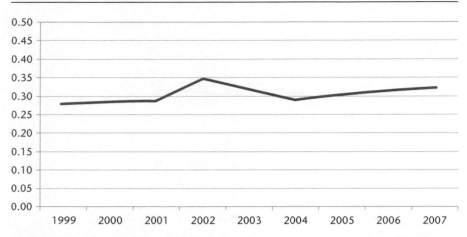

Figure 7.8. Aggregate-level correlation between trust in the EP and trust in national parliaments, 1999–2006 (all countries)

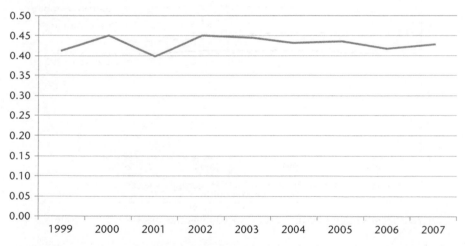

Figure 7.9. Aggregate-level correlation between trust in the EP and EU country benefit, 1996–2006 (all countries)

The figures collectively reveal a significant trend: while the correlation of EP with *EU membership benefit* is very *stable*, the *correlation* with the desired unification speed (the item used to measure affective support) *decreases* significantly. This indicates the decreasing relative importance of affective support over instrumental and political calculations during those years. Additionally,

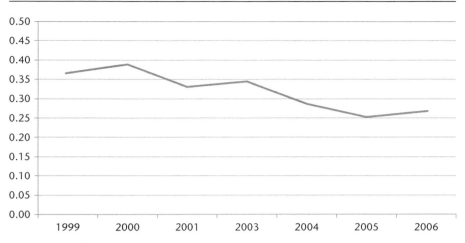

Figure 7.10. Aggregate-level correlation between trust in the EP and desired unification speed (affective support), 1999–2006 (all countries)

the correlation between trust in the EP and trust in national parliaments seems to be much more *unstable* and to offer distinctive fluctuation patterns, even though it remains fairly high overall. This evidence suggests that citizens may use these proxies when they are asked about their trust in the EP, but that they tend to use general support for the EU integration process less and less, thus giving more weight to subjective sociotropic instrumental evaluations and trust in their national parliaments. This confirms similar findings by other scholars studying general support for EU integration (Eichenberg and Dalton 1993; Anderson and Reichert 1996). While the *aggregate data* reported in Figures 7.8 to 7.10 seem to confirm the aforementioned trend, in the next section we refine the analysis and test whether the decreasing importance of affective support vis à vis subjective instrumental evaluations trust in the EP shows up at the *individual level* of analysis as well.

To what extent is this process the result of growing interest and/or political awareness in the EU in some of the countries under study? Lack of data prevents us from delving deeper into this topic (these items were only included in the surveys of 1994 and 2006). However, as can be seen from Figure 7.11, in 1994 there was a slight positive correlation between subjective instrumental evaluations and interest in politics, whereas affective support and interest were negatively correlated.[7] This evidence is already illustrative of the different natures of the two indicators. More important is the correlation between interest and subjective instrumental evaluations of the benefits of the EU, which rose markedly in 2006. The correlation here was statistically

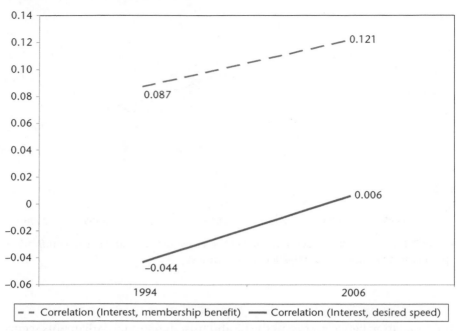

Figure 7.11. Change in the correlations between (a) interest in politics and EU membership benefit and (b) interest in politics and desired unification speed between 1994–2006

significant both for the countries included in 1994 (0.12) and for the larger group including post-communist latecomers (0.14), while the correlation between interest and affective support disappears altogether.

4. Models of trust in the EP: the waning impact of affective support

We argued in the previous section that citizens mainly rely on one heuristic and two political cues when asked whether they trust the EP: (1) trust in national institutions; (2) subjective sociotropic evaluations regarding EU membership; and (3) affective support for the integration process. In this section, we test different models to explain citizens' trust in the EP over time, using data from four selected Eurobarometer surveys: 1994 (EB 42.0), 1999 (EB 52.0), 2004 (EB 61.0), and 2006 (EB 66.1). There were three considerations in selecting the datasets, two of them practical and one substantive. The first was to ensure they covered the scope of our study. Second, they had to provide comparable data in the Eurobarometer series for the variables we were interested in. Third, they needed to encompass a crucial step in the integration process, namely the introduction of the euro. Availability of all the relevant variables determined the selection of these four specific surveys.

The three key independent variables to test these models were the same as in the analyses carried out in the previous section (trust in national parliament, country benefit, and desired unification speed). We also added a set of control variables that might influence the results. These included factors such as experience of living in the EU (age), cognitive mobilization (education and exposure to media information on TV),[8] and sex. As mentioned earlier, we considered that the process might be the result of the politicization of the EU integration issue by political parties (Hooghe and Marks 2008; Kriesi 2008) combined with an increasing awareness of the consequences of the EU integration process. Although it was not our intention to test the impact of this politicization process on the increasing instrumental nature of the EP support, we nevertheless had to control for its possible effects.

The use of the three proxy devices

Table 7.2 displays the results yielded by this model with all these variables for each of the selected years. The models displayed in this table show how the two political cues and the affective component, as predicted, actually play an important and separate role in explaining trust in the EP in the four years selected (1994, 1999, 2004, and 2006). Affective support for EU integration,

Table 7.2. Trust in the European Parliament: 1994, 1999, 2004 and 2006. (Logistic regression models, cluster-corrected standard errors)

	Model 1 1994 EB 42 b	Model 2 1999 EB52.0 b	Model 3 2004 EB61.0 b	Model 4 2006 EB 66.1 b
Age	−0.00	−0.00	0.00	−0.00
Male	−0.05	0.11	−0.21***	−0.05
Education		0.02	0.00	0.01
News on TV		0.12		
National parliament trust	1.78***	0.76***	1.16***	1.22***
Desired unification speed	2.17***	2.00***	1.76***	1.53***
EU membership benefit	0.91***	1.16***	1.53***	1.44***
Vote pro-European party		0.63***	0.60***	
Constant	−2.50***	−2.60***	−2.01***	−1.70***
N	7614	5434	6404	16,892
Log likelihood	−4013.27	−2780.64	−3051.43	−8943.20
df_m	5.00	8.00	7.00	6.00
chi2	320.60	1306.92	962.74	1933.09
Pseudo R2	0.21	0.20	0.23	0.19

* $p<0.1$; ** $p<0.05$; *** $p<0.01$

subjective benefit evaluation (as expressed by the perception of an actual benefit from the EU) and trust in national institutions all play a salient role in the models, with strong, highly significant coefficients. The impact of these variables remains strong despite the significant effect of the pro-/anti-European party-support variable present for the 1999 and 2004 data, a variable included to control for the effect of party cues that have been found to play an important role in shaping EU public opinion (Anderson 1998a; Ray 2003a; Hooghe and Marks 2005, 2008).

As Table 7.2 indicates, then, each of the three variables contributes to the explanation of trust in the EP.[9] These models are broadly consistent with the trends in the relative importance of these cues that we discussed previously, especially with regard to the decreasing coefficient for affective support (*desired unification speed*). Although the graphs and models are not directly comparable, conversion of these coefficients in Table 7.2 into odds ratios highlights the change. Here, the odds ratio for *desired unification speed* fell from 8.78 in 1994 to 4.63 in 2006. The reverse trend (albeit not so marked) emerged for instrumental support. Indeed, if we compare the odds ratios, affective support was 3.5 times stronger (8.8 versus 2.5) than instrumental support in 1999 but by 2006 there was little difference between the two kinds of support (4.63 vs 4.24, respectively).

The evolving determinants of trust in the European Parliament

Having shown that the three variables have a strong and statistically significant impact on trust in the EP, we further develop the analysis and directly test the indications we found in the aggregate graphs and in the models shown in Table 7.2. Our findings suggested a trend in the relative importance of these three heuristics that affect trust in the EP. Our hypothesis here, as noted earlier, is that *as citizens become more acquainted with the EP, they will rely more on instrumental support* (EU membership benefit) *and less on affective support* (desired unification speed). Thus as citizens gain a clearer sense of what EU institutions actually do, their evaluations should be more strongly linked to their fickle subjective evaluations of EU institutions' outcomes and other political and national institutional cues rather than to generic support for the integration process. We tested this hypothesis directly by pooling the four datasets and repeating the same analysis conducted in Table 7.2 in the pooled dataset. In doing so, we added two multiplicative interaction terms: one between time (years elapsed since 1992) and EU membership benefit; and one between time and desired unification speed. Any significant impact of the interactions would indicate an evolution in the influence of each of these cues on trust in the EP. The results in Table 7.3 confirm expectations: the interaction terms are both significant and run in the expected direction.

Table 7.3. The impact of the relationship between instrumental and affective support on trust in the EP, 1994–2006. (Logistic regression model, cluster-corrected standard errors)

	Pooled model 1994, 1999, 2004, 2006
	b
Age	−0.00
Male	−0.08**
National parliament trust	1.23***
Desired unification speed	0.32***
EU membership benefit	1.00***
Years since 1994	0.04**
Speed*Years	−0.01**
Benefit*Years	0.05**
Constant	−2.18***
N	39,049
Log likelihood	−20023.35
df_m	8.00
chi2	2607.12
Pseudo R2	0.20

* $p<0.1$; ** $p<0.05$; *** $p<0.01$

In 2006 the effect of *EU membership benefit* (instrumental support) was stronger than in 1994, while the contrary was true for affective support; its impact fell significantly throughout the 1994–2006 period.

To approach the actual trends expressed by these interaction terms, we repeated the analysis for selected pairs of years rather than for the whole period. Table 7.4 shows the results for the 1994–2006, 1999–2006 and 2004–6 models. It can be seen that the trend towards the growing role played by instrumental calculations was more marked than the waning impact of affective support for the EP, except for the short period between 2004 and 2006 when the biggest changes to EU institutions had already taken place (for example, the introduction of the euro)—a point we shall return to later on.

The predicted probabilities of trust in the EP as *EU membership benefit* and *desired unification speed* increase provide further evidence of this trend. The difference in predicted probabilities of trusting the EP between an average citizen wanting a freeze in EU unification to one wanting unification to advance as fast as possible fell from 0.42 in 1994 to 0.38 in 2006. This narrowing gap indicates the decreasing effect of affective support for the EU on trust in the EP. Comparing the degree of trust in the EP shown by citizens who believe their country has benefited from EU membership with that shown by citizens who hold the contrary view reveals a widening gap (from 0.20 in 1994 to 0.32 in 2006). Following Brambor, Clark, and Golder (2006: 74), we can illustrate the actual effects of the interaction terms by displaying

Table 7.4. Trends in the impact of the relationship between instrumental and affective support on trust in the EP, 1994–2006. (Logistic regression models, cluster-corrected standard errors)

	Model 1 1994–2006	Model 2 1999–2006	Model 3 2004–2006
	b	b	b
Age	−0.00	−0.00	−0.00
Male	−0.05	−0.05	−0.11**
National parliament trust	1.51***	1.02***	1.28***
Desired unification speed	2.10***	2.40***	1.85***
EU membership benefit	0.93***	1.38***	1.50***
Year	0.44*	0.50***	−0.06
Speed*Year	−0.08*	−0.13***	−0.05
Benefit*Year	0.62***	0.19*	0.06
Constant	−2.32***	−2.08***	−1.71***
N	18,634	20,962	21,493
Log likelihood	−9650.91	−10741.52	−10755.25
df_m	8.00	8.00	8.00
chi2	3483.52	1387.84	1347.39
Pseudo R2	0.21	0.19	0.21

* $p<0.1$; ** $p<0.05$; *** $p<0.01$

Table 7.5. Marginal effects of desired unification speed and perception of benefit on trust in the EP over time (and standard errors)

	1994	2006
Desired unification speed	0.50 (0.07)	0.43 (0.07)
EU membership benefit	0.22 (0.04)	0.20 (0.04)

the marginal effects of the constitutive variables (desired unification speed and EU membership benefit) as the modifying variable (year) changes. Table 7.5 shows these effects at the beginning and end of the period. As the signs of the interaction terms show, the effect of desired unification speed has fallen (despite the overall stability of this indicator noted earlier) while the contrary is true for EU membership benefit. However, the trend in the marginal effect is clearer for the former than for the latter.

The graphs in Figure 7.12 show that in 2006, the predicted probabilities of trust in the EP based on affective support rose at a slower pace than in 1994: the lines have a steeper slope in 1994 than in 2006. Also, the strongest effect of instrumental support is evident in the graphs, with a wider gap between the predicted probabilities in the case of those who thought EU membership had benefited their country (right-hand side of figure) than in the case of those who thought it had not (left-hand side of figure).

Table 7.6 shows the results of testing the impact of trust in the national parliament on trust in the EP from 1994 to 2006. Two opposing hypotheses

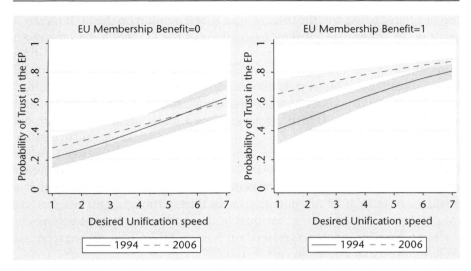

Figure 7.12. 95% confidence interval of the predicted probability of trusting the EP as instrumental and affective support change, 1994 and 2006

Table 7.6. Trends in the relationship between trust in national parliament and trust in the EP, 1994–2006. (Logistic regression models, cluster-corrected standard errors)

	Model 1 1994–2006	Model 2 1999–2006	Model 3 2004–2006
	b	b	b
Age	−0.00	−0.00	−0.00
Gender	−0.04	−0.05	−0.11**
Trust national parliament	1.80***	0.72***	1.25***
Desired unification speed	0.32***	0.34***	0.26***
EU membership benefit	0.92***	1.39***	1.50***
Year	0.77**	0.19	−0.08
Trust national parliament*Year	−0.50**	0.58***	0.05
Speed*Year	−0.10**	−0.12***	−0.05
Benefit*Year	0.64***	0.16*	0.06
Constant	−2.54***	−1.90***	−1.70***
N	18,634	20,962	21,493
Log likelihood	−9627.73	−10704.94	−10755.04
df_m	9.00	9.00	9.00
chi2	3486.02	1326.98	1445.14
Pseudo R2	0.21	0.20	0.21

* p<0.1; ** p<0.05; *** p<0.01

can be offered to explain the trend. One is that if opinion on the EU is merely a question of knowledge, citizens' evaluations of the EU should become more independent from national cues as they learn more about community institutions. If this is the case, one should find a *declining* influence of trust in the national parliament on trust in the EP, mirroring our finding regarding affective support. On the other hand, if the politicization hypothesis is right and attitudes towards the EU institutions are increasingly influenced by national political evaluations, the effect of the national cues should *increase* over time.

The results reported in Table 7.6 show that the interaction between *trust in national parliament* and the time variable takes a different sign in different models. This indicates that the influence of trust in national parliament as a predictor of trust in EP has fluctuated over time, although remaining strong overall. This in turn suggests that trust in the *national* parliament behaves in the same unstable manner as general support for EU unification—as reported by Ray (2003a and 2003b) in earlier studies.

5. Causal mechanisms underpinning the trend: institutionalization or cumulative knowledge?

How can we explain this pattern of changing effects over time and what are the causal mechanisms driving it? Our hypothesis states that as citizens become better acquainted with EU institutions (interacting with the EU politicization process), their evaluations tend to depend more on instrumental subjective evaluations and less on affective support for EU integration. Two causal mechanisms can be posited for this trend. First, it is possible that the institutional development of the EU, which is becoming more and more relevant to citizens' everyday lives, independently of the level of party politicization, makes citizens more aware of the actual performance of European institutions and how they are affected by them. The second possibility is that there is a more simple "time effect" linked to a process of cumulative acquisition of information about the EU by citizens. As time goes by, the continuous presence of the EU in the national media makes citizens increasingly familiar with the EU's institutional activity. This in turn enhances citizens' ability to base their evaluations on instrumental considerations rather than having to rely on affective support for the European integration to evaluate the workings and performance of EU institutions (Anderson and Kaltenthaler 1996).

Which of these two mechanisms explains the trend we have identified? Distinguishing between the two mechanisms is not straightforward, since they suffer from observational equivalence: both can be thought of as linear processes: as time goes by, both *institutionalization* and *cumulative knowledge* increase. How can the problem of observational equivalence be overcome, enabling these two causal mechanisms to be disentangled and tested independently? We came up with three observable implications of the two mechanisms that would permit an empirical analysis to distinguish between the two: (1) the effects of the introduction of the euro; (2) the consequences of different waves of accession; (3) the impact of the age of respondents.

The introduction of the euro

One can take advantage of a natural quasi-experiment[10] to overcome this problem, following a similar strategy to the one adopted by Ray (2003a: 989–90) for estimating the effects of the ratification of the Treaty on European Union in 1992. The introduction of the euro was the most visible form of the EU's "reinforced cooperation" as far as ordinary citizens were concerned. Joining the eurozone potentially had important consequences for many of the citizens of the participating countries. For example, the abandonment of long-standing national currencies could have repesented an important symbolic and cultural break or disruption for some citizens (Hymans 2006). It could also have been the case that the level of acceptance of the euro differed across European countries (Anderson 2006). The euro might also have had the most tangible and controversial consequences since the start of the European integration process,[11] given that it affected key exchange aspects of citizens' everyday lives (Fishman 2006: 2). In particular, the euro could reasonably be expected to have made the consequences of European integration much clearer to the average citizen. More than any other institutional development, the euro made people realize that the European project was developing in ways that they had not thought of before. The euro, in short, made Europe real (Risse 2006), and therefore increased the level of European awareness. This increased awareness allowed citizens to distinguish their diffuse/affective support for the EU from the evaluative/instrumental one, making them go beyond the so-called *permissive consensus* (Franklin, Marsh, and McLaren 1994; Ray 2003a). As we have said, the levels of both types of support may have changed little but the weight given by citizens to each of them when they expressed their views on the EU's institutional development and performance might have changed.

Given that our sample includes countries that adopted the euro (treatment group) and countries that did not (control group), we can test the effect of institutional development separately from the effect of time. If this is the relevant mechanism, the trend towards a greater impact of instrumental support should be clearer in the eurozone than in those countries in which the institutional development of the EU has been slower and/or less visible. Therefore, in Table 7.7 we replicate the analysis carried out in Table 7.2 separately for the eurozone and the remaining member states. If the

Table 7.7. Relationship between instrumental and affective support with trust in the EP in Eurozone and non-Euro countries, 1999–2006. (Logistic regression models, cluster-corrected standard errors)

	Model 1 Eurozone	Model 2 Non-Euro countries
	b	b
Age	−0.00	0.00
Male	−0.02	−0.13
Education	−0.00	0.01
National parliament trust	1.05***	1.16***
Desired unification speed	0.31***	0.34***
EU membership benefit	1.37***	1.40***
Year	0.55***	0.37
Speed*Year	−0.14***	−0.07
Benefit*Year	0.20**	0.20
Constant	−1.87***	−2.85***
N	15,654	4017
Log likelihood	−7900.60	−2163.14
df_m	9.00	1.00
chi2	1827.54	.
Pseudo R2	0.18	0.22

* $p<0.1$; ** $p<0.05$; *** $p<0.01$

institutionalization argument holds, the trend we observed before (i.e. towards a greater impact of instrumental support on trust and a diminishing impact of affective support) should be stronger in the eurozone than in the non-euro countries.

The results of the estimation of the models in Table 7.7 show how the trend identified in Table 7.2 is indeed concentrated within the eurozone and does not take place in the non-euro countries—both of the *Year interaction terms are non-significant in the non-eurozone equation. This result strongly supports the idea of institutional development and the awareness that goes with it as the driving force behind trends in the determinants of trust in the EP identified in the previous section.

The year of accession to the EU

A second way of distinguishing between the two mechanisms is based on the successive waves of EU accession. If the cumulative-knowledge hypothesis is correct, one would expect to see stronger affective support effects in newer EU members than in longer-standing EU countries. Conversely, the reverse should be true for the impact of instrumental support: it should be stronger in the older EU countries, since their citizens will have had more time to gain knowledge of the working of the EU institutions. Table 7.8 compares the odds ratios for every group of countries for the three years studied to ascertain

Table 7.8. Instrumental and affective support for the EP over time, by groups of countries (1994–2006)—Odds ratios

	1994		1999		2004		2006	
	Desired unification speed	EU membership benefit	Desired unification speed	EU membership benefit	Desired unification speed	EU membership benefit	Desired unification speed	EU membership benefit
Founders	7.72***	3.22***	10.23***	2.97***	4.55***	4.74***	3.97***	3.11***
UK, Ireland, DK	11.37***	3.22***	4.89***	5.73***	4.93***	5.82***	4.75***	6.71***
Southern Europe	6.15***	1.29	4.98***	3.90***	4.50***	6.05***	1.34	5.30***
Austria, Finland, Sweden	N/A	N/A	5.54***	5.73***	4.69***	3.55***	3.13***	5.20***
post-com	N/A	N/A	8.10***	3.23***	2.91***	2.90***	2.95***	5.16***

*** p<0.01

Note: Table entries are odds ratios for the effect of the two variables from a model where Trust in the European Parliament is the dependent variable; and age, gender, trust in national parliament, desired unification speed and EU membership benefit are the independent variables.

whether instrumental support really plays a bigger role in predicting trust in the EP in longer-standing EU members and whether affective support is stronger in the latecomers. As the table indicates, no clear pattern emerges: having been in the EU for longer does not make citizens more likely to base their views on political cues than on affective support. Likewise, there is no evidence that the trend exhibits systematic differences between the various groups. Belonging to the EU for longer therefore seems to have *no* impact on the relative weights given to subjective instrumental evaluation and affective support in determining citizens' trust in the EP.

Generational gap

Finally, we can also test for another possible implication of the "time effect": if knowledge accumulation is the mechanism weakening affective support and strengthening subjective instrumental support, we should see instrumental support having a greater impact among older generations than younger ones, given that the former have had more time to accumulate knowledge and were socialized in a different, more pro-EU context (see Anderson and Kaltenthaler 1996). Conversely, if the relevant mechanism is just institutional development, we should not find any significant age gap.

To test this implication, we divided the sample into two generational groups varying from country to country. One group included all those who, when their country entered the EU, were 25 or older and the other those who were under 25 at accession. The rationale behind this operationalization is that the accumulation of knowledge will be greater among those who were already adults when their country joined the EU and who have thus been exposed longer as adults to EU-related inputs. Then we re-estimated the models from Table 7.2 but included two interaction terms: one between generation (as defined here) and *EU membership benefit*, and the other one between generation and *desired unification speed*. Table 7.9 shows the results of the models.

Table 7.9 shows that there is some partial (although not completely consistent) evidence of this age gap: the effect of *EU membership benefit* appears to be stronger in those who were 25 or older when their countries joined the EU than for the younger generations. According to our argument, this might express a *knowledge-accumulation effect* that could help explain why we found instrumental support grew at the expense of affective support with time in explaining trust in the EP.

A post-communist effect?

There is, however, an additional aspect that should be tested in our argument. The level of political awareness of the EU issue seems to be higher in

Table 7.9. Generational gap in the relationship between instrumental and affective support with trust in the EP (1994–2006) (Logistic regression models, cluster-corrected standard errors)

	Model 1 1994	Model 2 1999	Model 3 2004	Model 4 2006
	b	b	b	b
Male	−0.05	0.03	−0.28***	−0.05
Education		0.02	−0.00	0.00
National parliament trust	−1.78***	0.77***	1.30***	1.23***
Desired unification speed	1.98***	2.12***	1.56***	1.49***
EU membership benefit	0.88***	1.17***	1.55***	1.29***
Generation	−0.54***	−0.39**	−0.29	−0.17
Benefit *Generation	0.08	0.43**	−0.00	0.53***
Speed* Generation	0.07	0.26*	0.35	0.07
Constant	1.22***	−1.73***	−1.32***	−1.62***
N	7616	8842	9471	16,892
Log likelihood	−4007.25	−4482.69	−4683.34	−8913.54
df_m	7.00	8.00	8.00	8.00
chi2	1037.66	5968.44	2904.23	2931.66
Pseudo R2	0.21	0.20	0.23	0.20

* $p<0.1$; ** $p<0.05$; *** $p<0.01$

post-communist countries. This could be due to the presence of distinctive ideological interpretations of the EU integration process and its consequences; the effects of particular national political cueing in those countries; variations in the dimensions of party competition; or the existence of different winners and losers associated with the integration process (Cichowski 2000; Tucker, Pacek, and Berinsky 2002; Rohrschneider and Whitefield 2004, 2006a, 2006b; Christin 2005; Marks et al. 2006). Therefore, evaluations of the EU and the integration process could be different in the post-communist countries and consequently the impact of subjective instrumental evaluations might be distinctive and clearer.[12] To test for this possibility, we repeated the model for 2006 with two additional variables, a dummy variable that identifies post-communist countries and interactions between each proxy and the post-communism dummy. The results of this model in Table 7.10 indicate that the interaction between post-communist status and the benefits term is positive and significant. Trust in the EP among post-communist citizens tends to depend more on instrumental cost–benefit calculations, although the differential effect is low (Christin 2005). Additionally, the coefficient of the other interaction goes in the expected direction and is negative: citizens of post-communist countries tend to depend less on affective heuristics but this is not statistically significant. In short, therefore, there are some indications that the impact on EP trust of subjective sociotropic evaluations vis à vis affective support is greater in post-communist countries

Table 7.10. Trust in the EP in post-Communist countries vs. the rest (2006) (Logistic regression model, cluster-corrected standard errors)

	2006 EB 66.1
	b
Age	−0.00
Male	−0.04
Education	0.01
National parliament trust	1.30***
Desired unification speed	1.50***
EU membership benefit	1.36***
Post-communist country	0.63
Speed* Post-Communist	−0.41
Benefit* Post-Communist	0.28*
Constant	−1.79***
N	16,353
Log likelihood	−8593.04
df_m	9.00
chi2	2113.98
Pseudo R2	0.20

* $p<0.1$; ** $p<0.05$; *** $p<0.01$

than in the other EU member states. This is consistent with the lower exposure to the traditional European ideology of these countries' citizens and the greater comparative impact of instrumental evaluations when it comes to explaining EU support (Cichowski 2000; Tucker, Pacek, and Berinsky 2002; Christin 2005; Marks et al. 2006). This evidence confirms our main findings and hypotheses that the changing nature of EU support depends on politicization and awareness.

Conclusions

How is European citizens' trust in EU institutions formed? The analysis here shows that Europeans fall back on the use of three attitudinal variables similar to the ones conditioning their support for the EU in general: affective support for the EU; subjective sociotropic evaluations of the integration process; and a set of national political cues. However, as noted in the analyses of the support for the EU integration process, the relative strength of these variables has been changing since the mid-1990s. Affective mechanisms of support, which were so powerful during the times of the *permissive consensus*, are being replaced by subjective instrumental calculations and national political cues. This process is the result of EU citizens' growing political awareness of the consequences of EU integration and its policies. In particular, we showed that this process is the result of the increasing awareness of EU integration fostered by the introduction of the euro. However, we are aware that this process is strongly linked to the increasing politicization of the EU issue in some of the EU member states. Subjective sociotropic evaluations and increasing use of national political cues are endogenous to the political system, and are induced by the conflicts and political discourses of party elites. At the same time, increasing political awareness of the consequences of EU integration is changing the nature of support, regardless of changing levels of politicization of the EU issue. As Hooghe and Marks (2008) have argued, we are in an era of *constraining dissensus* when it comes to the EU integration process. This helps to explain why increasing levels of political knowledge and awareness of the EU do not reduce the extent which people use their subjective evaluations of institutional performance or national political cues when they express their trust or distrust of EU institutions.

Notes

1. For the discussion of this concept, see Zaller (1992: 20–3).
2. For a different position on this deterioration process, see Janssen (1991).
3. In other words, there is an increasing level of politicization of the European integration process in some countries by some of the non-main parties taking advantage of the increasing visibility of some of the problems of integration and the passivity of the major political parties (Hooghe and Marks 2008; Kriesi 2008).
4. The question asked used to be: "Have you heard of . . . the European Parliament/the European Commission/the Council of Ministers/the Court of Justice/the European Ombudsman/the European Central Bank/the European Court of Auditors/the Committee of Regions/the Social and Economic Committee?"
5. We have selected the autumn round of EB studies for each year.
6. We should mention that there are two different indicators used in this series: for the years 1994, 1995, 1996 the data are obtained from a different question than for the rest of the years. For 1994–6: "Many important decisions are made by the European Union. They might be in the interest of people like yourself, or they might not. To what extent do you feel you can rely on each of the following institutions to make sure that the decisions taken by this institution are in the interest of people like yourself?" The European Parliament goes just after the question for the national government. For the remaining years "For each of the following European institutions please tell me if you tend to trust it or you tend not to trust it?" where the European Parliament is the first item in the battery of questions. This may affect the trends identified and should be taken into account.
7. Zaller (1992: 21–2) argues that political awareness is not the same as political interest and that the former can only be measured by factual political knowledge, but unfortunately this information was not included in these particular surveys.
8. This variable was only available for the 1999 survey.

9. To control for potential endogeneity problems, we replicated the models in Table 7.2 using maximum likelihood estimation of probit models for endogenous regressors with instrumental variables. The variables "desired unification speed" and "EU membership benefit" were instrumented using exogenous regressors (exogenous variables: age, gender, education, size of habitat, occupation, marital status, satisfaction with life, and country of residence). The results (not shown) revealed how the instrument for desired unification speed is a statistically significant predictor of trust in the EP for the four years covered by this study. By contrast, the instrumental variable for EU membership benefit had a significant impact in 2004 and 2006 but not in 1994 (in 1999 the model does not converge). These results are in line with what we find in Tables 7.3 to 7.9.

10. Certainly, this is far from being an experimental design as the selection of the treatment and control groups is not random, but linked to scepticism about the new currency in those countries that opted out of the euro (UK, Denmark, Sweden) and thus somewhat endogenous to the dependent and independent variables. However, it is harder to think of it as endogenous to the trends in specific and diffuse support regarding trust in the EP.

11. For an excellent controversy about this issue, see Fishman (2006) and Risse (2006).

12. However, it does not affect the findings on trends in the relative weights of the two proxies shown in Tables 7.2, 7.3, and 7.4, since in the merged models, we can only use those countries that were EU members over the whole period. Therefore, the only post-communist unit present in the diachronic analyses is East Germany.

8

Support for European Integration

Andrija Henjak, Gábor Tóka, and David Sanders

This chapter examines generalized support for the EU rather than attitudes towards specific institutions and policies. We subject theories about its origin to more comprehensive empirical tests than previous analyses attempted: we cover all member states from the 1970s to 2007 and simultaneously consider most micro- and macro-level explanations hitherto proposed in the literature. We argue that common typologies dividing empirical determinants of EU support into categories like rational cost–benefit calculus, identity, cue-taking from trusted sources and cognitive mobilization are rarely as clear cut as they are presented. Nonetheless, we attempt to operationalize a number of important theoretical claims about the sources of EU support.

We focus our efforts on three main theoretical perspectives. The first involves "hard" *instrumental rational choice* approaches that attempt to assess the effects of the utility calculations which citizens make about the relative costs and benefits engendered by EU membership. The core hypothesis is that support for the EU is likely to be strongest among those who perceive that they clearly benefit from it. The second approach involves "soft" *low information cueing rationality*, in which citizens use heuristic shortcuts to make judgements about the EU based on their assessments of more familiar institutions or actors. We distinguish between "transfer cueing", where citizens directly translate their positive (negative) assessments of national institutions into positive (negative) assessments of the EU, and "substitution cueing", where citizens' negative (positive) assessments of domestic institutions lead them to take a more positive (negative) view of the EU. The third approach is *cognitive mobilization*. The central idea here is that higher levels of education, political awareness, and engagement encourage people to be more cosmopolitan in their world views, thereby making it more likely that they will support supranational integration also in the European context.

In relation to each of these three approaches, it is by no means easy to find reliable operational measures of the signature concepts involved. Nonetheless, a plausible case can be made that the indicators we present below do capture key aspects of the concepts they purport to operationalize. The same cannot be said of a fourth perspective, the "identitarian" approach, which we deliberately exclude from our analysis. This exclusion does *not* reflect a conviction on our part that there is anything intrinsically wrong with identitarian theory— on the contrary, the idea that a stronger sense of European identity is likely to foster greater support for the EU has a good deal of face plausibility. Rather, it reflects the sparseness of suitable identity measures that we could incorporate in our empirical analysis. Although such measures do exist, they cover such limited time periods and so few countries (see Isernia et al. 2012) that our empirical analysis would be unacceptably impoverished were we to include them in our statistical estimations. However, in addition to considering the three core theoretical perspectives mentioned above, we do seek to assess the effects of several further possible causal factors that lie outside their ambit. We accordingly investigate the potential ad hoc effects on EU support of (a) the coincidence of a country's accession to the EU with its status as a "third-wave democracy"; (b) the extent to which each country exhibits centralized wage bargaining; and (c) the overall volume of EU legislation.

In Section 1, we update the available time-series data on EU support and highlight the main variations in support across member states and over time. Section 2 summarizes extant theories about the origins of this variation. Section 3 lists the specific theoretical propositions that we test, discusses their underlying assumptions, and outlines the operational measures that we deploy. Section 4 presents our empirical analyses of the changing economic and political circumstances as well as individual characteristics that account for variation in EU support across time, space, and individuals. The empirical results we report suggest that there is a clear explanatory role for all three of our main perspectives. However, our findings also indicate that the main drivers of EU support across time and space relate primarily to variations in economic and political conditions *within* nation states rather than in matters relating to the EU itself. Broadly, the better things are at home, the more people seem to value the EU; the worse things are, the less they value it.

1. Generalized support: measurement and trends

Our analysis, like most previous studies, relies on the Eurobarometer series, which has fielded surveys in all EC/EU member states every year since 1973 (cf. Schmitt 2003a). The Eurobarometers and the Candidate Countries Eurobarometers also provide similar survey data for new member states in the last (few) year(s) before their accession to the union. The differences between the multiple surveys conducted in the same country within the same calendar year are largely irrelevant and ignored here since quarterly or monthly data are only available for a few plausible determinants of EU support. Thus we pool together all such surveys and treat the nearly 500 individual country years—starting with nine observations in 1973 and ending with twenty-seven in 2007, corresponding to the number of member states in the given years—as the aggregate level in our analysis. We examine the factors that cause variation in EU support both across country years and across individuals nested within each of those country years.

The Eurobarometers feature several measures of generalized support for integration, but only one was administered in nearly all years, having been omitted only from the pre-1973 studies. Therefore this chapter, just like much of the literature, mostly relies on this item, which gauges support for membership by asking: "Generally speaking, do you think that [NAME OF RESPONDENT'S COUNTRY]'s membership of the . . . [COMMON MARKET, EUROPEAN COMMUNITY, EUROPEAN UNION] is a good thing, neither good nor bad, or a bad thing?" For ease of interpretation and analysis, we recode the responses to a 0–100 scale so that 100 and 0 stand for evaluating membership as "a good thing" and "a bad thing", respectively, with "neither good nor bad" coded as 50. "Don't know" and other missing responses were replaced using the multiple imputation procedure of the Amelia 2 software (see Honaker et al. 2007). This imputation is superior to ignoring such responses or replacing with the mean because non-responses to attitude items tend to come from somewhat distinct population groups in terms of opinion profiles (cf. Berinsky 2004). Imputation removes any comparability problems that could arise from variation across countries and years in the frequency and origin of non-responses.

The interpretation of our dependent variable as a measure of generalized support is relatively straightforward. Although the object of evaluation is not integration per se, we suspect that few ordinary citizens display the advanced sophistry of maintaining separate opinions about European integration in general on the one hand, and their own country's EU membership on the other. Rather, the EU membership question measures support for integration in the most natural way for citizens, exactly as they are most likely to encounter the issue in everyday discourse and political practice. The question wording is very general: unlike other similar items in the Eurobarometers, this one does not frame the issue through specific aspects like a given policy domain or the speed and extent to which integration should be advanced. Instead, it focuses on the general but nevertheless simple evaluation of EU membership of the respondent's own country. There is considerable merit in this very concrete question compared to asking citizens, as other Eurobarometer items do, about "further" and/or "faster" integration in some unspecified direction, which inevitably remains open to different interpretations by different respondents. It may be a limitation that the item focuses on a specific country's membership rather than the idea of European unity in general, or that the wording seems implicitly to invite rather utilitarian evaluations (Eichenberg and Dalton 2003). Yet the sample mean of this item correlates at $r = 0.93$ with the similar mean of an alternative item, which is available for 276 of the country years in our analysis, and asks "If you were to be told tomorrow that the... [COMMON MARKET, EUROPEAN COMMUNITY, EUROPEAN UNION] had been scrapped, would you be very sorry about it, indifferent or very relieved?" This strong correlation makes us confident that our dependent variable, at least at the aggregate level, is a highly reliable tool for detecting patterns in support for the EU.

It has been argued that support for the extension of EU competence into various policy domains is in fact a better measure of generalized support for integration than our dependent variable (cf. Magalhães 2012). We concur that there is only a moderately strong correlation between these two measures of EU support, and that—as a comparison between our results and those of Magalhães in this volume will demonstrate—opinions about membership may be more responsive to short-term factors than preferences about the EU's policy scope. This looks reasonable given that policy integration does not change its substantive meaning over time as much as EU membership. Integrating, say, foreign policy has carried more or less the same meaning since the early 1970s. In contrast, approving of France's membership in the Common Market in 1973 was not the same as approving of France's membership in the much larger, more elaborate, and much more closely integrated EU of 2007. It follows that, if preferences for the integration of *particular policies* were *unchanging*, support for *membership* would *decline,* as membership comes to entail a higher level of integration, which increasing numbers of people find exaggerated. Put differently, a constant level of support for membership in a deepening union means, implicitly, increasing support for policy integration, and thus membership support is indeed a somewhat misleading measure of support for integration. This said, membership does nonetheless have a distinct meaning and importance that emerge from the fact that it amounts to a holistic evaluation of the union, closely connected to voting behaviour in, for instance, accession referendums.

Table 8.1 illustrates this last point. Here we look at the impact of membership evaluation and preferences for policy integration on voting behaviour in the pre-accession referendums of the nine countries that joined in the 2004 accession wave (the data are not available for Cyprus). As is evident from Table 8.1, evaluation of membership shows a much stronger impact on vote choice in accession referenda than does Magalhães's (2012) summary

Table 8.1. The predictive power of evaluations of EU-membership and a summary of preferences regarding policy integration in models of Vote Choice (yes or no) in nine accession referendums, 2003

Predictor:	Membership good or bad	No. of policies to be integrated
Czech Rep.	0.71	0.25
Estonia	0.65	0.13
Hungary	0.57	0.16
Latvia	0.61	0.11
Lithuania	0.56	0.15
Malta	0.79	0.38
Poland	0.61	0.18
Slovakia	0.67	0.25
Slovenia	0.45	0.13

Notes: Table entries are Nagelkerke R^2 values from bivariate logistic regressions calculated by the authors using data from the October–November 2003 Candidate Countries Eurobarometer. The dependent variable is how the respondent voted in the national referendum on EU membership (Yes = 1; 0 = No).

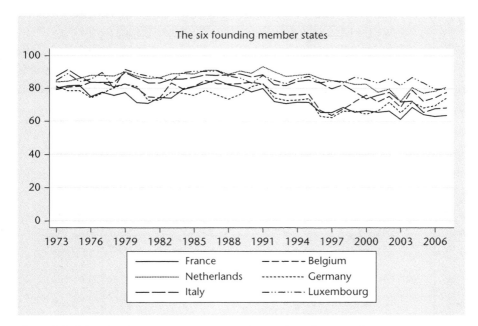

Figure 8.1. Membership support over time; the six founding member states

measure of preferences for policy integration. Thus, support for membership is naturally more than just a reflection of preferences for policy integration. In spite of its specificity, it is probably the most general evaluation of the EU that ordinary Europeans—who, after all, are citizens of the union only on account of their nationality—are ever likely to make as political actors.

We now proceed to a review of trends over time and across countries in generalized EU support. Figures 8.1 to 8.6 show the mean value of our

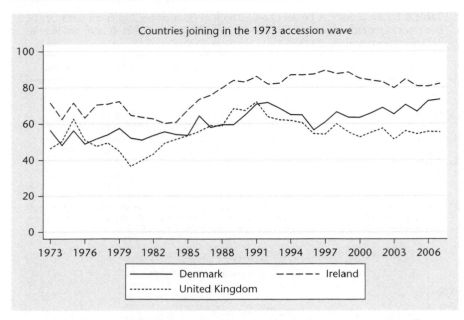

Figure 8.2. Membership support over time; countries joining in the 1973 accession wave

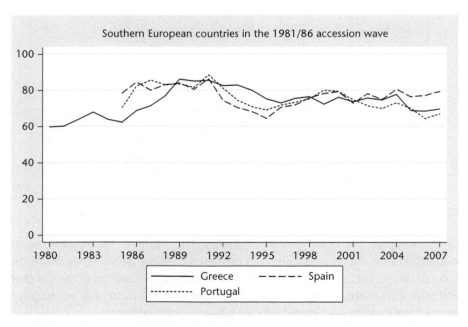

Figure 8.3. Membership support over time; southern European countries in the 1981/86 accession wave

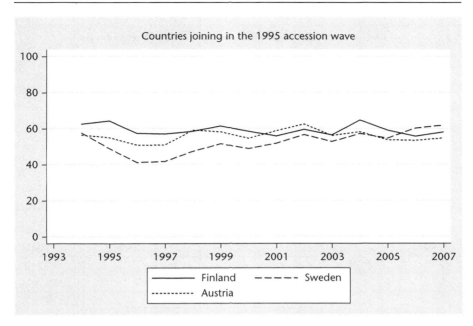

Figure 8.4. Membership support over time; countries joining in the 1995 accession wave

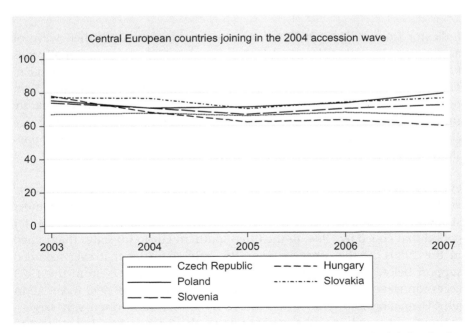

Figure 8.5. Membership support over time; central European countries joining in the 2004 accession wave

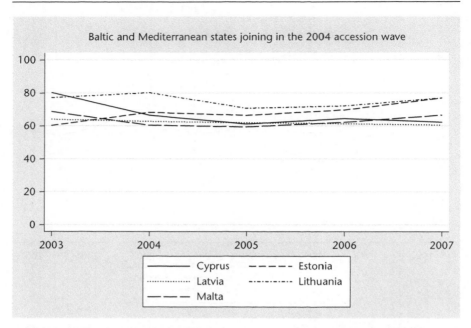

Figure 8.6. Membership support over time; Baltic and Mediterranean states joining in the 2004 accession wave

indicator from 1973 to 2007 for member states grouped by their wave of accession.[1] The first striking fact is that support only very exceptionally falls below 50 points, i.e. to the point where more people find membership a bad rather than a good thing. This only ever happened in Sweden and the UK, in both cases just for a few years following their entry in the union. It is hardly surprising, however, that support is more frequent than opposition: since accession is naturally tied to a democratic decision, the countries with opposition majorities are unlikely to join in the first place.

It is more remarkable that for most country years, support varies within the even further restricted range between 60 and 80 on our 100-point scale. Higher values than this were only ever recorded in the founding member states; then, in Ireland from the end of the 1980s; and, for a somewhat shorter period that ended by 1994, in the three Southern European states that joined in the 1980s. At the other extreme, the only countries that ever recorded support below the 60-point mark are Denmark and the UK from the 1973 accession wave and Austria, Finland, and Sweden from the 1995 wave. All in all, EU membership tends to be valued by a clear—and often very large—majority of the public in the member states, though it has rarely got close to being generally accepted.

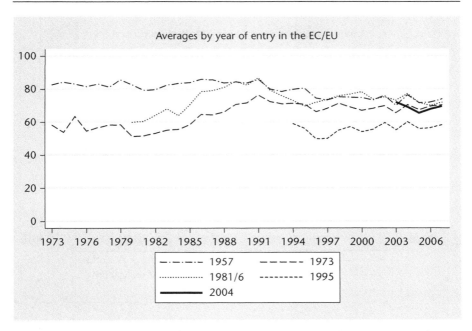

Figure 8.7. Membership support over time; averages by year of entry in the EC/EU

Since the early 1970s, support for membership gradually dropped in nearly all of the six initial members, but increased in the countries that joined in 1973 (see Figure 8.7). Elsewhere, only a few countries show either downward or upward movement over the whole period—Hungary and Portugal exemplify the first while Estonia, Greece, and Poland the second development—and trendless country-specific fluctuations rather than across-the-board trends prevail. In terms of EU support among citizens, the six founding members became more heterogeneous over time, while the countries in the different accession waves remained internally as diverse as ever, even if a few leap-frogged others in the degree of enthusiasm for membership.

All in all, a period of "permissive consensus" only ever existed among mass publics in the six initial members—all later entrants started off with significantly less enthusiasm for union than the EU6 displayed at the time of the first enlargement in 1973. Nonetheless, supporters came persistently to outnumber doubters in all member states—even, within two years of its accession, in the reputedly eurosceptic UK. As Figure 8.7 also shows, the initial differences between countries tended to persist, yet the low and high points of support in the series for a country are often separated by 20 or more points, as in France, Germany, Greece, Ireland, Sweden, and Italy. The figure also indicates that support for membership was less variable by accession wave in 2007 than in 1973. Indeed, the cross-country standard deviation in support was about half

177

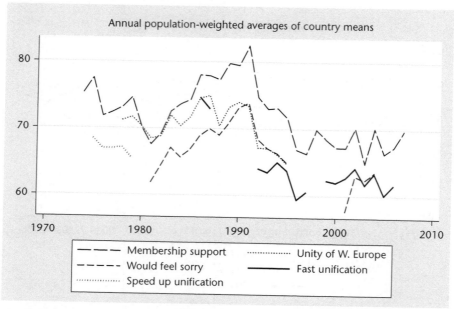

Figure 8.8. The all-EU trend in five measures of support; annual population-weighted averages of country means

as big in 2007 than at its historical peak, just before Greece's accession in 1981 (data not shown).

Figure 8.8 examines the over-time trend for the entire EC/EU and weights countries by their population size in calculating the all-union mean for each calendar year. It also shows the same population-weighted mean for all other indicators of generalized EU support available in the Eurobarometers, which were all converted to a 0–100 scale for the purpose of this comparison (for the wording of these items, see the Appendix). These other items solicit less EU enthusiasm than the question on membership support, but appear to reveal much the same temporal pattern. Support declined in the second half of the 1970s and the first half of the 1990s, but increased almost continuously throughout the 1980s. The last decade witnessed relatively minor and annually pulsating changes in the all-EU level. Overall, membership support was about 6 per cent lower in the EU as a whole in 2007 than in 1973. This decline occurred in spite of the relatively high levels of Euro support in 2007 in Spain, Poland, and Romania, the countries whose accession accounted for the bulk of the EU's population growth in the period.

Comparing our findings with the long-term trends reported by Isernia et al. and Magalhães in this volume, we observe that support for membership exhibited a probably larger temporal shift than the incidence of European identity or support for policy integration. Moreover, neither identification with Europe nor public support for the integration of policies with a high degree of "inherent internationalization" shows the significant decline over time that we see in the case of membership support. What this suggests to us is once again that membership support is more sensitive than European identity or support for policy integration to the changing meaning of union membership in the context of deeper and broader integration. The next section prepares the way for a multivariate analysis of the roots of EU support by reviewing the propositions of the previous literature about the factors that may explain variation across countries, time, and individuals.

2. Sources of public support for the EC/EU in the previous literature

The earliest studies of public opinion about European integration had little reason to probe the roots of cross-national and over-time variation as the core West European countries of concern at the time were all characterized by relatively high levels of support. Instead, these early studies focused on the role of individual-level factors (Inglehart 1970a, 1970b). However, subsequent enlargement waves and the Maastricht, Amsterdam, and Nice treaties deepened integration, and the political controversies that they triggered apparently ended the era of permissive consensus between political elites and mass publics over the nature of the integration process (Hooghe and Marks 2008). On Handley's (1981) account, this decline in EU support had already been foreshadowed by the recession of the 1970s and by the difficulties with the integration process that were being experienced at the time. In any case, a lively industry of studies, started by Inglehart and Rabier (1978) and extended by Eichenberg and Dalton (1993), has provided statistical tests for a variety of contextual influences on both the level and the within-country determinants of EU support. In addition, studies of individual-level correlates also suggest candidates for explaining cross-national and over-time differences in support, even though these rarely received attention in aggregate-level analyses (but see Duch and Taylor 1997; Janssen 1991; Netjes 2004).

The main shortcoming of previous research that this chapter aims to address is the lack of efforts at simultaneous testing of the diverse propositions in the literature. With the exception of a few studies on economic explanations (Çiftçi 2005; Eichenberg and Dalton 2007; Mikhaylov and Marsh 2009), previous analyses have failed to relate diverse theoretical propositions to data from all member states and for all time periods covered by currently available data. The diverse theories of the previous literature generally refer to one or more of three micro-logics allegedly used by citizens: the instrumental calculus of tangible benefits; expressive and/or instrumental judgements based on acquired taste (including sociopolitical identity); and cue-taking from trusted sources.[2] However, there are ambiguities about how these logics are linked to particular sources of EU support.

Advocates of the first micro-logic typically link support for market integration to the *capacity of citizens to benefit* from it, either personally or as members of a particular society or economic system. Economic theory is ambivalent about whether affluent or poorer countries could benefit more from EU integration, but the latter proposition receives more empirical support (Mikhaylov and Marsh 2009). From a functionalist perspective, however, it is clear that trade openness should be positively linked to support (Gabel and Palmer 1995), and several studies find impressive positive effects of within-EU trade on membership support (Anderson and Reichert 1996; Eichenberg and Dalton 1993; Gabel and Palmer 1995; Gabel and Whitten 1997; Mikhaylov and Marsh 2009; but cf. Çiftçi 2005; Eichenberg and Dalton 2007). The socioeconomic benefits of integration are, of course, not equal within countries and are likely to flow mostly to those groups and individuals that give a country a comparative advantage in integrated markets. Favourable labour market position as signalled by a person's education, professional status, and mode of employment is expected to increase EU support, especially in more highly developed countries that base their competitiveness on human capital. Meanwhile, manual workers may be more supportive in countries that have abundant cheap labour that can benefit from freedom of movement within the EU (Gabel 1998a, 1998b, 1998c; Gabel and Palmer 1995; Gabel and Whitten 1997).

Other sources of increased tangible benefits from integration explored in the literature include direct developmental assistance from the EU to one's country (Anderson and Reichert 1996; Bosch and Newton 1995; Carrubba 2001; Hooghe and Marks 2005; but cf. Eichenberg and Dalton 1993 and Duch and Taylor 1997 for negative findings); and the EU's supposed impact on macroeconomic performance as signalled by low inflation and unemployment and high growth in the member states (Anderson and Kaltenthaler 1996; Anderson and Reichert 1996; Bednar, Ferejohn, and Garret 1996; Eichenberg and Dalton 1993; Franklin and Wlezien 1997; Handley 1981; Inglehart and Rabier 1978; but cf. Duch and Taylor 1997; Gabel and Whitten 1997; Eichenberg and Dalton 2007).

The rationale for European integration has, of course, also been given in public discourse with reference to non-economic arguments, like the need to prevent wars in Europe, improve governance where this is less developed, and to consolidate democracy in Southern and Eastern Europe. In this context, Gabel (1998a) links membership support to the memory of Second World War casualties. In a similar vein, Sanchez-Cuenca (2000) links EU support to poor national governance (for example, involving high levels of corruption), which citizens in affected member states might expect to overcome through greater EU integration. Indeed, many scholars have suggested that support for the EU in third-wave democracies has been boosted by support for democracy. So far, the empirical literature does seem to support these ideas (see Çiftçi 2005, Gabel 1998a, and Gabel and Whitten 1997 regarding Second World War memories; Kritzinger 2003 and Christin 2005 on dissatisfaction with the national political system; and Rohrschneider 2002 and Rohrschneider and Whitefield 2006b on democracy support). Moreover, similar determinants of support have been found in both Eastern and Western Europe (Anderson 1998b; Cichowski 2000; Tucker, Pacek, and Berinsky 2002; Tverdova and Anderson 2004; Rohrschneider and Whitefield 2004).

Further instrumentally rational explanations implicitly or explicitly adopt the so-called *thermostat* model of public opinion towards policy instruments (cf. Çiftçi 2005; Franklin and Wlezien 1997). This model suggests that the greater supply of European integration—like the deepening of the union through Maastricht, the monetary union, and subsequent treaties—should have reduced citizen demand for integration (Eichenberg and Dalton 2007; Netjes 2004). Other writers suggest that *uncertain expectations* about future EU policies may also have an effect. Assuming that most citizens value the benefits of high welfare spending and centralized wage bargaining and expect them to be undermined by European integration, Brinegar, Jolly, and Kitschelt (2004) suggest that the presence of these factors will reduce EU support. In countries with a restricted welfare state they expect support for integration to be concentrated at the lower end of the socio-economic scale and on the political left. In contrast, in countries which have a comprehensive welfare state, support for integration should be stronger at the higher end of the socio-economic scale and on the political right (for similar arguments, see also Brinegar and Jolly 2005; Hix 2007; Hooghe and Marks 2005; Ray 2004).

Women and the elderly usually display below-average support for EU membership (but note Anderson and Reichert 1996 and Gabel 1998b for mixed or reversed findings regarding age). While the correlation with gender has usually been explained in terms of interest-based policy calculus (see Gabel and Whitten 1997; Gabel 1998b; Hix 2005; Nelsen and Guth 2000), the correlation with age often seems to invite explanations in terms of socialization, i.e. an acquired taste for more supranational governance among younger generations (Gabel and Whitten 1997; Inglehart 1970a, 1970b; Wessels 1995). Hix (2005), however, suggests that the age effect on EU support follows a life-cycle rather than a generational pattern, which is probably more consistent with instrumental calculus. For instance, the greater opportunities offered by an integrated labour market may appeal to the young and the middle-aged, while the feared impact of international labour mobility and a creeping internationalization of welfare systems may scare more risk-averse pensioners.

As we just saw, EU support has also been explained in terms of *acquired taste*. Thus the often-noted positive effects of a country's length of membership in the EC/EU on support is thought to emerge via socialization, identity building, and social learning regarding the benefits of integration (Anderson and Kaltenthaler 1996; Eichenberg and Dalton 1993; Inglehart and Rabier 1978; Mikhaylov and Marsh 2009). *Cognitive mobilization* theory is another example of an acquired taste-type explanation in that it explains the typically greater EU support among politically more attentive citizens either through differences in taste regarding supranational governance by degrees of parochialism, or by differences in socialization by degrees of exposure to the typically pro-EU elite discourse (Inglehart 1970a; 1970b; Gabel and Whitten 1997; Gabel 1998b). Acquired taste explanations are also advocated by the numerous studies that link EU support negatively to exclusive national identity, cultural homogeneity, and the perception of threat that European integration supposedly poses to *national identity* and culture (Carey 2002; Garry and Tilley 2009; Hooghe and Marks 2005; Lubbers 2008; McLaren 2002; van Kersbergen 2000; de Vries and van Kersbergen 2007). Unfortunately, data availability issues have restricted the testing of these identitarian explanations to one or just a few time points, in typically no more (and often fewer) than fifteen member states. For the same reason, we will not discuss them here any further.

A third micro-logic links EU support to *national political cleavages and cue taking* from national political elites or institutions. Anderson (1998a) suggests that citizens project their evaluation of the performance of their national political system and their trust in national institutions to the EU. Alternatively, Kritzinger (2003) argues that the "true" causal relationship runs in the opposite direction, though the relationship remains hidden (and perhaps never discoverable) by the endogeneity of EU support to satisfaction with national insitutions. In the discussion below, we retain Anderson's expectation, and only add the caveat that in countries where governance is relatively poor, this cue-taking effect may be counterbalanced by the utilitarian logic that generates a negative link between satisfaction with national institutions and EU support (cf. Christin 2005).

Cueing logic has also been employed in relation to the idea that EU support should be higher in countries that hold the presidency of the EU Council in any given period (see Magalhães 2012). A similar logic is also deployed in analyses that suggest that citizens follow the lead of trusted parties, i.e. use their partisanship and ideological attachments in developing their positions towards European integration (Anderson 1998a; Franklin, Marsh, and McLaren 1994; Gabel 1998b; Gabel and Scheve 2007; Lubbers 2008; Ray 2003a, 2003b; Rohrschneider 2002; Steenbergen, Edwards, and de Vries 2007; but cf.

Duch and Taylor 1997). Party preference may of course also act as a proxy (a) for policy preferences that are directly related to EU support, or (b) for the perceived probability that the EU's complex system of veto players will either increase or reduce the chances that one's preferences will prevail in the policy process (cf. Hix 2007). Supporters of parties that, in left–right terms, are far from the Europe-wide median (5 on a 0–10 scale) may be less supportive of the EU. This might be because they take cues from their parties; or because they support policies that are at odds with the integration process; or because they realize that the more complex web of veto players at the European as opposed to the national level gives them a lesser chance of prevailing in the former arena. A similar ambiguity is also present in the proposition that Catholics are more supportive of integration than Protestants (Hix 2005: 163; Nelsen, Guth, and Fraser 2001). We are nonetheless inclined to interpret above-average support for the EU among Catholics less as a sign of an acquired taste or peculiar policy preferences than of cue-taking related to the Catholic Church's traditional advocacy and practice of supranational governance, and do likewise with respect to left–right differences in EU support. We would draw the opposite inference with regard to the putative role of post-materialism, though (Inglehart and Rabier 1978), except that multiple studies have demonstrated in the meantime that it does not, in fact, have any noteworthy systematic effect on EU support (see Anderson and Reichert 1996; Anderson 1998a; Gabel and Whitten 1997; Janssen 1991).

3. Assumptions, testable propositions, and variables

Many of the general propositions outlined above fail to follow an integrated theoretical logic. They also give the impression that they have been largely inductively derived on the basis of largely ad hoc (and occasionally *sui generis*) theorizing. We suspect that these limitations arise quite naturally from the subject matter and that they should be recognized and accepted in its study rather than purged from it. The EU is a complex, dynamically evolving and self-reflexive organization that generates diverse, contradictory, and ever-changing expectations, which are unlikely to follow a unified logic or a given set of fixed preferences. For instance, Brinegar, Jolly, and Kitschelt (2004) argue that the most likely consequence of integration for welfare states in the eyes of the EU15 citizen population should be a slow convergence towards what Esping-Andersen (1990) called the "Christian-democratic" model of continental Western Europe. They then proceed to suggest that this should generate popular expectations of higher adjustment costs to such a change, and consequently lower EU support, in the populations of "liberal" and "social-democratic" welfare states; i.e. the UK on the one hand and the Nordic member states on the other. While their statistical analysis of fourteen states at one point in time appears to support this theory, one must wonder if integration is really expected by citizens to lead to any convergence of national welfare states (given that this domain is outside community jurisdiction) and in what direction. This example hints at the possibility that, depending on the peculiar communicative practices that characterize different political contexts, many factors may be related to EU support, and there cannot be a priori guarantees of temporal or cross-national uniformity in what factors become relevant. Our strategy in this and similar instances is accordingly to try to improve on previous analyses by covering as many data points and controls for alternative theories as possible. This allows for the possibility that any observed effects of, say, welfare spending are not spurious but indeed caused by (some) citizens' perception that European integration may have some impact on welfare provision after all.

Utilitarian, acquired-taste, and cue-taking explanations of EU support all make strong assumptions about exactly how citizens arrive at their evaluations of EU membership. It might seem prudent to replace some strong assumptions about citizens' knowledge and understanding of EU integration with the seemingly weaker assumption that their collective responses, assisted by the good work of competing opinion leaders and information shortcuts, can emulate informed behaviour even when (most) individual citizens remain information misers. However, this seemingly weaker assumption of collective rationality also leaves behind a huge burden of proof regarding the precise nature of the issue frames, information bites, and simplistic cues that citizens receive about the EU from competing political elites, interest groups, mass media, economic analysts, government agencies, and so forth. We can only leave it to further research to establish whether the preferences and/or communicative processes presumed by one or another proposition examined here have actually been in place in one country year or another. Our revisiting of these hypotheses merely focuses, therefore, on the statistical associations predicted by them, and benevolently ignores the possible problems associated with the underlying assumptions.

Developing testable propositions

We group the tested propositions around the three broad theoretical approaches outlined above: instrumental rationality, cognitive mobilization/ acquired taste, and heuristic cue-taking. We add a fourth "residual" ad hoc category for putative causal factors that do not obviously fit into any of these three categories. In presenting the propositions, we also distinguish among propositions that require testing at the micro or individual level; those that require testing at the macro or aggregate, country level; and those that imply a cross-level (macro*micro) interaction effect that combines both macro and micro levels. Most of our independent variables closely follow the extant literature and we add new ones only where the need is clearly implied by previous studies. The chief example here is the aggregate quality of governance, which, as we argue below, could act as either a "transfer" or a "substitution" cue. We further add a variable that stands for the annual number of regulations and directives adopted by the EC/EU (see Franklin and Wlezien 1997; Hix 2005). This variable refers to the "thermostat" model, which—admittedly adapted here to a different dependent variable than in its original exposition by Franklin and Wlezien—suggests that the more integrative activities the EC/EU provides at any given point in time, the less support there will be for integration, while falls in the supply of integration would prompt more popular demand for it, i.e. higher membership support. Following Magalhães (2012), we also include in our aggregate-level analyses a dummy variable identifying the two countries that held the EU presidency in either half of each year. Previous works with individual-level analyses suggested that cognitive mobilization, Catholicism, left–right extremism, and satisfaction with national democracy are significant predictors of EU support at the individual level. If the theories underlying these propositions were correct, one would also expect to observe these effects at the aggregate level. Therefore our aggregate-level analyses include the sample mean for each country year of the four respective individual-level variables that we could create from the Eurobarometer series. Last but not least, we aim at capturing the diminishing impact of the length of EU membership on support by a variable showing for each year the natural logarithm of the years that a country was member of the EC/EU until the given year.

Table 8.2 summarizes the various propositions that we seek to test and identifies the specific indicators that we deploy to operationalize each of them. The first segment of the table relates to the *instrumental rationality* approach. As noted above, the core intuition underpinning this approach is that people with certain characteristics and/or those living in countries with certain characteristics will be more likely to benefit disproportionately from (or believe themselves more likely to benefit from) their country's membership of the EU. The first set of variables in the instrumental rationality segment of Table 8.2 relates to the role of the *individual's labour market position,* as reflected in education, gender, age, and employment status. The basic claim of the individual-level hypotheses in this segment is that people who are relatively well placed in the labour market are more likely to be able to take advantage of the EU's common market for goods, capital, and labour than those who are less well placed; the former are accordingly more likely to

Table 8.2. Propositions tested

Propositions	Variables	Level
Instrumental rationality approach		
Vulnerable (advantageous) labour market position reduces (increases) support	education, managers, professionals, manual workers, farmer, self-employed, unemployed	micro
These effects are enhanced by welfare state development	SOCIAL EXPENDITURE*each of education, managers, professionals, manual workers, farmer, self-employed, unemployed	cross
The same effects are enhanced by economic development	GDP/CAPITA*each of education, managers, professionals, manual workers, farmer, self-employed, unemployed	cross
Women show less support	male	micro
Position in the life cycle influences support	age age-squared	micro
Relative economic development influences support	GDP/CAPITA	macro
Good economic performance increases support for integration	UNEMPLOYMENT INFLATION GDP GROWTH	macro
Within-EU trade increases support	INTRA EU TRADE	macro
Net transfers from European to national budgets increase support	NET EU TRANSERS	macro
Greater EU regulatory activity reduces support	EU LEGISLATION SUPPLY	macro
Relative welfare spending reduces support	SOCIAL EXPENDITURE	macro
High WW2 casualties increase support for integration	WW2 CASUALTIES	macro
Cognitive mobilization approach		
Cognitive mobilization increases support	education, political discussion, POLITICAL DISCUSSION	micro & macro
Cueing rationality approach		
Quality of governance reduces support	QUALITY OF GOVERNANCE	macro
Satisfaction with national political institutions increases support	democracy satisfaction DEMOCRACY SATISFACTION	micro & macro
Governance quality enhances the above effect	democracy satisfaction * QUALITY OF GOVERNANCE	cross
Left-right position influences support	left right ideology	micro
Welfare state development reduces support on the political left	left right ideology*SOCIAL EXPENDITURE	cross
Extreme political positions reduce support	left right extremes	micro & macro
Catholic religion increases support	catholic CATHOLIC	micro & macro
Length of EU membership increases support but less and less	EU MEMBERSHIP LENGTH	macro
Ad hoc *propositions*		
Council presidency by one's country increases support	EU COUNCIL PRESIDENCY	macro
Centralized wage bargaining reduces support	CENTRALIZED WAGE BARGAINING	macro
Democratic consolidation at time of accession increases support	THIRD WAVE DEMOCRACY	macro

Lower case variable names denote micro-level variables; UPPER case denotes macro-level variables.

support the EU than the latter. The aggregate-level "economic" hypotheses in this segment suggest that EU support is also likely to be higher among people living in countries that are more prosperous (measured by GDP per head), that are more integrated into the EU's trading regime (measured by intra-EU trade) or that receive net financial benefits from the EU (measured as net transfers from EU budget as a share of GDP). There are also macro-level hypotheses relating to the value of the EU in pre-empting intra-European war (support for the EU will be higher where Second World War casualties were highest); to the extent of domestic social welfare provision (support is expected to be highest where national social welfare expenditure is lowest); and to the "thermostatic" role of EU legislation (support is expected to decline, *ceteris paribus*, as the supply of EU legislation increases). Finally, the instrumental rationality segment of Table 8.2 contains two sets of cross-level interactions suggested by the previous literature—between the micro employment status variables and macro measures of prosperity and social welfare expenditure. In most of these cases, the theoretical expectation is that the effects of employment status will be greater where GDP per capita and social expenditure are higher; the only exception is that the negative effects of manual worker status may be attenuated where the economy is relatively weak (and, by implication, where wage rates are relatively low).

The second segment of Table 8.2 refers to the potential impact of *acquired taste/cognitive mobilization*. The key idea here is that as individuals become more educated and informed about politics, they acquire new, more cosmopolitan tastes and hence are more likely to register support for a supranational body like the EU. Two individual-level measures of such mobilization are employed—education and engagement in political discussion, with the expectation that both should exert positive effects on EU support. Note, of course, that education also features in the labour market position segment—a reflection of the fact that this variable is "claimed" by advocates of both instrumental rationality and cognitive mobilization explanations. Clearly, any observed empirical tendency for education to exert a positive effect on EU support must accordingly be interpreted as support for both of these accounts. Political discussion is also hypothesized to have an effect at the aggregate macro level, together with length of time that the individual's country has been an EU member state. This latter variable is included on the grounds that higher levels of cosmopolitanism will typically be associated with more extended exposure to EU policies, procedures, and practices.

The third segment of the table summarizes the putative *cue-taking* mechanisms that we explore. The core theoretical idea here is that citizens, confronted with a complex multilevel system of governance like the EU, are likely to make use of cognitive shortcuts or heuristics in order to make judgements about it. Three such heuristics are operationalized here at the micro level: Catholic religion, left–right ideology, and political performance evaluations. Following the logic outlined earlier, Catholics are expected to be more supportive of the EU on the grounds that the Church has traditionally advocated the merits and practice of supranational governance. The possible effects of ideological position are more ambiguous, given that the EU is supported by parties of both the centre left and the centre right. Nonetheless, the term that we include to describe those who take *extreme* positions on either left or right is expected to have a negative effect on EU support, on the grounds that both extreme left and extreme right parties have generally tended to be hostile to the EU project. The most ambiguous predictions for the direction of effects on EU support, however, derive from our two measures of domestic political performance: satisfaction with democracy and quality of governance. The existing literature, as noted previously, makes opposing claims about the likely consequences of strong domestic political performance, with some arguing that it spills over into greater support for the EU and others that it produces more cautious and more negative EU evaluations. In our view, this apparent contradiction can be resolved by recognizing that there are in fact two distinct sorts of cueing mechanisms that EU citizens might use in arriving at their EU evaluations. On the one hand, people who evaluate their own national institutions positively (negatively) may uncritically extend these evaluations to the supranational sphere and, as a result, also make positive (negative) evaluations of EU institutions. This *transfer effect* clearly implies a positive relationship between attitudes towards national and EU institutions. On the other hand, it is equally possible that people are likely to have more (less) confidence in EU institutions and processes precisely when they evaluate their own national institutions negatively (positively)—which implies a negative *substitution* relationship between attitudes towards national and EU institutions. We subject the rival claims of transfer and substitution cueing to empirical test at both the micro and macro levels. At the micro level we assess the extent to which individuals' sense of democracy satisfaction acts as a transfer or substitution cue in determining their EU evaluations. At the macro level we consider the equivalent effects of governance quality and aggregate-level democracy satisfaction.

The last segment of Table 8.2 identifies three additional ad hoc macro sources of EU support that have been suggested in previous studies, but which do not correspond to any particular theoretical perspective. The first refers to the putative effects of "third-wave" democratization, where the central claim is that EU support is higher in situations where (most) people see EU membership as important for consolidating the democratic process in their respective countries. The second relates to the idea that EU membership, given the union's myriad rules for ensuring competition in markets of all sorts, might pose a threat to centralized (national) wage bargaining. The key claim here is that countries with higher levels of wage-bargaining centralization should exhibit lower levels of EU support. Finally, as noted above, we include a term that measures whether or not a country has the EU presidency at a particular time. The assumption here is that having "our" leader as council president will tend to promote a more positive view of the EU among "our" citizens, however temporary any such effect might turn out to be.

The set of hypotheses shown in Table 8.2 clearly does not represent all of the possible hypotheses that could be tested against small spatial and/or temporal subsets of the available data on EU support. Nonetheless, we consider that the set is sufficiently comprehensive to mean that our analysis represents the most exhaustive thus far conducted.

This said, it is worth highlighting the hypotheses that we deliberately exclude from the analysis. First, we ignore the influence of a number of individual-level variables because recent Eurobarometers did not include the relevant measures and therefore entire countries would drop out of any analysis that included these factors. This applies in particular to measures of European and national identity, voting preferences, subjective economic evaluations, income, religiosity, and post-materialism. Second, while we aim to include all theoretically relevant macro variables that have been found to have effects on EU support in previous analyses, we take exception to the use of the large range of dummy and related variables, which identify particular periods or particular country years as "special". The chief examples include the timing of individual countries' accession (as, e.g., in Anderson and Kaltenthaler 1996), and particular events in the history of the community, like the 1979 European Parliament election, the adoption of the Single European Act, various referendums and treaty reforms, German unification, a country's entry into the monetary union, and the events of 9/11 (cf. Bednar, Ferejohn, and Garret 1996; Çiftçi 2005; Eichenberg and Dalton 1993, 2003, 2007; Netjes 2004). Such factors may no doubt have some effects on their own. However, the theoretical expectations about the direction and possible mechanisms of these effects are not so clear that they would identify where else we should expect to see similar effects. As long as this is the case, we fear that the inclusion of some opportunistically selected dummies to pick up the unique effects of some periods or country years just because something hits the eyes in the available time series is more likely to distort than advance our understanding of the underlying causal processes.

4. Empirical analysis

Our statistical analysis spans the period between 1975 and 2007 and includes all states that were full members of the EC/EU in each year. We conduct separate individual- and aggregate-level analyses because some technical characteristics make our dataset unusually large and complicated.[3] Indeed, we report our empirical findings under four main headings. We begin with *individual-level effects* in which we conduct 449 separate regression analyses—one for each of the 449 country years in our dataset. These analyses, using multivariate OLS regression, estimate the net impact of all available individual-level variables—age, age-squared, education, frequency of political discussion, satisfaction with democracy, left–right position, left–right extremism, and dichotomous variables identifying men, managers, professionals, non-agricultural manual workers, farmers/agricultural workers, the non-farming self-employed, the unemployed, and Catholics—on EU support for each country year separately. As will be recalled from earlier, missing values on all variables were replaced with multiple imputation via the Amelia II package.[4] We then report the summary pattern of these 449 sets of individual-level results. This summary pattern reveals considerable *variability* in the patterns of relationship across the various country years, though they also indicate a small number of *consistent and relatively robust effects* that seem to operate across a variety of temporal and spatial contexts.

The second phase of the empirical analysis involves supplementing our analysis of individual-level effects with a limited number of *cross-level effects*. This phase involves shifting our focus from 449 *separate* analyses of individuals sampled in different country years to an analysis of the pattern of *coefficients*—estimates of individual-level effects on EU support—observed in those separate 449 country years. In these analyses, we wish to know how far macro-level country characteristics can explain variations in coefficient signs and magnitudes across the 449 samples. This strategy of modelling coefficients, however, is complicated by the fact that, in order properly to analyse all of the available data, we need to use four distinct pooled cross-sectional time-series datasets. The four datasets in this context are: an unbalanced set covering the EU25 over the period 1975–2007; a balanced set for the EU9, 1975–2007; a balanced set for the EU12, 1986–2007; and a balanced set for the EU15, 1995–2007. In deference to the range of methods available for estimating both coefficients and standard errors with country-clustered time-series data, we estimate identical models of cross-level effects across all four datasets, using six different estimation methods. The summary results from these 6*4 = 24 sets of estimations are then used to evaluate the putative cross-level effects.

The third phase of the investigation switches to *cross-sectional, aggregate-level analysis of macro, time-invariant country characteristics* across the EU27. In this phase, we adopt a novel statistical approach in order to identify the optimal set of time-invariant country characteristics that explain national variations in EU support. We analyse five different cross-sections, defined by the timing of the five main waves of EU accession. The final phase of our analysis involves *testing macro time-series effects* using aggregate-level cross-sectional time-series data. We again deploy four different datasets, though here they are aggregate-rather than individual-level: one each for the EU25 (1975–2007 unbalanced), EU9 (1975–2007 balanced), EU12 (1986–2007) and EU15 (1996–2007).

Phase 1: Individual-level effects

Table 8.3 reports the results of an illustrative estimation of our individual-level model of EU support for one of the 449 country years. As the last two columns show, it makes no relevant difference in the results if we estimated the model with linear regression or ordered logit.[5] In this particular instance only a subset of the estimated effects is statistically significant, though most are signed as expected. The crucial question, however, is the extent to which significant effects are observed across all 449 country years for which data are available.

Table 8.4 provides summary statistics about these individual-level effects across the 449 samples. The first column of Table 8.4 shows the direction and size of each variable's net effect for the average country year. The figures are comparable in the sense that all these individual-level variables were scaled from 0 to 1 in the analysis—but not very usefully so since with the dichotomous variables (like male, manual worker, or Catholic) every respondent was coded either 0 or 1, while on continuous variables (like age, age squared, democracy satisfaction, or left–right ideology) few if any record either of these extreme values. Therefore it is more informative to read the last two

Table 8.3. Individual-level influences on EU support in France in 1990

	b	Standard error of b	T-value (OLS)	T-value (ordered logit)
Male	0.01	(1.24)	0.01	0.41
Age	−23.58	(20.24)	−1.17	−1.15
Age squared	23.20	(22.40)	1.04	1.03
Education	12.28***	(2.01)	6.10	5.59
Manager	−1.83	(3.46)	−0.53	−0.34
Professional	−1.67	(1.63)	−1.02	−0.92
Manual worker	−4.45**	(2.06)	−2.16	−2.42
Farmer	−13.43***	(4.57)	−2.94	−3.17
Self-employed	−0.69	(2.61)	−0.27	−0.07
Unemployed	−4.37*	(2.64)	−1.65	−1.94
Catholic	0.68	(1.60)	0.43	0.48
Political discussion	7.11***	(2.40)	2.96	2.82
Democracy satisfaction	21.42***	(2.10)	10.21	9.74
Left-right ideology	0.83	(2.92)	0.28	−0.01
Left-right extremes	−4.43**	(2.16)	−2.05	−1.81
Constant	66.42***	(4.58)	14.51	n.a.

***: p < 0.01; **: p < 0.05; *: p < 0.10.
Note: All table entries except the last column are based on linear (OLS) regression of EU-support on the variables listed on the left. The last column shows corresponding T-values from an ordered logit analysis of the same model.

Table 8.4. Summary of Individual-level influences on EU support in 449 country-year samples, 1975–2007

	Average effect (b) across 449 country-years	(Average standard error of b across country-years)	Standard deviation of b across country-years	% of bs that are positive and significant (p<0.05)	% of bs that are negative and significant (p<0.05)
Male	2.1	(1.6)	2.6	32.1	1.1
Age	−22.6	(22.2)	33.5	0.7	25.6
Age squared	17.2	(24.2)	33.8	18.3	1.1
Education	10.4	(2.9)	6.2	79.7	0.0
Manager	4.6	(5.8)	7.7	20.9	0.4
Professional	0.6	(2.1)	2.8	10.0	2.7
Manual worker	−3.0	(2.5)	3.4	0.9	26.5
Farmer	−3.9	(7.8)	12.4	7.3	14.0
Self-employed	0.1	(3.3)	4.2	4.9	4.7
Unemployed	−3.8	(3.9)	5.2	0.4	20.1
Catholic	2.5	(4.7)	6.8	19.2	2.6
Political discussion	5.3	(2.5)	4.2	49.4	0.9
Democracy satisfaction	23.0	(3.6)	9.9	95.0	0.0
Left-right ideology	10.0	(4.0)	21.4	41.8	16.8
Left-right extremes	−4.2	(2.6)	4.4	1.1	39.5

Note: Table entries are based on multivariate regressions of EU-support on the variables listed on the left run separately for each country-year.

columns first. These report the percentage of country years in which the variable in question records a statistically significant (net) effect. If a variable never had a real effect, then by chance alone we would expect a figure of about 2.5 (per cent) to appear in both columns. In reality, self-employed is the only variable that has about as many positive as negative significant effects, but since the percentage figures—4.9 and 4.7, respectively—clearly exceed 2.5, the correct interpretation appears to be that self-employment rarely has an effect on EU support, but when it does, the effect is as often positive as negative. All other effects, however, have a predominant direction, even if—as in the case of professionals, farmers, and especially left–right ideology—we see clear evidence that they can go either way depending on context. In fact, for most variables we see such a small percentage—1.1 per cent or less—of country years with significant effects going in the less common direction that these exceptions may well be provided merely by the statistically inevitable rogue samples. Hence we can conclude that men, the better educated, managers, those relatively satisfied with democracy in their own country, and those who discuss politics frequently are probably always more supportive of EU membership than the average citizen. In contrast, manual workers, the unemployed, and ideological radicals (i.e. those who place themselves far from the centre of the left–right scale) are always less supportive. It is just that these differences do not always reach statistical significance in polls due to their limited sample size. Only a little less universal is the above-average EU support among Catholics and the young.[6]

What is novel about all these findings is not the often reported main direction, but rather the relative invariability of these effects across periods and countries. For most variables, the standard deviation across the country years is less than one and a half times the average standard error (cf. columns two and three of Table 8.4). This means that the cross-contextual variance of these effects is barely more than the random noise introduced in the estimates by the inevitable sampling errors. Across Table 8.4 as a whole, only four variables produce an average estimated effect that is both (a) more than twice its average estimated standard error and (b) balanced predominantly toward either the positive or the negative. These are education, political discussion, democracy satisfaction, and left–right ideological position—all of which have consistently positive effects on EU support, but apparently bigger in some country years than others. There are five further variables which meet only criterion (b), that is, they display a clear "predominant balance" of either significant negative or significant positive effects and little variance in the size of the effect. Of these, unemployment, manual worker status, age, and ideological extremism all produce negative effects; being male and being Catholic produce a positive effect. The relatively consistent effects of manual work, unemployment, and education support one of the key hypotheses of the instrumental rationality approach—that labour market position affects EU support; the consistent effects of education and political discussion support the claims of cognitive mobilization theory; those of left–right ideology and democracy satisfaction support the cueing approach. The fact that the democracy satisfaction term is consistently positive rather than negative in this latter context implies that transfer, rather than substitution, cueing appears to be the dominant mechanism.

Phase 2: Cross-level effects

But if the effects of individual-level variables on EU support are relatively modest, is there any evidence that structural conditions in different countries might be responsible for the varying effects that we observe? It will be recalled from Table 8.2 that previous research has suggested the possible existence of a series of "cross-level interactions", particularly involving our various measures of labour market position. Previous research suggested, in essence, that the effects of certain individual-level variables on EU support might depend on variations in social welfare expenditure, the level of economic development, and the quality of governance. We investigated these possibilities by running a number of time-series analyses for each of the nine country-year-specific individual-level effects as the dependent variables and the relevant macro-level characteristics as the independent variables. Two models are bivariate: the individual-level effect of satisfaction with democracy on EU support is expected to depend on relative quality of governance, while the impact of left–right ideology on support is expected to vary by relative social welfare spending. The remaining seven models regressed the effects of education and employment status (measured with separate variables for managers, professionals, manual workers, farmers, self-employed, and unemployed) on relative economic development and relative social spending. We estimated all seven models for each of four panel datasets, and with each of six different specifications of model dynamics, unit heterogeneity, and other estimation details.[7] For reasons of space we do not present all 168 models and the tests of stationarity, autocorrelation, and unit heterogeneity that guided our choice between the six model specifications.[8] Instead, Table 8.5 presents only the relevant coefficients (omitting constants) for whatever seemed to be the most appropriate model specification for a given series in the complete dataset, i.e. the unbalanced panel of the EU27 from 1975 to 2007. We only briefly comment on results with other specifications or in other panels in the text.[9]

The first row of the table speaks to one of the characteristic propositions of the *substitution* logic argument, namely that good governance further *increases* the generally positive impact of satisfaction with democracy on EU support because in poorly governed countries the less satisfied will be most

Table 8.5. Key cross-level findings from regressing the effects on EU support of selected individual-level variables on theoretically relevant macro-level determinants

Level-1 effect	Level-2 predictor	Preferred model	b	standard error
Democracy satisfaction	Quality of governance	Fixed effects AR(1)	−3.85	(11.81)
Education	GDP/capita	Random effects AR(1)	0.41	(1.82)
Education	Social expenditure	Random effects AR(1)	0.18*	(0.09)
Manager	GDP/capita	Random effects GLS	−3.48*	(2.05)
Manager	Social expenditure	Random effects GLS	0.06	(0.11)
Professionals	GDP/capita	Random effects GLS	−1.12*	(0.59)
Professionals	Social expenditure	Random effects GLS	−0.09***	(0.03)
Manual worker	GDP/capita	Random effects GLS	−0.64	(0.89)
Manual worker	Social expenditure	Random effects GLS	−0.16***	(0.05)
Farmer	GDP/capita	Random effects GLS	−4.09	(3.06)
Farmer	Social expenditure	Random effects GLS	0.11	(0.16)
Self-employed	GDP/capita	Random effects GLS	−1.94**	(0.89)
Self-employed	Social expenditure	Random effects GLS	−0.02	(0.05)
Unemployed	GDP/capita	Random effects GLS	−1.92**	(0.91)
Unemployed	Social expenditure	Random effects GLS	−0.07	(0.05)
Left-Right ideology	Social expenditure	Random effects GLS	−0.24	(0.21)

***: $p < 0.01$; **: $p < 0.05$; *: $p < 0.10$.
Note: Table entries show results of one regression analysis for each of the nine individual-level effects in the unbalanced 1975–2007 panel of the EU27 using the model specification shown in the middle column. Constants not shown. N = 449 except when a level-1 variable was missing in the Eurobarometer series in some years.

supportive of EU integration on account of its expected benefits on political performance. Separate Woolridge and Hausman tests of the relevant regression of the level-1 effects of satisfaction with domestic democracy on governance quality shows significant, non-random unit effects and a lag-1 autocorrelation in the data. Therefore, our preferred model here is a fixed-effects regression with a first-order autoregressive term. When we re-estimate the regression with this specification, the relative quality of governance appears to *reduce* rather than *increase* the level-1 effect, both in the complete dataset (see the first row of Table 8.5) and in the balanced panels for the EU9, EU12, and EU15, although not significantly so. While the cross-level effect turns positive with a few other model specifications, it is always negative when—with two of the six model specifications, and only in the panel for the EU9 in 1975–2007—it reaches statistical significance. Hence the relevant hypothesis—expecting that the positive impact of satisfaction with national institutions on EU support would turn into its opposite where a low quality of governance may trigger a substitution logic in popular evaluations of the EU— is *not* supported. Instead, the transfer logic seems to be at work irrespective of the quality of governance in the member states.

Second, the expectation that the impact of labour market position (mostly positive for higher education, managers, self-employed, and professional positions, and negative for the other occupation dummies) increases with level of economic development is supported in the case of unemployment and the self-employed in the complete dataset with the preferred random-effect GLS model, and the signs of these effects remain largely consistent across panels and alternative model specifications. However, when we look at the effect of economic development on the level-1 impact of other occupational dummies on EU support, the effects, though they mostly run in the expected direction, rarely become significant, and some significant effects have the opposite sign than expected. Most notably, economic development significantly reduces the positive effect of being a manager or a professional worker on EU support in the 1975–2007 panel for the EU9, irrespective of model specification. Overall, then, the findings do not support the hypothesis that the domestic-class basis of EU support depends on whether a country is a potential labour or capital exporter within the EU.

The hypothesis that the impact of labour market position on EU support depends on the level of social welfare spending receives a bit more support from the data. Higher social spending relative to the EU average makes the impact of manual work on support for the EU even more negative, and that of education even more positive than usual. These effects are generally consistent and significant across model specifications and panels. Greater social spending also appears to reduce EU support among non-managerial or professional workers significantly and quite consistently across panels and model specification, which may or may not be considered consistent with the theory that seems underspecified in this respect. The effects of social welfare spending on the impact of unemployment, managerial, farming, and self-employed status on EU support are less consistent and relatively rarely significant, but at least do not contradict the theory in any panel or model specification.

Finally, there appears to be no support for the proposition that the domestic political basis of EU evaluations shifts from the left to the right as social spending increases relative to the EU average. The relevant coefficients run in different directions in different panels and model specifications, and none comes close to reaching statistical significance. Expectations about a possible convergence of social spending rates within the EU are clearly not what makes left–right differences in support for integration vary across country years.

Overall, then, with the partial exception of the impact of social welfare spending on the relationship between EU support and labour market position, the hypotheses of the political economy literature do not seem to take us far in understanding cross-contextual variation in which population segments show more or less support for the EU. Lack of sufficient time-series data on, say, party positions on EU integration, extreme nationalist mobilization, and immigration figures prevent us from examining if identitarian or cue-taking explanations might offer a better leverage on the same question. Yet some conclusions emerge quite clearly from our analysis of individual-level effects. At this level, support for the EU is a combination of rational calculation (based largely on labour market position), transfer cueing (satisfaction with domestic political conditions and left–right ideological position), and cognitive mobilization (education and engagement in political discussion). The only macro-level characteristic that appears to confound these generally consistent individual-level relationships is social welfare expenditure, which appears to intensify the effects on EU support of a limited set of labour market positions. Nonetheless, what is most striking about the results in Tables 8.4 and 8.5 is how similar the basis of EU support is across countries and over time. Virtually independently of the conditions of a country at a given point in time, it is the more politically engaged, better educated, ideologically more centrist, and— politically speaking—more satisfied citizens who are more likely to support the EU than the rest of the population, and this situation has remained unaltered by both the passing of time and subsequent waves of enlargement.

Phases 3 and 4: Aggregate-level analysis

Our analysis so far has focused on the individual-level sources of EU support and how such individual-level factors might be mediated by country-level characteristics. Yet regardless of the individual-level drivers of EU support, it is clearly the case that aggregate support levels differ both across countries and, within individual countries, over time. Our analysis turns now to analyse these macro-level variations in EU support and to assess how far our three main theoretical approaches can contribute to our understanding. The sources of differences in levels of support across the cross-national time series are analysed in two stages. First, we examine the impact of enduring country characteristics that change little or not at all over time, and then explore the roots of temporal change in support for EU membership. The separation of these two stages was necessary because the time-series data revealed a non-stationary process (a random walk with a drift) in how EU support evolved over time in most countries.[10] Therefore we prefer to first-difference the dependent variable in the subsequent time-series analysis. That is to say, the dependent variable in the second stage becomes the *change* of support level in 449 country years compared to the previous year's level in the same country. This means that all enduring cross-country differences in levels of support drop out of the time-series analysis due to the technical necessity of making the data stationary for time-series analysis. However, these enduring cross-country differences account for over two-thirds of the total aggregate-level variance in support across country years.[11] Rather than ignore these two-thirds of the variance or attribute it to the work of theoretically meaningless country dummies, we conduct a separate analysis of what may drive these enduring cross-national differences.

Phase 3: Time-invariant sources of aggregate variations in EU support

This part of the analysis focuses on five different cross-sections comprising the over-time averages of all macro variables for a given set of countries and period. The first covers the EU9 over the 1975–85 period, the second the EU12 in 1986–94, the third the EU15 in 1995–2003, the fourth the EU25 in 2004–6, and the fifth the EU27 in a single year, 2007. One candidate independent variable measuring supply of European legislation drops out of the analysis of static cross-sections because it does not vary across countries. Altogether then we have seventeen independent variables to account for variation in over-time averages of EU support across 27, 25, 15, 12 and 9 cases in the various cross-sections, respectively. Since it would be either meaningless or even impossible to run statistical analyses with such an un-favourable ratio of cases to variables, we devised a two-step procedure to develop a similar and theoretically plausible model for all five cross-sections, which assumes that the causal determinants of EU support remained relatively stable over time but permits the exact weight of individual factors to change over time as the population of member states becomes larger and larger. Our model selection procedure is admittedly ad hoc but it considers a vast amount of empirical evidence in a disciplined and systematic way where the only

Table 8.6. Two-step selection of variables that are most likely to have a non-zero effect on overtime average levels of EU support in member states, 1975–2007

	First Analysis		Second Analysis				
Variable	EU27	EU25	EU27	EU25	EU15	EU12	EU9
Democracy satisfaction	0.43	0.42	–	–	–	–	–
Left-Rght extremes	0.47	0.40	–	–	–	–	–
Catholics	0.44	**0.53**	0.38	0.45	0.27	**0.52**	0.37
Political Discussion	0.50	0.44	–	–	–	–	–
GDP/capita	0.47	0.47	–	–	–	–	–
GDP growth	0.47	0.44	–	–	–	–	–
Unemployment	0.45	0.41	–	–	–	–	–
Inflation	**0.55**	0.39	0.41	0.31	0.39	0.43	0.31
Intra-EU trade	0.48	**0.58**	0.46	**0.62**	0.51	**0.67**	**0.52**
Net EU Transfers	0.45	0.41	–	–	–	–	–
Quality of governance	0.46	0.42	–	–	–	–	–
Social expenditure	**0.71**	**0.75**	**0.81**	**0.92**	**0.90**	0.39	0.29
Wage Bargaining centralization	**0.65**	**0.66**	**0.68**	**0.61**	0.39	0.39	0.26
Third wave democracy	0.45	0.51	–	–	–	–	–
Wolrd War 2 casulties	0.49	0.49	–	–	–	–	–
EU membershp length	**0.65**	**0.80**	**0.66**	**0.91**	**0.95**	0.46	**0.92**
Council presidency	0.44	0.42	NA	NA	NA	NA	NA

Note: Table entries show the combined probability of the models including the given variable relative to the combined probability of all models that can be formed with the set of independent variables (17 in the first and six in the second analysis). Probability values above 0.51 indicated in bold.

alternative would be to improve theories—which we cannot undertake here—or to choose arbitrarily between them.

Instead, then, in the first step we regressed EU support on each of the 131,072 logically possible combinations of the seventeen independent variables in both the EU27 and EU25 cross-sections with the help of Clyde, Ghosh, and Littman's (2011) software for Bayesian model averaging. The relevant results are shown in the two leftmost columns of Table 8.6. The figures reported indicate the combined probability in each of the EU25 and EU27 cross-sections, of all the 65,536 models that *include* the given variable. Probability is estimated from statistical criteria of model fit and parsimony.[12] The combined probability of the other 65,536 models (which *exclude* the given variable) is, naturally, one minus the number shown in the table. So when one value is close to 0.5, then so is its counterpart, and there is little empirical ground to choose, either way, between models that include and models that exclude the variable. Crucially, we find just six variables—referring to the proportion of Catholics, annual inflation, the importance of within-EU trade for the national economy, social spending, centralization of wage bargaining, and the length of EU membership—for which our key statistic in the first two columns of the table is higher than 0.51 for either of the two cross-sections. For the other variables there seems to be little chance that their inclusion in the models for the EU27 and EU25 would improve model fit, and therefore we drop them from the subsequent analysis.[13]

The second step of this analysis repeats the first, except that now we focus only on the 64 possible combinations of the six variables selected in the first step, and run all these models for all five cross-sections, as shown in the "Second analysis" in Table 8.6. We find that there are three variables that have a more than fifty-fifty chance of improving model fit in a majority of the five cross-sections: *length of EU membership* (which we expect to impact either acquired taste for EU membership or a nation's ability to shape the union to its own liking, or both); *social spending* (which, assuming that more people prefer than oppose high levels of spending and that most expect integration to level out spending levels across countries, should create more liking for the integration of labour and capital markets in low- than in high-spending countries); and *within-EU trade* (which we expect to create a stronger preference for integration in countries that trade more with member states). Of the other variables, only centralized wage bargaining passes the same threshold in at least one cross-section. However, the average impact of this variable is in the opposite direction to that expected in the extant literature (data not shown), which we are inclined to count as a further reason for dropping this variable from any further analysis. Therefore we propose a model of enduring cross-national differences in EU support that includes only three variables. Table 8.7 presents simple OLS-regression results of this model for each of the five cross-sections as well as a pooled dataset comprising the five cross-sectional samples together.

Table 8.7. The performance of the selected model for enduring cross-national differences in EU Support in different cross-sectional data sets, 1975–2007: fit statistics and OLS regression coefficients

	EU27 in 2007	EU25 in 2004–06	EU15 in 1995–03	EU12 in 1986–94	EU9 in 1975–85	pooled dataset
Intercept	38.2***	25.4**	28.8**	25.2	−10.7	36.6***
	(11.3)	(12.1)	(11.4)	(17.3)	(15.7)	(6.7)
EU membership length	5.2**	5.4***	6.4***	3.9	21.0***	6.0***
	(1.9)	(1.2)	(1.4)	(3.3)	(3.4)	(0.9)
Intra-EU trade	0.2*	0.4**	0.3*	0.7**	0.5*	0.3***
	(0.1)	(0.2)	(0.2)	(0.3)	(0.2)	(0.1)
Social expenditure	−1.1***	−1.0***	−1.4***	−0.5	−0.9	−1.0***
	(0.4)	(0.3)	(0.3)	(0.7)	(1.0)	(0.2)
F-value	4.2**	8.39***	21.1***	3.4*	22.5***	16.5***
Adjusted R^2	0.27	0.48	0.82	0.40	0.89	0.35

***: $p < 0.01$; **: $p < 0.05$; *: $p < 0.10$.
Cell entries are regression coefficients, with standard errors in parentheses.

The F-test results, the explained variance, and the steady sign of each model variable's effect suggest that the model fits the data from all cross-sections reasonably well. Except for the unusual result for the variable measuring the length of EU membership and the intercept in the 1975–85 cross-section, the estimated effects all vary within the sampling error across the cross-sections. If we are to believe the pooled dataset, every percentage increase in within-EU trade increases EU support by 0.3 per cent and every percentage increase in social spending reduces it by one per cent. A one-logarithm increase in length of membership, in turn, increases support by 6 per cent— for comparison, the logarithm value of Hungary's four years of membership in 2007 is 1.38, Austria's 13 years is 2.56, that of Greece's 28 years is 3.33, Italy's 52 years is 3.95. Thus length of membership alone might produce a more than 7 per cent gap in EU support between Austria and Hungary but a less than 4 per cent difference between Greece and Italy. By and large, the model explains probably just over a third of the enduring cross-national differences with a parsimonious, theoretically plausible model, which yields believable coefficient estimates and broadly consistent results over time. Figure 8.9 plots the observed over-time averages of EU support against the predicted values based on these three-variable models and demonstrates that the model accounts for patterns in different groups of countries fairly evenly.

It would certainly be wrong to suggest that our data analysis rejects hypotheses about the impact of other variables than the three included in our final model, but we feel reasonably confident that from all seventeen variables that we could consider here, these are the most likely to have had a consistent effect on cross-national differences throughout all five periods, and that these three should certainly not be excluded from any comprehensive explanation of EU support. The substantive implications of the model are clear. Long-term national variations in EU support are attributable primarily to three sets of factors. First, EU support tends to be lower in countries where social welfare spending is already high—presumably because rational citizens in those countries tend to be disproportionately concerned about the risks to future social welfare provision that EU membership might bring. Second, EU support tends to be higher in those countries whose trade is focused mainly on other EU member states. This may again reflect rational calculations. Finally, length of membership in the union also stimulates EU support.

Phase 4: Time-series sources of aggregate variations in EU support

The final stage of our analysis concerns the sources of within-country variations in EU support over time. This issue is explored with time-series analyses summarized in Tables 8.8 and 8.9. As noted above, stationarity problems forced us to use annual change in EU support as the dependent variable in

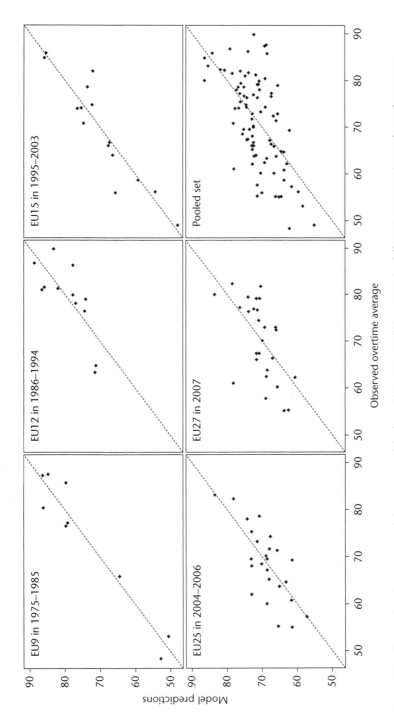

Figure 8.9. The explanatory power of the same model of overtime average EU support in different cross-sections of member states

Table 8.8. Time-series model of aggregate EU support in four data panels, 1975–2007

Differenced independent variables	EU25 1975–2007	EU9 1975–2007	EU12 1986–2007	EU15 1995–2007
Instrumental rationality predictors				
GDP/capita (change)	0.20**	0.21**	0.20*	0.33**
Intra EU trade (change)	0.09*	0.11	0.01	0.02
Net EU transfers (change)	0.06	0.10*	0.01	0.16*
GDP growth (change)	−0.01	−0.05	−0.05	−0.04
Unemployment (change)	−0.11**	−0.1	−0.18*	−0.13
Inflation (change)	−0.06	−0.07	−0.02	0.04
Social expenditure (change)	0.08**	0.08	0.01	0.1
Cueing rationality predictors				
Democracy satisfaction (change)	0.30***	0.27***	0.37***	0.36***
Governance Quality (change)	0.08**	0.03	0.07	0.01
Left-right extremes (change)	−0.02	−0.06	−0.01	−0.02
Cognitive mobilization predictors				
Log EU membership length (change)	−0.09*	0.12	0.03	0.10*
Political discussion (change)	0.10**	0.09	0.15**	0.09
Ad hoc *predictors*				
EU legislation supply (change)	0.05	0.08	0.07	0.08
Council presidency (change)	0.06*	0.06	0.06	0.11
Wage bargaining centralization (change)	0.10***	0.12*	0.04	0.04
Lagged dependent variable and constant				
Lagged dependent variable (change)	−0.19***	−0.25**	−0.20*	−0.24*
Constant	0.0	0.0	0.0	0.0

* $p<0.05$; ** $p<0.01$; *** $p<0.001$.
All variables are first differenced. OLS estimates with panel-corrected standard errors.

this analysis for all available panels (the EU9 1975–2007, EU12 1986–2007, EU15 1995–2007, and the EU25 1975–2007 unbalanced panel). Therefore long-term cross-national differences disappear from these data, except as far as trends in the mean and changes in variance are concerned. Since we are concerned with explaining change, the original independent variables were also first-differenced in this analysis, e.g. the relative quality of governance is replaced with the change in the relative quality of governance compared to a year earlier.[14]

In the absence of significant unit heterogeneity, variables like Second World War casualties (Gabel's indicator for fear of a European war), whether the country is a third-wave democracy, and the barely changing percentage of Catholics in the population stand no chance of revealing their true impact (if there is any) in this analysis. Therefore they are dropped from the list of independent variables here. Affluence, measured as GDP per head, is also dropped since its differenced value is equivalent to economic growth—a change variable that is already present in our model. However, the variables that vary little or nothing across countries but which do vary over time (such as the legislative activity of the EU or which countries provide the EU presidency) now get their chance to reveal the dynamic impact that they may have and are thus included in the models.

Time-series analysis results tend to be sensitive to seemingly technical details of model specification. It is therefore advisable to double-check the consistency of results obtained from any one model specification with a variety of plausible specifications (Wilson and Butler 2007). Evidence of spatial and temporal correlation, together with the dimensions of our dataset, delimited our choice set of plausible statistical models. Woolridge tests (Woolridge 2002) in all four balanced panels, with three different model specifications for each panel, rejected the hypotheses of no first-order autocorrelation in the residuals in ten out of the twelve resultant tests.[15] The possibility of no cross-sectional correlation was, in turn, consistently rejected by a similar series of Pesaran tests (Pesaran 2004). Since the number of time points is relatively small in most national series, we suspect that maximum likelihood models would not be a prudent choice and conclude that OLS models are most probably preferable to GLS estimation.

The model that we consider most appropriate is presented in Table 8.8. This specification uses OLS estimators and corrects for spatial autocorrelation and within-cluster correlation of residuals with the use of panel-corrected standard errors. The same model was re-estimated with eleven alternative estimation techniques, with the results largely concurring (see below). The model always included the predictors grouped under the four headings that we have employed before: instrumental rationality, cueing rationality, cognitive mobilization, and ad hoc variables. The dependent variable in each of the four panels is the year-on-year change in EU support. Looking at the pattern of significant coefficients across all four panels, it is clear that only two predictors consistently achieve statistical significance across all sets of estimations: one that reflects *instrumental rationality* (change in GDP) and one that reflects *cueing rationality* (change in average democracy satisfaction). Two other predictors yield significant effects which, though they do not occur in all models, are spread across at least three panels: change in unemployment (another instrumental rationality variable) and change in average political discussion (which reflects a cognitive mobilization effect). All other predictors fail to achieve significance across more than two panels, with some (such as change in EU legislation and changes in ideological extremism) failing to achieve significance in any of them. These observations apart, the general conclusion suggested by the table resonates with our earlier observation that different findings have been obtained in previous studies in part because those studies have analysed data from different groups of countries in different time periods. If we consider all of the different groups and periods simultaneously, as we do in Table 8.8, the only consistent pattern is that aggregate (over time) changes in EU support follow a transfer rather than substitution logic.

Table 8.9. Comparing alternative significance level estimates for the 1975–2007 unbalanced panel of the EU25

	Estimation method												N of times $p<0.05$
	1	2	3	4	5	6	7	8	9	10	11	12	
Instrumental rationality predictors													
GDP/capita	0.20**	**	***	***	***	**	**	***	***	***	**	***	12
Intra EU trade	0.09*		**	**	*		*	*	**	*		***	8
Net EU transfers	0.06					**					**	*	4
GDP growth	−0.01												0
Unemployment	−0.11**	*	*	*	*		*	*		**			7
Inflation	−0.06												0
Social expenditure	0.08**	**					*					**	
Cueing rationality predictors													
Democracy satisfaction	0.30***	***	***	***	***	***	***	***	***	***	***	***	12
Government quality	0.08						*					***	2
Left-Right extremes	−0.02												0
Cognitive mobilization predictors													
EU membership length	−0.09*	*	*	*	**	*		*					6
Political discussion	0.10**	**	*	*	**					*	*		9
Ad hoc predictors													
EU legislation supply	0.05												0
Council presidency	0.06*			*		*	*						3
Wage bargaining centralization	0.10***	**					*	*				**	4
Lagged dependent variable and constant													
Lagged dep. var.	−0.19***	**	***	***	***	*	***	***	***	***	*	***	12
Constant	−0.00												

* $p<0.05$; ** $p<0.01$; *** $p<0.001$.

All variables are differenced (change) variables. For an explanation of the estimation methods see the main text. A black entry in the matrix indicates that the relevant predictor had no significant effect.

EU support increases with rising rather than falling national GDP and satis-faction with democracy. Only very generic aspects of regime performance—i.e. growth, satisfaction with democracy—matter reliably, while more specific things like inflation or net EU transfers do not have similarly clear-cut effects.

It appears that the unbalanced EU25 panel represents our best chance to summarize the macro-level sources of EU support. This panel, though it con-tains varying numbers of cases for different groups of countries, is obviously the most comprehensive and inclusive of the panels we analyse. It is also clear from Table 8.8 that the pattern of significant effects in that panel is not wholly out of line with the results observed in the other panels. Viewed in this light, we consider that the EU25 panel offers the single best representation of the likely macro-level sources of EU support.

Table 8.9 reports the pattern of coefficient significance across the E25 panel using our twelve alternative estimation methods.[16] The first column of the table replicates the first column of Table 8.8 in order to indicate the signs and magnitudes of the estimated coefficients, which vary hardly at all across the different estimation methods. What change with the use of the different methods are the coefficients' estimated standard errors and their resultant significance levels. Table 8.9 shows that only two predictor variables are significant in all twelve estimations: change in GDP (which supports instru-mental rationality theory) and change in democracy satisfaction (which sup-ports the idea of transfer cueing). Three further variables achieve significance in more than half the estimated models: two that lend further support to instrumental rationality theory (change in EU trade and change in unemploy-ment) and one that supports cognitive mobilization theory (change in politi-cal discussion). The fact that this set of five predictors is both signed as theoretically expected and consistently significant across different estimation methods using the EU25 macro-level panel complements the broad conclu-sion that we drew earlier in relation to the individual-level sources of EU support. Taken together, they indicate the importance of taking an eclectic theoretical approach to the understanding of EU support. The results of the EU25 panel, in short, indicate that the origins of EU support lie in part in instrumental rationality; in part in the sort of cognitive shortcuts associated with cueing rationality; and in part in the changing taste patterns associated with cognitive mobilization. For all the remaining predictor variables in Table 8.9, we conclude that the case for their having an effect on changes in EU support is at best "not proven". Interestingly, none of the ad hoc predictors identified as important in previous studies appears to exert any consistent effect on EU support whatsoever. The theory that EU support is rooted in a substitution logic fares worse yet: all indications are that citizens support the EU when things are going well, rather than when things are going wrong in the domestic arena. This suggests that citizens may just see the EU and the nation state as part of the same political system, and responsible for much the same aspects of system performance.

Summary and conclusions

We have attempted here to subject the claims of three broad theoretical perspectives on EU support (instrumental rationality, cueing rationality, and cognitive mobilization) to more stringent empirical testing than was previously possible. We have simultaneously attempted to assess the explanatory power of a number of ad hoc hypotheses that have been advanced in previous studies to account for specific temporal or spatial variations in EU support patterns. Using the most comprehensive micro- and macro-level datasets available, we have sought to assess how far the signature variables of the various perspectives are capable of explaining both individual- and aggregate-level variations in EU support. Lack of suitable data has prevented us from assessing the value of other theoretical perspectives, such as identitarian theory. We have deliberately eschewed the development of a single, all-encompassing multilevel model of EU support because we are convinced that the technical difficulties associated with the simultaneous estimation of individual-level, cross-country, and within-country time-series effects (as well as any possible cross-level effects) are so great as to render any such estimation procedure meaningless. We have accordingly broken down the process of estimating different sorts of effect into four separate estimation procedures—one each for individual-level effects, cross-level effects, cross-country effects, and within-country time-series effects.

Table 8.10 summarizes the results of our endeavours. As the table indicates, we find evidence that at least one of the signature variables associated with each of the three theoretical perspectives is significant at both the micro and macro levels. At the micro level, for example, there are significant roles in the determination of EU support for instrumental rationality (five of the indicators of labour market position have significant, correctly signed coefficients), for cueing rationality (satisfaction with democracy, ideological position, and Catholic religion are all significant and plausibly signed), and for cognitive mobilization (engagement in political discussion and level of education are both significant and correctly signed). Similarly, in the macro time series, the set of significant predictors (changes in GDP, EU trade, unemployment, democracy satisfaction, and political discussion) indicates that each of the three perspectives contributes something to the explanation of EU support. Significantly, though, EU support is consistently increased, rather than decreased, by the kind of factors that can be expected to boost regime support

Table 8.10. Summary of empirical findings

	Individual-level support (Table 8.4)	Cross-level support (Table 8.5)	Cross-section support (Table 8.7)	Timeseries support (Table 8.9)
Instrumental Rationality	*Strong support* Education (+) *Moderate support* Unemployment (−) Manual worker (−) Age (−) Male (+)	Social expenditure: *Education (+) *Unemployment (−) *Manual worker (−) *White Collar worker (−)	Intra-EU trade (+) Social expenditure (−)	Changes in (log) GDP (+) Changes in intra-EU trade (+) Changes in Unemployment (−)
Cueing Rationality	*Strong support* Democracy satisfaction (+) Left-Right scale (+) *Moderate support* Catholic (+) Left-Right extreme (−)			Changes in Democracy Satisfaction (+)
Cognitive Mobilization	Political discussion (+) (Education +)		Length EU membership (+)	Changes in Political Discussion (+)
Ad hoc	—		—	—

at the national level. Hence, EU support is dominated by a transfer, rather than substitution logic.

Overall, Table 8.10 suggests the following conclusions. First, there is evidence for *instrumental rationality* in the determination of EU support at all four data-analytic levels. At the individual level, labour market position has clear and predictable effects on support: the educated, the young, and men are more likely to support the EU; the unemployed and manual workers are less likely to do so. As our analysis of cross-level effects shows, these labour market effects are strengthened by social welfare spending. Where spending is high, the positive effects of education and the negative effects of unemployment and manual work are all increased. In terms of relatively stable cross-country differences, EU support is highest where intra-EU trade is highest and where social welfare spending is lowest. We interpret these effects as rational responses, respectively, to the recognition of material economic interests and to the expectation that in the long term current national social welfare spending will converge across the EU. At the macro time-series level, EU support rises (falls) when the domestic economy, as reflected in GDP and unemployment, improves (declines); it also rises (falls) as a country's trade connections with other EU countries strengthens (weakens).

Second, Table 8.10 also indicates support for *cueing rationality*. At the individual level, there is strong evidence of "transfer" as opposed to "substitution" cueing. Across the EU, people who are satisfied with their national democratic institutions are significantly more likely to support the EU—as the transfer cueing hypothesis would suggest. In contrast to the claims of "substitution" cueing, it is *not* those who are most *dissatisfied* with their national democratic processes who are most likely to support the EU. There is also evidence for relatively modest individual-level cueing roles for left–right ideology (with people on the centre right tending to be more pro-EU than those on the centre left, but with those at both extremes tending to be *less* supportive of the EU project) and for religion (with Catholics being the most likely to be pro-EU). These individual-level cueing effects are complemented by a strong macro time-series effect in which changes in aggregate democracy satisfaction have consistent and positive effects on changes in EU support. Finally, Table 8.10 also shows the consistent importance of cognitive mobilization. At both the micro and macro levels, engagement in political discussion exerts a powerful positive effect. This is supplemented by the micro effects of education (effects that are also "claimed" by instrumental rationality theory) and the country-level effects of length of EU membership.

Perhaps the most important conclusion suggested by Table 8.10, however, is the simple observation that, when all of the relevant data sources are considered and no one estimation method is relied upon, the set of consistent influences on EU support is very limited. By no means do all signature variables associated with the three main theories achieve consistent statistical significance—and none of the ad hoc explanatory variables achieves this status. As we have repeatedly indicated, we make no claims to test all of the possible hypotheses that can be advanced about the sources of EU support: the lack of suitable data makes such a task impossible. However, our analysis shows the importance of treating "partial" empirical evidence—based on a restricted time period or on a limited group of countries—with considerable caution. Our analysis shows that what we actually *know* about the sources of EU support is quite limited and does not easily generalize from one period to another. We suspect that the key reason for this lies in the nature of the EU itself as a complex, dynamically evolving, and self-reflexive organization that generates diverse, contradictory, and ever-changing expectations, which are unlikely to follow a unified logic or a given set of fixed preferences. Appropriate empirical tests of this possibility—and significant further progress in individual, cross-national, and cross-temporal variation in support for the EU—can only be expected from further studies that can explicitly model the changing expectations towards the EU and how they transform the bases on which the EU is judged by its citizens. Yet the robust positive effect of satisfaction with domestic democracy and domestic economic performance on the over-time dynamics of EU support makes it far more likely that the global and European financial crisis that started in 2008 will reduce rather than ignite popular support for integration.

Notes

1. Previous time-series analyses mostly relied instead on the difference in the percentages of those who consider membership a good and a bad thing, respectively. While such details tend to make very little difference (cf. Eichenberg and Dalton 2007: note 7), our series makes a fuller use of the available information by taking both non-responses and neutral responses into account.
2. See Hooghe and Marks (2005) for a partly different classification and review of the relevant theories, and note that we subsume all identity-based reactions in our second category.
3. Recall that at the individual level we have a multiply imputed dataset for over 200,000 individuals, who form unequally sized samples of an unbalanced set of twenty-seven countries over a thirty-three-year period, and note that three of the individual-level variables in the analysis—satisfaction with democracy, left–right ideology self-placement, left–right extremism and religion—are missing for certain years in the Eurobarometer series.
4. The standard errors of these estimated effects were adjusted for the multiply imputed nature of the data using the *mim* package of Carlin, Galati, and Royston (2008).

5. This choice is prompted by the fact that the dependent variable is a three-point scale with a typically skewed distribution. Therefore we replicated all individual-level analyses reported in this chapter with both ordered logit and linear regression but found no systematic differences between them (these additional analyses are available from the authors upon request). For ease of interpretation, the rest of the chapter only shows linear regression results.

6. The effect of age is apparently not linear and therefore we included both age and age-squared among the predictors. For the interpretation of their effects note that the age variable in this analysis is measured in years divided by 100, and thus the extreme values of 0 and 1 on either the age or the age-squared variable refer to the— practically speaking fictitious—newborn and 100-year-old respondents. Consequently, in the average country year we expect that, *ceteris paribus*, a 100-year-old person (at 17.2–22.6 = –5.4 points) is just 1.6 points less supportive of EU membership than a 20-year-old (at 17.2*0.04–22.6*0.2 = –3.832 points), while a 50-year-old (at 17.2*0.25–22.6*0.5 = –7 points) is rather more markedly, namely 3.2 points, less supportive than the 20-year-old. While there is considerable variance across country years in the direction of the expected differences between the middle-aged and the old, the percentage of country years where either the middle-aged or the old is expected to be significantly more pro-EU than the young is just slightly higher than we would expect by chance alone. Nonetheless, the non-monothonic pattern of generational differences seems hard to explain either in terms of relative labour market positions, or cues, or "acquired taste" factors.

7. Since the dependent variables in these analyses were themselves statistical estimates rather than observations, it would be desirable to incorporate information about their level-1 standard errors in our level-2 time-series analyses as in two-step multi-level analyses. However, we are not aware of statistical software that could accomplish this task. We did find, however, that simple OLS regression analyses of our level-2 models produce virtually identical results as the FGLS analyses that adjusted for level-1 standard errors in the dependent variable as proposed by Lewis and Linzer (2005). Therefore we think that the validity of our time-series results is not undermined by the lack of adjustment for level-1 standard errors.

8. We conducted Fisher tests of unit roots in all panels and found that these do not raise concerns. Woolridge tests identified first-order autocorrelation in some panels for the first two level-1 effects. Hausman tests showed that all series display significant unit effects, and that these, except for the effect of satisfaction with democracy, are approximately random. Table 8.5 shows what level-2 model we considered most appropriate in the light of this for explaining the cross-unit variance in each of the nine level-1 effects.

9. For each dependent variable we estimated the following time-series models (with the names of relevant STATA commands in parentheses): fixed-effects regression with AR(1) (i.e. first-order autoregressive disturbance) and Driscoll and Kraay (1998) standard errors (xtscc); fixed-effects (within) regression with AR(1) (xtregar); random-effects GLS with AR(1) (xtregar); random-effects regression with clustered sandwich estimator of standard errors (xtreg); random-effects regression with conventional standard errors (xtreg); Prais–Winsten regression with panel-corrected standard errors and a lagged dependent variable (xtpcse).

10. Non-stationarity was tested separately in all four panels mentioned in the previous note with the augmented Dickey–Fuller unit-root test.

11. That is, a variance analysis with country as the only independent variable yields an adjusted R^2 of 0.72, 0.69, 0.64, and 0.86 in the EU27 unbalanced panel for 1975–2007, and the balanced panels for the EU9 (1975–2007), EU12 (1986–2007), and EU15 (1995–2007), respectively.

12. We replicated the reported analyses with six different ways of estimating probability (goodness of fit) but found no difference between the results. The tables present the results obtained with the hyper-g prior, while the alternatives that we tested are described in the documentation of the software as "EB-global", "ZS-null", "AIC", "BIC", and "g-prior".

13. These choices were supported by further evidence available on request about the average and overall distribution of T-values for each variable's effects, and additional Bayesian model averaging analyses that dropped all (but just one at a time) of the seventeen variables from the analysis reported here.

14. We took an exception with economic growth, which is already a change variable.

15. The first specification only including the substantively interesting independent variables among the predictors; the second added to this the lagged dependent variable (LDV); and the third added fixed effects for countries (but not the LDV). Only two models for the EU12 panel (1986–2007) gave support for the null hypotheses.

16. The twelve estimation methods, in order of their appearance in Table 8.9, were: pooled OLS regression with panel-corrected standard errors; pooled OLS regression with Driscoll–Kray standard errors; pooled OLS with robust standard errors and correction for clustering; population-averaged GLS with robust standard errors; pooled FGLS; pooled FGLS assuming heteroskedastic and correlated error structures; random-effects GLS with robust standard errors; fixed-effects GLS with robust standard errors; random-effects FGLS; random-effects FGLS assuming heteroskedastic and correlated error structures; fixed-effects OLS regression with Driscoll–Kray standard errors.

9

Europe à la Carte? Public Support for Policy Integration in an Enlarged European Union

Pedro C. Magalhães

To a large extent, every major step in the history of European unification—and much of the debate each of those steps generated—has concerned "policy integration", i.e. the "Europeanization" of particular domains of policy making by the transfer of competencies and prerogatives from national governments to EU institutions. The very inception of the European Economic Community involved the adoption of common trade and agricultural policies. One of the crucial changes brought about by the Single European Act was the addition of regional cohesion, scientific research, workers' rights, and environmental protection to the set of policies where supranational decision making at the European level was to take place. The Maastricht Treaty created nothing less than a European Monetary Union and a Common Foreign and Security Policy, while the Amsterdam Treaty brought political asylum, immigration, and judicial cooperation in civil matters under the supranational "community pillar". More recently, much of the political controversy around the draft for a new European Constitution or its revised version in the Treaty of Lisbon revolved precisely around which policies were to be assigned to each level of government, as well as the decision-making procedures to be adopted at the European Council in each policy domain, prolonging the debates generated by the subsidiarity principle enshrined in the Maastricht Treaty and its application (Sinn 1994).

However, most of the social-scientific research dealing with citizens' attitudes vis-à-vis the European Union has tended to focus on more generic objects of public support than on *policy integration* itself. Support for "Europe" has been most frequently assessed by analysing responses to survey questions about citizens' beliefs in whether their countries' membership in the European Union is "a good thing" or "a bad thing", what their feelings would be if the European Union was "scrapped", whether they support efforts being made to "unify Europe", the speed with which they desire integration to proceed, or whether they believe their country "has benefited" from integration. The extent to which all these different questions measure the same or different constructs, and particularly the extent to which they tap "specific" or "utilitarian" support versus "diffuse" or "affective" support, remains a matter of debate, with important empirical, theoretical, and normative implications (see, among many, Lindberg and Scheingold 1970; Inglehart, Rabier, and Reif 1991; Niedermayer 1995b; Gabel 1998b). However, there is clearly something of paramount importance that all those previous indicators do not seem to be capturing head on: European citizens' views about the transfer of policy prerogatives in specific areas from national or sub-national levels of government to the European level of government.

There are three main reasons why the relative neglect of this aspect of citizens' views may be unfortunate. First, there is compelling evidence that public attitudes towards Europe are multidimensional, and that support for policy integration constitutes precisely one of such crucial dimensions. Lubbers and Scheepers (2005), for example, show that while commonly used survey items such as the "membership as a good thing" or the "perceived benefits of integration" belong to a single dimension of "instrumental" attitudes—particularly pliable to short-term developments, attitudes, and perceptions concerning the economic consequences of integration (Gabel 1998c; Christin 2005)—support for joint decision making between national and European institutions constitutes a different dimension of support, more political in nature and potentially far more relevant to the legitimization of the European Union as a multilevel political system.[1] In fact, the claim that support for policy integration comes closer to tapping the fundamental legitimacy of the EU was made by Sinnott more than a decade ago: the "legitimacy of internationalized governance (. . .) depends on the relationship between the EU's claims at acquiring decision-making authority in different policy areas and public perceptions and expectations about such claims" (1995: 275).[2]

Second, there are good reasons to believe that even the distinction between "instrumental" and "political" dimensions of support for Europe may still be oversimplifying relevant differences between policy areas and political systems. On the one hand, while clear majorities among the European publics have consistently seen certain policy areas as ripe for some amount of centralization of authority in supranational European institutions—the cases of scientific research, foreign aid, environmental protection, and foreign policy, just to give a few examples—there are other domains—such as education, health and welfare, and cultural policies—in which clear majorities have consistently *rejected* such transfer of power (Sinnott 1995; Dalton and Eichenberg 1998; Lubbers and Scheepers 2005). On the other hand, regardless of those cross-policy differences, there is also a clear sense in the existing research

213

that cross-national differences in this respect are also particularly pronounced. While lack of support for policy integration seems widespread in countries such as Finland, the United Kingdom, Sweden, and Denmark, the opposite tends to happen in a country such as Italy. Furthermore, not all countries can be ranked in the same way concerning all types of policies. While citizens in countries such as Portugal and Greece emerge as having as many "sceptics" vis-à-vis the Europeanization of "international" policies as citizens in countries such as Denmark or the UK, their opposition to the Europeanization of "sociocultural policies"—education, health care, or culture—is clearly not as pronounced as in other countries (Lubbers and Scheepers 2005). In other words, even the distinction between "instrumental" and "political" support for integration is likely to be missing out on important variations that beg for an explanation.

Finally, there are signs that, by missing out on both this multidimensionality and on these cross-policy and cross-national variations, the literature on support for integration has also been missing out on one of the possible explanations of the current travails of the European Union, following the rejection of the European Constitution and the Treaty of Lisbon in popular referendums. Alesina and Wacziarg, for example, suggest the existence of a connection between a decrease in public support for the European project and the widening range of policy prerogatives transferred to EU institutions that has taken place in the last two decades (Alesina and Wacziarg 1999). Such widening has encompassed policies unrelated to the protection of free trade and free markets, and where the benefits of centralization at the supranational level of government, in terms of economies of scale and internalizing externalities, are smaller than the costs of imposing uniform policies on large populations with heterogeneous preferences. As a result, the benefits of economic integration have arguably been overshadowed by a growing resistance to political integration on the part of citizens "attached to their own national identities and preferences" and who have grown to fear excessive centralization (see also Alesina and Wacziarg 2008).

The purpose of this chapter is precisely to discuss mass attitudes in Europe concerning the assignment of responsibilities to European institutions in different policy areas, and what different factors are associated with trends and cross-policy and cross-national variations that can be observed in this regard. We are interested in answering three main questions. First, which policy areas tend to be seen by most European citizens as properly belonging to the exclusive decision-making domain of national governments, and which tend to be seen as requiring at least some amount of supranational centralization and coordination at the European level? Second, what causes citizens of some countries to be more supportive of allocating policy prerogatives to the European level of government than others? And finally, to what extent have Europeans' views about these issues changed through time?

In the following section, we will discuss several hypotheses about what may explain differences between policies, countries, and political and economic contexts in regard to the level of support for policy integration. In Section 3, on the basis of Eurobarometer and Candidate Country Barometer data, a cross-sectional analysis will be used to test a set of generic hypotheses about what explains cross-national and cross-policy differences in terms of the support for policy integration. In Section 4, using panel data, we will analyse the changes through time experienced in the levels of support for integration in a smaller set of policies and countries on which we have longer time series available. In the concluding section, we will discuss the implications of our findings for different views about the relationship between the pace of European integration and citizens' views about it.

1 Hypotheses

Three basic sets of hypotheses have been advanced about aggregate levels of mass support for policy integration. The first is related to the issue of why some policies might generally be seen by citizens as more adequately handled at a supranational level of government than at other levels. The second concerns the reasons why citizens of some countries might be more likely than their counterparts elsewhere to support a shift towards supranational decision making. Finally, some hypotheses have also been advanced concerning how and why levels of support for policy integration may have changed through time. We deal with each of these in turn.

Cross-policy differences

How can we distinguish policy areas from each other in a way that might be consequential in terms of the level of mass support for policy integration? The first and most common approach has been to focus on the nature of the problems and issues involved in each domain, and to distinguish them in terms of the extent to which, under some general and abstract criteria of efficiency or appropriateness, supranational decision making is required or desirable. Political scientists have tended to draw on neo-functionalist theory (Haas 1958) in order to think about policies in this way, identifying those that deal with problems that are difficult to solve exclusively at the national level and where gains from supranational coordination are more likely (Dalton and Eichenberg 1998: 254). This is what underlies the notion of "endogenous internationalization" advanced by Sinnott (1995). The issues that "require the intervention of internationalized governance if they are to be tackled at all", that "penetrate and transcend borders", and that "require a response at the international level" are the ones where a sort of "endogenous" or "inherent" internationalization is at stake (Sinnott 1995: 247–8).[3] In a similar vein, Wessels and Kielhorn distinguish policies in terms of the "global problem scope" they address, i.e. the extent to which "problems are border-crossing in their scope" (Wessels and Kielhorn 1999: 177). De Winter and Swyngedouw follow the same approach, by identifying issues that, besides their border-crossing nature, "require a larger-than-national scale in order to mobilize the resources necessary to solve the problem" (1999: 48).

Political economists have addressed the same sort of question under a different but related perspective, drawing on the theories of fiscal federalism (Oates 1972) in order to ascertain the optimal allocation of policies to different levels of government. This allocation has been discussed as resulting from a trade-off between (1) the benefits that centralization may bring in terms of internalizing externalities and reducing production costs by means of economies of scale; and (2) the welfare losses involved in centrally and uniformly providing public goods to large populations with heterogeneous preferences. Alesina and colleagues (Alesina and Wacziarg 1999; Alesina, Angeloni, and Schuknecht 2005) have discussed the desirable allocation of policy responsibilities among local, national, and EU levels from this point of view, and Hooghe has also drawn on this literature in order to distinguish policies from each other: "Europeanization may be advantageous to maximize economies of scale (. . .) or it may be desirable to internalize negative externalities. (. . . .) Where such economies of scale or policy externalities are weak (. . .), the relevant jurisdiction is national (or regional or local)" (Hooghe 2003: 287–8).

Operationalizing the "inherent internationalization" of policy areas or making judgements about their optimal allocation to different levels of government, far from being a straightforward task, is prone to over-extension, i.e. "to see virtually all problems as internationalized" (Sinnott 1995: 261), and is inevitably based on a number of simplifying and contestable assumptions (De Winter and Swyngedouw 1999: 51; Hooghe 2003: 288; Alesina, Angeloni, and Schuknecht 2005: 284). However, in spite of this, there is a considerable convergence in expert judgements in this respect. Table 9.1 presents the lists of policies that have been described as either high or low in terms of their "inherent internationalization" in different studies. It also presents Hooghe's "functionality" scale and the judgements made by Alesina, Angeloni, and Schuknecht (2005) about the areas where efficiency considerations suggest that all or at least some competencies should be allocated at the EU level.

There is not complete overlap in the range of policies assigned to the different categories in these different studies. Besides, a "medium" category is introduced in two of them, while another relies on a post-fieldwork coding

Table 9.1. Policies and levels of government: assessments of inherent internationalization, functionality or optimal allocation

	Inherent internationalization			Functionality/Optimal allocation	
	Sinnott 1995	Wessels and Kielhorn 1999	Winter and Swyndegouw 1999	Hooghe 2003	Alesina et al. 2005
Internationalization/EU Centralization	Crime Data protection Defence Drugs Environment Foreign aid Foreign policy Research Terrorism	Agriculture Currency Defence Environment Foreign aid Foreign Policy Immigration	Agriculture Crime Democratic assistance Drugs Environment Foreign aid Foreign policy Immigration Terrorism	Agriculture Currency Defence Environment Foreign aid Foreign policy Immigration/ Asylum	Common market Communications Competition Currency Defence Environment Foreign aid Foreign policy Global crime International trade Migration Subsidies Transportation
Medium/mixed		Crime Economy Media/press Research		Regional funds Research Social inclusion	Fiscal/tax
Nationalization/Decentralization	Education Energy Fighting poverty Unemployment Worker's co- determination	Education Health Regional funds Social policy Taxation Unemployment	Corruption Education Health Inflation Media/press Political institutions Rights Taxation Unemployment Welfare/equality	Education Employment Health	Agriculture Culture Education Employment Energy Health Local crime Regional funds Research Welfare

of respondents' open answers to a survey question (rather than a pre-prepared list of items). However, comparing the lists, only on two issues—agriculture and scientific research—do we find clearly contradictory assessments. This should not surprise us too much. On the one hand, treating agriculture as an "inherently internationalized" issue seems to flow much more from the very extensive competencies already enjoyed by the EU since the Treaty of Rome than from any consideration of the cost–benefit relationship involved in that centralization. And on the other hand, the different ways in which scientific and technological research is addressed reflects the controversy within the political economy literature on the issue (Breuss and Eller 2004). However, in all of the remaining policy areas, most authors that have tackled the subject from this point of view seem to have been able to largely agree on the kind of issues whose nature advises at least a partial shift of responsibilities from member states to a centralized European authority. Foreign policy, environmental protection, foreign aid, defence, fight against drugs, terrorism, immigration/asylum, currency, and terrorism emerge undisputedly as evoking interdependence concerns and suggesting that benefits may arise from some coordination at a supranational level. Conversely, on issues such as unemployment, education, health, cultural policy, media, regional development, poverty, taxation, and social inclusion, the verdict is either mixed or decidedly for national or even sub-national policy making.[4]

A rather different question is whether this broad convergence in the conjectures found in the literature coincides with the actual preferences of citizens regarding what the allocation of responsibilities for different policies should be. As Sinnott noted early on, inherent internationalization exists "whether or not it is perceived by the public" (1995: 247), and he even detected a number of issues—such as data protection, defence, and, in some countries, foreign policy—where, at least by the early 1990s, the level of public support for policy integration was lower than the nature of the issue seemed to impose. As it happens, there is some division in the literature on the question of whether the degree of "inherent internationalization" of particular domains tends to be acknowledged by the general public. Although there is agreement that political elites do seem to lend greater support to the Europeanization of "inherently international" policies (Wessels and Kielhorn 1999; Hooghe 2003), controversy ensues when mass attitudes are concerned. Several studies using Eurobarometer data have suggested that public support for the Europeanization of the policies in the "low inherent internationalization" list in Table 9.1 tends to be lower (Dalton and Eichenberg 1998; Alesina, Angeloni, and Schuknecht 2005; Lubbers and Scheepers 2005; Christin, Hug, and Schultz 2005), although this is more clearly the case in the EU15 members than in the ten new member states that entered the union in 2004 (Ahrens, Meurer, and Renner 2007). Using European Election Study data, De Winter and Swyndegouw also show that the inherent internationalization of problems, as they operationalize it, is one of the strongest predictors of European citizens' willingness to allocate responsibility for decision making to the EU level of government (1999: 64).

However, Hooghe (2003) reaches very different conclusions: once we control for other features of each policy domain, "functionality" or "inherent internationalization" considerations end up being a poor predictor of people's views about which level of government should do what (p. 292). What are the other aspects of policies and issues that seem to drive support for Europeanization? First, according to Hooghe, a "spending logic" is at stake from the citizens' point of view: policies where shifts of authority would involve greater distributional implications, potentially destabilizing the interests of powerful groups in society and the everyday policy delivery to citizens, are unlikely to receive public support for their Europeanization. These are the policies that involve greater financial flows from state to citizen, such as health, education, and social policies in general. Hooghe finds that support for policy integration among mass publics is lowest for those policies (2003: 282), echoing Dalton and Eichenberg's conclusion that public support should be lower in policies related to standards of living and the distribution of national welfare, a result of the potentially disturbing effect of Europeanization on "national welfare traditions and policies that represent historic (. . .) national compromises" (1998: 279).

A second potentially relevant attribute of policy areas is the extent to which they conform to a "social model" logic and how this is likely to increase citizens' support for their Europeanization (Hooghe 2003: 290–1). Since the 1970s, using a dynamic interpretation of the treaties, the EU engaged in a set of "new regulatory" policies, initially aimed at harmonizing national standards in a variety of areas where those standards could work as barriers to trade (Börzel 2005). However, with the Delors Commission, such prerogatives have increasingly developed also as "market-correcting" policies, i.e. as a means with which to face the detrimental effects of globalization on the political discretion of governments and the economic security of citizens. Areas such as regional asymmetries and development, employment, social inclusion, industrial regulation, scientific and technological research, and environmental or consumer protection fall into this category. Indeed, Hooghe finds that these "social model" policies also tend to elicit greater support for integration on the part of citizens (although not among elites), a finding that, again, Dalton and Eichenberg had already hinted at in their descriptive analysis of support for the Europeanization of employment policies: "citizens are receptive (. . .) to the EU's argument that the functioning of the single market requires economic mechanisms that reduce the uncertainties and costs of doing business in the market" (1998: 279).

A fourth and final feature of policy domains whose impact on citizens' views may need to be considered is related to the actual involvement of the EU in the different issue areas. Regardless of the judgements that can be made about the appropriateness of allocating policy responsibilities to the EU and any other issue-specific aspects, citizens may also be influenced in their evaluations by the extent to which those policy areas are already "claimed by some agency of internationalized governance as lying within its competence" (Sinnott 1995: 248). De Winter and Swyndegouw's analysis of European Election Study data—where respondents were asked to state their perception of what level of government at which issues were decided—lends support to this hypothesis: "the problem sectors that are already perceived as being most European-ized are at the same time those for which further Europeanization is demanded most" (1999: 58). Of course, such relationship, if it exists once other factors are taken into account, is neither necessarily deterministic nor unidirectional. As Dalton and Eichenberg note for the case of environmental policy, for example, public support for European action actually preceded the enhancement of EU responsibility in that area, an enhancement that can conceivably be seen as a result of mounting public and interest-group pressure (Dalton and Eichenberg 1998: 265–6).

Cross-national differences

As we saw early on, regardless of cross-policy differences, there is also a clear sense in the existing research that cross-national differences in this respect are particularly pronounced. One way of thinking about the sources of cross-national differences is to relate them to aspects of the domestic political system. In a widely cited article, Sánchez-Cuenca shows that citizens who live in more corrupt countries tend both to distrust their government and to place greater stock in the European project (2000: 159, 163). In other words, further integration is more desired when citizens have good reasons to be sceptical about domestic state capacities and the quality of national governance. Rohrschneider (2002) suggests a similar albeit conditional empirical relationship: living in countries with well-functioning institutions increases the extent to which perceptions of lack of representation by EU institutions depress support for an EU-wide government. It is true that the dependent variable in these studies did not consist in citizens' preferences for policy integration. However, examining precisely such preferences within the EU15 countries and comparing them with those in the countries that acceded the EU in 2004, Ahrens, Meurer, and Renner (2007) find that those countries with lower quality of national governance, measured by World Bank Governance Indicators (Kaufmann, Kraay, and Mastuzzi 2007), are precisely those that tend to display greater support for the allocation of policy responsibilities to the EU.

Population size is a second potentially relevant variable explaining cross-national differences in terms of support for policy integration. De Winter and Swyngedouw find that population size is negatively related to the assignment of policy responsibilities to the EU, with smaller and medium-sized countries displaying more pro-European attitudes than larger ones (1999: 65). Why might this be the case? Alesina and Wacziarg suggest that, by being over-represented in the European Council, smaller countries have more to gain from transferring policy prerogatives to the EU level, something that may indeed account for the fact that "popular support for European integration has traditionally been greater within Europe's smaller countries" (Alesina and Wacziarg 1999: 32). However, one can conceive of an alternative hypothesis. To the extent that smaller jurisdictions are likely to be both more homoge-neous and better able to satisfy the preferences of their populations, central-ization of policy-making authority at a higher level could be thought less likely to be seen as welfare enhancing and, thus, less desirable from the citizens' point of view (Breuss and Eller 2004). Thus, what we should expect about the impact of population size is unclear: although larger countries may be more reluctant to relinquish sovereignty to decision-making bodies where they are comparatively under-represented, smaller countries may also face greater potential incentives to preserve that sovereignty.

Arguments concerning timing of accession have been commonly framed in terms of how a longer duration of membership allows for the build-up of a larger reservoir of diffuse support for the EU (Inglehart and Rabier 1978). However, the relationship between membership duration and support for the EU seems to be undercut by other factors. Niedermayer (1995b) noted that the six original member states had reached, by the mid-1980s, "an upper limit in the level of public support" (1995: 64), while some of the later entrants—i.e. the United Kingdom, Denmark, and Ireland—displayed com-paratively lower levels of support. But when it came to the Southern European cases, their more recent European membership did not prevent them display-ing high levels of public support for integration from very early on. This phenomenon has been attributed to the role played by the EU in those countries' successful democratization processes and the consolidation of the new regimes (Niedermayer 1995b: 66), an argument that De Winter and Swyngedouw (1999: 65) restate as they analyse support for the Europeaniza-tion of policies. Extending this logic further, we should expect other new democracies to display favourable sentiments to EU decision making. With the exception of Malta, all countries that entered the EU in 2004 and 2007 are—together with Portugal, Greece, and Spain—"third-wave democracies" (Huntington 1992), where the prospects of integration and European conditionality policies have played an important role in the legitimization of democratic actors, the advance of economic reforms, and overall regime democratization (Whitehead 2001).

One final aspect that must be taken into consideration is each country's level of economic development. One possible argument regarding the relationship between development and support for policy integration or European integration in general is that voters in richer and more developed countries might be generally unwilling to endure an expected harmonization of policy making at lower standards of delivery that would follow from "Europeanizing" a particular policy domain. There is little evidence in the literature, however, that the wealth of countries exerts an independent effect on the extent to which their citizens express greater or lower support for European integration (Bosch and Newton 1995; Sánchez-Cuenca 2000). Nevertheless, differences between the most and least developed countries in the EU are likely to express themselves in subtler ways in what concerns the preference for Europeanizing particular policies. If, as we have seen, high-spending policies are generally less likely to receive support for their Europeanization, this may not be the case in all EU countries. As Dalton and Eichenberg suggest, citizens in poorer countries are actually more likely to perceive there is less to lose (and something to gain) from the harmonization of those policies whose delivery requires greater economic resources (1998: 280). From this point of view, the relationship between economic development and support for the Europeanization of policies can be hypothesized as a conditional relationship, contingent upon the nature of such policies: in what concerns "high-spending" policies, citizens of poorer countries may be more likely to support their Europeanization than citizens of wealthier EU member states.

Changes through time

Regardless of stable differences between policies and between countries, it is possible that levels of support for the allocation of policy-making responsibilities to the European level have also changed through time. A first conjecture, based on the existing research on "instrumental" attitudes such as support for membership or perception of benefits from integration, is that that such support may have shifted mostly on the basis of domestic economic performance. There is some evidence that, although citizens' subjective perception of economic performance seems to play a far stronger role in explaining support for European integration, objective economic performance also has a relevant positive effect (Eichenberg and Dalton 1993; Gabel and Palmer 1995; Bosch and Newton 1995; Gabel and Whitten 1997). It is at least conceivable that a similar phenomenon has taken place in what concerns support for joint decision making with the EU in particular policy areas. However, it is not clear that this role played by economic performance has persisted in the post-Maastricht era. Çiftçi (2005) shows, for example, that even in what concerns the explanation of aggregate generic "support for integration" in nine EU countries from the early 1970s until the late 1990s, growth, unemployment, and inflation have relatively small effects on the perception of membership as a "good thing". Eichenberg and Dalton (2007) suggest this is a specifically post-Maastricht phenomenon: the transition to monetary union has changed the criteria on the basis of which citizens evaluate integration, leading citizens to cease responding to improvements in economic conditions. Feeling that the monetary union process and the convergence criteria associated with it have affected government provision of social programmes, European citizens may have begun to perceive integration as having direct consequences on their day-to-day lives, ceasing to judge it primarily on the basis of the generic cues provided by domestic economic performance (Eichenberg and Dalton 2007).

All this has led to consideration of the integration process in itself—its stages, crucial events, and political developments—as creating different contexts and environments that can perhaps be themselves more important determinants of public attitudes than economic performance itself. There are at least three additional conjectures about trends in support for policy integration that can be made. First, support for EU decision making in all policy areas in general may have followed the same path experienced by generic support for European integration, and for the same reasons: i.e. a general post-Maastricht decline. Çiftçi (2005) finds that the signing of the Maastricht Treaty marks the beginning of a decline in the positive evaluations of membership in the EU, which is replicated in most examined member states (with Ireland as the single exception). According to Çiftçi, "the challenges posed to national sovereignty as well as the frustration caused by the increasing amount of supranational decision making (post-Maastricht era)" (2005: 484) are behind this trend. It is not inconceivable that the same frustration has spread to support for policy integration. This would correspond to a "too much too soon" hypothesis, with Maastricht triggering a general decline in support for awarding prerogatives to the EU across all policy levels, resulting from a generic public rejection of the "dramatic acceleration of the scope and depth of the integration process" (Eichenberg and Dalton 2007: 139).

Another possibility is that Maastricht has indeed triggered a decline in public support for policy integration, but a selective one, in some areas but not others. Eichenberg and Dalton (2007) advance a hypothesis as to what areas those might be: the ones related to or affected by monetary union. According to them, the adoption of a common monetary policy and the convergence criteria it entailed have brought real and perceived consequences in terms of government spending, particularly in what concerns budget austerity and cuts in redistributive policies. "As a result," they argue, "EMU is now debated as much for its impact on government spending as it is for its impact in the field of monetary policy" and "from the perspective of pensioners or recipients of health benefits (to name just two very large constituencies), little in this debate reflects positively on monetary union" (Eichenberg and Dalton 2007: 140). Thus, we should observe, since Maastricht, a decline in support for policy integration in areas such as health, welfare, social protection, and education—where the distributive implications of budget austerity are large—as well as in areas where integration can be seen as a direct culprit of budgetary constraints, such as monetary policy.

Finally, support for assigning policy prerogatives to the EU may indeed have declined only in some areas, but for reasons unrelated to the budgetary and redistributive consequences of monetary union. For Alesina and Wacziarg (1999), the crucial point is that centralization of policy-making authority in the EU is not equally beneficial in all policy areas. In some, externalities or economies of scale justify devolution to the European institutions, which is why the EU's policy activism designed to create a larger European free market and fostering "deep" economic integration seems to have been met with little public resistance: "as long as the European construction was primarily about establishing a single market, it tended to generate relatively little popular discontent" (Alesina and Wacziarg 1999: 28). They also argue, however, that "the widening of the range of the potential prerogative transfers in the early 1990s" has included areas where the benefits of centralization in a supranational authority do not compensate for the costs involved in shifting policy making further away from local or national heterogeneous interests (Alesina and Wacziarg 1999: 28; see also Alesina and Wacziarg 2008). This brings us back, in fact, to our earlier discussion about "inherent internationalization". In areas where such internationalization is high—such as defence, foreign policy, environmental issues, or monetary policy—we should not expect a significant public resistance to the transfer of policy prerogatives to the EU. In other areas, however—such as educational, cultural, and social policies (Alesina and Wacziarg 2008)—support for policy integration is likely to have declined, particularly if the devolution of prerogatives to the EU has been fostered. This is especially the case in the fields of health, employment, and social protection where, although the treaty-based competencies of the EU in these three areas have remained rather limited (especially in comparison with those deposited in domestic governments—Börzel 2005), there has been an intense regulatory activity on the part of the EU (Alesina, Angeloni, and Schuknecht 2005).

2 Data

The scarce existing research on attitudes vis-à-vis policy integration has typically resorted to data derived from survey questions in which respondents are asked about which level of government—national, European, and sometimes sub-national—should deal with particular "problems" or "policies". In the European Election Studies, for example, respondents have been asked, since 1994, to select what they think are the "most important issues or problems", a question followed by others in which they are asked to give their opinion about which level of government—regional, national, or European—deals with that problem and which would be the most appropriate to do so. A somewhat different approach has been followed in the Eurobarometer surveys. It consists in providing respondents with a pre-prepared list of problems/policies and then eliciting their response, for each of those items, as to whether they should be dealt with by member states acting independently or jointly within the European Union. The specific wording of the questions has changed considerably through time (see Sinnott 1995: 256), but has, since 1989 (EB 32), settled to a stable formulation:

> Some people believe that certain areas of policy should be decided by (National) government, while other areas of policy should be decided jointly within the European Community [later, Union]. Which of the following areas of policy do you think should be decided by the (National) government, and which should be decided jointly within the European Community [Union]?

What has been much less stable is the particular set of items/policies on which these preferences were measured. From 1989 until the time of this writing, more than sixty different policy domains have been used in different questionnaires, including, in some cases, substantial changes in wording used to describe similar policy areas. The problems this poses for detection of trends in citizens' attitudes are compounded by the comparability problems that arise when one tries to include in the analysis the twelve new member states that acceded to the EU in 2004 and 2007. The Candidate Countries Eurobarometers (CCEB) conducted from 2001 to 2004 did include questions on the desired integration of twenty-five policy areas. However, starting with EB 64 (autumn 2005), the second one conducted after the 2004 enlargement, the range of policy areas included in the surveys changed considerably. One of the consequences of these discontinuities is that the existing research on policy integration has typically been forced to balance the number of policy areas under analysis with the number of observations obtained in each policy area. Cross-sectional studies have managed to compare up to twenty-five policy areas (Christin, Hug, and Schultz 2005; Alesina, Angeloni, and Schuknecht

2005), while studies aiming at detecting trends have often been limited to no more than twelve policy areas (Dalton and Eichenberg 1998 and 2007).

In this chapter, I combine the two strategies. On the one hand, for the cross-sectional analysis of the determinants of support across policy domains and countries, I focus on two surveys, the Standard Eurobarometer 58 and the Candidate Country Eurobarometer 2002.2. There are two major advantages to this. First, in these two surveys, the question about the scope of government was applied in relation to twenty-five different policy areas in all current EU27 countries and using exactly the same wording. Second, unlike what occurred with later waves of both surveys with the same characteristics (namely EB 59, EB 60, and EB 62, and CCEB 2003 and 2004), both the EB and the CCEB surveys took place in all countries in exactly the same period, i.e. October–November 2002. In this way, we can be confident that any cross-national variations are not due to extraneous events that might affect a particular group of countries in one time period.

On the other hand, for a panel analysis of trends in net support for integration, I use all the Eurobarometer surveys conducted since 1989 in all twelve countries that were members of the EU from the beginning of the series. Given the frequent changes in the set of policy areas included in the surveys and in question wording, not many policies provide us with a long enough time series in order to test hypotheses related to the effects of economic performance or of changes in the contexts of integration. But there are several areas on which we have continuous observations of aggregate levels of support for Europeanization from at least 1989 and until at least 2004. These policies are "Health and social welfare"; "Protection of the environment"; "Scientific and technological research"; "Education"; "Currency"; "Security and defence"; "Foreign policy" and "Rules for broadcasting and press". To these, we will add "Unemployment" and "Immigration", two areas on which we have data since 1992 and at least up to 2007.

3 Cross-sectional analysis: differences between policies and between countries

In both EB 58 and CCEB 2002, respondents were asked about their preferences regarding the level of government in which twenty-five policies should be decided.[5] For the following analysis, I excluded six policies from that list, due to difficulties in measuring the relevant independent variables (more on this later). For each of the remaining nineteen policy areas and for each country, net aggregate levels of support for policy integration are measured by subtracting the percentage of respondents in each national sample who answered that decisions should be made by the national government (N) from the percentage of respondents who answered that decisions should be made jointly within the EU (J). Following Alesina, Angeloni, and Schuknecht (2005), I multiply this difference (J–N) by 1–U/100, with U equal to the percentage on DK/NA answers, in order to give a lower weight to the net balance whenever DK/NA responses are higher.

Figure 9.1 shows a box-and-whiskers plot of net support for policy integration, per policy, found in the EU27 countries. The EB 58/CCEB 2002 results in this respect are very much in line with earlier findings. Scientific research, foreign aid, environmental protection, and foreign policy have always been areas where, at least since the 1970s, support for Europeanization has been high, while it has been consistently low for education, health and welfare, and cultural policies (Sinnott 1995; Dalton and Eichenberg 1998; Lubbers and Scheepers 2005; Christin, Hug, and Schultz 2005). Thus, most of those policies where support was higher in the 1970s and 1980s remain those where support was high by the early twenty-first century, and the same stability seems to be in place in relation to low-support policies.

The plot also allows us to see that the former policy areas—together with organized crime, regional aid, and social inclusion—constitute today a set of core issues where we could find net positive popular support for integration in all or almost all EU27 countries. Only the UK, Finland, Sweden, and (in one case) Malta emerge as outliers, and only in some cases. Conversely, in the areas of culture, media regulation, and the police, integration is rejected by the majority of the population in the overwhelming majority of countries. In the remaining policy domains, the picture is somewhat more blurred: either dispersion between countries is very large (in unemployment, immigration, urban crime, welfare, and education) or the positive median net support is relatively narrow and mitigated by the existence of a significant number of countries where net support is negative or very negative (asylum, defence, and agriculture).

Figure 9.2 changes our point of view on the data, showing box-and-whiskers plots of average net support for policy integration found for the nineteen policies above, per country. As extant research already suggested, Finland, Sweden, the United Kingdom, and Denmark emerge as reliable redoubts of opposition to policy integration in most policy areas, joined, to a lesser extent, by Austria and one of the newer members, Malta (by then, still a candidate country). In this respect, however, Malta is exceptional among the new member states. Among the ten countries where greater support for Europeanization is found, seven are countries that entered the EU in 2004 or 2007. They are joined by three Southern European countries: Greece, Italy, and Spain. Finally, in the Czech Republic, Estonia, Lithuania, and Portugal—all "third-wave" democracies—net support is positive in more than three out of every four policy areas under consideration.

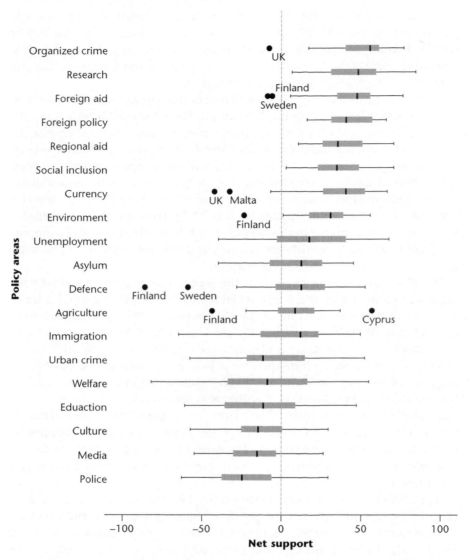

Figure 9.1. Net support for policy integration in 19 policy areas (EU27, EB58/CCEB 2002)

What emerges from an analysis of the determinants of these patterns? Let us focus, first of all, on cross-policy variations. Recall that, while part of the extant research tends to show a relationship between each policy area's "inherent internationalization" and citizens' support for centralized European policy making, Hooghe's multivariate analysis reveals such a relationship to be spurious. Rather, she finds that support is driven by whether a policy

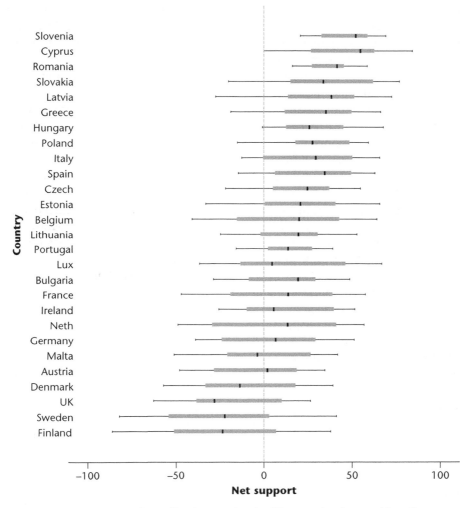

Figure 9.2. Net support for policy integration in 27 countries (across 19 policy areas, EB58/CCEB 2002)

involves fewer financial resources and by its "market-flanking nature" (Hooghe 2003). Thus, we simply replicate Hooghe's multivariate analysis, with two main differences: we include more policies and use a more completely specified model.

Hooghe's study provides measures of three crucial independent variables for thirteen policy areas. First, measures of "Functionality"—what we called "inherent internationalization"—in a scale of 1 (low) to 3 (high). In this case, we decided to rely instead on Alesina, Angeloni, and Schuknecht's (2005) dichotomous coding of policies in terms of their optimal "Centralized"

(European) or "Decentralized" (national or regional) allocation, since it was more exhaustive than Hooghe's, albeit based on the same theoretical framework. Second, she also includes a measure of "Government spending", from 1 to 5, with 1 being used for policies that represent less than 0.1 per cent of a country's GDP; 2 for equal or more than 0.1 per cent and less than 0.5 per cent of GDP; 3 for equal or more than 0.5 per cent and less than 1.5 per cent of GDP; 4 for equal or more than 1.5 per cent of GDP and less than 4.5 per cent of GDP; and 5 for all those representing 4.5 per cent of GDP or more. We used the same coding for all policies also discussed by Hooghe in her study, and relied on the same source (CEC 2002) to code all the remaining ones.[6] Hooghe also uses a dummy variable to signal a number of "social model/market-flanking policies": Environment, Research, Regional policy, Social inclusion, and Employment, and the same coding is used here. Finally, we included an additional variable: the actual competencies entrusted by the treaties to the EU in each policy area, on a scale of 1 (low) to 3 (high), following Alesina and Wacziarg (1999) and Ahrens, Meurer, and Renner (2007). Table 9.2 summarizes how each policy was coded from these points of view.

Table 9.3 shows the results of a linear regression analysis where the dependent variable is the average net support for policy integration in each area across the twenty-seven countries, while the variables measuring the attributes of each policy are used as explanatory variables. We can see, first of all, that only two attributes of policy areas seem to be consequential for the level of net average mass support for Europeanization: their "inherent

Table 9.2. Coding of policies according to four criteria

	Inherent internationalization	Government spending	Social model	Actual EU competencies
Agriculture and fishing	0	3	0	3
Cultural policy	0	3	0	1
Currency	1	1	0	3
Defence	1	4	0	1
Education	0	5	0	1
Environment	1	3	1	2
Fighting organized crime	1	3	0	2
Fighting urban crime	0	3	0	2
Foreign policy	1	1	0	1
Health and welfare	0	5	0	1
Humanitarian aid	1	2	0	2
Immigration	1	2	0	2
Police	0	3	0	2
Political asylum	1	2	0	2
Regional aid	0	3	1	2
Research	0	3	1	2
Rules for media	0	1	0	1
Social inclusion	0	5	1	1
Unemployment	0	4	1	2

Table 9.3. The impact of policy attributes on net support for their Europeanization

	b	Beta
Intercept	−7.04	
	(20.13)	
Inherent internationalization	26.04*	0.56
	(10.64)	
Government spending	−1.67	−0.09
	(3.54)	
Social model	32.46**	0.62
	(10.82)	
Actual EU competencies	4.35	0.12
	(5.64)	
R2	0.46	
N	19	

*p<0.05; **p<0.01; ***p<0.001.

Robust standard errors in parenthesis. Highest VIF: 1.55.

internationalization" and their "social model/market-flanking" nature. Net support for Europeanization is about 30 percentage points higher for these policies. While supporting Hooghe's findings about the special status enjoyed by some policy areas in the European public's perception—the "social model" ones—our results clearly disconfirm her findings about the public's insensitivity in relation to each policy's "inherent internationalization". Independently of other features of policy areas and of each country's socio-economic and political features, policies whose centralization brings benefits in terms of economies of scale and internationalization of externalities tend to elicit higher public support for dealing with them also at the European level.

Shifting our attention to cross-national differences, Table 9.4 shows the results of another linear regression analysis where, this time, the dependent variable is the average net support for policy integration, per country, across the nineteen policy areas. As follows from the discussion in the previous section, we included in the model a dummy for "third-wave democracies",[7] population size,[8] and measures of the "quality of governance" in each country. We use two alternative measures for this purpose. In Model 1, we use the Corruption Perceptions Index of Transparency International for each country in 2002, with scores ranging from 1 to 10, with 10 meaning maximum transparency (Transparency International 2008). In Model 2, we resort to the World Bank Governance Indices, which provide measures of six dimensions of governance in 212 countries for 2002 and afterwards (Kaufmann, Kraay, and Mastuzzi 2007).[9] In each case, the correlation between our two measures of the quality of governance in each of the twenty-seven EU member

Table 9.4. The impact of country attributes on net support for the Europeanization of policy areas

	Model 1		Model 2	
	b	Beta	b	Beta
Intercept	−186.55*		−207.09*	
	(69.92)		(78.28)	
Governance quality (Transparency)	−9.03***	−0.93	−	−
	(2.14)			
Governance quality (World Bank)	−	−	−99.99***	−0.83
			(23.46)	
Population size	−2.13	−0.16	−1.93	−0.14
	(1.21)		(1.49)	
Third-wave democracy	21.01**	0.54	29.20**	0.75
	(6.92)		(7.41)	
Economic development	28.51**	0.74	31.59**	0.81
	(7.93)		(8.60)	
R2	0.76		0.73	
N	27		27	

*p<0.05; **p<0.01; ***p<0.001.
Robust standard errors in parenthesis. Highest VIF: 4.28.

states is 0.93. Finally, we also include a variable measuring each country's level of economic development.[10]

Table 9.4 shows that three variables emerge as strong predictors of the average net support for Europeanization across the nineteen policies we are considering. First, quality of domestic governance, regardless of how we measure it, has a strong negative impact. In other words, mass support for having Europe—rather than national governments—decide on policies is lower in countries with better domestic governance institutions. Second, third-wave democracies, regardless of their level of development and the quality of their democratic institutions, tend to be more supportive of policy integration. These results lend additional plausibility to the notion that higher support for integration in these countries is linked to the special role played by the EU and European integration in democratic and economic reforms in these countries (Niedermayer 1995b; De Winter and Swyngedouw 1999). Finally, economic development has a strong positive effect in support for policy integration. The coefficient for population size has a negative sign—suggesting that the average net support for policy integration was lower among the largest countries in our sample—but fails to reach statistical significance.

Recall, however, that we had hypothesized an interaction effect: support for the Europeanization of "high-spending" policies should be contingent upon the countries' level of economic development. In order to model that effect, we shift to multilevel analysis. Since each observation of aggregate net support for each of the nineteen policies is nested within each country, the assumption that these observations are independent from each other is highly questionable. We thus treat country as a macro-level unit, and observations of aggregate support for the Europeanization of each policy in each country as lower-level observations made within each macro unit. Variables capturing attributes of countries are treated as macro-level (level-2) variables, while those capturing attributes of policies are treated as level-1 variables.

Table 9.5 shows the results of two models. The first is a random intercept and random slope model, where we allow for the possibility that the different attributes of policies affect net support for their Europeanization in different ways in different countries. As expected, only in relation to the government spending variable do we find significant random slope variance. The second model specifies a cross-level interaction between economic development and government spending. That interaction term is statistically significant and, as predicted, negative: among richer countries, net support for policy integration decreases as policies involve greater budgetary implications, as we had hypothesized.

Table 9.5. Multilevel linear regression analyses of support for Europeanization, EB58/CCEB 2002

	Model 1	Model 2
	b (SE)	b (SE)
Fixed effects Intercept	15.08 (1.76)***	15.08 (1.76)***
Country-level intercept effects		
Third-wave democracy	21.75 (6.04)**	21.53 (6.03)**
Population size	−2.19 (0.83)*	−2.11 (0.85)*
Governance quality (Transp.)	−8.35 (1.65)***	−8.86 (1.79)***
Economic development	27.55 (6.99)**	28.88 (7.04)**
Policy-level predictors		
Inherent internationalization	26.04 (2.34)***	26.04 (2.34)***
Government spending	−1.68 (1.21)	−1.68 (0.91)
* Economic development	—	−6.96 (1.84)**
Social model	32.46 (1.64)***	32.46 (1.64)***
Actual EU competencies	4.35 (1.05)***	4.35 (1.05)***
Random effects	Variance component	
Inherent internationalization	39.76	—
Government spending	18.75**	5.07
Social model	13.91	—
Actual EU competencies	2.01	—
Level 2 N	27 countries	
Level 1 N	513 observations	

*p<0.05; **p<0.01; ***p<0.001.
Robust standard errors in parenthesis; level-1 variables centered around group means and level-2 variables centered around grand means.

All the remaining results obtained confirm the previous analyses, with two exceptions. First, the negative relationship between population size and support for policy integration becomes statistically significant with $p<0.05$. Second, with a much larger number of country-by-country observations, the actual competencies exerted by the EU on a given policy area acquire a significant positive effect on net support for Europeanization. The effects of this policy attribute, however, remain much smaller than those of each policy's "inherent internationalization" or "market-flanking" nature. Furthermore, a question of potential reverse causality emerges in this case: the results support the notion that net support for Europeanization in a given policy is higher because the EU has more policy-making prerogatives, but also the opposite causal direction.

4 Panel analysis: trends in support for policy integration

By comparing the results displayed in Figures 9.1 and 9.2 with the findings of previous research on the matter, we have already noted that cross-policy differences in levels of mass support for integration seem to have remained largely stable in the period since comparable data have been available. However, this does not necessarily mean that such support has remained totally impervious to the passage of time. As we saw earlier, the literature suggests the possibility of some sort of post-Maastricht decline in support for policy integration, either across the board in all policy areas, in all areas directly or indirectly related to the common monetary policy and the convergence criteria (Eichenberg and Dalton 2007), or in all areas of low "inherent internationalization" (Alesina and Wacziarg 1999). What has indeed occurred?

There are eight policy areas that have been systematically included in the EB surveys since at least 1989 and until at least 2004:[11] scientific and technological research; protection of the environment; health and social welfare; education; currency (until EB 62, 2004); foreign policy (until EB 62, 2004); rules for broadcasting and press (until EB 62, 2004); and security and defence (until EB 62, 2004). Furthermore, on unemployment and immigration, we have Eurobarometer data since 1992 (immediately after the signature of the Maastricht Treaty). Although a specific "Maastricht effect" is very difficult to determine—as even the longer series have no more than five pre-Maastricht observations—we can at least look for general trends. This is our goal in this section.

These ten policies can be clearly contrasted in terms of their high or low inherent internationalization. Environment, currency, foreign policy, defence, and immigration belong to the "high" group, while the remaining five—media regulation, research, health and welfare, education, and

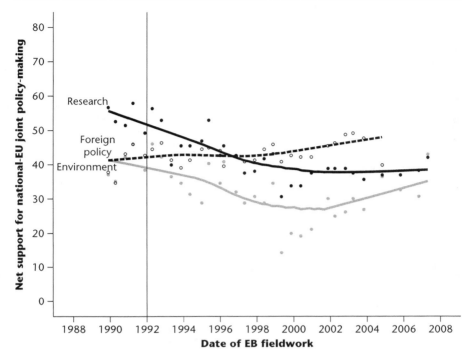

Figure 9.3. Trends in net support for policy integration, selected policies, EU12 weighted average

unemployment—are domains of low or at least contested inherent internationalization. The fact that the latter three also count among those policies whose distributive implications are more important also allows us, together with the inclusion of monetary policy, to test the hypothesis that the budgetary implications of Maastricht have driven down support for policy integration in these areas. Figures 9.3, 9.4, and 9.5 allow a preliminary visual inspection of the trends experienced in the period in which data is available, i.e. from late 1980s/early 1990s until the early twenty-first century. Figure 9.3 focuses on the three policy areas where the weighted average EU12 net support for policy integration has been highest: scientific and technological research, foreign policy, and environment. The graph plots the EU12 weighted averages against the final data of fieldwork for each Eurobarometer survey, also displaying smoothed local regression lines for each policy area.[12] A vertical reference line was placed in 1992, i.e. between the two EB surveys conducted immediately before and immediately after the signing of the Maastricht Treaty.

Just by looking at these three cases in Figure 9.3, it is easy to see that the hypothesis of a general decline in support for policy integration widespread to

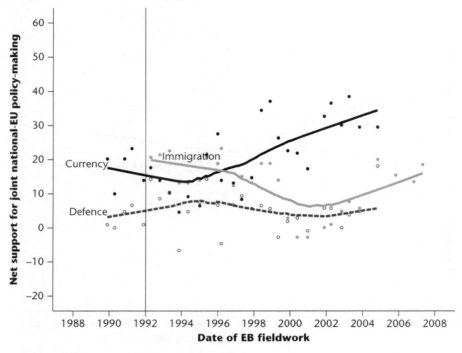

Figure 9.4. Trends in net support for policy integration, selected policies, EU12 weighted average

all policy areas does not seem to hold. While there is indeed a period in which support for integration seems to have declined in the cases of research and environmental policies, any such trend seems to have stopped or even to have been completely reversed by the end of the 1990s. And in the case of foreign policy, net support seems mostly trendless throughout the entire period.

Figure 9.4 presents the same sort of information for three additional policy areas where average support has been somewhat lower than for those presented in Figure 9.3: currency, immigration, and defence. Again, as in the case of foreign policy, support among the EU12 countries for joint national–EU decision making in the area of defence seems mostly trendless throughout the entire period. Conversely, in the cases of currency and immigration, any initial trends of decline were reversed at a later point in time. The case of currency is particularly interesting, since one of the hypotheses in the literature was that we should be observing a post-Maastricht decline in support for policy integration in this area, as a reaction against the budgetary consequences of the convergence criteria. However, whatever decline in support for joint national–EU decision making in monetary policy among the EU12 countries did occur seems to have been very short-lived.

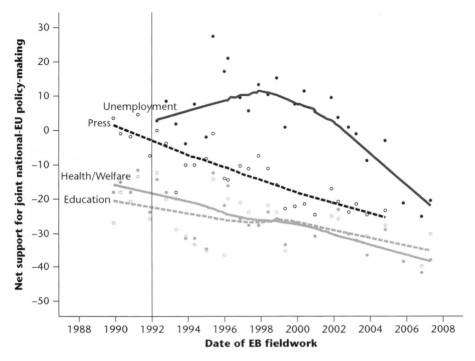

Figure 9.5. Trends in net support for policy integration, selected policies, EU12 weighted average

Figure 9.5 completes this overview for the remaining four policy areas under analysis: media regulation, health and welfare, education, and unemployment. These are the cases, in fact, where the notion of a secular decline in support for integration seems to be on firmer ground. By 2006–7, levels of net support for policy integration in these areas among the population of the EU12 countries was clearly lower than by the late 1980s/early 1990s.

In order to determine the existence of significant trends in the period, we created a pooled cross-sectional time-series dataset for each of the ten policy areas, containing all observations of net support for Europeanization available for all the EU12 countries and all EB surveys since 1989 (EB 32)[13] until at least 2004 (EB 62) and, when available, 2006 (EB 66). A "counter" variable, years (or fractions thereof) elapsed since the beginning of the series, allows us to look for trends. Additional variables include the yearly percentage change in GDP as well as a dummy variable with value 1 when a particular country was, at the time of the survey, serving as European Council president, testing the hypothesis that this particular role of the country at the time might have a short-term effect of increasing support for integration among its citizens.

Additional variables include all the already discussed determinants of cross-national differences: economic development, population size, third-wave democracy, and quality of governance, measured here by the Transparency International Corruption Perceptions Index. Since we only have measures of this last variable since 1996, we present two tables—Tables 9.6 and 9.7—where this variable is, respectively, excluded and included. In Table 9.6, all observations since the beginning of the series are used, while in Table 9.7, only observations since 1996 are used. We estimate the models with a Prais–Winsten regression and panel-corrected standard errors, addressing the auto-correlation problems detected in all series. Both tables display the results for all ten policy areas, divided in two groups: high and low inherent inter-nationalization areas.

Confirming what visual inspection has already suggested, different policies exhibit different trends in net support for their integration from the late 1980s/early 1990s until today. The areas where a secular trend of decline can be found are not those we would expect on the basis of popular rejection of or fear about the consequences of monetary union. While support for common education, health and welfare, and unemployment policies has indeed declined, support for a common monetary policy has experienced no such trend. Besides, a totally unrelated area—media regulation—has experienced the strongest decline since 1989 and the second strongest since 1996. The results are much closer to supporting the notion that decline mostly took place in areas of low inherent internationalization. Only in relation to scientific research policies do we lack strong evidence of a decline, at least in the more fully specified model addressing trends since 1996.

Another interesting finding concerns the absolute lack of any impact of economic performance, captured with our economic growth variable. Although there is some evidence of a positive effect of economic development in several of the "low-spending" areas, the results are much less clear than those obtained in the previous section where we used 2002 data for the EU27 countries. Similarly, the effects of third-wave democracy are only evident (and only in some policy areas) in the model displayed in Table 9.6, before quality of governance is taken into account. Recall, however, that restricting the analysis to the EU12 countries significantly limits our variance both in terms of economic development levels and in the number of new democracies in the sample, unlike what occurred in the cross-sectional analysis of the EU27 countries. In any case, one central finding persists here as strongly as before: quality of governance has a clear negative impact in support in nine of the ten policy areas examined.

Table 9.6. Net support for Europeanization, selected policies, 1989/92

	High inherent internationalization				
	Environment	Foreign Policy	Defence	Currency	Immigration
	b (SE)	b (SE)	b (SE)	b (SE)	b (SE)
Years since beginning of series (1989/1992)	-1.37 (0.39)***	0.08 (0.39)	-0.61 (0.69)*	1.04 (0.87)	-0.79 (0.76)
GDP growth	-0.84 (0.49)	0.02 (0.37)	-0.48 (0.61)	-0.55 (0.65)	-0.41 (0.68)
Council presidency	3.51 (1.65)*	2.81 (1.21)*	2.09 (1.74)	2.46 (1.58)	2.25 (1.70)
Economic development	42.08 (6.09)***	26.72 (7.78)**	91.89 (12.42)***	28.62 (11.88)*	24.84 (16.37)
Population size	6.35 (0.70)***	3.81 (0.85)***	7.34 (1.33)***	-0.18 (1.50)	6.19 (1.86)**
Third Wave Democracy	10.77 (2.94)***	-2.81 (4.59)	17.63 (6.06)**	5.06 (5.86)	17.97 (6.50)**
Constant	-490.35 (66.32)***	-292.24 (84.99)**	-1035.81 (136.07)***	-268.18 (133.85)*	-338.54 (183.30)
R-squared	0.17	0.14	0.19	0.07	0.06
Observations	372	348	336	348	312
Time period	1989–2006	1989–2004	1989–2004	1989–2004	1992–2006

	Low inherent internationalization				
	Health and welfare	Education	Research	Media regulation	Unemployment
	b (SE)	b (SE)	b (SE)	b (SE)	b (SE)
Years since beginning of series (1989/1992)	-1.24 (0.50)*	1.42 (0.44)**	-1.04 (0.47)*	-2.23 (0.50)***	-1.59 (0.95)
GDP growth	0.18 (0.56)	-40 (0.49)	-14 (0.43)	0.62 (0.51)	0.87 (0.92)
Council presidency	3.00 (1.64)	1.05 (1.78)	1.30 (1.10)	1.42 (1.76)	2.64 (1.84)
Economic development	13.09 (9.71)	23.23 (7.56)**	17.11 (7.84)*	30.88 (10.56)**	-5.39 (13.03)
Population size	2.71 (1.07)*	3.32 (0.87)***	-1.04 (0.93)	2.55 (1.01)*	1.90 (1.31)
Third Wave Democracy	28.43 (4.31)***	22.46 (3.36)***	1.42 (3.55)	16.87 (3.71)***	11.19 (5.82)
Constant	-201.31 (105.30)	-312.11 (84.45)***	-100.43 (88.30)	-356.58 (116.73)**	32.94 (144.76)
R-squared	0.15	0.13	0.26	0.10	0.08
Observations	372	372	372	336	300
Time period	1989–2006	1989–2006	1989–2006	1989–2004	1992–2006

*p<0.05; **p<0.01; ***p<0.001.
Robust standard errors in parenthesis

Table 9.7. Net support for Europeanization, selected policies, 1996–2006: panel corrected standard errors, Prais–Winsten regression, EU12 balanced panel

High inherent internationalization

	Environment b (SE)	Foreign Policy b (SE)	Defence b (SE)	Currency b (SE)	Immigration b (SE)
Years since 1996	−1.12 (0.75)	−0.36 (0.55)	−2.05 (1.22)	1.58 (1.38)	−0.85 (0.93)
Growth	−1.35 (0.73)	−0.14 (0.51)	−1.45 (1.00)	−1.28 (1.00)	−0.86 (0.79)
Council presidency	0.97 (2.22)	2.16 (1.67)	2.00 (2.20)	2.72 (2.14)	2.18 (1.90)
Economic development	24.61 (9.54)*	33.78 10.22)**	86.07 19.75)***	23.44 (15.24)	15.81 (19.44)
Population size	3.94 (1.17)**	2.87 (1.17)*	6.82 (2.07)*	−3.40 (1.98)	3.10 (2.38)
Third Wave Democracy	5.19 (4.11)	−4.13 (3.56)	13.58 (8.00)	−7.34 (7.41)	5.20 (7.36)
Transparency index	−0.81 (0.79)	−4.26 (.78)***	−2.90 (1.25)*	−6.73 (1.53)***	−5.40 (1.44)***
Constant	−266.10 (108.26)*	−311.89 (114.78)**	−937.62 (219.37)***	−113.60 (185.50)	−150.41 (211.13)
R-squared	0.19	0.34	0.17	0.17	0.12
Observations	240	216	216	216	240
Time period	1996–2006	1996–2004	1996–2004	1996–2004	1996–2006

Low inherent internationalization

	Health and welfare b (SE)	Education b (SE)	Research b (SE)	Media regulation b (SE)	Unemployment b (SE)
Years since 1996	−1.57 (0.47)**	−1.72 (0.59)**	−0.69 (0.61)	−2.31 (0.63)***	−2.90 (0.66)***
Growth	0.10 (0.56)	−0.63 (0.59)	−0.20 (0.60)	0.63 (0.66)	0.48 (0.61)
Council presidency	2.79 (2.01)	−0.29 (1.93)	1.34 (1.56)	−1.08 (2.24)	2.86 (2.09)
Economic development	5.84 (9.83)	21.87 (9.04)*	14.34 (10.88)	30.35 (11.09)**	−5.75 (9.67)
Population size	−0.58 (9.83)	1.78 (1.10)	−3.29 (1.23)**	0.14 (1.27)	−0.61 (1.01)
Third Wave Democracy	10.48 (4.01)**	6.89 (4.21)	−5.43 (4.36)	3.76 (3.98)	−4.98 (5.47)
Transparency index	−7.64 (0.85)***	−7.57 (0.68)***	−4.81 (0.82)***	−7.73 (0.76)***	−8.24 (0.89)***
Constant	−8.06 (112.51)	−208.95 (103.79)*	−2.59 (123.79)	−251.04 (127.41)*	161.33 (107.59)
R-squared	0.35	0.32	0.41	0.33	0.47
Observations	240	240	240	216	240
Time period	1996–2006	1996–2006	1996–2006	1996–2004	1996–2006

*p<0.05; **p<0.01; ***p<0.001. Robust standard errors in parenthesis

5 Discussion

We started this chapter by asking three main questions. Why do most European citizens believe that some policy areas should be decided at the European level while others should not? Why is support for policy integration higher in some countries than in others? And what trends can we find in support for policy integration?

The answer to the first question seems to lie mostly in three main features of policy domains themselves. First, it is related to whether they are "high inherent internationalization" issues. This finding is robust to the introduction of other features of policy areas as controls, confirming most of the previous scholarship on the issue (with the exception of Hooghe 2003). Second, Europeans also seem to desire the Europeanization of "social model" or "market-flanking" policies. Finally, to a much lesser extent, areas in which the already achieved levels of policy integration are higher also tend to be the ones where support for these is also higher. But this particular effect is much smaller than the previous ones, and the direction of causality is unclear.

The answer to the second question flows from a mix of utilitarian considerations as well as of other factors that are more difficult to disentangle or robustly confirm. The strongest finding, common to both the cross-sectional analysis of net support for policy integration in the EU27 countries in 2002 and the time-series cross-sectional analysis of EU12 countries since the late 1980s/early 1990s, is that, in countries where the domestic quality of governance is lower, more citizens tend to perceive benefits in shifting all sorts of policy responsibilities to the EU. In other words, we have good reason to believe that citizens engage in a "*political* costs and benefits" reasoning, rejecting centralization of policy making in the EU when domestic quality of governance is higher, and vice versa. The role of "*economic* costs and benefits" is less visible. Economic growth seems to have no effect on aggregate views about policy integration. However, although the analysis of the EU12 countries did not show this clearly, a focus on the broader set of EU27 countries suggests that citizens in poorer countries seem to perceive advantages in shifting those responsibilities in policy areas with greater budgetary and distributive implications.

The third question—trends in support—was discussed in the last section of the chapter. We found trends of declining support since the late 1980s, or since at least the mid 1990s, taking place mostly in areas where support was already low from the start and in all areas of low "inherent internationalization." In the remaining cases, no European-wide trends of decline were found.

What are the implications of these results? First, they confirm the convenience of making nuanced distinctions in relation to the objects of public attitudes of support for integration. The trends observed in the literature concerning "instrumental support" for membership or the perception of the benefits of such membership—a general decline specifically brought about by Maastricht (Çiftçi 2005)—are not confirmed for all policy areas in terms of support for policy integration. This lends further plausibility to earlier findings about the different micro foundations of different dimensions of support (Lubbers and Scheepers 2005). On the other hand, we found that even this distinction between "instrumental" and "political" support may be, for some purposes, excessively crude. Although individual support for integration in one policy domain may be strongly correlated with support for integration in another, aggregate levels of net support vary quite substantively from one policy area and from one member state to another.

The second implication of our findings is related to our overall conception of how citizens have reacted to developments in European integration. The fact that we find no evidence of negative reaction to monetary union, as Eichenberg and Dalton (2007) suggested might be the case, might lead us to conclude that a "permissive consensus", with disinterested and uninformed citizens, is still in place. However, other aspects of our findings suggest otherwise. Citizens in different countries display different preferences that are congruent with the performance of their own domestic political systems and the likely consequences of policy harmonization in some areas for their own standards of living. They make very stark distinctions between policy domains where they feel Europeanization makes sense and where it does not. Clearly, as Schmitt and Thomassen put it, "citizens are probably more knowledgeable about the logic of internationalization than is often assumed" (2004: 383). And they seem to be increasingly so. What we find are negative trends only in what concerns support for the Europeanization of policy domains where the benefits of Europeanization are more questionable, something much more akin to a "learning mechanism" than to either a blanket negative reaction to "too much Europe"—which has indeed been a reality in some policy areas but clearly not in others (Börzel 2005)—or to generic fears concerning the consequences of monetary union.

A final implication concerns the question of what kind of "Europe" European citizens seem to want, or more specifically, what kind of policy-making authority on the part of EU institutions they are likely to perceive as legitimate. At first sight, some of the results we obtained seem rather disturbing in terms of the possibility of achieving a minimal consensus about the political and institutional development of the EU's policy-making capabilities between twenty-seven different domestic public opinions and the governments that are directly accountable to them. Instead of buying or rejecting a generic idea of European unification, domestic public opinions want a "Europe à la carte", with more or less sovereignty and in different policy competencies depending on each country's political and economic situation.

Having said this, however, the extent of this dissensus should not be overestimated. In spite of cross-national differences, there are several policy areas in which clear majorities of citizens have remained supportive of EU policy making in all or almost all member states. What these areas have in common is either (and in some cases, both) the fact that the allocation of policy prerogatives to the European level is more likely to bring benefits in terms of internalizing externalities and taking advantage of economies of scale or (and in some cases, and) can be publicly framed as addressing the negative consequences of free markets and economic globalization. Fighting organized crime, protecting the environment, managing foreign policy and aid vis-à-vis non-EU countries, addressing regional asymmetries and social exclusion, and even a common monetary policy are areas where a core consensus for a EU policy-making role does seem to exist, in contrast to areas with direct implications on redistributive policies, cultural identity, and/or fundamental rights. In several of the former, such a role is already significant. If it is not more so, lack of cross-national public support is certainly not to be blamed.

Notes

1. For concurrent empirical findings about the dimensionality of attitudes towards Europe, see Chierici (2005).
2. For similar arguments, see De Winter and Swyngedouw (1999: 66–7) and Hooghe (2003: 283).
3. From here on, I will use the expression "inherent internationalization of policies" in order to avoid unnecessary confusion with the concept of "endogeneity" as it is used to describe the status of variables in a causal model. I thank David Sanders for this suggestion.
4. The apparently contradictory assessments made about crime probably result from a lack of distinction between "global" and organized forms of criminality and local delinquency.
5. Immigration; Political asylum; Fight against organized crime; Police; Justice; Accepting refugees; Juvenile crime prevention; Urban crime prevention; Fighting drugs; Exploitation of human beings; Defence; Environment; Currency; Humanitarian aid; Health and welfare; Rules for media; Poverty; Unemployment; Agriculture and fishing; Supporting poorer regions; Education; Scientific and technological research; Information about the EU; Foreign policy towards countries outside the EU; and Cultural policy. EB 58 also included "Fighting international terrorism" and "Tackling the challenges of an ageing population", but I excluded these for lack of comparability among the total EU27 countries.

6. However, we were unable to safely code, from this point of view, policies such as "Accepting refugees", "Juvenile crime prevention", "Information about the EU", "Justice", "Fighting exploitation of human beings", and "Fighting drugs". Thus, they were dropped from the analysis.
7. Greece, Spain, Portugal, and all 2004 and 2007 accession countries (except Malta).
8. The (log of) population size of each country, in millions, in 2002 (World Bank 2008).
9. The measure we employ is based on the first principal component of the six indicators (Voice and accountability; Political stability; Government effectiveness; Regulatory quality; Rule of law; and Control of corruption). This factor explains 85 per cent of the variance on the six indicators and correlates at more than .9 with five of them, the exception being Political stability.
10. Measured by the (log of) GDP per capita PPP in each country in 2002 (World Bank 2008).
11. Unfortunately, since 2004, foreign policy and defence ceased to be treated as separate policies in the EB surveys, while the entire gamut of policy areas included in the EB surveys was changed. Furthermore, in 1998, "Cooperation with Third World developing countries" was replaced by "Humanitarian aid". We therefore did not include this item.
12. Kernel function: Epanechnikov. Points to fit: 65 per cent.
13. For unemployment and immigration, since 1992 (EB 37).

10

Summary and Conclusions: Europe in Equilibrium—Unresponsive Inertia or Vibrant Resilience?

David Sanders, Pedro C. Magalhães, and Gábor Tóka

Political systems across Europe have experienced extraordinary changes in the last three decades. The process of globalization—which arguably began in the 17th century or earlier—has continued apace, fed by increasing levels of global trade and the revolution in information technology associated with the internet and the mobile phone. Across much of the world, the feminist revolution has radically changed the position and status of women as economic, social, and political actors. In Europe, the collapse of the Soviet Union and the end of the Cold War after 1989 have transformed the character of international relations—even though the emergence of loosely organized Islamic terrorism, focused on Al Qaeda and potential "rogue states", has ensured that "security" has remained a major preoccupation for both governments and mass publics. Increased personal mobility, as a result of expanding transport networks, and increasing concerns about the human rights of migrants of various sorts have produced a significant increase in immigration to many European countries, from both inside and outside the EU. The European Union itself has changed considerably since the late 1970s. From an organization of nine (West European) member states that focused primarily on developing a genuine "single market" for goods, capital, and labour whilst at the same time ensuring that agricultural production remained high and stable, the EU has evolved into a genuinely supranational system of governance that embraces twenty-seven democracies across Western, Central and Eastern Europe. This broadening and deepening of the EU has necessarily affected the formal decision-making autonomy of member-state governments. Since the Maastricht Treaty in 1992, notwithstanding the limited opt-outs secured by some member states, the range of policy areas where EU-level policies or directives hold sway over the preferences of national governments has gradually increased (Alesina and Wacziarg 1999). EU policy competence is now generally considered to be high in relation to agriculture/fisheries policy and currency policy—though this latter competence applies only to those seventeen member states that belong to the eurozone. It is also moderately high—and growing—in relation to the environment, policing and organized crime, humanitarian and regional aid, immigration/asylum, research, and unemployment (Ahrens, Meurer, and Renner 2007).

On the face of it, it might be expected that any or all of these long-term structural changes—which, for presentational purposes, we describe here as "exogenous"—could have affected the operation of democratic politics in Europe. Globalization, mass immigration, changing security threats, and reductions in national decision-making autonomy all potentially produce "winners" and "losers" at both the national and the individual level. Some societies and some individuals are less able to cope effectively with change than are others—especially if the changes involved are either undesired or unapproved. In these circumstances, it might be expected that, as a result of the exogenous macro-level political and economic changes outlined above, European mass publics—or some parts of those publics—might take a different view either of domestic politics in their own countries or of the EU itself. It is this mass public response to macro-level change that we have sought to describe and explain in this book. We begin this concluding chapter by restating the features of domestic, national-level and European Union-level politics that our analysis has sought to illuminate. Section 2 summarizes the key changes in mass public political attitudes and behaviour that have occurred across Europe in the last three decades or so. Section 3 reviews the central theoretical ideas that have been developed both in earlier studies and in this volume to explain why citizens change their political views and behaviours. Section 4 summarizes the results of our various empirical analyses and outlines the key individual- and macro-level drivers of changing (and sometimes unchanging) mass attitudes and behaviours. Two core substantive conclusions emerge from our analysis. First, the large-scale, external macro changes that have affected both national polities and the EU over the last thirty years have had relatively little enduring impact on the political attitudes and behaviours of European mass publics. Second, those changes that have occurred have been driven by a complex mixture of instrumental rational calculation, heuristic cue-taking, cognitive mobilization, and affective/emotional adjustments. In the final section of the chapter, we speculate as to whether the absence of major attitude change reflects a stubborn, unresponsive inertia or a vibrant resilience on the part of European mass publics. We conclude that it probably reflects a mixture of both.

1 The focus of our study: what we have been trying to explain

It is clearly not possible to identify and measure all the possible ways in which citizens in modern, complex democracies might respond to major political changes in their respective domestic and international environments. Indeed, bearing in mind the constraints of data availability, in order to make sense of citizens' responses, we have been obliged to focus on those attitudes and behaviours that are susceptible to systematic and sustained empirical examination across time and space. We have accordingly concentrated our efforts in two areas: on key attitudinal and behavioural features of national politics; and on attitudes towards the European Union.

In terms of national politics, our analysis has focused on two attitudinal and two behavioural variables. The first attitudinal measure concerns people's satisfaction with democracy. This is clearly one of the key expressions of popular support for the regime—indeed, on some accounts, it reflects the overall legitimacy of the political system itself. Regardless of what citizens think of the government of the day, it is vitally important that they remain committed to the democratic system itself. It is accordingly crucial to assess how far the sorts of exogenous macro-level changes outlined above might have affected their sense of democracy satisfaction. The second attitudinal measure analysed is left–right ideology, one of the crucial sources of division and differentiation in global twentieth-century politics. It is more than fifty years since Daniel Bell proclaimed "the end of ideology", yet still today many political parties, actors, and observers continue to think and speak in the language of "left" and "right". Several observers in the mid-1990s noted that, from the 1970s onwards, there was a period of "ideological depolarization", in which both parties and mass publics in Western Europe shifted their ideological positions towards the centre ground of democratic politics. Our analysis considers the extent to which these trends continued after 1990 and whether or not they were replicated in the new democracies of Central and Eastern Europe. It also assesses how far the ideological thinking of mass publics across Europe has been affected by exogenous macro-level change.

The two behavioural variables that we consider relate to formal and to informal political activity. On the formal side, our analysis has focused on the most common way in which most citizens participate in their respective political systems—by voting (or not) in national and in European elections. On the informal side, we would ideally have liked to look at a wide range of actions, such as participation in protests, petitions, boycotts, and political associations. However, given the absence of comprehensive cross-national time-series measures of these variables, we concentrate instead on a more general, but nonetheless crucial, measure of informal political engagement—the extent of people's participation in political discussion and persuasion. The key questions that we examine in relation to these two behavioural measures is how far they have varied systematically over time and whether or not any such variations can be linked to any of the exogenous macro changes that were identified earlier.

In terms of attitudes towards the European Union, we draw clear theoretical distinctions among four different categories of attitude. On our account, people exhibit generalized attitudes towards the EU which are captured by their sense as to whether their country's membership of the EU has been "a good thing" or "a bad thing". We distinguish this generalized sense of EU support, however, from three more specific sets of attitudes, which are probably causally prior to it and which in our view represent the three core dimensions of "European citizenship". The first of these concerns the extent to which people feel a sense of *European identity* or attachment. This sense of European identity may be in competition with, or complementary to, any national or sub-national identity that a particular individual may hold. The second attitude set—*EU policy scope*—refers to people's preferences about the policy competence of EU institutions in comparison with the competencies of national or sub-national levels of governance. The final attitude set—*EU representation*—relates to people's sense that they are "represented" or not by EU institutions, which we operationalize in terms of citizens' levels of "trust" in the key democratic institution of the EU, the European Parliament. In our view, although these four attitude sets may be empirically related to some degree, since they are conceptually distinct there is no ineluctable reason why they should move together over time. Accordingly, our analysis here considers how each of them has varied over the last three decades or so across different countries, and the extent to which any observed variations can be linked to exogenous macro changes at the national, European, and global levels.

2 How, if at all, have European mass political attitudes and behaviour changed?

Figures 10.1 to 10.8 provide graphical representations of the broad changes in European attitudes and behaviour (or lack of them) that have been described in this volume. Apart from the data for electoral turnout, the figures are all based on data from the long-running Eurobarometer series and, more recently, the European Social Survey. The use of this common source—nothwithstanding the additional sources cited in earlier chapters—ensures that the results reported are broadly comparable both across countries and over time. The idiosyncrasies of individual country patterns were described in previous chapters. Here, we focus on the general, pan-European pattern as a whole.

For each of Figures 10.1, 10.2, and 10.4–10.8, two graphs are reported. One shows the changes over time on the response measure for the "EU9" (the six founder members plus Denmark, Ireland, and the UK)—countries for which data are continuously available on an annual basis, for the majority of variables, since 1976. The other graph shows the picture for the EU as a whole at the time each survey was conducted—it includes an increasing number of countries as the number of member states progressively increased after 1973. No comparable over-time data on these measures are available for countries *before* they became EU member states. We accordingly report both sets of graphs here to show that the changes we describe are *not* a function of the changing pattern of EU membership. The graphs are all produced using data weighted by population size. With a few minor exceptions, the changes that we describe for all EU member states also occurred among the longstanding EU9. This suggests that the changes were not the result of the changing composition of the EU itself, arising from the accession of new member states, but rather reflect real variations in opinion and behaviour across Europe—real variations that, in the next section, we seek to explain.

Figure 10.1 reports variations in average Democracy Satisfaction across Europe for the period between 1976 and 2006. The figures reported are based on a simple scale index in which those "very satisfied" score 4, those "satisfied" score 3, "dissatisfied" score 2 and "very dissatisfied" score 1. The fact that the graph for all EU citizens falls in the wake of the collapse of the Berlin Wall could be construed as an artefact of the inclusion of the new states that were progressively included in the Eurobarometer series—especially after 1994. Such an inference would be mistaken, however. This is precisely why we include the figures for the EU9, where the same group of countries is being surveyed over time. The pattern for the EU9 shows exactly the same sort of post-1989 decline and subsequent recovery as the "all EU" series. This clearly suggests that there really was a decline in satisfaction with democracy in the

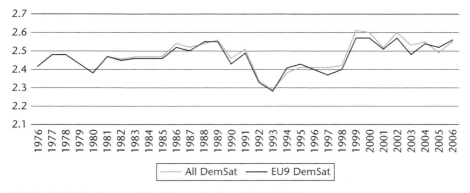

Figure 10.1. Democracy Satisfaction Index, 1976–2006

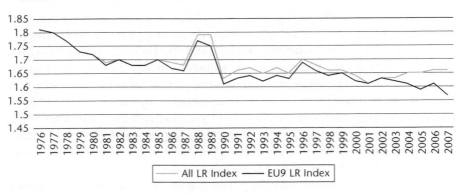

Figure 10.2. Index of left-right polarization, 1976–2007

wake of the end of the Cold War, but that by the late 1990s, satisfaction levels had re-established themselves at levels broadly similar to those observed up to the late 1980s.[1] We will examine the possible reasons for these changes in subseqent sections. We simply note here that, notwithstanding the changes in and external shocks to European societies that have occurred in the last three decades, mass satisfaction with the democratic process itself has certainly not declined—if anything, it has increased slightly from just under an index score of 2.5 in the 1970s to just over 2.5 in the 2000s.

Figure 10.2 reports the long-term changes in left–right ideological polarization that have occurred among European mass publics since the mid-1970s. The index numbers reported are calculated by measuring how far each individual's position deviates from the midpoint of the 1–10 left–right ideological scale. (The scale has a theoretical minimum of 0 and a theoretical maximum of 4.5.) These deviations are then averaged across the whole EU and across the EU9 to produce the graphs shown. A relatively high annual score on the index indicates that there were more people located towards the extremes of left and right; a lower score that fewer people took extreme views. As in Figure 10.1, there is no differentiation between the "all EU" and "EU9" graphs between 1976 and 1980—when the EU9 constituted the EU. Although minor differences in the two graphs develop after 1985, they clearly follow the same broad pattern, with sharp upward movements in 1988, followed by equally sharp declines in 1990. The only noticeable difference in the two graphs is towards the end of the series, when the EU9 graph falls below that for all EU countries. The flattening of the all-EU graph reflects the fact, noted in Chapter 4, that in Eastern Europe there has been a progressive polarization of opinon, rather than the general depolarization observed in the West. This produces an average figure that rises very slightly after 2001. The overall European-wide trend is clear, however. Across the EU as a whole, the period between 1976 and 2007 was one of declining ideological polarization—the index fell from above 1.8 in

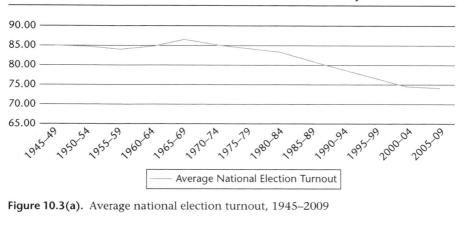

Figure 10.3(a). Average national election turnout, 1945–2009

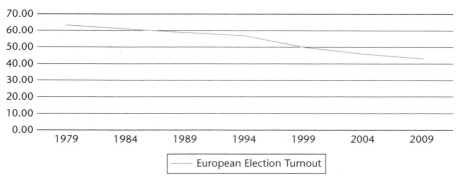

Figure 10.3(b). European election turnout, 1979–2009

1976 to around 1.6 by 2007. Whatever was responsible for this pattern of change—a question that we consider in the next section—it is clear that European mass publics (in the West at least) have progressively moved towards the political centre over the past thirty years or so.

Figures 10.3 shows the long-term changes in national and European election turnout that have occurred in European democracies since 1945. The data on national elections cover the fourteen largest West European countries for the period 1945–2009, while the line for European Parliament elections reports the figures for all EU member states (nine in 1979; ten in 1984; twelve in 1989; and so on) for the period since the first European Parliament elections in 1979. The implications are quite clear. European mass publics have become progressively less inclined to participate in both national and European elections. In 1945, average turnout in national elections in Western Europe was around 85 per cent; by 2009, it had fallen to 74 per cent. In 1979, over 60 per cent of eligible citizens turned out to vote in European Parliament elections; the corresponding figure in 2009 was 43 per cent. These progressive long-term

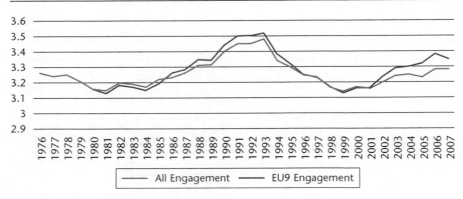

Figure 10.4. Index of informal political engagement, 1976–2007

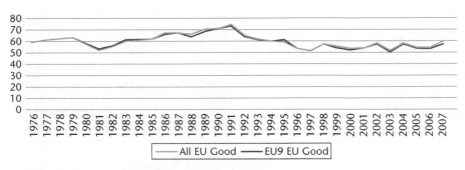

Figure 10.5. Percent believing the EU is a good thing, 1976–2007

declines, though by no means uniformly distributed across different countries (as we saw in Chapter 5), represent an important change in the way that many citizens exercise their most basic of civic duties—a change that, as discussed below, clearly demands some sort of explanation.

Figure 10.4 outlines the changes in *informal* political engagement during 1976–2007. The index used in the figure is described in detail in Chapter 3. The pattern is interesting, particularly in comparison with the declines in *formal* participation documented in Figure 10.3. Whereas formal participation clearly trends downward, informal engagement briefly rose quite markedly in the aftermath of the Cold War. Moreover, the levels of informal engagement are broadly the same at the end of the series as they were at the beginning, suggesting that informal engagement was not affected by whatever long-term factors were responsible for the decline in electoral turnout.

Figures 10.5 to 10.8 describe changes in various EU attitudes. The time periods vary as a result of variations in data availability. The general measure of EU support—the percentage of people who believe that on balance the EU has been "a good thing" for their respective countries—covers the period from

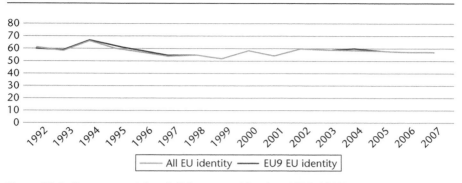

Figure 10.6. Percent partial or full European identity, 1992–2007

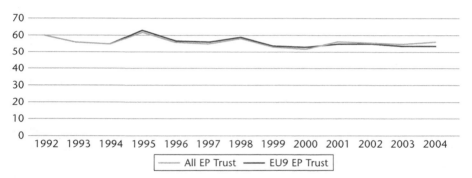

Figure 10.7. Average support for EU policy scope, 1992–2007

1976 to 2007. The more specific measures are available on a more restricted basis—the EU identity and EU policy scope data begin in 1992 and the European Parliament trust measure starts only in 1999. As Figure 10.5 shows, average general support for the EU varied in a similar way to informal political engagement. After an initial decline, support recovered, reaching a peak at around the end of the Cold War, and then subsequently fell back, with the consequence that support levels were marginally lower (around 55 per cent) at the end of the period than they had been at the beginning (support in 1977, for example, was 60 per cent). The decline in support that appears to have set in around 1992, after the signing of the Maastricht Treaty which was designed both to broaden and deepen the union, has been well characterized elsewhere as signalling the point at which the EU's mass public's "permissive consensus" over elite efforts to strengthen the integration process transmuted into a "constraining dissensus" that has exercised something of a brake on further efforts to develop the European project (Hooghe and Marks 2008). In any event, it is evident that mass support for the EU did decline at this time—and, again, this is certainly something that requires explanation. Figures 10.6, 10.7, and 10.8 respectively show little systematic trend variation

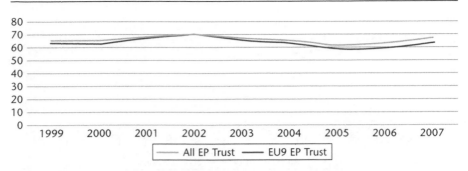

Figure 10.8. Percent trust in the European Parliament, 1999–2007

in levels of European identity, preferences for EU policy scope, or trust in the European Parliament. There are perhaps very slight declines in the identity and policy scope graphs, but they are so modest as to be barely visible. The safest inference from the three graphs, however, is that since the early 1990s, when systematic over-time measurement started, mass attitudes towards European identity, EU policy scope, and EU representation have changed very little.[2]

What conclusions, if any, are suggested by the trend evidence reported in Figures 10.1–10.8? While it is always dangerous to try to draw firm inferences from comparisons of different trends, the general impressions that trends provide can still be either interesting or useful. One obvious point of temporal symmetry in the various graphs is the increase–decline pattern that characterizes the graphs for EU support (Figure 10.5) and informal political engagement (Figure 10.4), since both rise to a peak in the early 1990s and then decline thereafter. However, this temporal similarity may mask rather different causal mechanisms. As implied earlier, the decline in general EU support is widely attributed to the effects of the Maastricht process, which began in 1992. As discussed below (and in Chapter 3), the rise in engagement appears to be linked much more directly to the end of the Cold War. Thus, the two trend patterns—though similar—may well be unrelated in terms of causal mechanisms. A second point of symmetry across the different graphs is the coincidence of a long-term trend *decline* in turnout (Figure 10.3) with long-term trend *increases* in democracy satisfaction (Figure 10.1) and *reductions* in ideological polarization (Figure 10.2).[3] A possible interpretation here is that the trends are causally linked. As voters become progressively more satisfied with democracy, and/or as they become less polarized and move to the political centre, they are less motivated to make the effort to choose between parties and they are therefore less inclined to vote. Again, however, such an inference could only be made with considerable caution, since it would require rather more careful, systematic analysis than the sort of impressionistic weighing of trends that we have provided here. This more systematic approach is precisely what we provided in the various substantive chapters of this volume—analysis that is reviewed in the remainder of this chapter. Note, finally, that the trends in the various graphs relating to EU attitudes are by no means coterminus. The EU support graph rises and falls. The identity and policy scope graphs fall very slightly. The trust in the European Parliament graph oscillates a little over time but finishes almost exactly where it starts. These differences are modest but nonetheless evident. They emphasize the idea that the different components of EU attitudes are not monolithic, but rather that they need to be differentiated from one another. What drives people's general support for the EU may not be the same as what drives people's sense of European identity, their preferences for EU policy competence, or their perceptions of the European Parliament. In short, the differentiated time-series patterns shown in Figures 10.5–10.8 demonstrate the importance of adopting a differentiated approach to the analysis of EU attitudes—exactly the sort of approach that has been adopted here.

3 Towards explanation: theoretical perspectives

In the previous section we cautioned against the employment of simple trend data for identifying possible causal relationships between variables. The substantive chapters of this book have instead used a range of theoretical perspectives to generate testable hypotheses about the phenemona that they have respectively sought to explain. Five main perspectives have been employed: cognitive mobilization; "hard" instrumental rationality; "soft" cueing rationality; identitarian attachment; and equity/fairness calculation. Here, we briefly review the core theoretical claims of each of these perspectives and illustrate the ways in which our substantive chapters employed them in their analyses.

Cognitive mobilization

The basic claim of cognitive mobilization theory is that, as people become more informed about politics through greater education and exposure to political information (the latter often through the mass media), they are more likely to take a more progressive, cosmopolitan view of politics, policy, and political institutions (Inglehart 1970a). Inglehart used cognitive mobilization theory in order to explain the developing sense of European identity that was emerging during the 1960s, arguing that rising levels of cognitive mobilization—of education and knowledge—were stimulating an increase in support for the then EEC.[4] This core idea is used in two of the chapters here—in the discussion of the sources of European identity in Chapter 6 and in the discussion of EU support in Chapter 8. Because Chapter 6 provides a purely aggregate-level analysis, it does not provide an empirical test of the effects of cognitive mobilization on identity. However, Chapter 8—since it provides an analysis at both individual and aggregate levels—is able to test the effects of cognitive mobilization on general EU support, by considering the extent to which educated and informed individuals exhibit higher levels of EU support than their less-educated and uninformed counterparts.

"Hard" instrumental rationality

The idea that people's views and preferences reflect rational, "economic" calculations about their own or their countries' interests is widespread in the analysis of public attitude formation and change. Instrumental or economic rationality assumes that, when faced with a choice, people will weigh the perceived costs and benefits of each option in order to judge between them. Since it is difficult directly to observe people engaging in this kind of "weighing" activity, individual- and aggregate-level research typically has to make assumptions in order to test for the effects of instrumental rationality. In Chapters 7 (trust in the European Parliament) and 8 (EU support), *individual-level* tests are conducted which assume either that instrumental rationality can be operationalized by examining people's beliefs about the relative costs and benefits that have accrued to their respective countries as a result of EU membership, or that likely individual benefits of integration can be captured through objective personal characteristics. The simple empirical proposition tested is that those who believe their country has benefited, or who are themselves more likely to benefit, will be more likely to support the EU than those who believe otherwise. It is also possible, however, to test the effects of instrumental rationality at the *aggregate level*. Three general sets of variables are deployed in the aggregate-level analysis conducted in this volume. The first set involves measures of economic performance, where it is assumed that good (bad) economic performance—specifically, higher GDP growth and lower unemployment—instrumentally encourages (discourages) satisfaction with current political institutions, at both national and EU levels. The effects of this sort of instrumental rationality are investigated in Chapters 2 (democracy satisfaction), 6 (European identity), 9 (EU policy scope), and 8 (EU support).

The second set of aggregate variables also refers to the economy, but focuses on the extent to which an individual's country is dependent on trade with other EU countries. This sort of measure is used in Chapter 6, where it is assumed that it is more rational to think in pan-European terms (in this case, to develop a sense of European identity) in countries with higher levels of intra-EU trade.

The final set of aggregate variables that captures important aspects of instrumental rationality focuses more on politics. The first of these is "quality of governance", where it is assumed that low-quality national governance is likely to elicit dissatisfaction with domestic political institutions (thereby reducing democracy satisfaction, as argued in Chapter 2) and a greater degree of sympathy for supranational decision making (thereby increasing support for EU policy scope, as argued in Chapter 9). The second aggregate "political" variable is ideological polarization, which elsewhere in this volume (Chapter 4) is treated as a dependent variable. In Chapter 3, the level of informal political engagement is regarded as a rational response to the level of ideological polarization: the greater (less) the level of polarization, the stronger (weaker) the incentive to discuss with and to seek to persuade others that it is important to adopt a similar ideological position to one's own.

"Soft" cueing rationality

In recent years, rational choice analysts have increasingly recognized the possibility that individuals with access to very limited information might still behave rationally, by using heuristics or "cognitive shortcuts" in order to make decisions. They might, in short, use "cues" with which they are relatively familiar in order to make judgements about issues and objects with which they are relatively unfamiliar. In electoral research, one classic heuristic or cue for individuals who have neither the time nor the inclination to familiarize themselves with the detailed policy stances of rival parties is to focus on the likely managerial capabilities of the rival party leaders. There are two main sorts of cueing effect that relate to mass attitudes towards the EU: substitution and transfer cueing. Substitution cueing occurs when an individual evaluates domestic institutional performance negatively (positively) and therefore assumes that it would be desirable (undesirable) for more (fewer) decision-making powers to be ceded to supranational institutions. Reasoning of this sort is assumed to operate in Chapters 6 and 9, where it is hypothesized that a measure of the quality of governance should exert *negative* effects, respectively, on European identity and EU policy scope. In both cases, the core idea is that if things are badly run at home, people are more likely to look to Europe; if they are well run at home, Europe is not so important. The second type of cueing is "transfer cueing". This sort of cueing is based on the idea that people who evaluate their own national institutions positively (negatively) may uncritically extend these positive evaluations to the supranational sphere and, as a result, also make positive (negative) evaluations of EU institutions. In contrast to substitution cueing, this *transfer effect* clearly implies a *positive* relationship between attitudes towards national and EU institutions. These sorts of transfer effect are hypothesized to operate in Chapters 7 and 8, where trust in domestic political institutions is hypothesized to have a positive cueing effect, respectively, on trust in the European Parliament and on general support for the EU.

Affective/identitarian factors

The suggestion that people might have affective feelings towards political objects that can influence their attitudes and preferences just as strongly as rational calculations is neither novel nor contentious. It is clear from a large number of psychological and attitudinal studies that people's feelings and sense of political and social identity can have profound effects on their political attitudes and choices. The notion of identity has been widely used in analyses of EU attitudes and it is used in three ways in the chapters in this volume. First, in Chapter 7, following Easton (1965), trust in the European Parliament is seen as a manifestation of "specific support" for EU institutions that itself stems from a deeper and more generalized, affective sense of "diffuse support" for the EU as a whole. The chapter uses people's preferences for a faster or a slower speed for integration as a loose indicator of their diffuse, affective support for the EU, which it predicts will have a positive effect on trust in the European Parliament. Second, in Chapter 6, which explicitly tries to specify the causal antecedents of European identity, the length of time that each member state has belonged to the EU is used to indicate the extent of people's exposure to EU norms and practices. It is predicted that, other things being equal, greater exposure is likely to generate a greater sense of affective identity towards the EU. Finally, Chapter 6 also sees a tension between a strong sense of national identity and the development of European identity, with the former acting as a direct impediment to the development of the latter. The expectation here is accordingly that strong national identity should exert a negative effect on identification with Europe.

Equity/fairness

One of the commonest factors that researchers in a wide range of fields have identified as motivating diverse forms of political action is a sense of relative deprivation or injustice (Gurr 1970; Sniderman, Brody, and Tetlock 1991). People who feel that either they or some group they care about are failing to benefit fully from the opportunities and/or rewards that society offers are more likely to be driven by a sense of injustice to challenge the political status quo. The reverse side of this discontent-driven sort of activity is that people who believe that the society or political system they live in is basically "fair" and/or "equitable" are more likely to be supportive of the status quo and for this to be expressed in their political attitudes. The notion of equity/fairness is used in several of the analyses developed in this volume. The most direct usage is in Chapter 2, where is it hypothesized that democracy satisfaction is likely to be higher, *ceteris paribus*, in countries where the electoral system is proportional, thereby ensuring a relatively fair distribution of seats in the legislative assembly. The idea of "fairness" is also employed in Chapter 3, where it is assumed that systems with relatively high welfare spending are likely to be perceived as being more equitable than those with low spending. It is further hypothesized that, net of all other effects, informal political engagement is likely to be higher in countries where equity/fairness in the form of social welfare spending is more deeply entrenched.

It is clear from the foregoing discussion that a range of theoretical perspectives have been used in a diverse set of ways in different chapters. We regard this eclectic approach as entirely appropriate. The phenomena that the different chapters seek to analyse, though often empirically related, are conceptually distinct. It would be decidedly odd if a single theoretical perspective—or even a single set of perspectives—could satisfactorily account for all of the cross-national and over-time patterns of change and variation that we have described in our substantive chapters. In the next section, we offer a summary account of the factors that each chapter has identifed as being responsible for the changing political attitudes and behaviours of European mass publics over the last three decades. As we will see, although the various theories outlined above all play a role, they by no means provide—even in combination—a full explanation of the complex and diverse pattern of change that we have outlined.

4 Core empirical findings: what explains variations in European political attitudes and engagement?

There are in principle three main types of variation in political attitudes and behaviour that require description and explanation: variations across individuals; across different geographical regions or countries; and, within any given region or country, over time. Because the sorts of statistical modelling techniques we have employed in the different chapters of this volume are capable of handling cross-national and over-time variations simultaneously, in our discussion we have distinguished mainly between micro- or individual-level factors and macro- or aggregate-level factors. Ideally, any analysis of either attitudes or behaviour should be conducted at both the micro/individual and macro/aggregate levels—and given perfect data availability, this is exactly what we would have attempted to do here. However, practical empirical analysis and hypothesis testing always involve a compromise between what is theoretically desirable and the availability of suitable, comparable, representative data. In our case, data constraints have forced different choices on the authors of different chapters. In the chapters on informal political engagement, EU support and turnout in EU elections, there are sufficient comparable individual- and aggregate-level data available over enough countries and time points to allow for the simultaneous estimation of a range of individual- and macro-level effects. For the chapter on trust in the European Parliament, the data available on suitable explanatory variables are far more restricted. In order to assess the consequences of the changes in the nature of the EU that have resulted from the process of monetary union, this chapter uses a quasi-experimental design that deploys individual-level data collected both before (in 1999) and after (in 2006) the introduction of the euro. The remaining chapters all use a purely aggregate-level approach. This necessarily involves making stronger assumptions about the precise mechanisms through which causal effects might operate than is the case with individual-level data. Nonetheless, in each of these chapters the aggregate-level approach enables important hypotheses about the sources of the various dependent variables to be systematically assessed empirically over both time and space.

Democracy satisfaction. Chapter 2 regards the extent to which people feel satisfied with democracy as a response to instrumental rational calculations about system performance. The core assumption, following valence theories of electoral politics (Stokes 1963; Clarke et al. 2009) is that the better the system performs, the higher the level of democracy satisfaction. The chapter considers system performance under three main headings: (1) the performance of *the economy*, which is measured in terms of growth in gross domestic product; (2) the extent to which the political system operates under the *rule of law*, which is operationalized in terms of the quality of governance within the state and public bureaucracy; and (3) the extent to which the legislative system delivers *political representation*, which is captured by whether or not the electoral system is based on proportional representation. Data constraints mean that the effects of these macro variables on democracy satisfaction can only be estimated across the whole of Europe for the period between 1994 and 2006. Although the time period covered in the analysis is relatively limited, the empirical results are robust. Economic performance clearly exerts a consistent positive effect on democracy satisfaction: across a wide range of institutional contexts, a stronger economy means more support for democracy. The same conclusion also holds with regard to the rule of law, where the quality of governance is used as an indicator: low governance quality (a weak rule of law) is consistently associated with lower levels of democracy satisfaction. Finally, democracy satisfaction is also found to be higher in systems with proportional representation. These findings clearly suppport the idea that people are instrumentally rational in their judgements about the democratic quality of their respective countries' political systems. They also indicate both the strengths and the vulnerabilities of contemporary European democracies. As long as they continue to perform well in terms of delivering prosperity, public probity, and electoral fairness, levels of democracy satisfaction will be maintained or even enhanced. In contrast, serious economic crisis, departures from the rule of law, or failures of political representation clearly threaten to weaken support levels.

Ideological polarization. Ideological polarization is the only area studied in this volume in which there appear to be major differences between Western and Eastern Europe. In the West, it is clear that ideological polarization has been in long-term *decline*, with mass publics in most countries moving towards the political centre, as the traditional left–right divide between capital and labour has diminished in importance. In the East, however, the picture is reversed. Here, since the establishment of democratic systems in the early 1990s, the tendency has been towards *greater* ideological polarization. This distinctive Eastern pattern probably reflects the effects of the emerging party systems in the post-communist countries, where parties have progressively found it useful to differentiate themselves in terms of left–right ideological appeals and have therefore been more inclined to structure their political discourses in ideological terms. This sort of party cueing has in turn affected the ideological thinking of East European mass publics. In contrast, in Western Europe, there has been a progressive weakening of mass affiliation to established left–right political parties—a long-term decline in levels of party identification with established left–right parties—and this in turn probably underpins the long-term decline in the ideological polarization of West European mass publics. These differences in the trends of ideological polarization in the Eastern and Western parts of Europe are complemented by the fact that different sets of factors appear to underpin variations in polarization in each. In the East, polarization is most strongly influenced by the age of the democratic regime and by the number of electoral parties. In the West, the main drivers are unemployment and the existence of federal political institutions. These differences almost certainly reflect the different levels of maturity of the political systems of Eastern *versus* Western Europe. In the West, party competition and left–right ideological thinking have been embedded in the practice of democratic politics for much of the period since 1945—or even longer; as a result, ideological thinking is less influenced by relatively short-term factors than it is in the East. Note, finally, that the discussion in Chapter 3 established an important differential *consequence* of ideological (de)polarization in the Eastern and Western parts of Europe. In the West, polarization has a positive causal effect on turnout—the long-term decline in polarization has accordingly been one of the key long-term factors responsible for declining levels of turnout in Western Europe. In short, as ideological differences have declined, citizens have had less incentive to bother to vote because there has been less at stake if one government rather than another is elected. In the East, however, the effect is reversed: polarization has a negative effect on turnout. Here, therefore, rising levels of polarization after 1990 have provoked a *decline* in turnout—perhaps reflecting the tendency for East European voters, given the years of ideologically-driven communist rule, to regard more intense ideological discourse as a disincentive to participate in electoral politics.[5]

Informal political engagement. Notwithstanding the trend decline in national election turnout across Europe that was documented in Figure 10.3(a), it is clear from Figure 10.4 that informal political engagement has not been subject to the same sort of linear trend decline. Rather, informal engagement—discussing politics and seeking to persuade others to change their views—has oscillated over the last three decades. Engagement declined slightly after 1976, recovered in the mid-1980s, reached a peak in the wake of the end of the Cold War, subsequently declined again, and then, after 1999, returned progressively to the levels of the mid-1970s. In attempting to explain both individual- and macro-level variations in engagement, Chapter 3 considered the rival merits of factors based on cognitive mobilization, equity/fairness and instrumental rationality. At the individual level, as cognitive mobilization theory predicts, education and employment status exert positive effects on engagement. At the macro level, as the equity/fairness model predicts, engagement is stimulated by higher levels of social welfare spending. The remaining effects, apart from those concerned with demographic and other controls, focus on the role of instrumental rationality. Higher levels of unemployment act as a demotivator and *discourage* people from informal engagement. Ideological polarization, in contrast, represents a sharpening of fundamental political divisions and accordingly provides a *greater* incentive for people to engage in informal political activity. As noted above, great events—in this case the end of the Cold War—also seem to stimulate greater levels of informal engagement, albeit temporarily, with an effect that produced a rapid increase in engagement in 1991, which then discounted over time. The analysis in Chapter 3 also produced an important "null" finding. It was expected that, given the considerable successes of the feminist movement across Europe after the 1970s, the negative effect on political engagement of "being female" would progressively reduce over time. No such effect was in fact observed. In spite of the increasing role that women play in many aspects of contemporary economic and political life, informal political engagement in Europe remains a predominantly male activity.

Formal political engagement: turnout in European elections. It was noted above that the general decline in turnout in national elections across Western Europe over recent decades is in part due to the long-term decline in ideological polarization that has also occurred over the same period. Indeed, it is likely that the same factors that have driven down national turnout have also been responsible for declining turnout in elections for the European Parliament. These elections, after all, are generally regarded as "second order"—that is to say, people vote in them primarily on the basis of national, domestic, rather than strictly "European", factors and calculations. This said, the analysis in Chapter 5 shows that, at the individual level, people's orientations towards the EU *do* have an effect on whether or not they decide to vote in elections for the European Parliament. Measures of EU support, affinity, or identity all consistently furnish significant, positive coefficients for EU parliamentary turnout over the 1979–2004 period. In short, people seem to be behaving rationally in the sense that the more positively they feel about the EU in general, the more likely they are to participate as citizens in the EU political process. The individual-level analysis in the chapter also shows that some of the standard drivers of national election turnout—age, interest in politics, and strength of party identification—also figure significantly in models of EU turnout. The significance of the "age" and "interest in politics" terms is clearly consistent with cognitive mobilization accounts of turnout. The significance of the strength of partisanship term indicates that EU turnout is also affected by "transfer cueing". Individuals who exhibit strong partisanship at home are likely to use the cues represented by such attachments to decide to vote in European elections. Taking all these factors together, it is relatively easy to appreciate why turnout in European elections has fallen progressively since 1979. Three of the key drivers of EU election turnout—the age profiles of European democracies, people's interest in politics, and general support for the EU—have, with minor variations in specific countries, been broadly constant over time. However, the two big drivers of turnout in all sorts of election—ideological polarization and partisanship—have witnessed secular declines over the last three or four decades in almost all the contexts in which they have been measured. Small wonder, therefore, that turnout has also declined in European elections.

European identity. One important conclusion drawn in Chapter 6 was that, contrary to the hopes of the EU's functionalist founding fathers, a strong sense of European identity has not developed amongst European mass publics as the EU itself has broadened and deepened. Using aggregate-level data, the chapter sought to explain why this should be the case. As in other chapters, a range of theoretical positions was brought to bear. The empirical analysis conducted in the chapter shows that instrumental rationality, substitution cueing, and affective attachments all play a role in the development of European identity. In terms of instrumental rationality, identity is strongly and positively influenced by public beliefs about the benefits of EU membership: the more that mass publics perceive that the EU brings benefits to their respective countries, the stronger the sense of European identity. In terms of substitution cueing, it is clear that the sense of European identity is far stronger in countries where the quality of governance is low: doubts about the effectiveness and probity of one's own political system clearly translate into a stronger sense of European identity. Finally, in terms of affective/identitarian considerations, there is a strong tendency for countries with a high proportion of immigrants to fail to develop a cosmopolitan sense of European identity, precisely because high levels of foreign immigrants engender a stronger, and competing, sense of national identity among indigenous populations. Again, in these circumstances it is easy to envisage why a greater sense of European identity has failed to develop over time. While there has been a slight growth in the proportion of people who consider that the EU has brought "benefits", the positive effects on European identity of such a development have been more than outweighed by the negative effects of mass immigration, which most European countries have experienced in recent years.

Trust in the European Parliament. Chapter 7 views levels of trust in the European Parliament as an indicator of European citizens' "specific support" for the institutions of the EU. It deploys three theoretical perspectives to account for variations in such support, over time, at the individual level. Instrumental rationality is captured through perceptions of the benefits that accrue (or fail to accrue) to the respondent's country as a result of EU membership. Transfer cueing is operationalized using people's levels of trust in their own national political insitutions. Affective attachments to the EU are measured through preferences for a "faster" or "slower" approach to EU integration ("EU speed"). The effects of these different stimulae, given the constraints of data availability, are tested against data for the period 1999–2006. The empirical results suggest three main conclusions. First, the measures of instrumental rationality, transfer cueing, and affective attachment all produce significant positive coefficients over the 1999–2006 period, supporting the idea that all three theoretical positions contribute to the explanation of European Parliament support. Second, the analysis shows that the effects of affective attachments weaken over time, whereas those associated with instrumental rationality strengthen. The third conclusion relates to the role of European monetary union. Several previous studies have suggested that the extension of EU policy competence to the monetary sphere after Maastricht— which culminated in the introduction of the euro as the official circulating currency of the "eurozone" in January 2002—engendered a more critical approach among European mass publics towards the EU. This was because Europeans gradually became more aware of the costs of EU membership that were associated with the budgetary and public spending disciplines imposed by membership of the eurozone. Chapter 7 uses the fact that several EU countries did *not* join the eurozone as a "natural experiment" to determine if the weakening effects of affective attachment were indeed due to the

Maastricht process. The findings show that the change in the relative effects of instrumental versus affective considerations was almost exclusively confined to eurozone countries; where the euro was *not* introduced, the balance of instrumental and affective effects on trust in the European Parliament remained more or less constant. This strong finding leads to the conclusion that the deepening of the EU integration process—in particular its extension to the field of monetary policy—has enhanced the role of instrumental calculation in people's evaluations of the union itself. If specific support for EU institutions is to increase in the future, they must deliver—and be seen to deliver—tangible benefits to citizens.

Support for the EU. Chapter 8 offers an analysis of the sources of general support for the EU. As in other chapters, theoretical ideas from instrumental rationality, heuristic or cueing rationality, and cognitive mobilization are used to develop explanations for variations in support across time and space. Data availability constraints mean that aggregate-level analysis is the most appropriate for evaluating the various theoretical claims that are made. A key feature of the chapter is its focus on the extent to which different causal factors operate uniformly or unevenly across geographical and temporal contexts. The empirical results indicate that, although instrumental rationality is an important driver of EU support in certain contexts, its impact varies considerably across time and space—and on occasion it disappears altogether. This variegated pattern contrasts strongly with the impact of cognitive mobilization and transfer cueing. The evidence reported suggests that these latter two mechanisms operate with remarkable evenness across contexts: where cognitive mobilization is high, the greater cosmopolitanism it engenders consistently seems to promote support for the EU; and where domestic politics works, people are more likely to be cued to support the EU. These results suggest that future generalized support for the EU will perhaps depend less on the performance of its own institutions than has sometimes been the case in the past. It will depend more on the continuing process of cognitive mobilization that has occurred as education levels across Europe have risen over the last fifty years, and more on the performance of domestic political institutions and their ability to provide their populations with transparent, fair government. Indeed, if EU policy makers are seriously interested in generating increased support for the EU in the future, they might well consider the benefits of developing processes that could ensure "more cognitive mobilization" and "better governance" at national and sub-national levels throughout the EU.

EU policy scope. The question of the policy competencies that should be the preserve of national as opposed to EU-level decision making has been at the heart of debates about the future of the European project since the 1950s. One important argument that has been advanced in this context is that there are certain policy areas (for example, the environment or the fight against organized international crime) that are "inherently internationalized", whereas others (such as education or health policy) are not (Hooghe and Marks 2008). Chapter 9 shows that a similar set of factors appears to drive popular preferences for EU competence in policy areas of both "high" and "low" "inherent internationalization". In line with previous arguments about "substitution cueing", people living in countries with relatively low quality of governance are more likely to want to see an extension of EU policy competence in all areas. EU mass publics also display practical common sense in recognizing that EU-level policy making is desirable in precisely those areas where competence has already been ceded to the supranational level. The chapter also finds evidence that the strongest support for EU competence is in those policy areas that correspond to the "European Social Model"—particularly in relation to the environment, regional policy, social inclusion, and policies for dealing with unemployment. Two of the more important "null findings" of the chapter are also worth highlighting. First, it is sometimes thought that it is instrumentally rational for people living in poorer EU countries to prefer EU to national policy making, on the grounds that an EU policy approach is more likely to provide subsidies from Brussels that will disproportionately benefit poorer regions and economies. The evidence provided in Chapter 9 shows clearly that this is only the case for those policy areas with high budgetary implications. In the remaining cases, economic development has a *positive* effect on preferences for EU policy competence, rather than the reverse. The second null finding relates to the role of Maastricht. As indicated above, in relation to trust in the European Parliament, the changing character of the EU since Maastricht has lead to some changes in the pattern of mass public support for the EU itself. Some authors have even gone as far as to identify a transition from a "permissive consensus", in which mass publics deferred to elite judgements about the future course of the union to a "constraining dissensus", in which increasing mass public doubt about the benefits of the union act as a brake on further integration. However, the evidence reported in Chapter 9 suggests that, as far as mass preferences for EU policy scope are concerned, the position is rather more complicated and inconsistent. Maastricht appears to have exerted little or no *general* effect on these preferences. In some policy areas support for Europeanization increased after 1992; in others it remained stable; in still others, it fell. In Social Model policy areas, mass publics appear to be just as committed to EU-level decision making as they were before the mid-1990s—even if they are more reticent about the benefits of EMU. As the title of the chapter suggests, mass publics are in fact quite discriminating in terms of the policy areas in which they wish to see the EU develop: they are instrumentally rational; they want a Europe à la carte, with more EU-level decision making in some areas—and less in others.

Postscript

This volume has covered a lot of empirical ground, embracing analyses of up to twenty-seven EU countries over a period of almost forty years. In spite of the large-scale changes that have occurred at the global and European levels—globalization, the end of the Cold War, the expansion of the EU, the introduction of the euro, and significant increases in migration both within and into the EU—the political attitudes and behaviours of European mass publics have changed relatively little. Indeed, it is tempting to conclude in this context that *plus ça change, plus c'est la même chose*. This is not to say, of course, that nothing (important) has changed. Turnout in both national and European elections has declined progressively over the long term, in part as a response to the systematic long-term decline in ideological polarization which has certainly occurred extensively in Western Europe. At the same time, however, democracy satisfaction has, if anything, increased—and *informal* political engagement is certainly no lower now than it was in the mid-1970s. Although levels of European identity have barely changed in four decades, attitudes towards the European Union have matured. Citizens are somewhat more sceptical towards the EU than they were in the 1970s, and—since the introduction of the single currency—they place more emphasis on instrumental rational considerations in evaluating institutions like the European Parliament than they did previously. They are also more inclined to differentiate their attitudes towards the EU, favouring more EU policy competence in some policy areas and less in others.

In order to explain these different changes and stages, we have employed a number of theoretical perspectives and identified several practical developments that appear to have had important empirical consequences. Instrumental rationality and either substitution or transfer cueing feature significantly in most of our statistical models. Cognitive mobilization and affective attachments play important roles in a substantial number of others. The effects of equity/fairness considerations are more limited but they nonetheless play a role in a minority of models. In contrast to these more deep-seated psychological mechanisms, the "great events" of the last three decades or so have played relatively minor roles in changing the political views and behaviours of Europe's mass publics. The end of the Cold War appears to have affected informal political engagement—but only temporarily. The Maastricht process of monetary union has affected EU-related attitudes towards institutions but not—in any consistent way—towards issues of EU policy competence. The inclusion of a new set of post-communist states in the European family has injected some new attitudinal patterns—Eastern European states, for example, have become more, rather than less, ideologically polarized since 1990. Yet the behaviour patterns of the new member states have been very similar to states that joined the EU in earlier accession waves—electoral turnout continues to decline almost everywhere.

All of this begs the question as to whether the relative lack of attitudinal change among European mass publics betokens a dangerous complacency in the face of potentially disruptive exogenous change or an adaptive resilience that refuses to be diverted from deeply held convictions when challenged. In many respects, the question is unanswerable, but there are two reasons for supposing that the "adaptive resilience" characterization may be the more important. The first is that there is a considerable degree of over-time stability across so many different attitudinal sets, covering both domestic and EU-related politics. The lack of marked linear trend change or instability in most of the attitude measures reviewed here suggests that European mass publics are not easily swayed in their fundamental political views by "events". We would argue that this stability of trend signifies a stability of view that is not easily shaken, rather than an indifference to the threats and challenges that exogenous change might engender. The second reason for supposing "adaptive resilience" relates to evidence that we present in a companion volume to this study. That study involved conducting two surveys of political opinion among European mass publics. The first survey was carried out in the spring of 2007—before the "credit crunch" of late 2007, which transmuted into a full-blown recession in 2008. The second wave of the survey—which asked an identical set of questions to the first—was conducted in the summer of 2008. These surveys covered the same set of issues analysed in this volume—satisfaction with national politics and democracy, political engagement, ideological positioning, European versus national identity, and attitudes towards the EU in terms of policy scope and representation. What is fascinating about the results is that although people's economic perceptions were transformed between 2007 and 2008 (becoming massively more pessimistic and negative), all of the key political and European attitudes examined here remained broadly stable—indeed, most of the marginal distributions were identical within the margins of sampling error across both survey waves. It is possible that the continuing economic uncertainties since 2008 will eventually provoke a change in the currently stable political attitude set that we have described. However, the fact that these attitudes did not change in the face of the most intense economic shock adminstered to Europe's political systems since 1945 suggests to us that they reflect, at heart, a deep-seated stability in European public opinion. This stability reflects a basic contentment—despite local and localized frustrations—with the way politics is practised in most of Europe and the EU. We do not know, particularly in the aftermath of the 2011/12 eurozone crisis, whether national political systems and the emerging EU political system will continue to deliver the kind of policy outcomes that

European mass publics favour and demand. But if they do, there is good reason to suppose that levels of satisfaction with national political systems and with the EU will continue to be maintained in the future.

Notes

1. This finding of a recovery in democracy satisfaction after the 1990s contrasts with the sort of analysis provided in Norris (1999a). It is perhaps the case that the rise of "critical citizens" or "dissatisfied democrats" that was described in that volume reflected changes during a specific time period, rather than an inevitable feature of mature democracies.
2. As pointed out in Chapter 9, there are also specific—and varying—trends in different policy areas.
3. The turnout graph, of course, covers a longer period than the polarization graph. The shorter time period for the polarization data is because they are available only since 1976. Note, however, that even for the period since 1976, both graphs clearly trend downward.
4. Inglehart's analysis also embraces the connected idea of post-materialism, which together with cognitive mobilization is seen as being responsible for increasing distrust of hierarchical institutions and an increasing disposition to engage in protest and other forms of unconventional political action (Inglehart 1977a; Barnes and Kaase 1979).
5. This, of course, is only one possible interpretation of these observed relationships. An alternative possible interpretation is that turnout is falling in both East and West because of "political normalization". Democracy pushes parties towards less polarized positions in advanced democracies. Economic growth and consolidation of democratic institutions such as a functioning party system help party politics to become less dramatic—and accordingly less mobilizing in terms of turnout.

Appendices

Note: An extended and continuously updated version of this appendix, with links to the principal datasets used in the analyses is available online at http://www.personal. ceu.hu/departs/personal/Gabor_Toka/INTUNE1.

Most analyses in this volume rely on two datasets: one formed by pooling individual-level survey data from the Eurobarometer series and the other by assembling country-level contextual indicators and matching them with aggregated survey data (typically, variable means for individual country years) from the Eurobarometer series. The general characteristics of these datasets and the variables appearing in them are discussed in the first two main sections of the appendix below. Chapters 2, 3, 4, 5, and 9 also rely on some other data sources and the variables appearing in those analyses are described in separate sections below.

The individual-level Eurobarometer data used in chapters 2–3 and 7–8

The principal micro dataset used in the analysis in this volume is Xezonakis's (2008) update on the Mannheim Eurobarometer Trend File 1970–2002 and is composed from surveys from the Eurobarometer survey series and the European Community survey from 1970 to 2007, with the exception of 1972, for which no data are available. The Xezonakis (2008) dataset was created for the IntUne project by pooling 113 individual Eurobarometer and European Community surveys and represents an extension of the Mannheim Eurobarometer Trend File 1970–2002 with Eurobarometer surveys from the 2003 to 2007 period. It also includes EU member states that joined in the 2004 enlargement wave as well as Romania and Bulgaria (also included from 2004). The total number of unweighted cases included in the full dataset is 1,798,481. The dataset includes all variables which were included in at least five different standard Euro-barometer surveys.

The dataset covers all countries that were members of the EU in the 1970–2007 period and for all years in which Eurobarometer surveys were conducted in these countries. Data from Belgium, France, Germany, Italy, Luxembourg, and the Nether-lands are included for the entire 1970–2007 period. Data from Denmark, the United Kingdom, and Ireland are included for the 1973–2007 period only. Data from Greece are available for 1980–2007, from Portugal and Spain for 1985–2007, from Austria, Finland, and Sweden for 1994–2007. The ten member states joining in 2004 are included, with data starting with 2004, as are Romania and Bulgaria. The actual data availability for particular years varies substantially across variables and this is reflected in the analysis in the individual chapters.

The following Eurobarometer and European Community Surveys are included in the pooled dataset: ECS 70, ECS 71, ECS 73, EB 2, EB 3, EB 4, EB 5, EB 6, EB 7, EB 8, EB 9, EB 10, EB 10A, EB 11, EB 12, EB 13, EB 14, EB 15, EB 16, EB 17, EB 18, EB 19, EB 20, EB 21, EB 22, EB 23, EB 24, EB 25, EB 26, EB 27, EB 28, EB 29, EB 30, EB 31, EB 31A, EB 32A, EB 32B, EB 33, EB 34, EB 34.1, EB 35, EB 35.1, EB 36, EB 37, EB 37.1, EB 38, EB 38.1, EB 39, EB 39.1, EB 40, EB 41, EB 41.1, EB 42, EB 43, EB 43.1, EB 43.1B, EB 44, EB 44.1, EB 45.1, EB 46, EB 46.1, EB 47, EB 47.1, EB 47.2, EB 48, EB 49, EB 50, EB 50.1, EB 51, EB 51.1, EB 52, EB 52.1, EB 53, EB 54, EB 54.1, EB 54.2, EB 55, EB 55.1, EB 55.2, EB 56, EB 56.1, EB 56.2, EB 56.3, EB 57, EB 57.1, EB 57.2, EB 58, EB 58.1, EB 58.2, EB 60, EB 60.1, EB 60.2, EB 60.3, EB 61, EB 62, EB 62.1, EB 62.2, EB 63.1, EB 63.2, EB 63.4, EB 64.1, EB 64.2, EB 64.3, EB 64.4, EB 65.1, EB 65.2, EB 65.3, EB 65.4, EB 66.1, EB 66.2, EB 66.3, EB 67.1, EB 67.2.

More details about the Mannheim Eurobarometer Trend File 1970–2002, the selection of variables, coverage, and the coding of variables are available at the GESIS Eurobarometer Data Service available at: http://www.gesis.org/en/eurobarometer/topics-trends/eb-trends/eb-trends-trend-files/mannheim-eb-trend-file

Individual-level variables in chapters 3, 7, and 8

AGE and AGE-SQUARED: the respondent's age (in years) and its squared value.

CATHOLIC: based on responses about the respondents' religious denomination; all respondents who declared themselves as Catholic coded 1 and all others as 0.

DESIRED UNIFICATION SPEED: is measured with an item asking respondent what their preference is about the speed of the advance of European integration, with answers coded on a seven-point scale where 1 means "standing still" and 7 means "moving as fast as possible".

EDUCATION: age of respondent when s/he completed full-time education.

EU DEMOCRACY SATISFACTION: is measured with an item asking: "On the whole, how satisfied are you with the way democracy works in the European Union? Are you...?" with answers coded as 1=very satisfied; 2=somewhat satisfied; 3=somewhat dissatisfied; 4=very dissatisfied.

EU MEMBERSHIP BENEFIT: is measured with an item asking respondent: "Taking everything into consideration, would you say that [OUR COUNTRY] 1=has on balance benefited or 2=has not benefited from being a member of the European Union?"

EU MEMBERSHIP SUPPORT: is measured with an items asking respondent: "Generally speaking, do you think that [COUNTRY]'s membership of the European union is 1=a good thing; 2=neither good nor bad; or 3=a bad thing?" The original 1–2–3 values were recoded into 100–50–0 in the analysis in Chapter 8.

FARMER: constructed from the occupation variable by coding the respondents who work in farming as 1 and all others as 0.

FEMALE: sex of respondent, coded 0 for male and 1 for female respondents.

GENERATION: indicates whether the respondent was older (coded as 1) or younger (coded as 0) than 25 when her/his country entered the EC/EU.

HOMEMAKER/RETIRED: constructed from the occupation variable by coding respondents who are retired or homemakers as 1 and all others as 0.

LEFT-RIGHT IDEOLOGY: is measured with an item asking respondent "In political matters people talk of "left" and "right". Where would you place your views on this scale?" (SHOW CARD with horizontal laid 1-10 ladder where '1' is labelled "left" and '10' is labelled "right".)

LEFT RIGHT EXTREMITY: is calculated from the above variable by taking the squared deviation of the left-right self placement from 5 (after recoding 10 to 9).

MALE: sex of respondent, coded 0 for female and 1 for male respondents.

MANAGER: constructed from the occupation variable by coding the respondents who are holding managerial posts as 1 and all others as 0.

MANUAL WORKER: constructed from the occupation variable by coding the respondents who are manual workers as 1 and all others as 0.

MEDIA CONSUMPTION: is measured by asking respondent how frequently he/she follows news on television. The variable is coded as 1=every day; 2=several times a week; 3=once or twice a week; 4=less often; 5=never.

NATIONAL DEMOCRACY SATISFACTION: is measured with an item asking "On the whole, how satisfied are you with the way democracy works in [OUR COUNTRY]? Are you...?" and coded as 1=very satisfied; 2=somewhat satisfied; 3=somewhat dissatisfied; 4=very dissatisfied.

POLITICAL ENGAGEMENT: an additive scale created by combining the *Political Discussion* and *Political Persuasion* variables as shown in Table 3.2.

POLITICAL DISCUSSION: is measured with an items asking respondent:"When you get together with friends would you say you discuss political matters 1=frequently; 2=occasionally; or 3=never?"

POLITICAL PERSUASION: is measured with an items asking respondent: "When you (yourself) hold a strong opinion, do you ever find yourself persuading your friends, relatives or fellow workers to share your views? Does this happen: 1=often; 2=from time to time; 3=rarely; 4=never?"

PROFESSIONAL: constructed from the occupation variable by coding the respondents who are employed as professionals as 1 and all others as 0.

SELF-EMPLOYED: constructed from the occupation variable by coding the respondents who are self-employed in non-farming sector as 1 and all others as 0.

UNEMPLOYED: constructed from the occupation variable by coding unemployed respondents as 1 and all others as 0.

TRUST IN NATIONAL PARLIAMENT: is measured with an item asking if the respondent can rely on decisions made by national parliament or not, coded as 1=can rely and 2=cannot rely.

TRUST IN EUROPEAN PARLIAMENT: is measured with an item asking if the respondent can rely on decisions made by European parliament or not; coded as 1=can rely and 2=cannot rely.

VOTING FOR A PRO-EU PARTY: is created by assigning to each respondent the position on European integration from Chapel Hill expert survey (Hooghe *et. al.* 2010; Marks and Steenbergen 2007) (ranging from 1 to 7) of the party he voted for at the last national elections.

Macro variables created by aggregating micro-level data

The following variables were created by aggregating individual-level variables from Eurobarometer surveys by aggregating data across individual-level observations and producing country-level averages or sums.

EU DEMOCRACY SATISFACTION—percentage of respondents satisfied (fairly or very) with the way democracy works in the EU.

EU MEMBERSHIP BENEFIT—percentage of respondents who think their own country benefited from the EU membership.

EU MEMBERSHIP SUPPORT—average score of respondents answering whether their county's membership in the EU is a good or bad thing, after the original responses were recoded as 0=bad thing, 100=good thing, 50=neither good nor bad.

FARMER: constructed from the occupation variable by coding the respondents who work in farming as 1 and all others as 0.

FEMALE: sex of respondent, coded 0 for male and 1 for female respondents.

GENERATION: indicates whether the respondent was older (coded as 1) or younger (coded as 0) than 25 when her/his country entered the EC/EU.

HOMEMAKER/RETIRED: constructed from the occupation variable by coding respondents who are retired or homemakers as 1 and all others as 0.

LEFT–RIGHT IDEOLOGY: is measured with an item asking respondent: "In political matters people talk of "left" and "right". Where would you place your views on this scale?" (SHOW CARD with horizontal laid 1–10 ladder where "1" is labelled "left" and "10" is labelled "right".)

LEFT–RIGHT EXTREMITY: is calculated from the above variable by taking the squared deviation of the left–right self-placement from 5 (after recoding 10 to 9).

MALE: sex of respondent, coded 0 for female and 1 for male respondents.

MANAGER: constructed from the occupation variable by coding the respondents who are holding managerial posts as 1 and all others as 0.

MANUAL WORKER: constructed from the occupation variable by coding the respondents who are manual workers as 1 and all others as 0.

MEDIA CONSUMPTION: is measured by asking respondent how frequently he/she follows news on television. The variable is coded as 1=every day; 2=several times a week; 3=once or twice a week; 4=less often; 5=never.

NATIONAL DEMOCRACY SATISFACTION: is measured with an item asking: "On the whole, how satisfied are you with the way democracy works in [OUR COUNTRY]? Are you ... ?" and coded as 1=very satisfied; 2=somewhat satisfied; 3=somewhat dissatisfied; 4=very dissatisfied.

POLITICAL ENGAGEMENT: an additive scale created by combining the Political discussion and Political persuasion variables as shown in Table 3.2.

POLITICAL DISCUSSION: is measured with an items asking respondent: "When you get together with friends would you say you discuss political matters 1=frequently; 2=occasionally; or 3=never?"

POLITICAL PERSUASION: is measured with an items asking respondent: "When you (yourself) hold a strong opinion, do you ever find yourself persuading your friends, relatives or fellow workers to share your views? Does this happen 1=often; 2=from time to time; 3=rarely; 4=never?"

PROFESSIONAL: constructed from the occupation variable by coding the respondents who are employed as professionals as 1 and all others as 0.

SELF-EMPLOYED: constructed from the occupation variable by coding the respondents who are self-employed in non-farming sector as 1 and all others as 0.

UNEMPLOYED: constructed from the occupation variable by coding unemployed respondents as 1 and all others as 0.

TRUST IN NATIONAL PARLIAMENT: is measured with an item asking if the respondent can rely on decisions made by national parliament or not, coded as 1=can rely and 2=cannot rely.

TRUST IN EUROPEAN PARLIAMENT: is measured with an item asking if the respondent can rely on decisions made by European parliament or not; coded as 1=can rely and 2=cannot rely.

VOTING FOR A PRO-EU PARTY: is created by assigning to each respondent the position on European integration from Chapel Hill expert survey (Hooghe et al. 2010; Marks and Steenbergen 2007) (ranging from 1 to 7) of the party he or she voted for at the last national elections.

Macro dataset in Chapters 2–3, 6–8, and 10

The aggregate-level data used in these chapters are Henjak (2009), compiled for the IntUne project from multiple sources. It includes the following variables, all observed for individual country years starting with 1973 and ending with 2007 and covering the unbalanced panel of EU member states.

ACCESSION WAVE: a set of variables coding countries according to their participation in different accession waves (1973, 1981/1986, and 2004), where countries are coded as 1 if they belong to any of these waves and 0 if they entered the EU at another time point.

BUDGET DEFICIT: budget deficit measured as % of GDP. Source: 1990–2007 EURO-STAT (undated); l 1973–89 Armingeon et al. (2008).

CATHOLICS: percentage of the sample who identified themselves as Catholics. Source: aggregated individual-level Eurobarometer data available in Xezonakis (2008).

COMMUNIST PAST: former communist countries coded as 1; all others coded 0.

COUNCIL PRESIDENCY: indicator of country holding EU presidency at the time expressed as 1 when country is holding EU presidency in a given year and 0 for all other time points. Source: Wikipedia (undated A).

DEMOCRACY DURATION: number of years a country was under democratic regimes since 1900, counted as all years for which country has Polity score of 6 or higher. Source: Marshall, Jaggers, and Gurr (2011).

DISPROPORTIONALITY: Gallagher's Least Squares Index of Disproportionality in previous national legislative election. Source: the authors' calculation for 1989–2007 and Armingeon et al. (2008).

EFFECTIVE NUMBER OF PARTIES: effective number of electoral parties. Source: Armingeon et al. (2008) for Western Europe in 1970–2007, and the authors' own calculation from official election results for all other country years.

END OF COLD WAR: variable coded as 1 for years in the period 1990–93 and 0 otherwise.

EU DEMOCRACY SATISFACTION: percentage of respondents satisfied (fairly or very) with the way democracy works in the EU. Source: aggregated individual-level Eurobarometer data available in Xezonakis (2008).

EU MEMBERSHIP BENEFIT: percentage of respondents who think their own country benefited from the EU membership. Source: aggregated individual-level Eurobarometer data available in Xezonakis (2008).

EU MEMBERSHIP LENGTH: length of membership of a country in the EU expressed as the number of years the country in question was a member of the EU in the given year.

EU MEMBERSHIP SUPPORT: average score of respondents answering the question about whether their county's membership in the EU was a good or bad thing, after the original responses were recoded as 0=bad thing; 100=good thing; 50=neither good nor bad. Source: aggregated individual-level Eurobarometer data available in Xezonakis (2008).

FAST UNIFICATION: average score of respondents answering the question about preferred speed of advancement of European unification; the answers range from 1=standing still to 7=moving as fast as possible. Variable is recoded so that preference for moving as fast as possible has a value of 100 and preference for keeping integration as it is has a value of 0. Source: aggregated individual-level Eurobarometer data available in Xezonakis (2008).

FOREIGN WORKERS: share (%) of foreign workers in total workforce. Available for the 1996–2005 period only. Source: OECD (2008).

GDP/CAPITA: GDP/capita in USD expressed in 2005 constant prices. Source: Heston, Summers, and Aten (2009). Note: Chapter 8 uses the logarithm of this variable.

GDP GROWTH: real annual GDP growth measured in %. Source: EUROSTAT (undated).

GOVERNANCE QUALITY (WB): quality of governance index created by combining World Bank governance indicators (available for 1996, 1998, 2000, 2002, and 2002–8) and the PRS governance indicators which are themselves composed from the average of PRS scores for corruption control, bureaucratic quality, and law and order (available between 1984 and 2007). This variable provides a single comprehensive measure of governance quality using the World Bank summary score of overall quality of governance and replacing its missing values with estimates. For the odd years between 1996 and 2002, the estimate equals the average score of the same country in the previous and subsequent even years. For years before 1996, the PRS overall quality of government scores were used to predict the missing data in the World Bank series on the basis of a bivariate regression of the World Bank indicator on the PRS summary measure through the country years for which both data were available. Source: Kaufman, Kraay, and Mastruzzi (2008) and Political Risk Service (undated).

IDEOLOGICAL POLARIZATION: calculated on the basis of left–right self-placement of respondents, aggregated across countries and measured as the standard deviation in individual scores. Source: aggregated individual-level Eurobarometer data available in Xezonakis (2008).

INFLATION: Inflation expressed as a % of change in prices from previous year. Source: EUROSTAT (undated).

INTRA-EU TRADE: measures the % of trade in goods each member country does with other member countries as % of total trade in goods. Source: IMF Statistics Department (1973–2008).

LIFE SATISFACTION: measured as the percentage of respondents answering "very" or "fairly" to the question: "On the whole, are you very satisfied, fairly satisfied, not very satisfied or not at all satisfied with the life you lead?" Source: aggregated individual-level Eurobarometer data available in Xezonakis (2008).

NATIONAL DEMOCRACY SATISFACTION: percentage of respondents satisfied (fairly and very combined) with the way democracy works in their country. Source: aggregated individual-level Eurobarometer data available in Xezonakis (2008).

NATIONAL EXPERIENCE DIVIDED GOVERNMENT: the proportion of time, in the period covered by the analysis for each country included, in which divided government occurred. Source: The authors' own coding.

NET EU TRANSFERS: measure of net transfers to (or from) EU budget expressed as % of GNI. Positive values indicate net contributions to EU budget and negative values indicate net benefits from EU budget. Source: 1993–2007 European Commission EU Budget Financial Reports 2002, 2006, and 2008 (European Commission 2002, 2006, 2008). The data for 1976–92 period are calculated on the basis of reported contributions and transfers to and from EU budget from same reports (expressed in millions ECU in current prices) from data provided in 2008 Budget report.

POLITICAL DISCUSSION: average score of responses across respondent to the question: "When you get together with friends, would you say you discuss political matters frequently, occasionally or never?" Source: aggregated individual-level Eurobarometer data available in Xezonakis (2008).

POPULATION SIZE: size of the population of a country measured in millions of inhabitants. Source: World Bank WDI (various years).

SOCIAL EXPENDITURE: total public social spending on transfer and services as % of GDP. Source: 1990–2007 EUROSTAT (undated); 1980–1989 OECD (2009); 1973–1979 Huber et al. (2004).

SPEED UP UNIFICATION: average score of respondents answering the question of whether the movement toward European integration should be 1=speeded up; 2=slowed down; 3=continued at its present speed. The variable is recoded so that preference of an increased speed has a value of 100, preference for slowing down has a value of 0, and preference for continuing movement toward integration at its current speed has a value of 50. Source: aggregated individual-level Eurobarometer data available in Xezonakis (2008).

SUPPLY OF EU LEGISLATION: number of EU directives (or regulations) enacted in a given year, calculated as a number of directives adopted in a given year according to EUR-lex database. Source: EUR-lex (undated).

TRUST IN EUROPEAN INSTITUTIONS: average number of EU institutions (from those mentioned at the relevant Eurobarometer battery) "trusted" by respondents. Source: aggregated individual-level Eurobarometer data available in Xezonakis (2008).

THIRD-WAVE DEMOCRACY: dummy variable marking as 1 countries democratizing in third wave of democratization (Greece, Portugal, Spain, Cyprus, Poland, Hungary, Slovenia, Lithuania, Czech Republic, Slovakia, Latvia, Estonia, Romania, and Bulgaria) and coding all else as 0.

TRADE OPENNESS: measures the % of combined export and import of goods and services as % of GDP. Source: 1990–2007 EUROSTAT (undated); 1973–1989 Armingeon et al. (2008).

TURNOUT: turnout in last national legislative elections in % of the number of registered voters. Source: Pintor and Gratschew (2002), with additional data for following years from IDEA (undated).

UNEMPLOYMENT: Unemployment as % of the labour force. Source: 1990–2007 EUROSTAT (undated); 1973–1989 OECD (undated).

UNITY OF WESTERN EUROPE: average score of respondents answering the question of whether they are for or against efforts to unify Western Europe, with answer options 1=for, very much; 2=for, to some extent; 3=against, to some extent; 4=against, very much. Variable is recoded so that the highest level of support for unification has a value of 100 and the lowest level of support has a value of 0. Source: aggregated individual-level Eurobarometer data available in Xezonakis (2008).

YEAR OF ACCESION: the year the country in question became an EU member.

VOLATILITY: electoral volatility (calculated with the Pedersen index) in previous national legislative elections. Source: the authors' calculation.

WAGE BARGAINING CENTRALIZATION: measure of centralization of wage bargaining with five-point classification created by Jelle Visser, where 5 = economy-wide bargaining, based on a) enforceable agreements between the central organizations of unions and employers affecting the entire economy or entire private sector, or on b) government imposition of a wage schedule, freeze, or ceiling; 4 = mixed industry and economy-wide bargaining: a) central organizations negotiate non-enforceable central agreements (guidelines) and/or b) key unions and employers associations set pattern for the entire economy; 3 = industry bargaining with no or irregular pattern setting, limited involvement of central organizations and limited freedoms for company bargaining; 2 = mixed industry- and firm-level bargaining, with weak enforceability of industry agreements; 1 = none of the above, fragmented bargaining, mostly at company level. Source: Visser (2009).

WORLD WAR 2 CASUALTIES: casualties suffered in Second World War as a % of 1939 population. Data from Slovenia, Czech Republic, and Slovakia are based on figures for Yugoslavia and Czechoslovakia. Source: Wikipedia (undated B).

WOULD FEEL SORRY: average score of respondents answering the question of how they would feel if they were told that the EU would be scrapped tomorrow. The answer options are 1=very sorry; 2=indifferent; 3=relieved. Variable is recoded so that feeling regret has a value of 100, feeling indifferent a value of 50, and being relieved a value of 0. Source: aggregated individual-level Eurobarometer data available in Xezonakis (2008).

Appendix to Chapter 2

Wording of the items from the European and World Values Surveys, 1999–2002, which were included in the factor analysis shown in Table 2.1:

BELONGING TO A POLITICAL PARTY: responses to a question on "Please look carefully at the following list of voluntary organizations and activities and say... which, if any, do you belong to?" recoded as 1=did mention "a political party"; 0= did not claim belonging to "a political party".

CONFIDENCE IN CIVIL SERVICE: variable measuring trust in civil service with an item asking respondent: "Please look at this card and tell me, for each item listed, how much confidence you have in [CIVIL SERVICE]" with answers coded as 1=great deal; 2=quite a lot; 3=not very much; 4= none at all.

CONFIDENCE IN JUDICIARY SYSTEM: variable measuring trust in judicial system with an item asking respondent: "Please look at this card and tell me, for each item listed, how much confidence you have in [JUDICIARY SYSTEM]" with answers coded as 1=great deal; 2=quite a lot; 3=not very much; 4= none at all.

CONFIDENCE IN PARLIAMENT: variable measuring trust in national parliament with an item asking respondent: "Please look at this card and tell me, for each item listed, how much confidence you have in [NATIONAL PARLIAMENT]" with answers coded as 1=great deal; 2=quite a lot; 3=not very much; 4= none at all.

CONFIDENCE IN POLICE: variable measuring trust in police with an item asking respondent: "Please look at this card and tell me, for each item listed, how much confidence you have in [POLICE]" with answers coded as 1=great deal; 2=quite a lot; 3=not very much; 4= none at all.

DEMOCRACY IS THE BEST FORM OF GOVERNMENT: measured with an item asking respondent: "Democracy may have problems but it's better than any other form of government" with answers coded as 1=agree strongly; 2=agree; 3=disagree; 4= strongly disagree.

HAVE A DEMOCRATIC POLITICAL SYSTEM: measured with an item asking respondent: "I'm going to describe various types of political systems and ask what you think about each as a way of governing this country. For each one, would you say it is a very good, fairly good, fairly bad or very bad way of governing this country?... Having a democratic political system?" with answers coded as 1=very good; 2=fairly good; 3=bad; 4=very bad.

INTEREST IN COMPATRIOT'S CONDITIONS OF LIFE: measured with an item asking respondent: "Do you feel concerned about the living conditions of your fellow countrymen?" with answers coded as 1=very much; 2=much; 3=to a certain extent; 4=not at all.

LEFT–RIGHT IDEOLOGY: measured with an item asking respondent: "In political matters, people talk of "the left" and "the right." How would you place your views on this scale, generally speaking? (originally coded from 1=left; ... 10=right, recoded into 1=placed her/himself somewhere on the 1–10 scale and 0=did not place her/himself on the 1–10 scale).

NATIONAL PRIDE: measured with an item asking respondent: "How proud are you to be a [NATION] citizen?" with answers coded as 1=very proud; 2=quite proud; 3=not very proud; 4=not at all proud.

SATISFACTION WITH THE WAY DEMOCRACY HAS DEVELOPED: measured with an item asking respondent: "On the whole are you very satisfied, rather satisfied, not very satisfied or not at all satisfied with the way democracy is developing in our country?" with answers coded as 1=very satisfied; 2=rather satisfied; 3=not very satisfied; 4=not at all satisfied.

SATISFACTION WITH GOVERNMENT PERFORMANCE: measured with an item asking respondent: "People have different views about the system for governing this country. Here is a scale for rating how well things are going: 1 means very bad; 10 means very good. Where on this scale would you put the political system as it was ... [in former communist countries: under the communist regime]; [in countries where recently a change of regime has taken place: under the xxx regime;]; [in countries where no regime change has taken place: ten years ago]?"

TURNOUT: responses to a question on: "If there were a national election tomorrow, for which party on this list would you vote?" recoded as 1=would vote [for a party or other candidate] 0=would not vote, do not know, no answer.

Appendix to chapter 4

The dependent variable
IDEOLOGICAL POLARIZATION (IP): the authors' own calculation of the ideological spread of the relevant political parties in 135 national elections held in 18 countries. Relevance was defined by obtaining legislative representation in the given election. IP was calculated from individual-level survey data about the left–right (in the USA liberal–conservative) self-placement of each parties' voters—and, in the case of the CSES data used in Figure 4.7 and in the validity tests reported, from the voters' placement of political parties on the same scale—using the following formula: IP= $(\sum|$LRm–LRpx$|*$EPpx$)$ / IPmax, where: LRm=the numerical centre of the left–right scale; LRpx=the mean position of party x's voters on the left–right scale (alternatively all voters' mean placement of party x on the left–right scale in the analysis of CSES data); EPpx=party x fractional share of the valid vote in the last election; and IPmax= maximal ideological polarization defined by two equally strong parties that are located at opposite poles of the ideological spectrum. The data source for the calculation is the True European Voter database (see Thomassen 2005b, 2005c) expanded by the authors. Table 4.1 lists the country years covered by this expanded data set.

Note that there are alternatives in calculating country-specific levels of ideological polarization and their evolution over time (for a review see Laver 2001). First, we could have used party manifesto data (Budge et al. 2001; Klingemann et al. 2006). Although the availability of this type of data could allow us to analyse long time series, the fact that the meaning of left and right varies across countries and over time renders any fixed assignment of coding categories to either the left or the right side of the ideological spectrum problematic. Consequently, polarization scores based on those at least partly erroneous estimates of party positions tend to be misleading. A second option would have been to use expert surveys data to locate parties along the left–right continuum (see, for example, Benoit and Laver 2006), and then compute the polarization index on this basis. A third solution would have been to use electors' perceptions of parties' locations in the left–right dimension (see Berglund et al. 2005; Freire 2008; Knutsen and Kumlin 2005), and then compute the polarization index. Both options two and three were excluded because neither expert surveys nor mass surveys with questions about voters' perceptions of parties' ideological placement cover all the countries analysed, and even for the countries they cover only a few time points spanning a short period of time. Thus, a fourth option was chosen, which was explained above in detail. Namely, we use electors' left–right self-placement in each country, segmented by party, and then compute the polarization index from this. This is more appropriate than content analysing party manifesto data, and is available for many more country years than expert survey data or voter perceptions of party positions.

Although this solution is widely used in the literature for identical purposes (see, for example, Klingemann 1995, and Sani and Sartori 1983), doubts could be raised about the validity of using data on electors' ideological placement to describe parties' ideological placement. Thus, to cross-validate the use of data on voters to measure parties' positions, we compared the levels of polarization in six countries across time using both voters' left–right self-placement (segmented by party) and voters' perceptions of parties' location on the left–right scale (see the results in the online appendix). We chose these six countries because they have had national election studies for a long time, and in several of these mass surveys we can find both voters' left–right self-placement and their perceptions of the parties' location on the left–right scale (see Thomassen 2005a). A careful comparison reveals two things. First, data based upon voters' perceptions of the parties' locations on the left–right scale usually show lower levels of polarization than data based upon the voters' left–right self-placement. Second, the trends in the levels of polarization across time are basically similar, independent of the type of data used to compute the polarization indexes. Thus, we can conclude that voters' left–right self-placements (segmented by party) provide a reliable measure of ideological polarization at the party system level, especially if we are interested in trends across time.

Macro-level independent variables used in Chapter 4

CLEAVAGE STRENGTH: Pseudo-R^2 from multinominal logistic regressions of vote choice on social structural characteristics. Source: the author's own calculation from national election studies.

DISPROPORTIONALITY: Gallagher's Least Squares Index of Disproportionality between the percentage distribution of votes and seats across parties in previous national legislative election. Source: Gallagher (undated).

DIVIDED GOVERNMENT: variable coded as 0 for the absence of divided government and 1 for the presence of divided government either as divergent majority in bicameral parliament and for divergent majorities between presidency and parliament in presidential and semi-presidential system. Source: The authors' own coding.

EFFECTIVE NUMBER OF PARTIES: effective number of electoral parties. Source: Gallagher (undated).

EU MEMBERSHIP LENGTH: length of membership of a country in the EU expressed as the number of years the country in question was a member of the EU in the given year.

FEDERALISM: variable measuring degree of federalism coded as 0 for unitary countries, 0.5 for semi-federal countries (Spain only), and 1 for federal countries. Source: The authors' own coding.

GDP GROWTH: real annual GDP growth measured in %. Source: EUROSTAT (undated).

INFLATION: inflation expressed as a % of change in prices from previous year. Source: EUROSTAT (undated).

NATIONAL EXPERIENCE DIVIDED GOVERNMENT: the proportion of time, in the period covered by the analysis for each country included in which divided government occurred. Source: The authors' own coding.

NUMBER OF VETO PLAYERS: Sum of veto players present in the political system. Calculated by adding one point for the presence of each of presidential or semi-presidential form of government, federalism, and bicameral parliament. The variable ranges from 0 to 3. Source: The authors' own coding.

ONE-PARTY MAJORITY: measure of one-party majority government at the time of elections, coded as 0 for absence of one-party majority government and 1 for the presence of one-party majority government. Source: The authors' own coding.

QUALITY OF DEMOCRACY: the "overall score" from the Economist Intelligence Unit's Index of Democracy 2008. Source: EIU (2008).

TYPE OF PARLIAMENT: variable coded as 0 for unicameral parliament and 1 for bicameral parliament. Source: The authors' own coding.

TYPE OF REGIME: variable measuring type of political regime coded as 0 for parliamentary regime, 0.5 for semi-presidential regime and 1 for presidential regime. Source: The authors' own coding.

TURNOUT: turnout in last national legislative elections in % of the voting age population. Source: IDEA (undated).

UNEMPLOYMENT: Unemployment as % of the labour force. Source: 1990–2007 EUROSTAT (undated); 1973–1989 OECD (undated).

YEARS DEMOCRATIC: Number of years, at time of election, under democratic rule since 1945. Source: The authors' own coding.

YEAR OF ELECTION: The year of the election in question (see Table 4.1).

Appendix to Chapter 5

Macro-level variables appearing in Tables 5.1 to 5.6

COMMUNIST PAST: indicating former communist countries coded as 1; all others coded 0.

COMPULSORY VOTING: indicating if country has compulsory vote requirement, coded as 1 for countries which have compulsory voting and 0 for others. Source: UNDP (undated).

FIRST EP ELECTION: dummy variable marking the year when each country had its first election to the European Parliament; coded as 1 for year when the country in question had its first EP election and 0 for all other years.

LEFT–RIGHT POLARIZATION: national mean score of the LEFT–RIGHT EXTREMITY micro variable (see below).

SATISFACTION WITH DEMOCRACY: national mean score of the Satisfaction with democracy micro variable (see below).

SIMULTANEOUS NATIONWIDE ELECTIONS: coded as 1 for each country year when the EP election was held simultaneously with national elections and 0 for all other years.

SUNDAY VOTING: indicating if elections in a country are held on Sunday, coded as 1 for countries which have Sunday voting and 0 for others. Source: UNDP (undated).

SUPPORT FOR EU MEMBERSHIP: national mean score on the Support for EU membership micro variable (see below).

TIME: the number of years passed since the first European Parliament election in 1979.

TIME TO FIRST-ORDER MID-TERM: The variable is continuous and is based on the distance in months of a European Parliament election from the mid-term of the national parliament election cycle. As length of national election cycles vary from country to country the variable has been transformed to a scale between 0 and 1. It is 0 if a European Parliament election is held exactly at the mid-term of the national parliament election cycle. It is 1 if a European Parliament election is held simultaneously to the national parliament election in the respective country. Source: own calculation.

TURNOUT IN EUROPEAN PARLIAMENT ELECTIONS: official turnout in European Parliament elections in a given country as reported by the statistical offices of the EU and the member states. Source: Pintor and Gratschew (2002), Nordsieck (undated).

TURNOUT IN NATIONAL PARLIAMENT ELECTIONS: official turnout in national legislative election in a given country, as reported by the statistical offices of the EU member states. Source: Pintor and Gratschew (2002), Nordsieck (undated).

Micro-level variables appearing in Tables 5.7 to 5.10

The following Eurobarometer Surveys and European Election Surveys conducted in years when elections for European Parliament are held are included in the dataset used in the analysis in Chapter 5: EB 12 (1979), EB 22 (1984), EB 31A (1989), EB 41-1 (1994), EES 1999, EES 2004, EES 2009.

AGE: age in years (non-eligible respondents excluded).

CLASS: this variable is based on the following question in the EB/EES: "If you were asked to choose one of these five names for your social class, which would you say you belong to? 1=middle class; 2=lower middle class; 3=working class; 4=upper class; 5=upper middle class." The answers were recoded as: 0=working class; 0.25=lower middle class; 0.5=middle class; 0.75=upper middle class; 1=upper class. Variable not available in 1979 and 1984.

EDUCATION: this variable is based on the following question in the EB/EES: "How old were you when you stopped full-time education?" Due to strong differences in education systems the answer provided by the respondents was recoded: 1=low: minimum through 14 years; 2=medium: 15 through 17 years; 3=high–lower: 18 through 20 years; 4= high–upper: 21 through maximum.

EXTERNAL EFFICACY: this variable is based on the following question in the EB/EES: "The EU Parliament considers concerns of EU citizens". Answers are coded as 1= strongly agree; 2=agree; 3=neither agree nor disagree; 4=disagree; 5=strongly disagree.

The variable has been recoded to a scale from 0=no external efficacy at all to 1=highest level of external efficacy. This item has been created by using the following surveys and variables: Variable available only in 2009.

INTERNAL EFFICACY: this index is based on the following questions in the EES: 1) "Sometimes politics is so complicated that someone like me just cannot understand what is going on" with the answers coded as 1=strongly agree; 2=agree; 3=disagree; 4=strongly disagree. 2) "So many people vote in elections that my vote does not matter" with the answers coded as 1=strongly agree; 2=agree; 3=disagree; 4=strongly disagree. The index is an average of both items after both have been recoded to a scale from 0=no internal efficacy at all to 1=highest level of internal efficacy. Variable available only in 1999.

INTEREST IN POLITICS: this variable is based on the following question in the EB/EES: "To what extent would you say you are interested in politics?" With answers coded as 1=a great deal; 2=to some extent; 3=not much; 4=not at all. The categories were recoded to a scale from 0=not at all to 1=a great deal. Variable not available for 1979, 1984, and 1989.

LEFT–RIGHT EXTREMITY: this variable is based on the following question in the EB/EES: "In political matters people talk of 'the left' and 'the right'. How would you place your views on this scale? 1= left; 10=right." Left–right polarization is calculated by computing absolute values for the difference between 5.5 (mid-point of the scale) and the answer given by the respondents. This results in a variable that ranges between 0 (respondent's left–right self-placement is in the centre of the scale (since left–right self-placements are asked using a scale without mid-point the empirical minimum of that scale is 0.5, 0 is just a theoretical value)) and 4.5 (most extreme left–right self-placement).

MALE: variable coded as 0=female; 1=male.

MATERIALISM: this index is based on the following questions in the EB: "There is a lot of talk these days about what the country's goals should be for the next ten or fifteen years. On this card are listed some of the goals that different people say should be given top priority. Would you please say which one of them you yourself consider most important in the long run? And what would be your second choice? 1=maintaining order in the nation; 2=giving the people more say in important government decisions; 3=fighting rising prices; 4=protecting freedom of speech." The rank order provided by the respondents was used to create the following index: 0= post-materialist (answers 2 +4); 0.33=leaning post-materialist (answers 2 or 4 as first priority, answers 1 or 3 as second priority); 0.66=leaning materialist (answers 1 or 3 as first priority, answers 2 or 4 as second priority); 1=materialist (answers 1+3). Not available for 1999, 2004, and 2009.

MEDIA CONSUMPTION: this index is based on the following questions in the EES: 1) "[NORMALLY] How many days of the week do you watch the news on television? 0–7 days." 2) "[NORMALLY] How many days of the week do you read a newspaper? 0–7 days." Both items have been recoded to a scale ranging from 0=no media consumption to 1=highest level of media consumption. The index is the average of both recoded items (with the exception of 2009) and thus ranges from 0 to 1, too. Variable not available in 1979, 1984, 1989, and 1994.

Appendix to Chapter 6

European Identity Questions in the European Community Study (ECS), the Eurobarometers (EB), the World Values Surveys (WVS) and the International Social Survey Programme's "National Identity" module

Question theme/Source/Survey Year	Question wording and response options
(QW1) GEOGRAPHICAL BELONGING ECS: 1971, 1973, EB: 6–1976, 10A–1978, 12–1979, WVS: 1981, 1982, 1990, 1995, 1996, 1997, 1999, 2000	To which of these geographical groups would you say you belong first of all? And the next? – Locality or town where you live, – Region or country where you live, – Your country as a whole, – Europe, – The World as a whole
(QW2) THINKING OF SELF AS EUROPEAN (a) EB: 17–1982 (b) EB: 19–1983, 24–1985, 26–1986, 37–1992 (c) EB: 27–1987, 30–1988, 31–1989, 33–1990 (d) EB: 36–1991, 37–1992, 64.2–2005, 66–2006 (e) EB: 41.1–1994	(a) Do you ever think of yourself as a citizen of Europe? Often, sometimes, or never? (b) Do you ever think of yourself not only as a (nationality) citizen but also as a citizen of Europe? Often, sometimes, or never? (c) Does the thought ever occur to you that you are not only (nationality) but also European? Does this happen often, sometimes, or never? (d) Do you ever think of yourself as not only (nationality), but also European? Does this happen often, sometimes, or never? (e) Does the thought ever occur to you that you are not only (nationality) but also a European? (SHOW CARD with 10-point scale: 1=not at all … 10=very much so)
Question theme/Source/Survey Year *(QW4) NATIONAL VERSUS EUROPEAN* (a) EB: 37.0–1992, 40–1993, 42–1994, 43.1–1995, 44–1995, 46.0–1996, 47–1997, 49–1998, 50–1998, 52–1999, 53–2000, 54–2000, 56–2001, 57–2002, 58.1–2002, 59.1–2003, 60.1–2003, 61.0–2004, 62.0–2004, 64.2–2005, 67.1–2007 (b) EB: 61.0–2004 (c) EB: 62.0–2004	*Question wording and response options* (a) In the near future do you see yourself as: (nationality) only, (nationality) and European, European and (nationality), or European only? (b) In the near future do you see yourself as: (nationality) only, (nationality) and European, or European only? [split ballot with version (a) in EB 61] (c) In the near future do you see yourself as: (nationality) only, firstly (nationality) and then European, firstly European and then (nationality), or European only? [split ballot with version (a) in EB 62]
(QW5) PROUD TO BE EUROPEAN (a) EB: 54–2000, 56–2001, 57–2002, 60–2003, 62–2004, 64.2–2005 (b) EB: 66.1–2006	And would you say you are very proud, fairly proud, not very proud, or not at all proud to be European? (a) very proud, fairly proud, not very proud, not at all proud? (b) very proud, fairly proud, not very proud, not at all proud ["I do not feel European" recorded as separate response option if spontaneously volunteered]

OPINION LEADERSHIP: this index is based on the following questions in the EB: 1) "When you yourself hold a strong opinion, do you ever find yourself persuading your friends, relatives or fellow workers to share your views? If so, does this happen often, from time to time, or rarely?" with the answers coded as 1=often; 2=from time to time; 3=rarely; 4=never. 2) "When you get together with your friends, would you say you discuss political matters frequently, occasionally, or never?" with the answers coded as 1=frequently; 2=occasionally; 3=never. Both items have been recoded to a scale from 0=never to 1=frequently/often. The index is the average of both recoded items and thus ranges from 0 to 1. Variable not available in 1994, 1999, 2004, and 2009.

RELIGIOSITY: this variable is based on the following question in the EB/EES: "Do you attend religious services several times a week, once a week, a few times a year, once a year or less or never?" with the answers coded as 1=several times a week; 2=once a week; 3=a few times a year; 4=once a year or less; 5=never. The answers were recoded to a scale ranging from 0=never to 1=several times a week. Variable not available in 1984.

SATISFACTION WITH DEMOCRACY: this variable is based on the following question in the EB/EES: "On the whole, are you very satisfied, fairly satisfied, not very satisfied or not at all satisfied with the way democracy works [IN YOUR COUNTRY]?" The answers are coded as 1=very satisfied; 2=fairly satisfied; 3=not very satisfied; 4=not at all satisfied. Response categories have been recoded to the following format: 0=not at all satisfied; 0.33= not very satisfied; 0.66=fairly satisfied; 1=very satisfied.

SUPPORT FOR EU MEMBERSHIP: this variable is based on the following question in the EB/EES: "Generally speaking, do you think that [YOUR COUNTRY'S] membership of the European Community/Union is 1=a good thing; 2=a bad thing; 3=neither good nor bad?" Response categories have been recoded to the following format: −1=a bad thing; 0=neither good nor bad; 1=a good thing.

STRENGTH OF PARTISANSHIP: this variable is based on the following questions in the EB/EES: 1979–94: "Do you consider yourself to be close to any particular party? If so, do you feel yourself to be very close to this party, fairly close or merely a sympathizer?" Answers are coded as 1=very close; 2= fairly close; 3=merely a sympathizer; 4=close to no particular party. 1999–2009: "Do you consider yourself to be close to any particular party?" If a party was mentioned, respondents were asked the following question: "Do you feel yourself to be very close to this party, fairly close, or merely a sympathizer?" For the analysis, strength of party identification has been recoded: 0=close to no particular party; 0.33=merely a sympathizer; 0.66=fairly close; 1=very close.

URBANIZATION: this variable is based on the following question in the EB/EES: "Would you say you live in a . . . 1=rural area or village; 2=small or middle-size town; 3=large town?" The answers were recoded to a scale from 0=rural area or village to 1=large town.

Appendix to Chapter 9

ACTUAL EU COMPETENCIES: variable measuring competencies assigned to EU in accordance with EU treaties in each policy area. The variable is coded on a scale where 1 indicates low EU competencies and 3 indicates high EU competencies, and 2 indicates equal EU and national competencies. The value assigned to each policy area in indicated in Table 9.2, Chapter 9.

GOVERNANCE QUALITY (WB): quality of governance index created by combining World Bank governance indicators (available for 1996, 1998, 2000, 2002, and 2002–8) and the PRS governance indicators which are themselves composed from the average of PRS scores for corruption control, bureaucratic quality, and law and order (available between 1984 and 2007). This variable provides a single comprehensive measure of governance quality using the World Bank summary score of overall quality of governance and replacing its missing values with estimates. For the odd years between 1996 and 2002, the estimate equals the average score of the same country in the previous and subsequent even years. For years before 1996, the PRS overall quality of government scores were used to predict the missing data in the World Bank series on the basis of a bivariate regression of the World Bank indicator on the PRS summary measure through the country years for which both data were available. Source: Kaufman, Kraay, and Mastruzzi (2008) and Political Risk Service (undated).

GOVERNANCE QUALITY (TI): perception of corruption measured with Transparency International Corruption Perception Index (available between 1995 and 2008). Source: Transparency International (1995–2008).

GOVERNMENT SPENDING: indicates the size of the spending on a given policy area as a size of GDP. The variable is coded from 1 to 5 where 1 indicates policies spending less than 0.1% of GDP; 2 indicates more or equal than 0.1% and less than 0.5% of GDP; 3 indicates equal or more than 0.5% and less than 1.5% of GDP; 4 indicates equal or more than 1.5% of GDP and less than 4.5% of GDP; and 5 indicates 4.5% of GDP or more.

INHERENT INTERNATIONALIZATION: measure of likely internationalization of policy area (the degree to which policy can effectively be implemented only at the international/European level). Variable is constructed in a way that each policy area is coded dichotomously into categories indicating whether policies can be more effectively implemented at centralized (European) or decentralized (national) level. The allocation of individual policy areas into categories is described in Table 9.2 in Chapter 9.

LOG GDP/CAPITA: The log of PPP GDP/capita in USD expressed in 2005 constant prices. Source: Heston, Summers, and Aten (2009).

POPULATION SIZE: size of the population of a country measured in millions of inhabitants. Source: World Development Indicators (various years).

SOCIAL MODEL: variable indicating policy areas considered to be defining national social model (environment, research, regional policy, social inclusion, and employment). These policy areas are coded as 1 and other policy areas are coded as 0.

THIRD-WAVE DEMOCRACY: dummy variable marking as 1 countries democratizing in third wave of democratization and coding all else as 0.

YEARS SINCE BEGINNING OF THE SERIES (1989/1992): the number of years that passed since 1989 or 1992 (depending on which is the starting year of the series under analysis).

References

Aarts, K. and Thomassen, J. (2007), 'Satisfaction with Democracy: Do Institutions Matter?', *Electoral Studies*, 27, 5–18.

Achen, C. (2000), 'Why Lagged Dependent Variables Can Suppress the Explanatory Power of Other Independent Variables', *Annual Meeting of the Methodology Section of the American Political Science Association* (UCLA).

Adolph, C., Butler, D.M., and Wilson, S.E. (2005), 'Like Shoes and Shirt, One Size Does not Fit All: Evidence on Time Series Corss-Section Estimators and Specification from Monte Carlo Experiment', (Seattle: Department of Political Science, University of Washington).

Ahrens, J., Meurer, M., and Renner, C. (2007), 'Beyond the Big-Bang Enlargenment: Citizens' Preferences and the Problem of EU Decision Making', *Journal of European Integration*, 29, 447–79.

Albritton, R.B., Bureekul, T., and Gang, G. (2005), 'Context of Asian Democracy: A Cross-National, Within-Nation Analysis of Asian Countries', (Irvine: Center for the Study of Democracy, University of California).

Alesina, A., Angeloni, I., and Schuknecht, L. (2005), 'What Does the European Union Do?', *Public Choice*, 23, 275–319.

—— and Wacziarg, R. (2008), 'Europe Was Going Too Far', <http://www.voxeu.org/index.php?q = node/1258>, accessed 23. June.

—— —— (1999), 'Is Europe Going Too Far?', *Carnegie-Rochester Conference Series on Public Policy*, 51, 1–42.

Almond, G. and Verba, S. (1963), *Civic Culture: Political Attitudes and Democracy in Five Nations* (Princeton: Princeton University Press).

Almond, G., et al. (eds.) (2006), *European Politics Today* (New York: Pearson/Longman).

Ammendola, T. and Isernia, P. (2005), 'L'Europa vista dagli italiani: i primi vent'anni', in M. Cotta, P. Isernia, and L. Verzichelli (eds.), *L'Europa in Italia* (Bologna: Il Mulino).

Anderson, C.J. (1998a), 'When in Doubt, Use Proxies: Attitudes Toward Domestic Politics and Support for the European Integration', *Comparative Political Studies*, 31, 569–601.

—— (1998b), 'Parties, Party System, and Satisfaction With Democratic Performance in The New Europe', *Political Studies*, 46, 572–88.

—— (2001), 'Political Satisfaction in Old and New Democracies', (Binghamton: Binghamton University, Center on Democratic Performance).

—— (2006), 'Consent and Consensus: The Contours of Public Opinion toward the Euro', in R.M. Fishman and A.M. Messina (eds.), *The Year of the Euro: The Cultural,*

Social and Political Import of Europe's Common Currency (Notre Dame: University of Notre Dame Press), 111–30.

—— and Guillory, A. (1997), 'Political Institutions and Satisfaction with Democracy', *American Journal of Political Science*, 91, 66–81.

—— and Kaltenthalter, K. (1996), 'The Dynamics of Public Opinion Toward European Integration, 1973–1993', *European Journal of International Relations*, 2, 175–99.

—— and Reichert, S. (1996), 'Economic Benefits and Support for Membership in the EU: A Cross-National Analysis', *Journal of Public Policy*, 15, 231–49.

—— et al. (2005), *Losers' Consent: Elections and Democratic Legitimacy* (Oxford: Oxford University Press).

APSA (1950), 'Toward a More Responsible Two-Party System', *American Political Science Review*, 22, 475–510.

Armingeon, K., Gerber, M., Leimgruber, P., Beyeler, M., and Menegale, S. (2008), 'Comparative Political Data Set 1960–2005.' Available from http://www.ipw.unibe.ch/content/team/klaus_armingeon/comparative_political_data_sets/index_ger.html accessed on 15 December 2009.

Arter, D. (2006), *Democracy in Scandinavia: Consensual, Majoritarian or Mixed* (Manchester: Manchester University Press).

Bandeli, N. and Radu, B. (2006), 'Consolidation of Democracy in Postcommunist Europe', (Irvine: Center for the Study of Democracy, University of California).

Barnes, S.H. (2002), 'Left and Right in Old and New Democracies', *Central European Political Science Review*, 3, 6–15.

—— and Kaase, M. (1979), *Political Action: Mass Participation in Five Western Democracies* (Beverly Hills: Sage Publications).

—— McDonough, P., and Pina, A. (1985), 'The Development of Partisanship in New Democracies: The Case of Spain', *American Journal of Political Science*, 29, 695–720.

Bartolini, S. and Mair, P. (1990), *Identity, Competition and Electoral Availability: The Stabilization of European Electorates, 1885–1985* (Cambridge: Cambridge University Press).

Battistelli, F. and Bellucci, P. (2002), 'L'identità degli italiani tra euroscetticismo e europportunismo', *Il Mulino*, 1, 77–85.

Beck, N. (2001), 'Time-Series-Cross-Section Data: What Have we Learned in the Past Few Years?', *Annual Review of Political Science*, 4, 271–93.

—— (2006), 'Time Series Cross Section Methods'. (New York: New York University).

—— and Katz, J.N. (1995), 'What to Do (and Not to Do) with Time-Series Cross-Section Data', *American Political Science Review*, 89, 634–47.

—— —— (2004), 'Random Coefficients Models for Time-Series-Cross-Section Data', *Working Papers* (California Institute of Technology).

Bednar, J., Ferejohn, J., and Garret, G. (1996), 'The Politics of Europan Federalism', *International Review of Law and Economics*, 16, 279–94.

Bell, D. (1960), *The End of Ideology: On the Exhaustion of Political Ideas* (Glencoe: Free Press).

Benoit, K,, and M. Laver. 2006. *Party Policy in Modern Democracies*. New York: Routledge.

Berglund, F., et al. (2005), 'Party Identification and Party Choice', in J. Thomassen (ed.), *The European Voter: A Comparative Study of Modern Democracies* (Oxford: Oxford University Press).

Berinsky, A. (2004), 'Can We Talk? Self-Presentation and the Survey Response', *Political Psychology*, 25, 643–59.

Bielasiak, J. (2002), 'The Institutionalisation of Electoral and Party System in Post-communist States', *Comparative Politics*, 34, 189–210.

Blais, A. (2000), *Vote or Not to Vote? The Merits and Limits of Rational Choice Theory* (Pittsburgh: University of Pittsburgh Press).

Blondel, J., Sinnott, R., and Svensson, P. (1998), *People and Parliament in the European Union: Participation, Democracy and Legitimacy* (Oxford-New York: Oxford University Press).

Börzel, T. (2005), 'Mind the Gap! European Integration Between Level and Scope', *Journal of European Public Policy*, 12, 217–36.

Bosch, A. and Newton, K. (1995), 'Economic Calculus or Familiarity Breeds Context', in O. Niedermayer and R. Sinnott (eds.), *Public Opinion and Internationalized Governance* (Oxford: Oxford University Press), 73–104.

Brambor, T., Clark, W.R., and Golder, M. (2006), 'Understanding Interaction Models: Improving Empirical Analysis', *Political Analysis*, 14, 63–82.

Breakwell, G.M. and Lyons, E. (1996), *Changing European Identities: Social Psychological Analysis of Social Change* (Oxford: Butterworth).

Breuss, F. and Eller, M. (2004), 'On the Optimal Decentralization of Government Activity: Normative Recommendations for the European Constitution', *Constitutional Political Economy*, 15, 27–76.

Brewer, M.B. (2005), *Self and Social Identity* (Malden: Blackwell).

Brinegar, A.P. and Jolly, S.K. (2005), 'Location, Location, Location: National Contextual Factors and National Support for the European Integration', *European Union Politics*, 6, 155–80.

—— —— and Kitschelt, H. (2004), 'Varieties of Capitalism and Political Divides Over European Integration', in G. Marks and M. Steenbergen (eds.), *European Integration and Political Conflict* (Cambridge: Cambridge University Press), 62–98.

Bruneau, T.C., et al. (2001), 'Democracy South European Style', in N.P. Diamandorus and R. Gunther (eds.), *Parties, Politics and Democracy in New Southern Europe* (Baltimore: The John Hopkins University Press), 16–45.

Bruter, M. (2005), *Citizens of Europe?: The Emergence of a Mass European Identity* (Basingstoke: Palgrave Macmillan).

Budge, I., Klingemann, H., Volkens, A., and Bara, J. (2001), *Mapping Policy Preferences: Estimates for Parties, Electors and Governments 1945-1998*. Oxford: Oxford University Press.

Budge, I., et al. (2001), *Mapping Policy Preferences: Estimates for Parties, Electors and Governments 1945–1998* (Oxford: Oxford University Press).

Campbell, A., et al. (1960), *The American Voter* (New York: John Wiley & Sons).

Carey, S. (2002), 'Undivided Loyalties: Is National Identity and Obstacle to European Integration', *European Union Politics*, 3, 387–413.

References

Carlin, J.B., Galati, J.C., and Royston, P. (2008), 'A New Framework for Managing and Analyzing Multiply Imputed Data in Stata', *Stata Journal*, 8, 49–67.

Carrubba, C.J. (2001), 'The Electoral Connection in European Union Politics', *Journal of Politics*, 63, 141–58.

Castano, E. (2004), 'European Identity: A Social Psychological Perspective', in R.K. Herrmann, T. Risse, and M.B. Brewer (eds.), *Transnational Identities: Becoming European in EU* (Lanham: Rowman & Littlefield), 40–58.

Castillo, A.M.J. (2006), 'Institutional Performance and Satisfaction with Democracy: A Comparative Analysis', *Comparative Studies of Electoral System Conference* (Seville, Spain).

Chierici, C. (2005), 'Is There a European Public Opinion? Public Support for the European Union, Theoretical Concepts and Empirical Measurements', Working paper, POLIS (Paris).

Christin, T. (2005), 'Economic and Political Bias of Attitudes Towards the EU in Central and East European Countries in the 1990s', *European Union Politics*, 6, 29–57.

—— Hug, S., and Schultz, T. (2005), 'Federalism in the European Union: The View from Below', *Journal of European Public Policy*, 12, 488–508.

Cichowski, R. (2000), 'Western Dreams, Eastern Realities: Support for the European Union in Central and Eastern Europe', *Comparative Political Studies*, 33, 1243–78.

Çiftçí, S. (2005), 'Treaties, Collective Responses and the Determinants of Aggregate Support for European Integration', *European Union Politics*, 6, 469–92.

Citrin, J. and Sides, J. (2004b), 'Can There be Europe without Europeans? Problems of Identity in Multinational Community', in R.K. Herrmann, T. Risse, and M.B. Brewer (eds.), *Transnational Identities: Becoming European in the EU* (Oxford: Rowman & Littlefield), 161–85.

—— —— (2004a), 'More than Nationals: How Identity Choice Matters in the New Europe', in R.K. Herrmann, T. Risse, and M.B. Brewer (eds.), *Transnational Identities: Becoming European in the EU* (Lanham: Rowman & Littlefield Publishers), 161–85.

Clarke, H., Dutt, N., and Kornberg, A. (1993), 'The Political Economy of Attitudes Toward Polity and Society in Western European Democracies', *Journal of Politics*, 55, 998–1021.

—— Mishler, W., and Whiteley, P. (1990), 'Recapturing the Falklands: Models of Conservative Popularity 1978–1983', *British Journal of Political Science*, 20, 63–82.

—— et al. (2009), *Performance, Politics and the British Voter* (Cambridge: Cambridge University Press).

Clarke, H.D., et al. (2004), *Political Choice in Britain* (Oxford: Oxford University Press).

Clogg, R. (1987), *Parties and Elections in Greece: The Search for Legitimacy* (London: Hurst & Co.).

Clyde, M., Ghosh, J., and Littman, M. (2011), 'Bayesian Adaptive Sampling for Variable Selection and Model Averaging', *Journal of Computational and Graphical Statistics*, 20, 80–101.

Converse, P.E. (1972), 'Changes in the American Electorate', in Campbell A. and P.E. Converse (eds.), *The Human Meaning of Social Change* (New York: Russell Sage), 263–331.

Crozier, M.J., Huntington, S.P., and Watanuki, J. (1975), *The Crisis of Democracy: Report on the Governability of Democracies to the Trilateral Commission* (New York: New York University Press).

Curtin, R. (2002), 'Psyhology and Macroeconomics: Fifty Years of the Survey of Consumers', (Ann Arbor: Institute for Social Research, University of Michigan).

Dalton, R.J. (1999), 'Political Support in Advanced Industrial Democracies', in P. Norris (ed.), *Critical Citizens: Global Support for Democratic Governance* (Oxford: Oxford University Press).

—— (2004), *Democratic Challenges, Democratic Choices: The Erosion of Political Support in Advanced Industrial Democracies* (Oxford: Oxford University Press).

—— (2006), 'Social Mobilization and the End of Ideology Debate: Patterns of Ideological Polarization', *Japanese Journal of Political Science*, 7, 1–22.

—— and Eichenberg, R.C. (1998), 'Citizen Support for Policy Integration', in W. Sandholz and A. Stone Sweet (eds.), *European Integration and Supranational Governance* (Oxford: Oxford University Press), 250–82.

—— Flanagan, S.C., and Beck, P.A. (1984), 'Political Forces and Partisan Change', in R. J. Dalton, et al. (eds.), *Electoral Change in Advanced Industrial Democracies: Realignment or Dealignment?* (Princeton: Princeton University Press), 451–504.

—— and Tanaka, A. (2007), 'The Patterns of Party Polarization in East Asia', *Journal of East Asian Studies*, 7, 203–23.

—— and Weldon, S. (2007), 'Partisanship and Party System Institutionalization', *Party Politics*, 13, 179–96.

De Vries, C. and van Kersbergen, K. (2007), 'Interests, Identity and Political Allegiance in the European Union', *Acta Politica*, 42, 307–28.

De Winter, L. and Swyngedouw, M. (1999), 'The Scope of EU Government', in H. Schmitt and J. Thomassen (eds.), *Political Representation and Legitimacy in the European Union* (Oxford: Oxford University Press), 47–73.

Della Porta, D. (2000), 'Social Capital, Beliefs in Government and Political Corruption', in S. Pharr and R. Putnam (eds.), *Disaffected Democracies: What's Troubling the Trilateral Countries?* (Princeton: Princeton University Press), 202–29.

Deschamps, J.C. (1977), 'Effect of Crossing Category Membership on Quantitative Judgement', *European Journal of Social Psychology*, 7, 122–6.

Deutsch, K.W. (1957), *Political Community and the North Atlantic Area: International Organization in the Light of Historical Experience* (Princeton: Princeton University Press).

Díez Medrano, J. (2003), *Framing Europe: Attitudes to European Integration in Germany, Spain, and the United Kingdom* (Princeton: Princeton University Press).

—— and Gutierrez, P. (2001), 'Nested Identities: National and European Identity in Spain', *Ethnic and Racial Studies*, 24, 753–78.

Downs, A. (1957), *An Economic Theory of Democracy* (New York: Harper).

Driscoll, J.C. and Kraay, A. (1998), 'Consistent Covariance Matrix Estimation with Spatially-Dependent Panel Data', *Review of Economics and Statistics*, 85, 549–60.

Duch, R. and Taylor, M. (1997), 'Economics and the Vulnerability of the Pan-European Institutions', *Political Behavior*, 19, 65–79.

Duchesne, S. and Frognier, A.P. (1995), 'Is there a European Identity?', in O. Niedermayer and R. Sinnott (eds.), *Public Opinion and Internationalized Governance* (Oxford: Oxford University Press), 193–226.

Duverger, M. (1951), *Les Parties Politiques* (Paris: Armand Collin).

Easton, D. (1975), 'A Re-Assessment of the Concept of Political', *British Journal of Political Science*, 5, 435–57.

Easton, D. (1965), *A Systems Analysis of Political Life* (New York: Wiley).

Eichenberg, R.C. and Dalton, R. (1993), 'Europeans and the European Community: The Dynamics of Public Support for European Integration', *International Organization*, 47, 507–34.

—— —— (2003), 'Post-Maastricht Blues: The Welfare State and the Transformation of Citizens Support for European Integration 1973–2002', (Tufts University).

—— —— (2007), 'Post-Maastricht Blues: The Transformation of Citizen Support for European Integration, 1973–2004', *Acta Politica*, 42, 128–52.

EIU (Economist Intelligence Unit). (2008), 'The Economist Intelligence Unit's Index of Democracy 2008.' Available from http://graphics.eiu.com/PDF/Democracy%20Index%202008.pdf accessed on 15 December 2009.

Esping-Andersen, G. (1990), *The Three Worlds of Welfare Capitalism* (Princeton: Princeton University Press).

European Commission. 2002, 'EU Budget 2002: Financial Report.' Bruxelles: European Commission.

—— . 2006, 'EU Budget 2006: Financial Report.' Bruxelles: European Commission.

—— . 2008, 'EU Budget 2008: Financial Report.' Bruxselles: European Commission.

—— . undated. 'EUR-lex Database, Access to European Law.' Available from http://eur-lex.europa.eu/en/index.htm accessed on 15 December 2009.

EUROSTAT. undated. 'EUROSTAT Statistics Database.' Available from http://epp.eurostat.ec.europa.eu/portal/page/portal/statistics accessed on 20 October 2008.

Fauvelle-Aymar, C. and Stegmaier, M. (2008), 'Economic and Political Effects on European Parliamentary Electoral Turnout in Post-communist Europe', *Electoral Studies*, 27, 661–72.

Fiorina, M.P. and Levendusky, M. (2006), 'Disconnected: The Political Class Versus the People', in P.S. Nivola and D.W. Brady (eds.), *Red and Blue Nation? Characteristics and Causes of America's Polarized Politics* (Washington D.C./Stanford: Brookings Institution Press/Hoovers Institution Press), 49–71.

Fishman, R.M. (2006), 'Introduction', in R.M. Fishman and A.M. Messina (eds.), *The Year of the Euro: The Cultural, Social and Political Import of Europe's Common Currency* (Notre Dame: Notre Dame University Press), 1–11.

Flickinger, R.S. and Studlar, D.T. (2007), 'One Europe, Many Electorates? Models of Turnout in European Parliament Elections After 2004', *Comparative Political Studies*, 40, 383–404.

Franklin, M.N. (1996), 'Electoral Participation', in L. LeDuc, R.G. Niemi, and P. Norris (eds.), *Comparing Democracies: Elections and Voting in Global Perspective* (Thousand Oakes: Sage), 216–35.

—— (2001), 'How Structural Factors Cause Turnout Variations at European Parliament Elections', *European Union Politics*, 2, 309–28.

—— (2002), 'The Dynamics of Electoral Participation', in L. LeDuc, R.G. Niemi, and P. Norris (eds.), *Comparing Democracies 2: New Challenges in the Study of Elections and Voting* (London: Sage), 148–68.

—— Mackie, T., and Valen, H. (eds.) (1992), *Electoral Change: Responses to Evolving Social and Attitudinal Structures in Western Countries* (Cambridge: Cambridge University Press).

—— Marsh, M., and McLaren, L. (1994), 'Uncorking the Bottle: Popular Opposition to European Unification in the Wake of Maastricht', *Journal of Common Market Studies*, 32, 455–72.

—— and Wlezien, C. (1997), 'The Responsive Public: Issue Salience, Policy Change and Preferences for European Integration', *Journal of Theoretical Politics*, 9, 347–63.

Freire, A. (2006b), 'Bringing Social Identities Back In: The Social Anchors of Left-Right Orientations in Western Europe', *International Political Science Review*, 27, 359–78.

—— (2006a), 'Left-Right Ideological Identities in New Democracies: Greece, Portugal and Spain in the Western European Context', *Pole Sud—Revue de Science Politique de l' Europe Meridionale*, 25, 153–73.

—— (2008), 'Party Polarization and Citizens Left-Right Orientations', *Party Politics*, 14, 189–209.

—— Costa Lobo, M., and Magalhães, P. C. (2009), 'The Clarity of Policy Alternatives, Left-Right and the European Parliemant Vote in 2004', *The Journal of European Integration*, 31, 665–83.

—— and Teperoglou, E. (2007), 'European Elections and National Politics: Lessons from the "New" Southern European Democracies', *Journal of Elections, Public Opinion and Parties*, 17, 101–22.

Frognier, A. (2002), 'Identity and Electoral Participation: For a European Approach to European Elections', in P. Perrineau, G. Grunberg, and C. Ysmal (eds.), *Europe at the Polls: The European Elections of 1999* (New York, Houndmills: Palgrave), 43–58.

Fuchs, D., Guidorossi, G., and Svensson, P. (1995), 'Support for Democratic System', in H.-D. Klingemann and D. Fuchs (eds.), *Citizens and the State* (Oxford: Oxford University Press), 323–53.

—— and Klingemann, H.-D. (1995), 'Citizens and the State: A Relationship Transformed', in H.-D. Klingemann and D. Fuchs (eds.), *Citizens and the State* (Oxford: Oxford University Press), 419–43.

Gabel, M.J. (1998a), 'Economic Integration and Mass Politics: Market Liberalization and Public Attitudes in the European Union', *American Journal of Political Science*, 42, 936–53.

—— (1998b), 'Public Support for European Integration: An Empirical Test of Five Theories', *Journal of Politics*, 60, 333–54.

—— (1998c), *Interests and Integration: Market Liberalization, Public Opinion, and European Union* (Ann Arbor: University of Michigan Press).

—— and Palmer, H.D. (1995), 'Understanding Variation in Public Support for European Integration', *European Journal of Political Research*, 27, 3–19.

—— and Scheve, K.F. (2007), 'Mixed Messages: Party Dissent and Mass Opinion on European Integration', *European Union Politics*, 8, 37–59.

—— and Whitten, G.D. (1997), 'Economic Conditions, Economic Perceptions, and Public Support for European Integration', *Political Behavior,* 19, 81–96.

Gabriel, O.W. and Van Deth, J. (1995), 'Political Interest', in H.-D. Klingemann and D. Fuchs (eds.), *Citizens and the State* (Oxford: Oxford University Press), 323–53.

Gallagher, M. (1991), 'Proportionality, Disproportionality and Electoral Systems', *Electoral Studies,* 10, 33–51.

Gallagher, M. undated. 'Electoral Systems Website.' Available from http://www.tcd.ie/ Political_Science/staff/michael_gallagher/ElSystems/index.php accessed on 15 December 2009.

Garry, J. and Tilley, J. (2009), 'The Macroeconomic Factors Conditioning the Impact of Identity on Attitudes towards the EU', *European Union Politics,* 10, 361–79.

Geys, B. (2006), 'Explaining Voter Turnout: A Review of Aggregate-level Research', *Electoral Studies,* 25, 637–63.

Green, D.M. (2007), *The Europeans: Political Identity in an Emerging Polity* (Boulder: Lynne Rienner).

Green, D.M. (2000), 'On Being European: The Character and Consequences of European Identity', in M. Green Cowles and M. Smith (eds.), *The State of European Union: Risks, Reform, Resistance and Revival* (Oxford: Oxford University Press), 292–322.

Green, D.P., Kim, S.Y., and Yoon, D.H. (2001), 'Dirty Pool', *International Organization,* 55, 441–68.

Guetzkow, H. (1955), 'Multiple Loyalties: Theoretical Approaches to a Problem in International Organization', *Center for Research on World Political Institutions* (Princeton: Princeton University).

Gunther, R. and Kuan, H-C. (2007), 'Value Cleavage and Partisan Conflict', in R. Gunther, J.R. Montero, and Puhle H.-J. (eds.), *Democracy, Intermediation and Voting on Four Continents* (Oxford: Oxford University Press), 255–320.

—— and Montero, J.R. (2001), 'The Multidimensionality of Attittudinal Support for New Democracies: Conceptual Definition and Empirical Refinement', *Workshop of the Comparative National Election Project* (Santiago, Chile).

Gurr, T.R. (1970), *Why Men Rebel?* (Princeton: Princeton University Press).

Haas, E.B. (1958), *The Uniting of Europe* (Stanford: Stanford University Press).

Handley, D.H. (1981), 'Public Opinion and the European Integration: The Crisis of the 1970s', *European Journal of Political Research,* 9, 335–64.

Henjak, A. (2009), 'Contextual Data for INTUNE Project: Country-level Economic, Political and Institutional Data.' Budapest: Central European University.

Herrmann, R.K. and Brewer, M.B. (2004), 'Identities and Institutions: Becoming European in the EU', in R.K. Herrmann, T. Risse, and M.B. Brewer (eds.), *Transnational Identities: Becoming European in the EU* (Lanham: Rowman & Littlefield), 1–23.

—— Risse, T., and Brewer, M.B. (eds.) (2004), *Transnational Identities: Becoming European in the EU* (Latham: Rowman & Littlefield).

Heston, A., Summers, R., and Aten, B. (2009), 'Penn World Table Version 6.3.' Available from http://pwt.econ.upenn.edu/ accessed on 15 December 2009.

Hewstone, M. (1986), *Understanding Attitudes to the European Community* (Cambridge: Cambridge University Press).

Hirschmann, O. (1970), *Exit, Voice or Loyalty* (Cambridge, Mass.: Harvard University Press).

Hix, S. (2005), *The Political System of the European Union* (2 edn.; London: Palgrave Macmillan).

—— (2007), 'Euroscepticism as Anti-Centralization: A Rational Choice Institutionalist Perspective', *European Union Politics*, 8, 131–50.

Hooghe, L., Bakker, R., Brigevich, A., de Vries, C., Edwards, E., Marks, G., Rovny, G., Steenbergen, M., and Vachudova, M. (2010), 'Reliability and Validity of Measuring Party Positions: The Chapel Hill Expert Surveys of 2002 and 2006,.' *European Journal of Political Research* 42: 684–703.

Hooghe, L. (2003), 'Europe Divided?: Elites vs. Public Opinion on European Integration', *European Union Politics,* 4, 281–304.

—— and Marks, G. (2004), 'Does Identity or Economic Rationality Drive Public Opinion on European Integration', *PS: Political Science and Politics*, 37, 415–20.

—— —— (2005), 'Calculation, Community and Cues: Public Opinion on European Integration', *European Union Politics*, 6, 419–43.

—— —— (2008), 'A Postfunctionalist Theory of European Integration: From Permissive Consensus to Constraining Dissensus', *British Journal of Political Science,* 39, 1–23.

Howard, M. (2007), 'The Politics of Immigration and Citizenship in Europe', in C. Swain (ed.), *Debating Immigration* (Cambridge: Cambridge University Press), 237–56.

Huber, E., Ragin, C., Stephens, J.D., Brady, D., and Beckfield, J. (2004), 'Comparative Welfare States Data Set.' Available from http://www.lisproject.org/publications/welfaredata/welfareaccess.htm accessed on 15 December 2009.

Huckfeldt, R. and Sprauge, J. (1995), *Citizens, Politics and Social Communication: Information and Influence in an Election Campaign* (New York: Cambridge University Press).

Huddy, L. (2001), 'From Social to Political Identity: A Critical Examination of Social Identity Theory', *Political Psychology*, 22, 127–56.

Hug, S. and Sciarini, P. (2000), 'Referendum and European Integration: Do Institutions Matter in the Voter's Decision', *Comparative Political Studies*, 33, 3–36.

Huntington, S. (1992), *The Third Wave, Democratization in the Late Twentieth Century* (Norman: University of Oklahoma Press).

Hurwitz, J. and Peffley, M. (1987), 'How are Foreign Policy Attitudes Structured? A Hierarchical Model', *American Political Science Review*, 81, 443–68.

IDEA (International Institute for Democracy and Electoral Assistance). undated. 'Voter Turnout Data.' Available from http://www.idea.int/vt/ accessed on 15 December 2009.

IMF (International Monetary Fund) Statistics Department. 1973–2008. 'Direction of Trade Statistics; Yearbooks 1973 through 2008.' Washington, D.C.: International Monetary Fund, Statistics Department.

Inglehart, R. (1970a), 'Cognitive Mobilization and European Identity', *Comparative Politics*, 3, 45–70.

—— (1970b), 'Public Opinion and European Integration', *International Organization*, 24, 764–95.

—— (1977a), *The Silent Revolution: Changing Values and Political Styles Among Western Publics* (Princeton: Princeton University Press).

—— (1977b), 'Long-Term Trends in Mass Support for European Unification', *Government and Opposition*, 12, 150–77.

—— (1990), *Culture Shift in Advanced Industrial Society* (Princeton: Princeton University Press).

—— (2006), 'Democracy and Happiness: What Causes What?', *Conference on Human Happiness* (Notre Dame University).

—— and Rabier, J.-R. (1978), 'Economic Uncertainty and European Solidarity: Public Opinion Trends', *Annals of the American Academy of Social and Political Science*, 440, 66–97.

—— —— and Reif, K. (1991), 'The Evolution of Public Attitudes Toward European Integration 1970–86', in K. Reif and R. Inglehart (eds.), *Eurobarometer: The Dynamics of European Public Opinion* (London: Macmillan).

Isernia, P. (2008), 'Present at Creation: Italian Mass Support for European Integration in the Formative Years', *European Journal of Political Research*, 47, 383–410.

Jacobson, G. (2000), 'Party Polarization in National Politics: The Electoral Connection', in J.R. Bond and R. Fleisher (eds.), *Polarised Politics: Congress and the President in a Partisan Era* (Washington: QC Press), 9–30.

Janssen, J. (1991), 'Postmaterialism, Cognitive Mobilization and Public Support for European Integration', *British Journal of Political Science*, 21, 443–68.

Judson, R.A. and Owen, A.L. (1999), 'Estimating Dynamic Panel Data Models: A Guide for Macroeconomics', *Economic Letters*, 65, 9–15.

Kaase, M. and Marsh, A. (1979), 'Political Action: A Theoretical Perspective', in S.H. Barnes and M. Kaase (eds.), *Political Action: Mass Participation in Five Western Democracies* (Beverly Hills: Sage).

—— Newton, K., and Scarbrough, E. (1996), 'A Look at the Beliefs in Government Study', *PS: Political Science and Politics*, 29, 226–8.

Kaina, V. (2009), *Wir in Europa. Kollektive Identität und Demokratie in der Europäischen Union* (Wiesbaden: VS Verlag für Sozialwissenschaften).

Karp, J., Banducci, S., and Bowler, S. (2003), 'To Know is to Love It? Satisfaction With Democracy in the European Union', *European Journal of Political Research*, 36, 271–92.

Kaufmann, D., Kraay, A., and Mastuzzi, M. (2007), *A Decade of Measuring the Quality of Governance* (Washington: The World Bank).

—— (2009), *Governance Matters VIII: Aggregate and Individual Governance Indicators, 1996–2008* (26 August 2009).

Kelman, H.C. (1969), 'Patterns of Personal Involvement in the National System: A Social Psychological Analysis of Political Legitimacy', in J.N. Rosenau (ed.), *International Politics and Foreign Policy: A Reader in Research and Theory* (New York: The Free Press), 276–88.

Kirchheimer, O. (1965), 'Der Wandel des westeuropaischen Parteiensystems', *Politische Viertejahresschrift*, 6, 20–41.

Kirkpatrick, E.M. (1971), 'Toward a More Responsible Two-Party System', *American Political Science Review*, 72, 165–77.

Kittlel, B. (1999), 'Sense and Sensitivity in Pooled Analysis of Political Data', *European Journal of Political Research*, 23, 225–53.

Kleinhenz, T. (1995), *Die Nichtwähler: Ursachen der sinkenden Wahlbeteiligung in Deutschland* (Opladen: Westdeutscher Verlag).

Klingemann, H.-D. (1995). 'Party Positions and Voter Orientations.', in H.-D. Klingemann and D. Fuchs (eds) *Citizens and the State* (Oxford: Oxford University Press), 183–205.

—— (1999), 'Mapping Political Support in the 1990s', in P. Norris (ed.), *Critical Citizens: Global Support for Democratic Governance* (Oxford: Oxford University Press), 31–56.

—— (2005), 'Political Parties and Party Systems', in J. Thomassen (ed.), *The European Voter: A Comparative Study of Modern Democracies* (Oxford: Oxford University Press), 22–63.

—— and Fuchs, D. (eds) (1995), *Citizens and the State* (Oxford: Oxford University Press).

—— Volkens, A., Bara, J.L., Budge, I., and McDonald, M.D. (2006), *Mapping Policy Preferences II: Estimates for Parties, Electors and Governments in Eastern Europe, European Union, and OECD 1990–2003* (Oxford: Oxford University Press).

Kluth, C. (2005), 'Eurobarometer 63.4 Public Opinion in the European Union. Spring 2005. National Report. Executive Summary. Germany', *Eurobarometer Survey Series* (European Commision Representation in Germany).

Knutsen, O. (1995), 'Left-Right Materialist Value Orientations', in J. Van Deth and E. Scarbrough (eds.), *The Impact of Values* (Oxford: Oxford University Press).

—— and Kumlin, S. (2005), 'Value Orientations and Party Choice', in J. Thomassen (ed.), *The Europan Voter: A Comparative Study of Modern Democracies* (Oxford: Oxford University Press), 125–66.

Kornberg, A. and Clarke, H.D. (1994), 'Beliefs About Democracy and Satisfaction with Democratic Government: The Canadian Case', *Political Research Quarterly*, 47, 537–63.

Kriesi, H. (2008), 'Rejoinder to Liesbet Hooghe and Gary Marks, 'A Postfunctional Theory of European Integration: From Permissive Consensus to Constraining Dissensus", *British Journal of Political Science*, 39, 221–4.

—— and Lachat, R. (2004), 'Globalization and Transformation of the National Political Space: Switzerland and France Compared', *Workshop on the Analysis of Political Cleavages and Party Competition* (Duke University).

Kristensen, I.P. and Wawro, G. (2003), 'Lagging the Dog? The Robustness of Panel Corrected Standard Errors in the Presence of Serial Correlation and Observation Specific Effects', (New York: Columbia University).

Kritzinger, S. (2003), 'The Influence of the Nation-State on Individual Support for the European Union', *European Union Politics*, 4, 219–41.

Lachat, R. (2008), 'The Impact of Party Polarization on Ideological Voting', *Electoral Studies*, 27, 687–98.

Laver, M., ed. 2001. *Estimating the Policy Position of Political Actors*. London: Routledge.

References

Lazarsfeld, P.F., Berelson, B., and Gaudet, H. (1968), *The People's Choice: How the Voter Makes Up His Mind in a Presidential Campaign* (3 edn.; New York, London: Columbia University Press).

Lewis, J.B. and Linzer, D.A. (2005), 'Estimating Regression Models in Which the Dependent Variable is Based on Estimates', *Political Analysis*, 13, 345–64.

Lewis-Beck, M. and Stegmaier, M. (2000), 'Economic Determinants of Electoral Outcomes', *Annual Review of Political Science*, 3, 189–219.

Lijphart, A. (1999), *Patterns of Democracy: Government Forms and Performance in Thirty-Six Countries* (New Haven: Yale University Press).

Lindberg, L.N. and Scheingold, S.A. (eds.) (1970), *Europe's Would-be Polity: Patterns of Change in the European Community* (Englewood Cliffs, N.J.: Prentice-Hall).

Linde, J. and Ekman, J. (2003), 'Satisfaction with Democracy: A Note on a Frequently Used Indicator in Comparative Politics', *European Journal of Political Research*, 42, 391–408.

—— —— (2005), 'Institutional Trust and Democracy in the New EU Member States', *XIV Nordic Political Science Association Conference* (Reykjavik, Iceland).

Linz, J. and Stepan, A. (1996), *Problems of Democratic Transition and Consolidation: Southern Europe, Southern America and Post-Communist Europe* (Baltimore: John Hopkins University Press).

—— and Valenzuela, A. (eds.) (1992), *The Faliure of Presidential Democracy* (Baltimore: The John Hopkins University Press).

Lipset, S.M. and Rokkan, S. (1967), *Party Systems and Voter Alignments: Cross-National Perspectives* (2 edn.; New York, London: The Free Press/Collier-Macmillan).

Lockerbie, B. (1993), 'Economic Dissatisfaction and Political Alienation in Western Europe', *European Journal of Political Research*, 23, 281–93.

Lubbers, M. (2008), 'Regarding the Dutch "Nee" to the European Constitution: A Test of the Identity, Utilitarian and Political Approaches to Voting "No"', *European Union Politics*, 9, 59–86.

—— and Scheepers, P. (2005), 'Political Versus Instrumental Euro-scepticism: Mapping Scepticism in European Countries and Regions', *European Union Politics*, 6, 223–42.

Luebbert, G. (1986), *Comparative Democracy* (New York: Columbia University Press).

Luskin, R.C. (1987), 'Measuring Political Sophistication', *American Journal of Political Science*, 4, 856–99.

Maddala, G.S. (1971), 'The Use of Variance Components Models in Pooling Cross Section and Time Series Data', *Econometrica*, 39, 341–58.

Mainwaring, S. and Torcal, M. (2005), 'Party System Theory and Party System Institutionalization after the Third Wave of Democratization', *Political Science Seminar of the Social Sciences Institute of the University of Lisbon* (Lisbon).

Mainwaring, S. and Zoco, E. (2007), 'Political Sequences and the Stabilization of Interparty Competition: Electoral Volatility in Old and New Democracies', *Party Politics*, 13, 155–78.

Malang, T. (2010), 'National Institutional Performance in Uncertainty Reduction and its Effects on the Attitudes Toward European Integration', *ECPR Joint Sessions of Workshops* (Munster, Germany).

Marks, G. and Hooghe, L. (1999), 'National Identity and Support for European Integration', (Wissenschaftszentrum Berlin fur Sozialforschung).

—— et al. (2006), 'Party Competition and European Integration in the East and West: Different Structure, Same Causality', *Comparative Political Studies*, 35, 155–75.

Marshall, M.G., K. Jaggers, and T. D. Gurr. 2011. 'Polity 4 Dataset, Political Regime Characteristics and Transitions, 1800–2006.' Available from http://www.systemic-peace.org/polity/polity4.htm accessed on 11 March 2011.

Martinotti, G. and Stefanizzi, S. (1995), 'Europeans and the Nation State', in O. Niedermayer and R. Sinnott (eds.), *Public Opinion and International Governance* (Oxford: Oxford University Press), 163–89.

Mattila, M. (2003), 'Why Bother? Determinants of Turnout in the European Elections', *Electoral Studies*, 22, 449–68.

McAllister, I. (1999), 'The Economic Performance of Governments', in P. Norris (ed.), *Critical Citizens: Global Support for Democratic Governance* (Oxford: Oxford University Press).

McLaren, L. (2002), 'Public Support for the European Union: Cost/Benefit Analysis or Perceived Cultural Threat', *Journal of Politics*, 64, 551–66.

—— (2006), *Identity, Interests and Attitudes to European Integration* (London: Palgrave Macmillan).

Mikhaylov, S. and Marsh, M. (2009), 'Policy Performance and Support for European Integration', in J. Thomassen (ed.), *The Legitimacy of European Union After Enlargement* (Oxford: Oxford University Press), 142–64.

Miller, W.E., et al. (1999), *Policy Representation in Western Democracies* (Oxford: Oxford University Press).

Mishler, W. and Rose, R. (2001), 'Political Support for Incomplete Democracies: Realist vs. Idealist Theories and Measures', *International Political Science Review*, 22, 303–20.

—— (2002), 'Learning and Relearning Democracy', *European Journal of Political Research*, 41, 5–36.

Montero, J.R. and Gunther, R. (1994), 'Democratic Legitimacy in Spain', *IPSA world congress* (Berlin).

Moreno, A. (1999), *Political Cleavages. Issues, Parties, and the Consolidation of Democracy* (Bolder: Westview Press).

Morlino, L. (2003), 'What is a "Good" democracy? The Theory and the Case of Italy', *South European Society and Politics*, 8, 1–32.

Mummendey, A., Wenzel, M., and Waldzus, S. (2007), 'Subordinate Identitites and Intergroup Conflict: The Ingroup Projection Model', *European Review of Social Psychology*, 18, 331–72.

Mungio-Pippidi, A. (2006), 'Corruption: Diagnosis and Treatment', *Journal of Democracy*, 17, 86–99.

Nadeau, R., et al. (2000), 'Elections and Satisfaction with Democracy', *APSA Annual Meeting* (Washington, D.C.).

Nelsen, B.F. and Guth, J.L. (2000), 'Exploring the Gender Gap: Women, Men and Public Attitudes toward European Integration', *European Union Politics*, 1, 267–91.

—— —— and Fraser, C.R. (2001), 'Does Religion Matter? Christianity and Public Support for the European Union', *European Union Politics*, 2, 191–217.

Netjes, C. (2004), 'All Aboard? Explaining Public Support for European Integration in a Post-Maastricht Era', *Second Pan-European Conference, ECPR Standing Group on EU Politics* (Bologna).

Newton, K. (2006), 'Support for Democracy, Social Capital, Civil Society and Political Performance', (Berlin: Wissenschaftszentrum Berlin fur Sozialforschung).

—— and Norris, P. (2000), 'Confidence in Public Institutions', in S. Pharr and R. Putnam (eds.), *Dissaffected Democracies: What's Troubling the Trilateral Countries* (Princeton: Princeton University Press).

Niedermayer, O. (1995a), 'Trends and Contrasts', in O. Niedermayer and R. Sinnott (eds.), *Public Opinion and Internationalized Governance* (Oxford: Oxford University Press), 53–72.

—— (1995b), 'Trust and Sense of Community', in O. Niedermayer and R. Sinnott (eds.), *Public Opinion and Internationalized Governance* (Oxford: Oxford University Press), 227–45.

—— and Sinnot, R. (1995), 'Democratic Legitimacy and the European Parliament', in O. Niedermayer and R. Sinnott (eds.), *Public Opinion and Internationalized Governance* (Oxford: Oxford University Press), 277–308.

—— and Westle, B. (1995), 'A Typology of Orientations', in O. Niedermayer and R. Sinnott (eds.), *Public Opinion and Internationalized Governance* (Oxford: Oxford University Press), 33–50.

Nordsieck, N. undated. 'Parties and Elections in Europe.' Available from http://www.parties-and-elections.de/ accessed on 15 March 2010.

Norris, P. (1999a), *Critical Citizens: Global Support for Democratic Governance* (Oxford: Oxford University Press).

—— (1999b), 'Conclusions: The Growth of Critical Citizens and its Consequences', in P. Norris (ed.), *Critical Citizens: Global Support for Democratic Governance* (Oxford: Oxford University Press), 257–72.

—— (1999c), 'Introduction: The Growth of Critical Citizens?', in P. Norris (ed.), *Critical Citizens: Global Support for Democratic Governance* (Oxford: Oxford University Press), 1–29.

—— (2006), 'Support for Democratic Governance: Multidimensional Concept and Survey Measures', *LAPOP-UNDP workshop on Candidate Indicators for the UNDP Democracy Support Index* (Center for the Americas, Vanderbilt University, Nashvillle).

Oates, W.E. (1972), *Fiscal Federalism* (New York: Horcourt Brace Jovanovich).

OECD (Organization for Economic Co-operation and Development). 2008. 'Database on Immigrants in OECD Countries.' Available from http://www.oecd.org/document/51/0,3746,en_2649_33931_40644339_1_1_1_1,00.html accessed on 20 December 2008.

—— . undated. 'OECD Main Economic Indicators.' Available from http://stats.oecd.org/mei/default.asp accessed on 15 December 2008.

—— . (2009), 'OECD Social Expenditure Database.' Available from www.oecd.org/els/social/expenditure accessed on 15 December 2009.

Oppenhuis, E. (1995), *Voting Behavior in Europe: A Comparative Analysis of Electoral Participation and Party Choice* (Amsterdam: Het Spinhuis).

Pappi, F.U. and Schmitt, H. (1994), *Parteien, Parlamente und Wahlen in Skandinavien* (Frankfurt: Campus).

Pattie, C., Seyd, P., and Whiteley, P. (2004), *Citizenship in Britain: Values, Participation and Democracy* (Cambridge: Cambridge University Press).

Pelizzo, R. and Babones, S. (2007), 'The Political Economy of Polarized Pluralism', *Party Politics*, 13, 53–67.

Pharr, S. and Putnam, R. (2000), *Dissaffected Democracies: What is Troubling the Trilateral Countries* (Princeton: Princeton University Press).

Pintor, R. L. and Gratschew, M. (2002), *Voter Turnout since 1945: A Global Report*. Stockholm: IDEA International Institute for Democracy and Electoral Assistance.

Plümper, T., Troeger, V.E., and Manow, P. (2005), 'Panel Data Analysis in Comparative Politics: Linking Method to Theory', *European Journal of Political Research*, 44, 327–54.

PRS (Political Risk Services). undated. 'International Country Risk Guide - Researchers Dataset.' Available from http://www.prsgroup.com/prsgroup_shoppingcart/pc-32-6-researchers-dataset-icrg-t3b.aspx, accessed on 15 December 2009.

Ray, L. (1999), 'Conversion, Acquiescence or Delusion: The Contingent Nature of the Party Electorate Link', *Political Behavior*, 21, 325–47.

—— (2004), 'Don't Rock the Boat: Expectations, Fears and Opposition to EU-Level Policy Making', in G. Marks and M. Steenbergen (eds.), *European Integration and Political Conflict* (Cambridge: Cambridge University Press), 51–61.

—— (2003b), 'Reconsidering the Link Between Incumbent Support and Pro-EU Opinion', *European Union Politics*, 4, 259–79.

—— (2003a), 'When Parties Matter: The Conditional Influence of Party Positions on Voter Opinion About European Integration', *Journal of Politics*, 65, 978–94.

Reif, K. (1984), *European Elections 1979/81 and 1984: Conclusions and Perspectives from Empirical Research* (Berlin: Quorum).

—— and Schmitt, H. (1980), 'Nine Second-Order National Elections: A Conceptual Framework for the Analysis of European Election Results', *European Journal of Political Research*, 8, 3–44.

Risse, T. (2005), 'Neofunctionalism, European Identity, and the Puzzles of European Integration', *Journal of European Public Policy*, 12, 291–309.

—— (2006), 'The Euro Between National and European Identity', in R.M. Fishman and A.M. Messina (eds.), *The Year of the Euro: The Cultural, Social and Political Impact of Europe's Common Currency* (Notre Dame: Notre Dame University Press), 65–80.

Rohrschneider, R. (2002), 'The Democracy Deficit and Mass Support for an EU-Wide Government', *American Journal of Political Science*, 46, 463–75.

—— (2005), 'Institutional Quality and Perceptions of Representation in Advanced Democracies', *Comparative Political Studies*, 38, 850–74.

—— and Whitefield, S. (2006a), 'Political Parties, Public Opinion and European Integration in Post-Communist Countries: The State of the Art', *European Union Politics*, 7, 141–60.

—— —— (eds.) (2006b), *Public Opinion, Party Competition and the European Union in Eastern Europe* (London: Palgrave Macmillan).

—— —— (2004), 'Support for Foreign Ownership and Integration in Eastern Europe: Economic Interests, Ideological Commitments and Democratic Context', *Comparative Political Studies*, 37, 313–39.

Rose, R. and Munro, N. (2003), *Elections and Parties in New European Democracies* (Washington: QC Press).

Rosema, M. (2007), 'Low Turnout: Threat to Democracy or Blessing in Disguise? Consequences of Citizens' Varying Tendencies to Vote', *Electoral Studies*, 26, 612–23.

Rosenstone, S.J. and Hansen, J.M. (1993), *Mobilization, Participation and Democracy in America* (New York: Macmillan).

Rubenson, D., et al. (2004), 'Accounting for the Age Gap in Turnout', *Acta Politica*, 39, 407–21.

Ruiz Jiménez, A. M., et al. (2004), 'European and National Identities in EU's Old and New Member States: Ethnic, Civic, Instrumental and Symbolic Components', *European Integration Online Papers*, 8.

Sánchez-Cuenca, I. (2000), 'The Political Basis of Support for European Integration', *European Union Politics*, 1, 147–71.

Sanders, D. (2000), 'The Real Economy and the Perceived Economy in Popularity Functions: How Much Data do Voters Need to Know?; A Study of British Data 1974–1997', *Electoral Studies*, 19, 275–94.

Sani, G. and Sartori, G. (1983), 'Polarization, Fragmentation and Competition in Western Democracies.' In *Western European Party Systems: Continuity and Change*, edited by H. Daalder and P. Mair. Beverly Hills, CA: Sage, pp. 307–341

Sartori, G. (1976), *Parties and Party Systems: A Framework for Analysis* (Cambridge: Cambridge University Press).

Sayrs, L.W. (1989), *Pooled Time Series Analysis* (London: Sage).

Scharpf, F. (1999), *Governing in Europe* (Oxford: Oxford University Press).

Scheuer, A. (2005), *How Europeans See Europe: Structure and Dynamics of European Legitimacy Beliefs* (Amsterdam: Amsterdam University Press).

Schmitt, H. (2001), *Politische Repräsentation in Europ* (Frankfurt: Campus).

—— (2003a), 'The Eurobarometers', *European Union Politics*, 4, 243–51.

—— and Mannheimer, R. (1991), 'About Voting and Non-voting in the European Parliament Elections of June 1989', *European Journal of Political Research*, 19, 31–54.

—— and Thomassen, J. (2004), 'Democracy and Legitimacy in the European Union', *Tidsskrift for Samfunnsforskning*, 45, 375–408.

—— and van der Eijk, C. (2003), 'Die politische Bedeutung niedriger Beteiligungsraten bei Europawahlen. Eine empirische Studie über die Motive der Nichtwahl', in F. Brettschneider, J. van Deth, and E. Roller (eds.), *Europäische Integration in der öffentlichen Meinung* (Opladen: Leske + Budrich), 279–302.

—— and Wessels, B. (2005), 'Meaningful Choices: Under What Conditions do General Elections Provide a Meaningful Choice Set, and What Happens if They don't', (Third Wave of the Comparative Study of Electoral Systems).

—— and Wust, A.M. (2006), 'The Bundestag Election of 2005: The Interplay of Long-term Trends and Short-term Factors', *German Politics and Society*, 24, 27–46.

Schmitt, L. (2003b), 'Vertrauenskrise in der EU? Ausmaß, Struktur und Determinanten des Vertrauens in die zentralen Institutionen der EU unter besonderer

Berücksichtigung des Europäischen Parlaments', in J. van Deth and E. Roller (eds.), *Europäische Integration in der öffentlichen Meinung* (Opladen: Leske + Baldruch), 57–82.

Sheperd, R.J. (1975), *Public Opinion and the European Integration* (Farnborough: Saxon House).

Sinn, H-W. (1994), 'How Much Europe? Subsidiarity, Centralization and Fiscal Competition', *Scottish Journal of Political Economy*, 41, 85–107.

Sinnott, R. (1995), 'Policy, Subsidiarity, and Legitimacy', in O. Niedermayer and R. Sinnott (eds.), *Public Opinion and Internationalized Governance* (Oxford: Oxford University Press), 246–76.

Sniderman, P.M., Brody, R.A., and Tetlock, P.E. (1991), *Reasonng and Choice: Explorations in Political Psychology* (Cambridge: Cambridge University Press).

Steenbergen, M., Edwards, E., and De Vries, C. (2007), 'Who's Cueing Who? Mass-Elite Linkages and the Future of European Integration', *European Union Politics*, 8, 13–35.

Steenbergen, M. and Marks, G. (2007), 'Evaluating Expert Surveys.' *European Journal of Political Research* 46: 347-366.

Steinbrecher, M., Huber, S., and Rattinger, H. (2007), *Turnout in Germany: Citizen Participation in State, Federal, and European Elections Since 1979* (Baden Baden: Nomos).

—— and Rattinger, H. (2012), 'Explaining Turnout in European Parliament Elections', in P. Belluci, et al. (eds.), *The Europeanization of National Politics? Citizenship and Support in a Post-Enlargement Union* (Oxford: Oxford University Press).

—— —— (2007), 'Satisfaction with Democracy at the EU and the National Level', *IntUne papers*.

Stimson, J. (1985), 'Regression in Space and Time: A Statistical Essay', *American Journal of Political Science*, 29, 914–47.

Stokes, D. (1963), 'Spatial Models of Party Competition', *American Political Science Review*, 42, 97–116.

Tajfel, H. (1981), *Human Groups and Social Categories: Studies in Social Psychology* (Cambridge: Cambridge University Press).

—— and Turner, J.C. (1979), 'An Integrative Theory of Intergroup Conflict', in A.G. William and S. Worchel (eds.), *The Social Psychology of Intergroup Relations* (Monterey: Brooks/Cole), 33–47.

Thierlaut, S. (2008), *Polarisation in Congress* (Cambridge: Cambridge University Press).

Thomassen, J. (2005a), *The European Voter: A Comparative Study of Modern Democracies* (Oxford: Oxford University Press).

—— (2005b), 'Modernization or Politics', in J. Thomassen (ed.), *The European Voter: A Comparative Study of Modern Democracies* (Oxford: Oxford University Press), 254–66.

—— (2005c), 'Introduction', in J. Thomassen (ed.), *The European Voter. A Comparative Study of Modern Democracies* (Oxford: Oxford University Press), 1–21.

—— and Schmitt, H. (1999), 'Introduction: Political Representation and Legitimacy in the European Union', in H. Schmitt and J. Thomassen (eds.), *Political Representation and Legitimacy in the European Union* (Oxford: Oxford University Press), 3–20.

Tiersky, R. and Jones, E. (eds.) (2007), *Europe Today: A Twenty First Century Introduction* (Lanham: Rowman & Littlefield).

Toka, G. (1995), 'Political Support in East-Central Europe', in H.-D. Klingemann and D. Fuchs (eds.), *Citizens and the State* (Oxford: Oxford University Press), 354–82.

Topf, R. (1995a), 'Beyond Electoral Participation', in H.-D. Klingemann and D. Fuchs (eds.), *Citizens and the State* (Oxford: Oxford University Press), 52–92.

—— (1995b), 'Electoral Participation', in H.-D. Klingemann and D. Fuchs (eds.), *Citizens and the State* (Oxford: Oxford University Press), 27–51.

Torcal, M. and Montero, J.R. (2006), 'Political Dissatisfaction in Comparative Perspective', in M. Torcal and J.R. Montero (eds.), *Political Dissatisfaction in Contemporary Democracies: Social Capital, Institutions and Politics* (London: Routledge), 3–20.

Transparency International. 1995–2008. 'Corruption Perceptions Report.' Available from http://www.transparency.org/policy_research/surveys_indices/cpi accessed on 10 December 2009.

Tsebelis, G. (1995), 'Decision Making in Political Systems: Veto Players in Presidentialism, Parliamentarism, Multicameralism and Multipartyism', *British Journal of Political Science,* 25, 289–325.

—— (1999), 'Veto Players and Law Production in Parliamentary Democracies: An Empirical Analysis', *American Political Science Review,* 93, 591–608.

—— (2002), *Veto Players: How Political Institutions Work* (Princeton: Princeton University Press).

Tucker, J.A., Pacek, A.C., and Berinsky, A.J. (2002), 'Transitional Winners and Losers: Attitudes Toward EU Membership in Post-Communist Countries', *American Journal of Political Science,* 46, 557–71.

Turner, J.C., et al. (1987), *Rediscovering the Social Group: A self-categorization Theory* (Oxford: Blackwell).

Tverdova, Y. and Anderson, C.J. (2004), 'Choosing the West? Referendum Choices on EU Membership in East-Central Europe', *Electoral Studies,* 23, 185–208.

Tworzecki, H. (2002), *Learning to Choose: Electoral Politics in East-Central Europe* (Stanford: Stanford University Press).

UNDP (United Nations Development Programme). undated. 'Administration and Cost of Elections Project - Electoral Knowledge Network.' Available from http://www.gaportal.org/organizations/ace-electoral-knowledge-network accessed on 15 December 2009.

Uslaner, E.M. (2004), 'Trust and Corruption', in J. Lambsdorff, M. Traube, and M. Schramm (eds.), *Corruption and the New Institutional Economics* (London: Routledge).

—— (2006), 'Corruption and Inequality', (Department of Government and Politics, University of Maryland, Baltimore).

van der Eijk, C., Franklin, M.N., and Marsh, M. (1996), 'What Voters Teach Us About Europe-Wide Elections: What Europe-Wide Elections Teach Us About Voters', *Electoral Studies,* 15, 149–66.

—— Schmitt, H., and Binder, T. (2005), 'Left-right Orientation and Party Choice ', in J. Thomassen (ed.), *The European Voter: A Comparative Study of Modern Democracies* (Oxford: Oxford University Press), 167–91.

van Deth, J. and Elff, M. (2004), 'Politicisation, Economic Development and Political Interest in Europe', *European Journal of Political Research,* 43, 477–508.

van Kersbergen, K. (2000), 'Political Allegiance and European Integration', *European Journal of Political Research,* 37, 1–17.

Verba, S. and Nie, N.H. (1972), *Participation in America: Political Democracy and Social Equality* (New York: Harper & Row).

—— Schlozman, K., and Brady, H. (1995), *Voice and Equality: Civic Voluntarism in American Politics* (Cambridge, Mass., London: Harvard University Press).

Visser, J. 2009. 'Database on Institutional Characteristics of Trade Unions, Wage Setting, State Intervention and Social Pacts in 34 countries between 1960 and 2007' Available from http://www.uva-aias.net/208 accessed on 15 December 2009.

Wagner, A.F., Dufor, M., and Schneider, F. (2003), 'Satisfaction not Guaranteed—Institutions and and Satisfaction with Democracy in Western Europe', (CESifo).

Waldon-Moore, P. (1999), 'Eastern Europe at the Crossroads of Democratic Transition: Evaluating Support for Democratic Institutions, Satisfaction with Democratic Government, and Consolidation of Democratic Regimes ', *Comparative Political Studies*, 31, 32–62.

Walduzs, S. and Mummendey, A. (2004), 'Inclusion in Superordinate Category, In-Group Prototypicality and Attitudes Toward Out-Groups', *Journal of Experimental Social Psychology*, 40, 466–77.

Weiler, J.H. (1999), *The Constitution of Europe: Do the New Clothes Have an Emperor? and Other Essays on European Integration* (Cambridge: Cambridge University Press).

Wenzel, M., Mummendey, A., and Waldzus, S. (2007), 'Superordinate Identities and Intergroup Conflict: The Intergroup Protection Model', *European Review of Social Psyhology*, 18, 331–72.

Wessels, B. (1995), 'Development of Support: Diffusion or Demographic Replacement', in O. Niedermayer and R. Sinnott (eds.), *Public Opinion and Internationalized Governance* (2; Oxford: Oxford University Press), 105–37.

—— and Kielhorn, A. (1999), 'Which Competencies for Which Political Level?', in R. S. Katz and B. Wessels (eds.), *The European Parliament, the National Parliament, and European Integration* (Oxford: Oxford University Press), 174–96.

Westle, B. (2003a), 'Europäische Identifikation im Spannungsfeld regionaler und nationaler Identitäten: Theoretische Überlegungen und empirische Befunde', *Politische Vierteljahresschrift*, 44, 453–82.

—— (2007), 'European Identity and European Democracy: Analyses Concerning the "Democratic Dilemma" of the European Union', *IntUne Working Paper* (Marburg: University of Marburg).

—— (2010), 'Identity, Social and Political', in B. Badie, D. Berg-Schlosser, and L. Morlino (eds.), *Encyclopedia of Political Science* (Thousand Oaks: Sage).

—— (1999), *Kollektive Identität im vereinten Deutschland—Nation und Demokratie in der Wahrnehmung der Deutschen* (Opladen: Leske + Budrich).

—— (2003b), 'Universalismus oder Abgrenzung als Komponente der Identifikation mit der Europäischen Union?', in F. Brettschneider, J. W. Van Deth, and Roller E. (eds.), *Europäische Integration in der öffentlichen Meinung* (Opladen: Leske + Budrich), 115–52.

Whitehead, L. (2001), 'Democracy by Convergence: Southern Europe', in L. Whitehead (ed.), *The International Dimensions of Democratization: Europe and the Americas* (Oxford: Oxford University Press), 261–84.

References

Wikipedia. undated A. 'Presidency of the Council of the European Union.' Available from http://en.wikipedia.org/wiki/Presidency_of_the_Council_of_the_European_-Union accessed on 25 December 2009.

——. undated B. 'World War II Casualties' Available from http://en.wikipedia.org/wiki/World_War_II_casualties accessed on 15 January 2010.

Wilgden, J.K and Feld, W.J. (1976), 'Evaluative and Cognitive Factors in the Prediction of European Unification', *Comparative Political Studies*, 9, 309–34.

Wilson, S.E. and Butler, D.M. (2007), 'A Lot More to Do: Sensitivity of Time-Series Cross-Section Analysis to Simple Alternative Specifications', *Political Analysis*, 15, 101–23.

World Bank. various years. 'World Development Indicators.' Available from http://data.worldbank.org/indicator/SP.POP.TOTL accessed on 15 September 2008.

Wolfinger, R.E. and Rosenstone, S.J. (1980), *Who Votes?* (New Haven: Yale University Press).

Woolridge, J. (2002), *Econometric Analysis of Cross Section and Panel Data* (Cambridge: MIT Press).

Xezonakis, G. 2008. 'The Updated Mannheim Trend File from the Eurobarometer series prepared for the IntUne FP6 project.' Colchester: University of Essex.

Zaller, J. (1992), *The Nature and Origins of Mass Opinion* (New York: Cambridge University Press).

Index